GOING ABROAD

Stoneware ; with the K... ... furnitu.
Sale to commence at Twelve o'clock Noon.
BARCLAY & SKIRVING, AUCTIONEERS.

PUBLIC SALE OF
GROCERY GOODS, SHOP FURNITURE,
COFFEE MILL, SUGAR MILL, &c.
AND SHOP TO LET
To be sold, in No. 147 Foot of Saltmarket Street, on Thursday
next, the 6th September.
The Whole STOCK of GROCERY GOODS and SHOP
FURNITURE, of Mr. John McGibbon, who is going Abroad,
consisting of Teas, Coffees, Spices, Sugars, Messina Nuts, Soap,
Starch, Oils, Candles, and other Grocery Goods, Sugar and
Coffee Mills, Counter Beams and Scales, Tobacconist's Sign, Oil
Cisterns, Shop Drawers, Counter and Shelving, &c. &c.
Sale to begin at Twelve o'clock.
BARCLAY & SKIRVING, Auctioneers.

SHOP TO LET.
To Let, the SHOP, for Three years' Lease, with Fittings
and a Tenant might still have the Stock at valuation.

MONTHLY SALE OF PIECE GOODS, CLOTHS &c. &c.
MESSRS. CAMPBELL & CO.,
SUCCESSORS TO:
... beg to intimate that their nex
... GOODS, &c. takes place vi

Glasgow Herald, 3 September, 1849

Best wishes Willie

John McGibbon

JOHN MacGIBBON & SONS,

GENERAL MERCHANTS

Grain Dealers, Commission Agents, &c.,

MATAURA, GORE, and GORDON.

AGENTS FOR

SAWMILLS, BRICKFIELDS,

National Fire and Marine Insurance Company,

&c., &c.. &c.

Stones Directory, 1888

Foreword

The Otago settlement opened in 1848 as a 'class settlement' under the colonising system devised by Edward Gibbon Wakefield and the New Zealand Company. It was also seen as a religious settlement, by emigrant members of the newly formed Free Church of Scotland, who considered themselves to be a latter-day band of Pilgrim Fathers.

The New Zealand Company, in cooperation with the Lay Association of Members of the Free Church of Scotland, sought to transplant Scottish society to the antipodes – to recreate a society and preserve its gradations of social class, capital and labour, laws, customs and attitudes. It would not, of course, have any of the contemporary drawbacks: the urban overcrowding, slums, disease and poor working conditions. It was all part of building a Better Britain in the South Seas, and, like all utopian ideas, it didn't work.

As well as pitching dreams of a better life to the working classes, Otago scheme promoters targeted the capitalist class. This class would buy property from the New Zealand Company, and part of the purchase price would be ploughed back into the colony – subsidising passages for workers and paying for schools, churches (Free Church, of course), roads and bridges. The land would be sold at a 'sufficient price', i.e. high enough to discourage workers from becoming landowners too soon and upsetting the socio-economic equilibrium.

Wealthy capitalists were a target, and it was hoped that some would buy substantial landholdings in Otago, while remaining in Scotland themselves. Few took the bait, and most 'capitalists' who bought into the scheme – particularly those who emigrated to the colony – were people of moderate means. People like my namesake and great-great-grandfather, John MacGibbon, a merchant from Saltmarket Street in Glasgow.

John MacGibbon fitted neatly into the emigrant capitalist mould. He was respectable, and as a small businessman he was in a position to invest in the colony and employ labour. His Glasgow business was in decline, and he needed to take drastic action or face the possibility of slithering down to the lower ranks of society – a common middle class fear which emigration promoters openly played upon. Being a devout member of the Free Church, his religious credentials were impeccable.

John MacGibbon and his family began a new life at the 'Ends of the Earth' in 1849. This book looks at why they did it, how they did it and how they managed in their new country – first in Dunedin and later in Eastern Southland. MacGibbon family members are central to the story, but they are not the only characters in the plot. *Going Abroad* attempts to give a broad picture of the emigration and early colonial experience of the Scots who emigrated to New Zealand's deep south.

While the book contains a good deal of carefully researched detail, the primary aim has been to give readers an easily digestible slice of the life of the times – to recreate, as far as possible, the *flavour* of the emigration and colonial experience. The first section, set in Glasgow, is written as semi-fiction while the balance of the book is historical journalism.

The book's title is taken from an advertisement John MacGibbon placed in the Glasgow Herald to sell his business. 'Going Abroad' has a nicer ring to it than 'emigrating', and it was a common euphemism of the period.

I did not footnote the text, because the magazine format of the book would have made it impractical. Information sources are listed in the bibliography, and readers who wish to follow up any topic are welcome to contact me.

John MacGibbon
Wellington, September 1997
johnmacg@actrix.gen.nz

Acknowledgements

No-one can write something like this and claim it's all his or her own work. Many people have helped the book on its way, generously giving information, time and encouragement. So many, in fact, that a list is bound to miss some people out, and I regret that. My heartfelt thanks to you all.

On the family side of things, I've enjoyed an extraordinary amount of help and hospitality. Winifred Goddard, our oldest surviving relative (and still one of our liveliest) has been an amazing fount of family knowledge. As have been Ann, Angus and Bruce MacGibbon, and Margaret Royds. Many family members lent photo collections, and a particular treasure trove came from John Shanks in Christchurch. Peter MacGibbon pitched in with computer graphics, Stephen MacGibbon helped with National Archives research, while Shona MacGibbon dug out land records in Southland. Heather Moodie and Carey Carey made useful comments on drafts I foisted on them. Alastair MacGibbon's eagle-eyed proof reading was invaluable.

In Glasgow, I received wonderful help from David Stevenson of Strathclyde University, Douglas Murray of the University of Glasgow, and library staff at the University of Glasgow and Mitchell Library. I visited these people in person, but also via the Internet, which was the glue that held the research effort together over an extended period. I was fortunate that this project coincided with the dawn of the information superhighway.

Here in New Zealand, I received assistance of incalculable value from Rosemarie Smith, now living in Haifa, and her parents, Jean and Hallam Smith, of Gore. They were my main link with Southland, and encouraged me to expand the horizons of this endeavour. Similar encouragement and comment came from Bill and Kay Carter, of Paraparaumu. Thanks must go to Andrew Devon for his excellent drawings, and to Philippa Sargent for her expert sub-editing of my manuscript.

For keeping the pioneer MacGibbons and other Southland pioneers alive into the 20th century, I pay due homage to the sterling efforts of the Mataura Ensign's old-time reporter, Herries Beattie. I have drawn extensively on Beattie's work, and thank the Ensign for letting me reproduce great chunks of it. Another excellent source of Southland information was the *History of Mataura*, edited by Charles Muir. Tom Brooking of the History Department at Otago University, and George Griffiths from Otago Heritage Books, gave useful information and encouraging comments. Diane Daly and Bob McNeil laboriously transcribed the diary of Mooltan passenger F S Pillans, from a version held at the Hocken Library. Permission to optically scan their typescript was greatly appreciated. Florence Chuk, of Ballarat, Victoria, was very helpful with information on emigration voyages.

Institutions whose staff and collections I have drawn on include the Otago Settlers Museum, Hocken Library, National Archives, Gore Museum, Honeysuckle Historical Cottage in Mataura, National Library, Alexander Turnbull Library, libraries at Otago, Victoria and Massey universities, and the Family History Library at the Hataitai branch of the Church of Latter Day Saints.

Finally, to my wife Elizabeth, the greatest thanks of all – you couldn't choose your in-laws, and you've had to share our home and my attention with a much larger family than you ever expected. Your forbearance and help are infinitely appreciated.

GOING ABROAD

Part one: Scotland

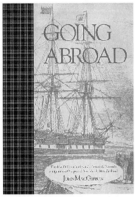

Cover: *The MacGibbon family and 152 other emigrants left Greenock docks for New Zealand on 11 September 1849. Their ship, the Mooltan, would have looked similar to this vessel. The family is a sept of the Buchanan clan, whose tartan is on the left.*

Written and edited by John MacGibbon

ISBN 0-473-04752-7

Designed and typeset by John MacGibbon, Infomedia Associates.

Ngaio Press

▪ Contents

John, Jane & Thomas in Glasgow

THE **LARGER CATECHISM**, AGREED UPON BY THE ASSEMBLY OF DIVINES AT WESTMINSTER, WITH THE ASSISTANCE OF COMMISSIONERS FROM THE CHURCH OF SCOTLAND, AND Approved, Anno 1648, by the GENERAL ASSEMBLY of the Church of Scotland, to be a Directory for Catechising such as have made some proficiency in the knowledge of the grounds of Religion. WITH REFERENCES TO THE **PROOFS FROM SCRIPTURE.**

Religion & social control, page 29

OTAGO, NEW ZEALAND

A Ship is under survey with a view to its being despatched from the CLYDE to OTAGO, and the other SETTLEMENTS of the NEW ZEALAND COY., on the 11th Sept. 1849.

To Suit the Circumstances of every CLASS of CAPITALISTS, IMPORTANT ALTERATIONS have been made on the TERMS of PURCHASE of LAND in this Settlement. A PROPERTY of 60¼ Acres in RURAL, SUBURBAN, and TOWN ALLOTMENTS, may be obtained for 40s. per acre, or £120, 10s., with a RIGHT of PASTURAGE over the unappropriated Land within the Original Block of 400,0000 acres, and over an Additional Block of 600,000 acres; Or, separately, A RURAL ALLOTMENT of 25 Acres for £50, with a similar RIGHT of PASTURAGE; or A SUBURBAN ALLOTMENT

Advertising the odyssey, page 46

Living in the slums, page 12

"I did not believe, until I visited the wynds of Glasgow, that so large an amount of filth, crime, misery and disease existed on one spot in any civilised country."

"These places are generally, as regards dirt, damp and decay, such as no person of common humanity to animals would stable his horse in."*

This is a 'close' behind Saltmarket Street in the old part of Glasgow, where John McGibbon sold groceries and dealt in tea and coffee. The McGibbon family probably lived in much better conditions, but they would have had contact with this kind of scene.

■ In 1849, only half of all children born in Glasgow could expect to live beyond five years.

■ In early 1849, a cholera epidemic swept through the city.

■ In September 1849, the McGibbon family emigrated to Dunedin, New Zealand.

19th century living in downtown Glasgow

A 'better' type of Glasgow close, ca 1868

*Reports from Assistant Hand-Loom Weavers Commissioners, 1839.

Photo by Thomas Annan.

GETTIN' OOT O' GLASGOW

The grocer's shop at 147 Saltmarket Street, Glasgow, had always given customers value for money. Not that you got a scrap more than you'd paid for in full and never a farthing's credit, but the price was fair. Never as fair as this! Today everything was free for the taking, and Sean O'Reagan was taking everything that could be stuffed into his ragged trousers and grasped in his grubby mitt.

Taking an alternative view of the value of his goods was the shop's proprietor, John McGibbon. At least his perspective on the matter *would* have differed, but John was in no position to talk terms of trade. Slumped senseless behind the counter, he was one of the first victims of Glasgow's unemployed worker riots of March 1848. And Sean, like the fifty other 'customers' in the shop, had no mind for the niceties of commercial exchange.

Half an hour earlier, John McGibbon had gone to his wife Jane in the tea and coffee blending room out the back, and remarked: "I dinna like the sound of that bunch o' rogues around the corner on the Green."

Robb's Close, which led off 122 Saltmarket Street. Drawn by David Small for his 1887 book, "Sketches of Quaint Bits in Glasgow". By that time, most of the old Saltmarket Street slums had been demolished.

"Och, they're just doin' the usual – letting off a wee bit of steam, dinna fash yerself, man," came Jane's response as she weighed twelve pounds of John O'Gaunt into the mix they sold proudly as Monarch Tea.

"Weel they're getting verra rowdy," said her husband, breaking open a chest of Pekoe for the blend. "Mrs Murdoch was in the shop a wee minute ago. She'd just come up past the Green and she said the gatherin' was awfu' stirred up. They were waving the usual Chartist banners and such, and George Smith and the other rabble-rousers were ranting awa' in fine style. Reckons she heerd talk about marchin' through town to make a point of it all and takin' food by the strong hand. They had sticks wi' them, and the police seemed to be giving up and clearing oot.

"If they're going to march thro' the City, they'll be coming up the Saltmarket. We're the first grocery shop, and they'll be hungry as weel as angry. Best keep an eye out and be ready to lock up."

John walked to the front of the shop. "Andrew! Will ye help me move our goods from the footpath, and then get ye down to the Green please and watch that crowd for us?" Together they moved the barrels and baskets of produce inside, and then Andrew, the messenger boy, slipped out the door and made his way down Saltmarket Street toward Glasgow Green, barely a stone's throw away. Half an hour later, the doorbell clanged as Andrew stumbled inside all excited and exclaiming, "The mob's moved to Jail Square, there's a awfu' bunch o' them, and they're cursin' and throwin' stones. They'll be over this way any minute."

John went into the street and looked to his left. Sure enough, Glasgow's poor and disorderly were on the move, and making a lot of noise with it. "Andrew – get ye away hame the noo: there's nae mair business tae be had here the-day, and it may not be too safe hereaboots." Having observed the crowd close-up, the lad needed no encouragement to absent himself, and as he scarpered up the

Saltmarket toward his home in High Street, his employer locked the front door and pulled the blinds down on the windows.

Beside them, Robert Gemmell was closing his bakery up. So were businesses all along the street.

"Jane – there's a bunch of them coming round the corner the noo! Leave off the tea blending and get thee and the weans upstairs out of harm's way."

The weans, consisting of six-year old Jessie and four-year old Jeannie, had seen the goings-on from their first-floor window and had come to the workroom, very frightened, to ask what it was all about. Their nine-year old brother Thomas was not with them, being away at Mrs Colquhoun's educational establishment in George Street – hopefully far enough from the current action for safety. Anyway, nothing could be done about Thomas for the moment. Their problem was at hand and it was imminent.

Down in the street, raised voices and police whistles could be heard. Peeking a look, John watched a rough looking group stalking along barefoot, gathering cobblestones as they went.

London grocer's shop drawn by caricaturist George Cruikshank in 1842. The McGibbon grocery at the foot of Glasgow's Saltmarket may have looked similar, though it was probably a bigger establishment. John McGibbon was also a tea and coffee dealer.

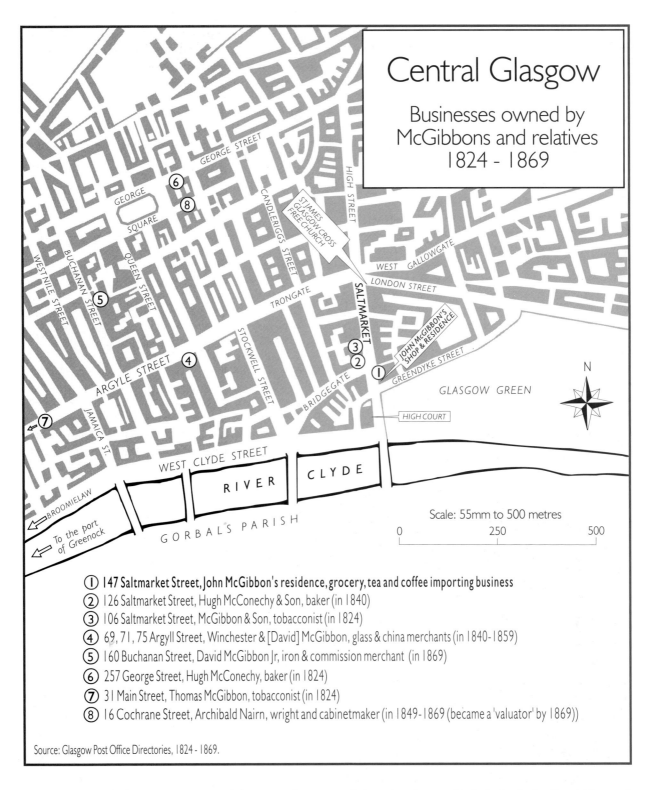

Central Glasgow

Businesses owned by McGibbons and relatives 1824 - 1869

① 147 Saltmarket Street, John McGibbon's residence, grocery, tea and coffee importing business

② 126 Saltmarket Street, Hugh McConechy & Son, baker (in 1840)

③ 106 Saltmarket Street, McGibbon & Son, tobacconist (in 1824)

④ 69, 71, 75 Argyll Street, Winchester & [David] McGibbon, glass & china merchants (in 1840-1859)

⑤ 160 Buchanan Street, David McGibbon Jr, iron & commission merchant (in 1869)

⑥ 257 George Street, Hugh McConechy, baker (in 1824)

⑦ 31 Main Street, Thomas McGibbon, tobacconist (in 1824)

⑧ 16 Cochrane Street, Archibald Nairn, wright and cabinetmaker (in 1849-1869 (became a 'valuator' by 1869))

Source: Glasgow Post Office Directories, 1824 - 1869.

The group quickly became a torrent of the most abject humanity he had ever laid eyes on – haggard, abandoned, ferocious-looking men and women, crawled out of Glasgow's most neglected haunts of misery and crime. He saw a few of them them pause in front of Mary McCurtan's wine and spirits shop and eye her merchandise. A fusillade of stones later, that merchandise was going down their gullets. On either side of her, grog shops owned by James Ballantyne and George Ross were also falling to the rioters.

"There's nae shortage of whisky in this street, if that's what they're after," said John to himself, hoping the rioters would pass him by. Indeed, nearly one in every three shops in Saltmarket Street sold alcohol, which offered Glasgow's impoverished classes a cheap, if temporary, escape from the dreadful reality of inner city life. "Drunk for a penny; dead drunk for tuppence," it was said. Well they weren't dead drunk yet, and there was more than drink on the minds of these rioters. Thousands of them were out of work and suffering genuine starvation, as Glasgow went through a severe business depression.

Across the street, sticks and stones did their work on the window of James Weir's bakery. Two minutes later, a swinging barrel stave stilled all objections from the proprietor of 147 Saltmarket Street and his shelves were laid bare.

Thomas Annan

Saltmarket Street from the corner of Bridgegate Street, almost opposite John McGibbon's grocery shop at number 147. The building on the extreme right is number 139. Unfortunately no Victorian photograph showing number 147 has been found, and the 1849 building is long gone. The photograph was taken in 1868 by Thomas Annan, who was commissioned to photograph slum areas of the city which had been earmarked for demolition. Annan's prints are held at the Mitchell Library in Glasgow.

Tuesdays were quiet in the Saltmarket, and extended afternoon teas in the blending room at the back of number 147 had become a tradition. Tuesday was when the McGibbons roasted their coffee, and the cosy atmosphere and delicious aroma usually drew a few neighbouring shopkeeper friends in for a cuppa. It was a good excuse to test new tea and coffee blends, and they could usually expect something tasty from Robert Gemmell's bakery next door .

Today there was a good complement of business people from this end of the street. Robert was in, and so was William Shaw, who had brought a bag of sweets from his confectionery shop at number 148. Also there, sitting at the work table, were Jane McGibbon's good friends, Lilly Gemmell, and victualler Agnes Pender. Beside them were Hugh Rowan, the watchmaker from across the street, and James Lynch, the undertaker.

Jane, as usual, was 'playing Mither': fussing around her guests and keeping their tea and coffee cups full.

"Looks as though ye're aboot to be mother in another way," commented Agnes, looking at Jane's heavily pregnant form. "When's the wean due? Looks awfu' close."

"Ay, it canna be far awa'," replied Jane as she struggled past an equally portly Mr Shaw to refill Agnes's cup.

"Have ye sorted out a name for the wee bairn yet?"

"Ay – it's Catherine we'll call her if it's a girl. But our last two bairns have both been lassies, and this one will turn out a wee laddie, I'm sure. We'll name him after his da', seein' as he'll be our third son. Thomas was named after John's father, then Hugh was named after my father."

Jane paused. "But you'll not be knowin' Hugh – he was only with us four months, puir wee laddie. He'd be coming up eight years now if he was still alive."

"I'm awfu' sorry to hear that, Jane. Still, it's a lucky family that keeps all its bairns, and we've all lost a few along the way."

Indeed they had. In the 1840s, half of Glasgow's children died before they were five, particularly from tuberculosis, 'fever', bowel disease, measles, and in epidemics of typhus and cholera. Middle class children fared better than average, but it was a rare family which didn't lose at least one child.

Agnes continued, "'Tis good ye'll be following the old

naming tradition though, calling the third one after his da'.'" Turning to John McGibbon, she added, "Sure it's a fine name – and if I may say so, today's coffee is a verra fine brew. My compliments."

"Aye, it's a guid one," said John, with a touch of irony. "The name and the coffee – this is a verra special blend of Jamaica Fine, Mocha and Ceylon. I believe we got the proportions just right."

The McGibbon emporium was known for its excellent tea and coffee, and as well as selling direct to customers, John had developed a small wholesale trade with nearby grocers. His dealings, written up in a leather-bound notebook with the date 1801 on the spine, recycled from his late father's tobacco business, showed that today's blend retailed for 1s 10d per pound, yielding a profit of 5¾d per pound, or 35 per cent. It was pure quality coffee, but he had cheaper blends which were cut with chicory and cheaper coffees. His most expensive ingredient, Mocha coffee, was imported through Gowland Brothers of London and cost 1s 6½d a pound, including freight, duty and toasting. Chicory was only 6d a pound, and most customers didn't seem to taste the difference. The cheapest blend sold for 1s 4d a pound, but actually yielded a higher profit, at 41 per cent.

The teas were pricier. Monarch Tea, made up of John O' Gaunt, William Gillies, Marmion and Pekoe, sold for 4s 10d a pound and yielded a profit of 10d or 22 per cent. The blend still wasn't quite right, wrote John in his workbook: "The above did not please so generally; it appears that the Pekoe flavour was too strong for the other Tea; therefore to give preponderance to the Congo flavour we need to add to 40 lb of the above, 16 lb of Marmion and 8 lb of William Gillies."

Everything was calculated to the last fraction of a farthing. Minute fractions, in fact. With the help of his ready-reckoner tables, John would work out ingredient costs to figures like 1s 2¾$\frac{323}{427}$ d. Jane was quite mystified by this devotion to accuracy, and had more than once questioned the need for it. "Ah – 'tis best to get it right," John would say. "Ye ken what they say: monie a mickle makes a muckle." To which, Jane would grumble that less time spent on the books and more time spent behind the counter in the shop might not go amiss either, and anyway, they could lose an awful lot of 427ths of a penny before joining the slippery slope to penury.

Hugh Rowan leaned back on his chair and lifted his cup. "D'ye realise it's almost a year now, since those mucklets around the corner? It still just seems like yesterday."

"You're not proposin' a toast to that event are ye, Hugh?" responded James Lynch. "It's somethin' I'm wanting to forget."

"Well I can understand that, James, although you even made a bit of money out of that kerfuffle, didn't you? The rest of us had to shut up shop for a couple of days, and John

was attacked and cleaned right out," said Robert.

It was true that James had profited a little from the disturbances. One day after the riot, the protesters had gathered again, but this time, the police were joined by armed cavalry. When a factory was attacked, firing started and the rampage petered out with six people – including some bystanders – dead from gunshot wounds, many wounded, and 64 arrests. Two of the dead were prepared for eternal rest at the James Lynch Funeral Parlour.

Ship's Bank, the first locally owned bank established in Glasgow. It was on the corner of Bridgegate and Saltmarket streets – just across the road from John MacGibbon's grocery shop. (David Small)

"Well thank the Lord those scum have calmed down a wee bit since then," said James, helping himself to one of Mr Gemmell's pastries. "It was guid to see the authorities putting them in their place and packin' a wheen 'o them off to Australia."

The authorities had shown no sympathy for the protesters' plight. Sentencing George Smith to 18 years' transportation for mobbing, rioting and theft, the judge, Lord Medwyn, said he hoped the punishment would be a "warning to the operative classes of this great city, whenever there occurs a depression in trade, and a consequent failure in employment, and the distress which accompanies such a state of things, that they should not listen to the bad advice of designing men, preaching to them about their 'rights'."

Rather, his honour advised, the "operative classes" should put their trust in the benevolence of the rich. And they should accept such crumbs from rich men's tables "...thankfully and gratefully, patiently enduring what is so inevitable, 'till the state of trade again admits of their full employment."

With no proper system of poor relief available, benevolence was the best most of Glagow's unfortunates could hope for – and this charity was a hit or miss affair at best.

Close leading off High Street, Glasgow, ca 1867. Note the gas light, which probably would not have been in an area such as this as early as 1849.

but we had some luck wi' it. Our stock was fairly low at the time, and we had a deal of fresh tea, coffee, sugar and flour sitting down at my brother David's warehouse on the Clyde. And David hisself gied me a wee loan to get me on my feet again.

"We're getting by now, but it's hard. It'll be hard for all of us though – I'll wager none of ye are making a fortune.

"I canna see things getting any better in this part of Glasgow. It's really gone to the dogs."

There were gloomy nods of agreement all round. John picked up an old clay pipe from a small wooden case with the name McGibbon and Sons on the lid, pressed some tobacco into it, lit a wax taper in the roasting oven and lit up. Through a cloud of pungent smoke he continued, "It certainly wasna like this in the auld days. Saltmarket was a bonny place 20 years ago when I was in my Da's tobacco business just up the street."

"Aye, we had a guid class of person here then," William Shaw agreed. "But most of them have packed up and moved west now. The grog shops are taking over, and what's really wrecking this neighborhood are all them paddies moving in."

"That, and the clearances pushing people down here out of the hielands. Still, at least the hielanders are Scots, even if they are a bunch of ignorant teuchters," John said.

"Well you'd best not be too tough on them, John. With a name like McGibbon, it's likely your lot were hielanders at one time."

"Aye – I believe they may have been. But that would be two hundred years ago at least. My grandfather moved here from Dumbarton about 70 years ago, and his parents and grandparents came from Bonhill, up near Loch Lomond. But going 'way back, the family was supposed to have been living near Doune, up in Perthshire. They might have been living further back in the hielands earlier than that.

"I trust you'll agree we've become a mite more civilised since then, man?"

The shop bell jangled and the proprietor rose to attend to business. Returning five minutes later, he resumed his chair and continued, "That was a good example of what we've been saying. I just sold four pounds of tea and a flagon of vinegar to Alex Buchanan. You'll ken Alex, he used to live up the street near the Cross, but he moved across to Blythswood a couple of years ago. Alex wasna in the shop

The Scottish poor law did not apply to the unemployed, and assistance via churches was rarely available to newcomers, who during this period of hardship were still flooding into Glasgow, mainly escaping the Irish potato famine, at up to 1,000 a week. Within a year, the rate would rise to 2,500 a week.

❧

"How are things with you, these days, John?" asked Robert Gemmell. "The business seems to be back on its feet again, no?"

"Hmmph," responded the grocer, fingering the deep scar behind his left ear that would be a permanent reminder of the big riot.

"It's nae been easy, I'll tell ye. I was out cold on the floor for a long while, and when I came to, the crowd had scarpered, and Jane was attending to an awfu' lot o' blood and gore. And there was precious little left on the shelves for selling to anyone.

"I tell ye, we came awfu' close to going out of business,

himself though – he ne'er comes any more. But he still sends his maid to buy things frae us. There's plenty who don't."

"Aye, it's a worry," said Robert. "We need customers with a wee bit of money at least. I don't see many of the new folk in our shops – they seem to buy mostly at the weekly market, and nearly all of it's oatmeal and potatoes. They're buying precious little bread from me, and I doubt there's many of your goods they'll be buying, John."

"Och, they wadna know what to do wi' a some of what I have on my shelves. But it's a worry, now that our usual trade is moving away. Part of me says the new folk should stick to their ain hovels and keep their filth and disease away from my shop. But gentility will ne'er boil the pot – I have to make a living."

John McGibbon and his merchant neighbours were typical of their class, and not embarrassed to wear such prejudice on their sleeves. But they did have reason for concern. Saltmarket Street had lost its former genteel character, and the profusion of grog shops and their clientele gave everyday offence to Free Churchers like the McGibbons.

J ohn and Jane McGibbon knew they were lucky compared with the neighbours they despised so much. Leading off Saltmarket Street, and other main streets in this old district of central Glasgow, were narrow wynds and closes which led into rabbit warrens of dense and airless housing – ancient dwellings and behind them, rackrent tenements crammed into former garden spaces. Few 'homes' were more than a single three by four metres room.

Almost opposite the McGibbon shop was the intersection of Saltmarket and Bridgegate streets. Bridgegate, or Briggate as it was usually called, was an Irish ghetto, notorious for some of the worst slum conditions in Glasgow. From their upstairs window, John, Jane and the children could see intoxicated men and women carousing on the street at all hours and in all weathers. Anything rather than stay inside their mean dwellings.

Sean O'Reagan was one of last night's revelers. Just for a while, life had seemed rosy as he jigged on the cobblestones with a flagon of whisky in his hand and sang the songs of County Mayo. But the 12 months since he called on John McGibbon had not been easy, and events were about to turn for the worse.

Last year's riot hadn't been fun, but at least it was a change from lounging around, visiting the soup kitchen, doing an occasional day of labour on the relief gangs, working on the bottle and slapping his wife a bit when she complained. For a while it had seemed the Chartist revolution might even happen, and Sean and his family had supper that night, thanks to the involuntary generosity of that shopkeeper in Saltmarket Street. Life had seemed fairer the further they moved along the streets, yelling Vive la Republique and looting food shops, jewelers and gunsmiths.

Extract from Gorbals Burying Ground Records, December 1848, listing deaths from cholera, croup, inflammation and consumption.

The best part of the day had been building the barricade at Glasgow Cross. That was real proletariat action – like the European revolutions those people talked about on Glasgow Green. The pity of it was the police had gone back to their barracks, and what was the point of a barricade if there was no-one to defend it against? Then, when he and his companions came out again next day, the cavalry beat them back and shot them up before they had a chance to be heroes.

Nothing much seemed to happen after that. There

Thomas Annan – 118 High Street

was another big meeting on the Green a month later, and suggestions of forming a Chartist National Guard. But it never caught on. The Chartist leaders could never agree among themselves, and when they started talking about *working* with the middle classes instead of fighting them, that was an end to it. It was back to the old Briggate routine.

In a few hours, the springtime sun would begin to warm Glasgow, but not Sean's close. In fact, the sun only ever shone there in the middle of summer, for a few hours a day. The flagstoned wynd leading into the close was a narrow lane, just wide enough for a small dung cart to pass – and it was enclosed by soot-stained stone walls, towering four stories high. An open drain along one side of the wynd was but a slight concession to sanitation.

In the early morning gloom, Sean staggered barefoot down the reeking wynd, picking his way around splodges of crap with only moderate success, and partly ducking a cascade of unmentionable matter from the fourth floor. "Why don't they empty their chamberpots on the dunghill out the back?" he asked himself – and then admitted his own disinclination to carry a smelly pot down four flights of uneven, slippery stairs and over to that unspeakable mound of excrement.

He reached the end of the wynd, entered a six metre square close, and carefully picked his way around the resident dunghill to an opening in the far wall. He entered, and staggered down a long dank corridor to another courtyard. A further doorway led directly to a dark staircase which Sean climbed with difficulty, to reach an attic room above the fourth floor of the building. He pushed the door open and immediately sensed that things were more desperate than usual.

"About time you came home too, you drunken shit!" were the first words he heard. This was from Colleen McBride, one of three lodgers who shared the room and took turns to doss on a pile of straw and rags in a corner.

A pale little girl in a torn grey shift threw herself at Sean and cried, "Da'! Where have you been? If you were only here before – Mammy's sick. There's a mess in the bed and she won't get up or do anything."

In the pale light from a single flickering farthing candle, Sean could see his wife, Maureen, doubled up on their narrow cot beside the fireplace, groaning and holding her stomach. Her face seemed shrunken and there was an unnatural blueness about her features. He hurried to her.

"What's wrong, Maureen? When did it start?"

"In the middle of the night. It... it just came on me."

With difficulty she raised herself a little, reached weakly for his hand and whispered, "It's the cholera, Sean."

She collapsed back on the filthy pillow. "Mind you look after the children, then."

Later that day, Maureen and several other Briggate residents made a one-way trip across the Clyde River to the Gorbals Burying Ground. They were bundled, with minimal ceremony, into a common grave for victims of the city's cholera epidemic. Within two days, three of their five children, plus Colleen the lodger, also paid a final visit to the Gorbals.

Oot 'n aboot on business

"I'll be off tae bank the takings and order in some new stock," said John McGibbon as he finished a lunch of fried herrings with oatcakes and drained his cup of tea. "I expect I'll be back aboot three o'clock. Will ye see to it that young Andrew is scrubbing up them barrels oot the back while I'm awa'?"

John stepped out of the shop and took a jaunty course up Saltmarket Street toward Glasgow Cross. It was a bright day in late winter, in fact the first time in several weeks that a sustained burst of sunlight had penetrated the Glasgow gloom. Even the dark stone tenements looked more optimistic than usual.

Original: People's Palace Museum, Glasgow

John Knox's painting, "The Trongate of Glasgow", probably in the early 1800s. The St James Church (which was not built until 1845), would have been just 'off-camera' in London Street at the bottom left of the picture. The painter is working from Gallowgate and looking west over the Cross to Trongate. High Street goes off to the right, beside the distinctive Toolbooth Steeple in the foreground. Saltmarket Street goes to the left opposite High Street. The steeple, built in the 14th century, was once the site of a 'tron' or weighing scales, where goods entering the town were weighed for taxation purposes. The massive statue of a toga-clad King William of Orange astride his charger can be seen a short distance along Trongate. This is very much how the area would have looked in 1849, when the McGibbon family emigrated to New Zealand. All that remains of this scene today are the Toolbooth Steeple, and the Tron Kirk Steeple on the left of the picture.

It should have taken only a few minutes to reach the Cross, for Saltmarket Street is not very long. Indeed, John had every intention of doing his business on the trot. But to walk down a street which had seen McGibbons in various shops for most of the century was to meet business colleagues and acquaintances. So, as usual, John was led astray from his best intentions.

He walked quickly past the first dozen or so businesses, which were mostly seedy little grog shops. But at number 107 he met a grizzled old fellow sweeping the footpath in front of his shop, and stopped for the first chat of the day. The old man

Close off 28 Saltmarket Street, near Glasgow Cross, ca 1868 (Thomas Annan)

was tobacconist William McWhinnie, a contemporary of John's late father. Thomas and William had been business rivals and firm friends.

Half an hour later, reminiscences ringing in his ears and a fresh plug of tobacco in his pocket, John went directly to the Cross, avoiding seven more spirit dealers, the Odd-Fellows Tavern, and sundry small businesses including victuallers, a candlemaker, confectioner, baker, bookseller, clog maker, iron merchant, surgeon and toy merchant.

At the Cross, he moved left into a more impressive thoroughfare: Trongate.

The broad street was a hive of activity: people and still more people, hurrying about on business; standing talking in pairs and groups. Men and grubby urchins moving goods in carts and barrows. Servant women with baskets, carrying clothes to the washing ground at Glasgow Green. Hucksters selling vegetables, oysters, mussels and fresh 'caller' herrings from barrows and trestle tables. Raggedy little girls with pinched, anxious faces, offering bunches of flowers. Men on horseback. Dogs underfoot. Everyone milling over the entire street, moving hastily out of the way of horse-drawn cabs, coaches and carts. A constant clop of hooves on cobblestones.

Like Saltmarket, this famous street had seen better days. No longer were its 'plainstanes' footpaths the exclusive paradeground of scarlet-coated and bewigged Tobacco Lords, whose grip on Glasgow's commercial power had faded after they lost their American estates in the War of Independence. But Trongate was still the financial heart of the city and still boasted good addresses.

John looked across to the Tontine Reading Room, which he had visited recently as a guest of his elder brother David, a glass and crockery merchant who was doing well in the thriving business of Winchester and McGibbon. The brothers had taken a 'meridian' glass of claret, like the elite merchants of yore who had brought fame to the establishment. In the old tradition, they read newspapers brought that day by coach from London and Edinburgh. John felt just a wee bit superior, although he knew that even David would not have visited the Tontine in its heyday.

On either side of the Reading Room were famous city landmarks. On the corner of the Cross was Glasgow's oldest building, the Tollbooth Steeple, while a short distance down Trongate to the left was the large statue of King William of Orange, dressed in a Roman toga and astride a rampant charger. King Billy was much admired by the Protestant majority, particularly those Orangemen who liked to celebrate Hogmanay by smashing whisky bottles on the statue's base. The statue held understandably less appeal for the Irish community.

As well as its monuments to local salubrity, Trongate had 30 taverns and nine wine and spirit dealers along its half kilometre length. These were just the legal drink outlets. As in the Saltmarket, illicit activity was just around the corner. If John were to venture down the narrow wynds leading off Trongate's respectable facade, he would find plenty of illegal stills and grogshops known as shebeens. And a host of thieves and prostitutes besides.

Even in Trongate proper, the crowds were not all honest and industrious, and John clutched his purse tightly as he walked to a small branch of the Union Bank.

"Good day to ye, and a verra fine day it is, no?" said John as he lifted his purse and shook the previous day's takings onto the counter. "Hmmph," came the reply from the manager, George Renton, who was not given to displays of enthusiasm. Sequestered in his sombre, dark panelled bank, Renton would hardly have noticed the fine weather

---

---

anyway. There would be no time-wasting conversation with this dour little money-man who habitually treated his customers as potential thieves.

"Ye dinna hae a deal to gie me the day, Mr McGibbon. I don't know why ye bothered to come," said the banker.

"Well, ye know what business is like, we're not takin' as much as we used to. But I'd rather it was in the bank than under my pillow."

"Ay, these are difficult times, but not all businesses are doin' it hard," said the banker as he gathered in the slim takings and wrote a receipt in precise copperplate style. "You'll ne'er do weel tryin' to keep a respectable shop in those parts. The Saltmarket has gone doon, and it'll stay doon, I'll warrant ye that."

"Your optimism is appreciated as always, Mr Renton," was John's sardonic reply as he left the bank, his mood somewhat dulled by the encounter.

Resuming his walk, John reached the entrance to Laigh Kirk Close and was nearly bowled over by a pair of ruffians pursued into Trongate by a whistle-blowing constable. Not an unusual event for this close, which as well as accommodating hundreds of citizens, also hosted three shebeens and 20 brothels.

A few doors further on he came to another local landmark, the old Tron Church. Crossing the street at this point, he walked past a few more doors, including Mrs McLaren's famous Rob Roy Tavern, before heading down Candleriggs Street to do the main business of the day.

Candleriggs was a cheerful, busy little street whose occupiers were mainly providoring warehouses and small manufacturers. There was an air of purpose about the place, with goods being loaded and unloaded from carts, and barrels being rolled along the street by workmen in coarse-wool trousers, rough linen shirts and dark jackets.

First stop was Walter Roberts' wholesale grocery, where he settled his account and ordered six sacks of potatoes, seven sacks of oatmeal, six dozen candles and quantities of sugar and starch. Next, at drysalter William Paterson's emporium, he ordered two cases of salted herrings, a crock of acetic acid, four stoneware flagons of white wine vinegar, a sack of salt and an assortment of pickles.

Along the street to William Adams and Son, ham curers: "… I'm not selling as much as I used to, Billy, but if you'll deliver half a dozen gammons to my shop the morrow I'll be obliged to ye."

Beside the City Hall was the Candleriggs Bazaar, Glasgow's equivalent of Covent Garden. Vegetables and flowers were displayed in the open air on tables and in barrows, and there was much shouting and carry-on from the hawkers. John wasn't interested in their offerings today, but he followed a pungent dairy aroma into a

Recipe for vinegar from the McGibbon business cashbook, dated 1846. The true vinegar content is somewhat 'cut' with a solution of acetic acid and water. Was this standard practice or sharp practice?

warehouse next door, where, as his eyes adjusted to the dim light, he could see rows of big round cheeses on well-scrubbed shelves.

William Dick came forward to welcome his old client and invite him out the back for a whisky. "This is a fine wee drappie, and I have just the right accompaniment for it," said the cheese merchant. "Alex Lindsay was up from Ayrshire yesterday and he brought this verra fine aged Dunlop cheese wi' him. I'm picking you'll be wanting to sell it."

After ordering butter and some cheeses, among them Lindsay's new product, John's business in the Candleriggs was finished. That didn't prevent him calling on his good friend and fellow grocer Roy Andrew, for tea and a long chat about business and the sudden turn of fine weather.

Back into Trongate, he walked briskly west. Soon Trongate became Argyll Street, and he arrived at his brother David's premises at number 71.

"If it's yer brither you're lookin' for, he's oot the back," advised George Winchester in the front office.

"Efternuin to ye," greeted David McGibbon, coming from behind a stack of wooden packing cases, broken open to display a new consignment of china from the potteries at Stoke on Trent.

The brothers passed smalltalk back and forth for several minutes before John got to the main point of his visit, which was to make final payment on the loan David had given him a year earlier. That was sufficient excuse for a further drop of whisky.

"How's business now that you've put all that unpleasantness behind ye?" asked David.

"Weel ye know it's not sae guid, an' just today George Renton at the bank was reckoning things will ne'er come richt again in the Saltmarket."

"Mr Renton is a gloomy auld gowk, but he does ken the richt side o' a shillin'," replied David. "I'm thinking you need to get awa' from there too. Canna ye look for a business up this way, or ower towards Buchanan Street?"

"Dinna ye think I've not been looking into it, David, but I'm not sure if we can afford to buy something new just yet."

"I understand, John, but ye maun do it suin, or it will be too late," advised David.

"I'd better be gettin' along then. I told the guidwife I'd be back by three, and it's already past that time."

In Buchanan Court, close by Winchester and McGibbons, was the Glasgow Courier newspaper office. John went in to buy the morning paper. Leaving the Court, he passed a man declaiming about a "new Scotland in the South Seas." John took a proffered handbill which read: "*Emigration to New Zealand – important meeting to discuss the new Scottish settlement. Tron Church, 7.30pm, Saturday 24 February. For more information, apply to the Lay Association for Promoting the Settlement of Otago, 3 West Nile Street.*"

The timing was right. The notion of emigration had not previously occurred to John McGibbon, but today's talk with his brother and the bank manager had helped make up his mind about their future in the Saltmarket. He knew he had to sell up, but really, could he afford

anything better in this city? Emigration had to be an option. A new start, a new land of opportunity. Well it wouldn't hurt to visit those offices in Nile Street and find out a little more.

Crossing Argyll Street, he walked up Queen Street past Bayley and Ferguson's music shop and the Royal Exchange Square with its temple-like Exchange Building and fine statue of the Duke of Wellington. He reached the corner of St Vincent Street and George Square. Over his right shoulder were the square's imposing buildings, and the dominating statue of Sir Walter Scott atop a 25 metre column.

Going along St Vincent Street, he crossed swanky Buchanan Street with its fashionable people in fashionable carriages, and found his destination at the next intersection. Number 3 West Nile Street was not an imposing address; it was the office of Charles Pendler, a commission agent who sublet a small room to the Lay Association of the Free Church of Scotland.

Entering the offices, John went up to a clerk seated at a high desk and stated his business. Reluctant to admit his own interest at this point, he requested any information that might be available about the Otago settlement, "...on behalf of an acquaintance".

"That will not be a problem Sir, but do you know there is a public meeting about the settlement this Saturday night?" replied the clerk.

"Ay, I do know aboot that, but my friend is anxious to read aboot the scheme afore he goes to the meeting."

"Very well Sir. May I suggest you purchase the Otago Journal. It is published by the Lay Association in conjunction with the New Zealand Company and has the very latest and best information on the subject. We also have a few general booklets about emigration to New Zealand. I would recommend Mr Earp's Emigrant's Guide."

"Thankye, I'll tak both o' them," said John, and handing over some coins, he walked out into the street with the slim volumes under his arm. Back in Buchanan Street on the way home, he went into a coffee house – partly because he felt the need of a cup, but mostly because he was eager to look at the emigration literature.

Glancing through the booklets with increasing

interest, he resolved to be at the Tron Church on Saturday and take a serious look at the proposition. He then retraced his steps home, scarcely noticing the streets and their occupants, but somewhat aware of the late hour and the likelihood of a wifely tongue-lashing. However he did think he saw a familiar looking girl at Trongate's West Port public well, a traditional meeting place for Glasgow maidservants. Wasn't it their Jenny cavorting among them? No, it couldn't be – she was still on duty.

Back at the shop, he was keen to take Jane for a short walk and tell her about the emigration idea. Neighbour Lily Gemmel was behind the counter, but there was no sign of Jane.

"It's a surprise to see you here, Lily – where is Jane?"

"Oh Mr McGibbon, thank heavens you're hame. Jane's in such a state. Your maid up and left this efternuin and I've come in to help out so Jane could attend to the bairns and cook the dinner."

He hurried up the stairs, to find Jane weeping as she attended the evening meal, cooking in pots on hooks over an open fireplace. The heavily pregnant woman turned on John and demanded to know why he was so late home.

"...and when I needed to have you here too. Just after you went off on your business, oor Jenny started cursing an' yelling. Said she was leavin' and wasna going tae be servant tae oniebodie. She just up and went awa' without so much as by your leave."

"The stupit young lass, she was aye lucky to have a position wi' us here," said John. "But we'll get anither maid, dinna ye fret."

"It's all verra weel for you to say that," sobbed Jane. "You don't have to find a decent lassie and keep her under control. We'll just get anither Godless hizzie oot o' the slums who doesn'a have the first notion aboot keepin' things clean. Sometimes I wonder why we even have a servant. They ne'er stay lang, and I'm always doin' half their work anyway, as weel as working in the shop. Scrubbing, dusting, keeping the fires going, doing the cooking and the washing and looking after the children. I'm at my wits' end now, an' soon there'll be anither bairn to worry aboot."

"Jane, it's nae so bad as that. And I've come home wi' a grand idea to put to ye. Will ye come oot fur a wee walk while I tell ye aboot it?"

"You and your ideas! Would ye have me going oot the noo when I'm up to my eyes in cooking your meal? If ye

have somethin' tae say to me, say it here and now."

"Not in front of the bairns, Jane. We'll talk later, then."

"What is it you're sayin', man! Are you askin' me tae live amang savages on the other side of the warld? Where was it ye said?"

"New Zealand is where it is, Jane. By all accounts it's a grand country, and there's a place for us in a town called Dunedin. They're building a new Scottish society there, and it's the Free Kirk that is doin' it. And we wouldna be amang savages – we'd be amang God-fearing fowk who believe what we believe. There's more savages in this part of Glasgow."

"But why would we want to leave the place we were born in – where we belang? The place where all our friends and relations live? Would we ever see them again?"

"We canna byde where we are, Jane. You've been sayin' yourself that the Saltmarket will ruin us if it doesna kill us first. And ye know full weel that we canna afford to set up business in a better part of town. It's you that's doin' the household budgeting – you know how things are."

"It's just not right – how can ye ask me to leave all we have here to go chasin' after something that could be waur than we already have?"

"All I'm sayin' Jane, is that we should tak' a look at the notion. Will ye come wi' me to the meetin' tomorrow night?"

"Ye'll be goin' on yer own, guidman!"

Next morning, John McGibbon was up early as usual, but after breakfast, instead of going down to the shop, he repaired to his comfortable armchair in the sitting room. In an uncharacteristic concession to his wife's condition and mood, he had made his own cup of tea, and now he settled down to study the emigration literature in greater depth. Jane fussed about the apartment, cleaning, tidying and keeeping the children away from her husband.

"It wilna do for the bairns to ken what is on their

SPIRIT CELLAR TO LET.

A LICENSED SHOP, of Moderate Rent, in an excellent and respectable locality, doing a good business, well fitted up, and the fixtures &c., to be taken along with the Shop.

Apply by Letter addressed to G. A. S., Herald Office.

TO LET,

THE JENNY LIND TAVERN, 85 NELSON STREET.

Apply to Mr. Thos. Whitaker, at 85 Nelson Street.

WINE AND SPIRIT CELLAR TO RENT.

A LICENCED neatly fitted up, SHOP, in one of the busiest thoroughfares of the City ; the present Proprietor retiring.

Apply, by Letter addressed W. C. D., Herald Office.

Glasgow, September 3, 1849.

DOG CART, BY AUCTION

MESSRS HUTCHISON & DIXON will Sell, at their Rooms, on Thursday 6th September, at One o'clock, a Handsome New DOG CART, well-found and finished.

May be seen on the Morning of Sale.

(Glasgow Herald, 3/9/1849)

faither's mind," she thought. "Not for a while, anyway. It's bad enough me knowin'."

Two hours later a hammering on the shop door summoned John to his commercial duties, which he carried out distractedly for the rest of the day. Jane remained upstairs, her mind churning over servant problems and the awful prospect of leaving Glasgow for the wilds of the Antipodes. She was still angry, but as the day wore on, her Victorian sense of wifely duty got the better of her. At noon she went down to the shop, faced John across the counter and announced, "Och weel, I suppose I'd better come wi' ye tonight and find oot what it's all aboot. Now come on up for lunch – I've made some pease brose for ye."

That evening, leaving the children in the care of Jane's friend Lily, the couple set out for the emigration meeting.

They were not on their own. Saturday night was the night to be out and about in Glasgow. There was no work in the factories and offices tomorrow, and even if people had nowhere in particular to go, walking the streets was better than being at home. Saltmarket Street's cobbled surface would be trod by thousands of jostling promenaders this night.

The McGibbons turned up their coat collars and shivered as a clammy miasma swirled out of the Clyde and around their ears. The narrow street seemed to close in, squeezed between tall buildings which faded above to nothingness in the foggy gloom. A soft glow from gas flares dimly marked the way ahead.

Outside the dark entrance to a nearby close stood a group of women chattering, cackling and cursing. Some were holding babies wrapped in filthy shawls. One woman, well in her cups, was stumbling about with a bottle in her hand, trying to dance a reel. As John and Jane approached, she slipped in front of them, the bottle splintering on the cobbles and splashing Jane's coat with cheap wine.

Ladies of the night were hustling shilling-a-screw customers down dark alleys to the sordid warrens of single room apartments that often did double duty as brothels.

A fight had broken out between a couple of sailors, egged on by the passers-by. Unconscious whisky drunkards sprawled against buildings, pushed casually aside by the street walkers.

Further along, John and Jane passed the brightly lit Odd-Fellows Tavern and Music Hall, advertised by a pair of illuminated globes and a clutter of patrons spilling out the doorway. Raucous song and conversation came from within. Two laughing boys and their mangy dog pushed through the crowd, chasing each other into the tavern.

Were John and Jane to have entered, they could have joined a singalong of sentimental songs led by popular comedian John McGregor, or watched Mr Baylis exhibit his ingenious automata.

Across the street, at the Jupiter Tavern, they could have joined in similar song and frivolity, listened to singer Miss Coutts, and watched in amazement as Alister McLean played the pipes and danced the highland fling, both at the same time.

At the nearby Shakespeare Tavern they would have heard the comic duet singers Mr Dalhousie and and Miss Annie Grant, while a few doors along at the Sir Walter Scott Tavern, amongst the general song and dance, they would have witnessed novelty performances by the resident Female Ethiopian Serenader.

John and Jane McGibbon never took part in the Saturday night revelries, although, being raised in the street, they were well aware of what went on. It didn't suit their current temperament or moral stance, though they were not teetotallers and were happy to take the odd drop of whisky, sherry or claret – in moderation of course. But usually on a Saturday night they would firmly barricade themselves from the street throngs, behind stout wooden shutters.

As they reached the head of the street, a small barefoot girl in a flimsy dress and carrying a broom came up to Jane and asked, "Can I sweep the crossing for ye Ma'am, only a penny?"

"Thank you, child," said Jane, reaching in her pockets for a coin.

The pair followed the sweeper across the street and moved on to Trongate, which was equally full of Glasgow humanity. It was only a short distance now to the meeting in the Tron Church – only four more taverns to pass...

Winding up the new Pilgrim Fathers

At 7:30 pm, the Tron Church was half full with a cross-section of decent Glasgow society. In the back pews were men and women from the respectable working classes, wearing their best clothes and glancing nervously at each other. John and Jane McGibbon had settled themselves closer to the front, among their own kind – mostly small businessmen who, though somewhat better-heeled, looked less affluent than the clergy and wealthy business people in the front rows.

Shortly after, when it was clear no more people would turn up, proceedings were opened with a prayer by Reverend Dr Robert Buchanan, minister of the kirk.

".....Heavenly Father ..... we beseech.....we are unworthy.....amen.

"Now I have great pleasure in introducing our two speakers, who are both from the Association of Lay Members of the Free Church of Scotland.

"On my left, from Edinburgh, is the man whose vision and industry are energising the great venture you have come to hear about tonight: John McGlashan, secretary of the Association. On my right is Dr Aldcorn, who is secretary of our local branch of the Association, and Mr Hutcheson, who runs the Association's office in Nile Street.

"Dr Aldcorn."

The Glasgow secretary moved to the pulpit.

"Thank you Dr Buchanan, and may I extend a warm welcome to everyone. Thank you for coming out on this cold night. You would never think spring is with us, the way winter is clinging on with its icy grip.

"But that is all the more reason for moving to Otago, and leaving Scotland's cold weather behind you.

"We are here tonight to commend the Otago settlement to your attention, and Mr McGlashan has very kindly travelled from Edinburgh to explain the background to the scheme, and the advantages it offers.

"Not all of you will know about the Lay Association. It is an association which lay members of the church set up in 1845 to promote the idea of a special Free Church settlement in Dunedin. In this we have the full support of the Church's General Assembly.

"The Lay Association is working alongside the New Zealand Company, which is, without doubt, the most

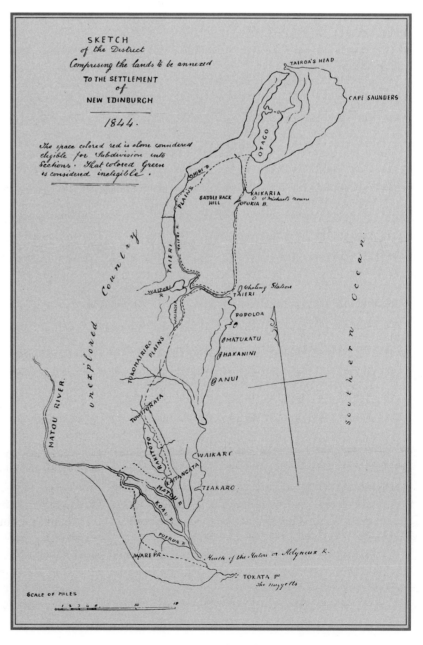

experienced and far-sighted agency ever established for British colonial development. The company has a special relationship with New Zealand. This relationship has been established by an Act of Parliament.

"Those of you who decide to emigrate to Otago will be joining a settlement which is not only Scottish in character, but more importantly, is following the beliefs and doctrines of the Free Church of Scotland.

"In moving to a settlement of such a character, you will be following in the footsteps of that brave and principled group of settlers who sailed in the Mayflower to Plymouth, Massachusetts, in 1620. They were called the Pilgrim Fathers, and their destination was then known as the New World.

"You will be travelling to an even newer world, on the other side of the globe – a much longer journey than the Pilgrim Fathers. They sailed for 65 days; you may be on the water for up to 120 days. That is something to think about, but I know I would rather take the longer voyage. The modern emigrant ships which sail today to New Zealand are three times as big as the Mayflower, and they have every comfort imaginable.

"The first two ships were despatched to our settlement at the end of 1847. The John Wycliffe dropped anchor at Otago on 22 March 1848, while the second ship, the Philip Laing arrived three weeks later. Since that time, six more ships have set sail for Otago. There is now a thriving settlement of about 700 men, women and children, under the able leadership of Captain William Cargill, who has been associated with this venture from its early days.

"Captain Cargill's chief associate here in Scotland is the man before you today: Mr John McGlashan.

"I give you Mr McGlashan."

As Aldcorn resumed his seat, the Edinburgh lawyer took over the meeting.

"Your words are too kind, Dr Aldcorn, but I thank you for them nevertheless. And may I also extend warm greetings to all of you who strayed from your warm hearths to learn about the new land that awaits us.

"Ladies and Gentlemen – by the infinite grace of our Lord and Maker, we are witnessing the beginning of one of Mankind's great endeavours."

The Lay Association's chief proselytiser paused, placed his hands on both edges of the lectern and looked toward the ceiling of the church, as though to seek affirmation from on high, and also to allow the import of his statement to sink into the audience.

"Otago represents the full flowering of the best principles of British colonial endeavour. It is the most advanced of the New Zealand Company's colonisation schemes. But it is much more than that.

"Dr Aldcorn spoke of the Pilgrim Fathers, and as God-fearing people we are proud to follow in the footsteps of that remarkable band of men.

"But the Otago Settlement offers superior possibilities, because it combines the highest standards of moral principle – within the Free Church framework – with a most enlightened system of social and economic organisation.

"The Pilgrim Fathers carried firm and admirable religious principles to America, but their endeavour would have been more successful had they paid more attention to the temporal needs of their people. We are not making that mistake.

"Our object is to transplant Scottish society to the new land. A Scottish society with all its levels of rank and organisation in their proper proportions. We are transferring our laws, our customs and our associations. We are taking our habits, manners and feelings with us. In other words, we are taking everything that is good about Caledonia except the soil itself. And we're setting it down to flourish in this new and most promising land.

"We are casting the foundations of a country that in a few generations will offer a counterpart of Britain to the world. A counterpart with the most cherished peculiarities of our own social systems and national character, as well as our wealth and power.

"But we are not taking everything with us. No nation can claim to be perfect, and we are glad to leave some aspects of Great Britain behind. We hold no brief for the intemperate elements in our society, for the slums, the overcrowding in our cities and the diseases. We can do without the poor working conditions and long working days which some have to endure.

"God willing, and in the fullness of time, I have every confidence that most of these problems will be dealt with in the home country.

"However in New Zealand, we have a clean slate to

John McGlashan

work with, and that is to the infinite advantage of the intending colonist.

"Many of you will know that Otago is one of a series of settlements which the New Zealand Company has promoted in that land of abundance. The Company has been remarkably successful, and it has given a start to thriving settlements at New Plymouth and Wellington in the North Island, and Nelson in the Middle Island. Dunedin is now established as the fifth settlement.

"As we speak, a sixth settlement is being planned near Port Cooper in the Canterbury region of the Middle Island. It is on the east coast, about halfway between Nelson and Otago. This Canterbury settlement will be English in character, and it will be promoted in connection with the Established Church of England.

"But I am getting away from what you came to hear. We must return to Otago to discuss the climate and the bounty of the land. Then I'll explain how all social classes can take advantage of the opportunities for their mutual betterment. Finally, I will invite any questions you may care to ask.

"Of all the areas of the world which Britain has favoured with its colonial endeavours, New Zealand has the best combination of climate and land.

"The climate is most salubrious, and perfectly suited to men and women of British stock. It is free from excessive heat in summer, and cold in winter. It is not too wet in any season, but it does not suffer from the droughts which are such a problem in Australia.

"Temperatures are generally a little lower in Otago than in the North Island, but the difference is not great. A great many people have praised the Otago climate – even the weather in winter."

McGlashan reached into his leather portmanteau and drew out a handful of slim magazines. Flourishing them above his head he continued:

"I am holding the January 1848 edition of the Otago Journal, and it contains some interesting observations from Dr Munro. Copies of this publication will be available at the conclusion of this meeting. The price is a very reasonable twopence, and I would urge all of you to make arrangements to secure a permanent subscription."

Opening the journal, the promoter read: "The extreme loveliness of the weather at Otago in the middle of winter, as described by Dr Munro – the surprising richness of the winter pastures, from the trickling down of the melted snows from the hills – the green, fresh growth of the potato-stems at the season answering to the very end of October, or the beginning of November, in this country – the fact of both Europeans and natives growing wheat of the finest quality, far in the interior behind, and to the south of Otago, and also at the Bluff Harbour, at the very southern extremity of the Island, in Foveaux Strait – and, to mention no more, the number of parakeets that are to be seen flying about in the depths of winter amongst the evergreen woods of Stewart's Island (the South Island), and also its being the haunt of the cassowary – these are sufficient proofs that no part of the Middle Island, not even the South Island, is severe in point of climate. Its coldest parts are greatly milder than the south of France, which is in the same latitude."

McGlashan placed the journals on the table beside him, and as he did so, a short, earnest looking man leaped to his feet. The interjector raised his top hat, waved it to gain attention, and stabbed the air with his free hand in the direction of McGlashan.

"How can you stand there an' tell us the weather is sae fine in Otago after the terrible time the first settlers had of it last year? My brither sailed to Dunedin on the Philip Laing, and here is a letter he wrote to us. He says the winter were awfu' wet an' cauld. He says they were promised housing, but it wasna there. They had to bide a lang time on the ship until the authorities built a rough barracks with grasses and bullrushes. It were draughty an' it didna keep the rain oot, and everyone had a hard time of it, especially the mithers and bairns.

"Why should we believe anythin' ye tell us?"

The audience began to murmur, but were stilled as

THE

EMIGRANT'S GUIDE

TO

NEW ZEALAND:

COMPRISING EVERY REQUISITE INFORMATION FOR

INTENDING EMIGRANTS,

RELATIVE TO THE

SOUTHERN SETTLEMENTS OF NEW ZEALAND.

BY

A LATE RESIDENT IN THE COLONY.

———

" Her Majesty's Government may rest satisfied that there will be soon no more prosperous nor contented Settlements than those which have been established in the Southern District of New Zealand."—*Governor Grey.*

———

THIRD EDITION.

LONDON:
W. S. ORR AND CO., AMEN CORNER, & 147, STRAND.
———
1848.

McGlashan raised his hand and fixed the dissenter with an imperious stare.

"Thank you for your question Mr..."

The dissenter leaped to his feet again. "McCallum, Sir. George McCallum."

"Well, Mr McCallum, you should be careful not to take an exception and call it the rule. I have any number of reports, going back over a number of years, which attest to the benign climate which Otago enjoys."

"What aboot the accommodation that ye promised to those settlers?"

"There were…..er, extenuating circumstances which led to a slight and temporary problem. But I can assure you that this is no longer an issue, and everyone can be sure of superior accommodation when they arrive. The settlers *are* expected to secure or build permanent housing in the fullness of time, but they are certainly given adequate shelter when they first arrive.

"Now if you'll permit me, Mr McCallum, I'll move along to the things these people have come to hear. Mr Hutcheson, may we have the blackboard?"

Hutcheson brought a large blackboard and easel to the centre of the stage. McGlashan took a piece of chalk and in a few quick lines drew a crude map.

"The New Zealand Company has sole rights to sell land in the Otago Block, which it is situated here on the east coast of the Middle Island, about 150 miles south of Banks Peninsula.

"The block is 400,000 acres, and it extends fifty to sixty miles, from this bump on the coastline known as the Otakou Peninsula, south to Nugget Point. It extends inland for an average of seven miles. It is perfectly free for settlement. The British Government purchased the block from the Maori owners in 1844, for two thousand, four hundred pounds.

"The Otago Block is blessed with an abundance of fertile land. Typically this is in open grassy natural pastures. The pastures are interspersed with trees, so there is an adequate supply of wood for fuel and building purposes.

"Running up the centre of the block is a navigable inland waterway called the Taieri River, with rich land lying on either side of it. There is an ample field of coal.

"To the west, stretching away to the feet of snowy mountains, is an unbounded sheepwalk which is open to farmers and flock-owners."

McGlashan tapped the blackboard with a riding crop.

"This is the Otago Peninsula, where you'll make land after the great voyage. The Peninsula contains a noble harbour, which runs in a north to south direction. Unlike most of the Otago Block, the Peninsula is covered in dense woods, which reach to the water's edge. It is hilly, but not as steep as the hills at Port Nicholson where the Wellington settlement is.

"The head of the harbour, here, is where we have established the capital town

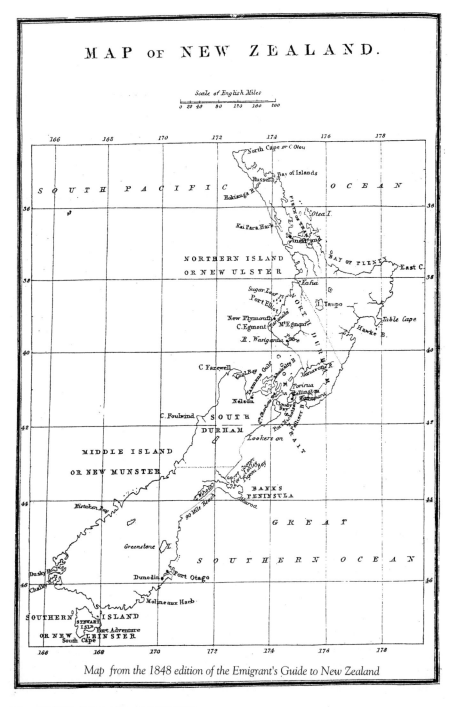

Map from the 1848 edition of the Emigrant's Guide to New Zealand

of Dunedin – or New Edinburgh, as it has been called. The settlement faces north, in a situation of great natural beauty. Here the hills have flattened off, and the land lies in long slopes and downs, generally covered in grass mixed with shrubs. Dunedin is perfectly placed to connect the sea port with the rural land of the interior.

"That covers some of the physical characteristics of the new colony. Now let me give you two more points which favour Otago over other destinations for emigrants.

"First, let us consider the question of the native population. Let me be quite clear: the natives are absolutely no impediment to settlement. It is true that in some overseas colonies, and even in the north of New Zealand, British settlers have endured difficulties with the aboriginal inhabitants. This is not a problem in Otago, because there are almost no natives, and the few who live near Dunedin are both friendly and helpful. You have nothing to fear from land claims, or from any annoying attempts at extortion.

"And nor will you mix with the undesirable elements of British society, as you certainly do in the Australian colonies. New Zealand has never been, and nor will it ever be, a dumping ground for the criminal classes.

"Altogether, the Otago Block presents a unique combination of advantages such is rarely seen in the world today. We are very fortunate to be in a position to take advantage of this opportunity."

"

"*Dunedin already has an able and energetic minister in the person of the Reverend Thomas Burns, who was formerly Minister of the Free Kirk at Monkton.*"

"Let us now talk about the arrangements for purchasing land," continued McGlashan.

"The block contains 400,000 acres, and at present we are offering 144,600 acres for sale. All is suitable for tillage. It is divided into 2,400 properties, and each property consists of three allotments: 50 acres of rural land, ten acres of suburban land, and a quarter acre of town land.

"The price for each property of is £120 10s, which works out to be 40 shillings an acre. Now I won't claim that is cheap, but nor is it expensive: it is a *sufficient* price for our purpose. If land were simply granted to settlers for little or no cost, everyone would want to be a landowner. Capitalists, or employers of labour, would not be encouraged to emigrate. The settlement would be held back through lack of capital, and lack of labour for development.

"Our sufficient price will prevent people buying more land than they can properly use, yet it is low enough to make buying and actually *using* land one of the most productive ways to employ capital.

"Because properties are small, they will suit the emigrant of moderate means. But any person with a large amount of capital is free to buy any number of properties and join them together to form a larger block.

"Some uninformed people have claimed that our land policy discriminates in favour of the wealthy. But look more closely and you will see this is not the case. Our policy benefits all classes of society. That is because

we are setting aside three-eighths of all purchase money to directly assist emigration. In practice, this means that every time a property is purchased, two labourers receive free passage to the colony.

"This is by no means the only excellence of our plan with respect to the working classes. Wage rates are higher in New Zealand, and any labourer who is capable of normal thrift should be able to save enough wages to buy land in his own right. And of course each time he does this, more money goes into the fund to assist more of Scotland's poor people to make a better life for themselves in Otago.

"Part of the land price also goes toward other vital community needs: communications, churches and schools.

"Fully one-quarter of the money from land sales is to be spent on roads and bridges, and we also expect to provide a steam-boat to work in the Otago Harbour.

"One-eighth of the price of land is reserved for the development of educational and religious institutions in Otago run by the Free Church of Scotland.

"Why only the Free Church? The reason is that if all denominations shared in the funds, those funds would be spread too thinly to be of practical benefit.

"Our solution has been to nominate the Free Church from the outset. We believe settlers prefer the certainty of having adequate churches and schools, even if these might not conform with their own ideas in every way. However, it goes without saying that other denominations are free to provide their own institutions should they think fit.

"Dunedin already has an able and energetic minister in the person of the Reverend Thomas Burns, who was formerly Minister of the Free Kirk at Monkton.

The Otago Journal,

No. I.   JANUARY 1848.   Price 2d.

CONTENTS.

Reverend Burns reached the new colony eleven months ago, just three weeks after the first ship, so you can see that from the very beginning, we have placed the highest priority on safeguarding the moral and religious interests of the settlers.

"Our first schoolmaster, Mr Blackie, arrived with Mr Burns and has established an excellent little school for Dunedin youngsters. This is just the beginning of our educational plans. We intend to establish a full academy which will have very highly qualified staff under the direction of a headmaster of the highest attainment and respectability.

"We will provide a liberal education which is both solid and substantial. An academy which befits a colony which aspires to be the focus for civilisation in the Southern Hemisphere. Indeed, we expect Dunedin to become a centre of education for the broader antipodean regions, and the academy will take in students of high respectability from countries such as India, Australia and Van Diemen's Land.

"Education in Otago is naturally conducted on Christian principles, and the students are carefully inculcated with the doctrines and duties of religion.

"Ladies and Gentlemen, you can see how we are determined that the Otago settlement will not lack for moral and religious support, or in sound mental culture. Alongside these requirements, we shall place health of the body.

"Good health and a long life are blessings you can almost be guaranteed of. As I have already mentioned, the climate is most salubrious. It is comparatively free from disease and perfectly adapted to British constitutions.

"In letter after letter, labouring men are telling relatives that their working conditions are far less arduous than the toil they knew in Scotland, and they are working generally in the open air.

"Here at home, our towns and cities are overcrowded, and workers and capitalists alike suffer from oppressive anxieties and difficulties – from the ruinous competition of both capital and labour. We are filling our hospitals and lunatic asylums with illness and insanity.

"The very opposite applies in the invigorating climate and way of life which you will enjoy in New Zealand.

"Good people – you have listened long and attentively tonight, and I won't keep you much longer. But before I throw the meeting open for questions, we must consider two related topics: who should emigrate to Otago, and who should invest their capital in that settlement.

"It is obvious that our respectable labouring classes should seriously consider emigrating to Otago. I have already adduced a number of compelling reasons why they should do this, and I don't propose to go into them again.

"Any number of letters from Otago are expressing sentiments like, "Come out to us, why will you stay at home and starve, when you might place yourself in a position to command your own self–respect, and the respect of those around you.

"The classes for whom most openings are available are agricultural, farm and other labourers, shepherds and domestic servants. Almost free passages are generally available for these emigrants, although you should be aware that for male labourers, we give preference to to those who are married.

"The married man has many advantages over the single man, and in the colonies his home will always contrast favourably with a bachelor's home. Not only is his happiness enhanced and his labour cheered, but an active woman does many things for her husband which

---

EVIDENCE FOUNDED ON TWELVE MONTHS EXPERIENCE OF OTAGO

(Answered by Captain Thomas.)

Question 1. What is the character of the Agricultural Land of the Otago Block; are there indications of fertility of the soil, and what are they?
Answer 1. Good—as indicated by crops of wheat and barley, excellent potatoes, and vegetables of all kinds.
Q. 2. What is the nature of the climate,—is it mild and equable, and fit for raising and ripening all the cereals and other crops of Great Britain?
A. 2. The climate is very healthy. I should say more mild than of the southern part of England.
Q. 3. Are any of the lands thickly wooded—is there plenty of wood on them, generally for all purposes for which wood will be required, including houses, fences, and fuel?
A. 3. The very great proportion of the settlement is clear of timber. At present there is sufficient for the purposes of fuel, building and fencing.
Q. 4. Is there much and good pasturage on the waste lands within, and surrounding the settlement, and what are the general features of these lands?
A. 4. There is excellent pasturage, on the adjoining waste lands which are hilly.
Q. 5. Is there plenty of water, everywhere in the Otago district, at all times, fit for man and beast?
A. 5. Plenty of good water in every part of the settlement.
Q. 6. Are fish plentiful on the coast, in the harbour of Otago, and in the rivers within the district?
A. 6. Fish are plentiful both on the coast and in the harbour of excellent quality : in the rivers and lakes, eels and smaller fish.
Q. 7. Is the harbour of Otago a good one, and is it likely to be frequented by vessels in the whaling trade and others?
A. 7. The harbour of Otago is good, and is now frequently visited by whalers and coasters.
Q. 8. Is Otago on the whole, in your opinion, a place where capital and labour are likely to meet with their due reward, and desirable as a home?
A. 8. I consider Otago a place where industry and capital are likely to meet a due reward, and where all emigrants will have a healthy climate secure from disturbances by natives.

(The Otago Journal, June, 1848)

he has neither the time nor the inclination to do himself.

"So we say to all intending settlers: before you go out, find yourself a really useful woman for a wife – but before you marry, be sure to tell her what kind of life she may expect, so she can make an informed decision before it is too late.

"Single women may be quite sure that they will be well looked after during the voyage. Every attention given to the safety and sanctity of their persons."

At this remark, a matronly, black-garbed member of the audience rose and pointed her umbrella at the speaker.

"My name is Caroline Rennie, sir, and I wish to ask aboot the single womenfolk. There has been talk that depravities and indignities have been visited on young women aboard emigrant ships, by the ships' officers and crew. Even the doctor was blamed. Can ye guarantee the safety of oor lasses?"

"I most certainly will guarantee you that. Impure conduct simply cannot take place on New Zealand Company ships. For a start, the companies we charter vessels from take care to engage only the best type of seafarers. And we select only the most respectable people to be emigrants. But as well as that, our accommodation arrangements simply do not allow such a situation to exist. We have a matron in the single women's quarters, and the single men are quite separate. The long cabin for married couples and their families is between them."

"But where there's a will, young folks will often be finding a way. There's aye plenty of time for both to develop on a long voyage," the woman protested.

"Not on *our* ships, Mrs Rennie. I do recall a rumour of the situation you have spoken of, and it may have happened on a vessel taking a large complement of single women to the Australian colonies. It was a very different situation, and the emigration company undoubtedly did not apply the high standards you rightly expect of the New Zealand Company."

The woman resumed her seat: "Hmmph....I suppose we have to take your word for it, Mr McGlashan, but decent folks maun keep an eye on the situation. I would think twice before sending my gels to the other end of the earth on one of them boats."

"Thank you for raising the matter, Madam. Your concern for the welfare of the fair sex cannot be faulted, even though it is certainly misplaced in respect of *our* operations. Now if we may move on, I wish to discuss the emigration imperative for those of you who are in the middle classes.

"Twenty or thirty years ago, there was considerable opportunity for people to advance themselves and build up capital. These opportunities are diminishing daily, and there is a very real danger that people whose capital is small and dwindling may sink down to the level of the labouring man. There is a clear tendency in this direction.

"Unless you employ considerable skill and prudence, small capital is something which will only put off the evil day of poverty. If you do survive to old age in this unhealthy climate, there is a high chance you will see poverty. If you do not experience poverty, your children almost certainly will.

"By way of fortunate contrast, small capital is a foundation for wealth in the colonies.

"If you are prudent and prepared to work hard, you can scarcely fail to do well. The virgin soil does not require expensive modes of cultivation, and its fertility ensures excellent crops. Opportunities for pastoral pursuits, such as sheep farming, are as unbounded as they are profitable.

"There are none of the absurd elegances of life which in Great Britain drain capital from those who can least afford it, but who feel they must keep up appearances to maintain a certain station in life.

"Taxation, and its concomitant evils and annoyances, have all been left behind.

"Emigrate to New Zealand, or at least help your children to do so. You will improve your own position, and as I mentioned earlier, you will also help the lower classes escape degradation. At the same time, you'll be ensuring the labouring support you need to develop the new land.

"Finally, I must point out that the Otago settlement is also a fine investment for men of capital who would remain in Scotland. If you purchase and amalgamate several contiguous blocks, you will have a sizeable property that can only increase greatly in value. You will have no difficulty in renting land, or you may wish to work the land with the help of a local manager.

"Your investment would be socially beneficial, because it would provide free passages for workers and their families, who you could recommend from your own neighbourhood or estate."

McGlashan pulled a gold watch from his waistcoat pocket, glanced at it and declared his address at an end.

"I fear I've spoken longer than I should, and on this occasion we won't have time for the many questions you may have. Be assured, though, that the answers are all contained in our literature.

"Before we call the meeting to an end, though, I will ask Mr Dunlop to give you some of the details that intending emigrants will need: how to book your passage, how much it will cost, and what preparations you should make for the voyage and your arrival in the new colony.

"Finally, I would like to underline the extent of my commitment to the Otago colony. I'm prepared to put my body where my mouth is, so to speak, because I have every intention of joining the settlers before long. Thankyou for your generous indulgence."

An hour later, John and Jane McGibbon made their way home through the Saturday night throng, with a great deal on their minds.

On the Seventh Day

Summer mornings began early for Scottish children before daylight saving reined in the rising sun. Youngsters might wake at four in the morning, in spite of heavy curtains on their window. Smaller varieties of child, sent to bed early the previous evening, showed negligible interest in sleeping in, and faced a long wait until breakfast. Games and chatter could help fill in the time, but it was important not to disturb slumbering parents.

This morning the McGibbon offspring woke early again. After a short and ineffectual attempt to lie quietly, they pattered one by one to the kitchen, drank from the big white water pitcher in the pantry, and helped themselves to an oatmeal bannock from the biscuit box by the hearth. Shortly afterwards, they began to do what bored children do. Play.

Suddenly the door to the children's bedroom opened, and Father, in a white nightshirt, stood glowering at his offspring.

"What is it that *you're* doing, then? Would ye seek to profane the Lord's day? Would ye bring doon the wrath of the Almighty with this vile construction and evil commotion?

"What in Heaven's name d'ye think it is that you're doing then, Tummas?"

Father McGibbon strode across the room and cuffed his son Thomas from a chair which was doing double duty as a coachman's perch. In front of the chair, connected by cords, was a rocking horse, while the back of the coach was a large toy chest containing passengers, Jeannie and Jessie. The journey had become rather exciting, and the children's exclamations had woken their father.

"Canna ye think of anything better to do on this day?"

Well no, they couldn't really. Possibilities for childish fun were necessarily restricted in a four-room apartment, and playing imaginary games with the materials on hand was often the best they could do. Thomas and his sisters were flying across an English moor, hotly pursued by the redoubtable Dick Turpin and his cracking pistols. Earlier, Thomas had read the exciting tale to his sisters from a tupenny popular edition borrowed from Agnes McDonald, the family's daytime maid.

Reading and acting out Dick Turpin would not have been considered grossly evil yesterday, nor on the previous five days – although the senior McGibbons would have condemned the book as common and frivolous. But this was Sunday, and activities and books which were acceptable all week, were now temporary agents of Beelzebub.

Before going to bed the previous evening, the children had gathered up their books, their marbles and their skipping ropes, and hidden them from sight in a big sea-chest in the parlour. Their father, and most other business-men in the street, had drawn the blinds on his shop windows, so that Sunday churchgoers would not be distracted by the spectacle of worldly goods.

The children leaped from their coach and scrambled back to bed. Flailing about like Jesus among the money-lenders, their father destroyed the wicked construction. Sighting the slim Turpin tome, he snatched it up and ripped it from cover to cover.

"Tummas – I would hae expected better of ye. Is this the example you should be giving to your sisters? Now get this clutter

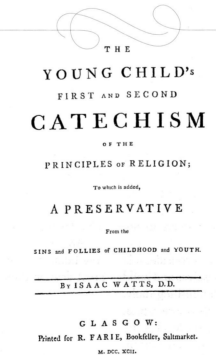

THE

YOUNG CHILD's

FIRST AND SECOND

CATECHISM

OF THE

PRINCIPLES OF RELIGION;

To which is added,

A PRESERVATIVE

From the

SINS and FOLLIES of CHILDHOOD and YOUTH.

By ISAAC WATTS, D.D.

GLASGOW:
Printed for R. FARIE, Bookseller, Saltmarket.

M. DCC. XCII.

(Price Two-pence.)

tidied up, and help the girls with their studies.

"I'll be asking you about the Fourth Commandment after breakfast, and I expect ye to ken the answers. Jessie, what does the Fourth Commandment tell us, then?"

"R-r-remember the Sabbath day to k-keep it holy, Da'," stammered the cowering seven-year old.

"That is correct. Kindly remember it in future if ye please, my gel. And now I'm awa' back to my bed, and I dinna expect to hear onie more nonsense from this direction. Guid mornin' t'ye!"

The children guiltily restored their bedroom to the approved sabbath state and moved to the big deal table in the kitchen to study the commandment in question. Thomas took the big leather bound family bible and a slim volume, The Young Child's First and Second Catechism on the Principles Of Religion, with its bonus section, A Preservative from the Sins and Follies of Childhood and Youth. Each child carried the Shorter Catechism.

"I will read the commandment to ye, and then we'll study its meaning," said Thomas.

"Remember the Sabbath day to keep it holy. Six days shalt thou labour and do all thy work; but the seventh day is the sabbath of the Lord thy God: in it thou shalt not do any work, thou, nor thy son, nor thy daughter, thy man-servant, nor thy maid-servant, nor thy cattle, nor thy stranger that is within thy gates. For in six days the Lord made heaven and earth, the sea, and all that in them is, and rested the seventh day : wherefore the Lord blessed the sabbath-day, and hallowed it."

Thomas paused and read from the catechism: "How is the sabbath or the Lord's Day to be sanctified? And Jessie answered: "By a holy resting all the day, not only from such works as are at all times sinful, but even from such worldly employments and recreations as are on other days lawful, and making it our delight to spend the whole time (except so much of it as is to be taken up in the

works of necessity and mercy), in the public and private exercises of God's worship."

"But Thomas," piped up little Jeannie, "You said we canna do any work on the Sabbath, and we do not. But what about our maid? Agnes cooks our meals, and so does Miss Murdoch at Uncle David and Auntie Jessie's house."

Thomas had asked his father the same question several years before, and could parrot the stock answer: "The Lord tells us that it is permitted to work on the Sabbath day when it is a matter of necessity or mercy."

Jeannie and her sister accepted the explanation, as Thomas had earlier done. It was a convenient hypocrisy, readily adopted by the rising Glasgow's middle classes, who were strong supporters of the newly established Free Church of Scotland.

For the next two hours, the children discussed points raised in the catechism and looked up references in the illustrated family bible. Thomas played father, to give his sisters a taste of the coming examination. He gave Jessie a passing grade, but it was obvious that four-year old Jeannie had only a vague idea what the fuss was all about.

"That is enough of the Fourth Commandment for now, but I think we should also have a look at the Fifth Commandment, because our Da' will likely ask us about that too."

"What is the Fifth Commandment?" asked Jeannie.

"Next to the Fourth Commandment, it is the most important commandment for us to know this morning," replied Thomas, who was beginning to vision himself at the high pulpit, guiding his flock in the tradition of the famous preacher, Reverend Thomas Chalmers – and of course Dr Brown at St James Glasgow Cross, where the family worshipped.

"But what does it say?" pressed Jeannie.

"It says honour thy father and thy mother, that thy days may be long upon the land which the Lord thy God giveth thee."

The children were reminded by their catechisms that they must honour and obey their parents. But it was more

THE

LARGER CATECHISM,

AGREED UPON BY

THE ASSEMBLY OF DIVINES

AT WESTMINSTER,

WITH THE ASSISTANCE OF

COMMISSIONERS FROM THE CHURCH OF SCOTLAND,

AND

Approved, *Anno* 1648, by the GENERAL ASSEMBLY of the CHURCH of SCOTLAND, to be a Directory for Catechising such as have made some proficiency in the knowledge of the grounds of Religion.

WITH REFERENCES TO THE

PROOFS FROM SCRIPTURE.

TO WHICH IS PREFIXED,

A RECOMMENDATORY PREFACE,

BY MANY EMINENT DIVINES OF THE LAST AGE,

AND THE

DIRECTORY FOR FAMILY WORSHIP.

PRINTED BY AUTHORITY.

ABERDEEN:
GEORGE KING, ST. NICHOLAS STREET.
1840.

complicated than that, according to the 'divines' of Westminster who had written the catechism two centuries earlier. They had taken it on themselves to expand the commandment into an instrument of social control, with a detailed description of how various ages and ranks in society should relate to one another. Everyone should know their place and honour their superiors in the home, the church, and in government.

Wives were to submit to their husbands, servants to masters and everyone should pay obeisance to authority figures such as ministers and magistrates. To show contempt, rebelliousness or even plain envy toward superiors would be considered "refractory and scandalous carriage". There was no Colonial Jack to look his master in the eye.

The catechism backed up its interpretations of the fifth commandment with 125 biblical references for further study.

By breakfast, Thomas and his sisters were thoroughly reminded of their place in the scheme of things spiritual, temporal and familial, and were ready for the parental inquisition. In the event, question-time was less of a fire and brimstone business than the children feared, and their strict father agreed they had passed the test.

"But see ye mind these truths, and be sure to live by them all your lives until the good Lord takes the last breath from ye," he warned.

Meanwhile Jane, who by reason of necessity had set aside the no-work stricture, announced that breakfast was ready, and would the children move the books from the table so they could eat. She gave the black pot a final stir with her big wooden spurtle, and poured out platefuls of steaming parritch.

But the children still had to wait for their father's lengthy grace, which thanked the Lord for the oatmeal they were about to consume, and offered grovelling apologies for the morning's spiritual lapse. After what seemed an eternity, John's amen permitted five hungry heads to be lifted. Breakfast was eaten in silence – the rule for all Sunday meals – and then Jane nursed the recent addition to the family, baby John Junior.

With breakfast over and the dishes stacked aside for later attention by Agnes, it was time for more bible study, with the Book of Ezekiel chosen by John McGibbon for its particular references to cessation of labour on the Sabbath.

This phase of the Seventh Day ended at 10 am, when each of the member of the family began the important task of dressing up in best clothes for church.

❧

THE

SUNDAY-SCHOLAR'S

GIFT;

OR,

A PRESENT

FOR A

GOOD CHILD.

╌╌╌╌╌

WELLINGTON, SALOP:
Printed & sold by F. Houlston & Son.
Sold, also, by all other Booksellers.
——
Price Two-Pence.

Shortly before 11am, kirk bells rent the air, calling Glasgow's faithful to forenoon church services. The McGibbon family and their maid stepped out of the front door and joined dutiful worshippers issuing from tenement doors and lanes all along the Saltmarket.

It was a quiet, dignified stream which proceeded the short distance to Glasgow Cross and walked through the door of St James. Husbands in their best black suits and tall top hats, wives in best black outfits with voluminous skirts, plaid shawls and dark bonnets, and the children looking much like their parents, but without the top hats.

Less dignified was the scene at the Sir Walter Scott Tavern, where the carousing establishment was doing its noisy best to beat the Sunday gloom. Indeed, several revellers were out on the street, happily desecrating the Sabbath in full view of scandalised churchgoers, who, huddling children to their skirts, hurried past with eyes directed firmly toward the spiritual haven.

It was a problem which had long irked Glasgow's pious classes. They regularly complained, and in a year's time, Sunday-school teachers would successfully petition the city council to close public houses on the Sabbath. That was by no means the only example of Victorian 'moral majority' standover tactics. Three years earlier, Sunday train services between Glasgow and Edinburgh had ceased after pressure from the churches – particularly the sterner evangelical churches such as the Free Church of Scotland.

The general view was that public transport should not operate on a Sunday. People were greatly discouraged from all forms of private perambulation – be it recreational walking or anything to do with horses or trains. Games, laughter and frivolity were simply not tolerated among the pious, and they did their best to prevent anyone else having fun.

There were exceptions to the rules – you were allowed to walk, if it was to the church, and transportation in cases of necessity or mercy was permitted. Few of the strictures were written into law, but they were generally observed. One visitor was to report that Glasgow's streets were "...as deserted and still during the hours of divine service, as a City of the Dead".

In 1863, the gates of Edinburgh's fine botanic gardens were closed on Sundays at the behest of all the main presbyterian churches, including the Free Church. This effectively excluded the working classes, who worked every other day of the week. The by-law was not overturned until 1889.

The McGibbon family walked into the church without speaking, although John nodded to a couple of business acquaintances. Arriving at the rented family pew, he removed his top hat and stood aside to let Jane, the children, and Agnes file in.

A heavy silence prevailed in the plain, undecorated church. When everyone was seated, the bulky, red-faced and desperately solemn church precentor, Robert McGillivray, stood before them to begin the service with the 23rd Psalm.

The congregation stayed seated while McGillivray led proceedings by 'lining out' – singing a line at a time for them to repeat. The discordant responses were unaccompanied. No new-fangled kist o' whistles – no such agent of Satan – would desecrate the Scotch Church!

The psalm had ended, and everyone stood as Reverend Dr David Brown Doctor of Divinity, climbed gravely to the pulpit to deliver his first prayer. Twenty minutes later the supplication ended, and his audience was permitted to sit. Now the black-robed minister lectured his audience on the import of Isaiah V.

"...woe unto them that are mighty to drink wine, and men of strength to mingle strong drink..."

Dr Brown was a fearsome sight: white knuckles grasped the high pulpit as he strained toward the body of the church. Silver hair, aquiline nose, rising complexion and roving eyes that swept the congregation, selecting particular sinners for meaningful stares.

The lecture over, McGillivray led a second psalm – Number 107 – about ancient sinners who "...reel to and fro, stagger like a drunken man and are at their wits' end." Then all stood for another prayer, before being seated for the main sermon of the day.

"Dearly beloved brethren in the Lord..." began Dr Brown, after his audience had shuffled their posteriors into as comfortable position as was possible on the hard pews, and settled down for an hour of scholarly discourse.

Today's subject of the evil of intemperance and associated soul-damaging activities had been the theme of many sermons at St James, and his audience knew what to expect.

"...and there is no evil habit equal to imbibing of the demon drink, in the efficacy and certainty of its power to bring rapid and hopeless ruin upon the community," he thundered.

At this point in proceedings, the adults were attentive. So, to a fair extent, were the children, although the younger of them were influenced more by the occasion, and family solidarity, than by the rhetoric, which was mostly incomprehensible to them.

"In this world of change we are exposed to many vices. There are many opportunities – and there are varied opportunities – for corruption of both our bodies and our immortal souls.

"But of all vices, pay the greatest heed to intemperance. Other vices are but fruits of disordered affections, but the vice of drunkeness is a vice that banishes all reason.

"Intemperance paves the way for all vices, for he who is a drunkard is qualified for all vice."

The minister was well into his stride, but after nearly an hour of intellectual abstractions stitched together by sermonising clichés, even the well regulated children in

the McGibbon pew had lost their battle with boredom. Jessie and Jeannie were squirming, and had to be treated with sweets from the bag their mother always carried for this purpose.

"...each of these sinful habits bears directly against the very life of religion in the soul..."

The sweets passed down the pew again.

"Cease not from the prayer, 'Lead us not into temptation', and next to praying for grace, see that you put yourselves in the way of grace."

"It is in vain that I study the subject of the Scotch Church. I have heard it ten times over from Murray, and twenty times from Jeffrey, and I have not the smallest conception of what it is all about. I know it has something to do with oatmeal, but beyond that I am in utter darkness."
Sydney Smith (quoted in his biography by Lady Holland, 1855)

We cannot for a certainty tell
What mirth may molest us on Monday;
But, at least, to begin the week well,
Let us all be unhappy on Sunday.
Charles, Lord Neaves (Songs and Verses, 1872)

"Th' approach of Sunday still I can't but dread,
For still old Edinburgh comes into my head
Where on that day a dreary gloom appears
And the kirk bells ring doleful in your ears."
James Boswell

"A Sunday in Scotland is for the traveller like a thunderstorm at a picnic."
Thedor Fontane (Beyond the Tweed, Pictures and Letters from Scotland, 1860)

"[The Scots] have a superstitious reliance on the efficacy of going constantly to church. Many of them may be said to pass their lives there; for they go almost without ceasing, and look so sorrowful...as if they were going, not only to bury their sins, but themselves."
Captain Edward Topham (Letters from Edinburgh, Written in the Years 1774 and 1775)

"The impression which I first received from hearing the singing in the Scottish churches was by no means a pleasant one, at least in regard to musical effect....no solemn instrumental symphony opens the concert with that sure and exact harmony which proceeds from an organ, but a solitary clerk (they call him precentor) who is commonly a grotesque enough figure, utters the first notes of the tune in a way that is extremely mechanical and disagreeable. The rest of the congregation, having heard one line sung to an end, and having ascertained the pitch, then strike in...there are generally so many with bad ears, that the effect, on the whole, is dissonant."
John Gibson Lockhart, Peter's Letters to his Kinsfolk, 1819

Soon it would need more than confectionery to still the squirming.

Dr Brown had moved onto the subject of salvation.

"I want to see in each one of you, a simple and serious desire to become wise unto salvation. A deep-felt desire for goodness in your souls. A desire that is grounded in a deep sense of your souls' exceeding worthlessness, while understanding the exceeding worth and magnitude of their eternity."

Thomas, who was earlier carried along by the strength of the minister's delivery, and had even for a while imagined *himself* at the ranting pulpit, was now plain bored and had begun to exchange furtive glances with his friend James Gow across the aisle. His father saw him and delivered a ferocious dig to the ribs, after which Thomas regained a sullen level of concentration.

The sermon was ending... "May these true sayings of God sink deep into your hearts, and may the Spirit so press them home, that they be to you the bearers of peace with God and of life everlasting, and to His name be praise."

The congregation rose again for prayer, which included the words, "And we pray for our church at Dunedin, far away in the colony of New Zealand. We pray for Captain William Cargill and the Reverend Thomas Burns, and all the brave pioneers who are building a new community based on the principles of the Free Church."

Another psalm, a benediction, and the two-hour service was over.

It was now one o'clock, and after a lunch of broth, bread and cold meat, devotions resumed with prayers and a family discussion of points raised in the morning's sermon. Then everyone made their way to St James again for the 2:30pm service. This was the last service the children and their mother would attend, but John would be off again at 6:30pm for the evening service.

The evening service had a more evangelistic purpose, with working people encouraged to attend in their ordinary clothes. Few of the working class, other than families of skilled craftsmen, ever came to daytime services, partly because they felt out of place among the dressed-up middle classes, and partly because few could afford the high rents demanded for pews. Although free and cheap pews were available at the back of the church, most were empty because people were too proud to be seen accepting charity.

In the last few years, the evangelising churches had worked hard, though with limited success, to draw the 'sunken portion' toward salvation. As an elder of the parish, John had often talked about encouraging the lapsed masses to attend church, and Jane was on a women's committee which lent acceptable church-going clothes to respectable members of the lower classes.

After the afternoon service was over, John had only a short time at home to organise more prayers and religious studies. Then he was out in the streets as a door-knocking missionary.

Jane and her children may not have attended evening service, but their devotions were far from over. After an early tea of bread, milk and brown sugar, Jane led a further round of bible study, based on her well-worn copy of The Mother's Catechism. At 7:30pm the girls were finally released to bed, and Jane and Thomas settled down to the only recreational reading permitted on this day: Milton's Paradise Lost, and Bunyan's Pilgrim's Progress. Neither book would disturb their moral equilibrium.

No picture of St James' Glasgow Cross Free Church has been found. It may have been similar to this church, the Buchanan Memorial, which is typical of Free Church buildings erected in central Glasgow last century.

A GLOSSARY OF SCOTTISH WORDS AND PHRASES

afore before

aft often

ain own

amang among

an' and

an aw as well, to

anither another

auld old

aw all

awa away

awthegither altogether

ay yes

aye always

bairn child

belang belong

ben mountain

bide/byde stay

bodie person

bonnie beautiful

brae hill

braw fine

bricht bright

brither brother

caller fresh

cannie careful

cauf calf

cauld cold

close enclosure, courtyard; entry, alley; accessway to common stair

coo cow

couthie friendly, sympathetic

cuik cook

dinna do not

dochter daughter

doon/doun down

dour sullen

drap/drappie drop

efternuin afternoon

faither father

fash annoy, inconvenience

fash yersel to worry

faut fault

fess fetch, bring

forbye also, as well, too

forenicht early evening

forenoon late morning

fou full

fowk people, family

frae from

fricht fright

fur for

gab talk

gane gone

gang go

geggie travelling theatre

gie give

glaikit foolish

gomeral fool

gowk fool

gret great

guid good

guidman husband

guidwife wife

hae have

hame home

havers nonsense

hied head

ken know

kenspeckle conspicuous

kimmer young girl

kirk church

kye/kyne cows, cattle

lad, laddie boy

lang long

lass, lassie girl

lave leave

loch lake

Losh! Lord!

mair more

maist most

man/mon man, husband

maun must

micht might

mickle small quantity

mind remember

mither mother

monie many

morn morning

muckle big, great, large, much

nae no, not

naethin' nothing

nicht night

nou now

o' of

onie any

oniebodie anyone

oor our

oot out

ower over

ower muckle too much

puir poor

richt right

richt nou/awa immediately

sae so

sassenach English person

stramash uproar, disturbance

suin soon

syne ago, then, since

tae to

tak' take

the day today

the morn/morra tomorrow

the nou just now

thegither together

thrang busy

vennel narrow alley or lane between buildings

verra very

wark work

warld world

watter water, river

waur worse

wean child

wee little, small

wee bit a little

weel well

wheen, a a few

wheesht be quiet, shut up!

wi' with

wumman woman, wife

wynd narrow, winding street

ye you

"We're going abroad"

"Losh, man, I canna believe what you're tellin' me! Would ye leave all that's grand in bonnie Scotland to live amang a bunch o' heathen cannibals doon at the ends of the earth? Are ye quite oot of your heid?"

The exclamation from David McGibbon was directed at his younger brother John, who had just arrived with his family by horse-drawn cab. A few days before, John had called at Winchester and McGibbons and told David there was a matter of family importance he and Jane wished to discuss with him.

"Well, what is it – ye can tell me now, can't ye?" David asked.

"The guidwife and I want to speak with you and Jessie together," said John, to which David replied: "Then you'd better all be coming to my house and doin' it properly. Bring the family along this Saturday forenicht and we'll talk afore dinner."

Now the adults were conversing in the drawing room of a terrace house in Hamilton Crescent, a newly developed street at the genteel end of Partick suburb. Bordering on Dowanhill, it was not the best address in Glasgow's superior west end, but good enough at present for a family rising in the world of commerce and finding a place in bourgeois society.

David, a glass of sherry in his hand, was leaning against the large Cararra marble and Minton-tiled fireplace. John and Jane McGibbon were on a leather settee, while next to them, seated on a high backed devotional chair in rosewood and horsehair, was the matron of the house, Jessie McGibbon.

It was a large Victorian room whose furnishings spoke clearly of the family's comfortable status. Next to David, sundry ornaments and a glass-covered Regency clock crowded the mantelpiece below a huge gilt-framed plate glass mirror. Further along was a large framed engraving of Wellington and his Generals, while elsewhere on the richly wallpapered walls were more engravings and paintings including a view in oils of Bonnie Prince Charlie's highland army and its camp followers, cresting a mountain pass amid towering bluffs and lowering mists.

Beside bay windows framed by heavy damask curtains in deep malachite green was a well-draped Bacchus and Venus in stucco, on a floor carpeted in Brussels tapestry-weave. There was no shortage of seating, with the sofa, seven chairs, an ottoman and a variety of stools and hassocks. Scattered about the room were many small tables – card tables, tea tables, occasional tables and Pembrokes. There was a japanned birchwood flower stand in the window, baby grand piano, whatnot, and davenport. A mahogany bookcase contained popular novels of Sir Walter Scott and the newly fashionable Charles Dickens, and a variety of religious books: the big family bible, a bible dictionary, prayer books, catechisms and collections of sermons.

Other books on the shelves and scattered on tables

Hamilton Crescent, Partick, where the David McGibbon family lived in 1849. This view was taken later in the century – possibly around 1870.

included the Reverend George McAlister's account of a visit to the Holy Land, art collections and a half morocco-bound edition, well-thumbed by McGibbon children, of travel writer William Beattie's *Scotland Illustrated*. "Most loyally and respectfully dedicated to her most excellent Majesty, Victoria the First", it was typical of the contemporary British mania for highland romance. The book was a family favourite, and it combined locality descriptions with tales of former heroes such as Prince Charlie, William Wallace, Robert the Bruce and Rob Roy. The splendid engravings featured heroic mountains, lochs, castles, and men in kilts and plaid.

Almost every square centimetre of level surface in the

room hosted some form of object or ornament. As befitted the nature of David's business, most were ceramic – vases and figurines from Chelsea, Dresden and the Far East. There were also glass vases, many brass and bronze objects, a brace of stuffed birds and a bowl of wax fruit.

A large deerskin sprawled in front of a fireplace with a Berlin black iron grate, and a banner firescreen hand-sewn by Jessica McGibbon.

"Why!?" demanded the elder brother.

"It's a deal better than goin' doon the drain in Saltmarket Street," John responded. "New Zealand is the land of the future, an' people are sayin' it will be the new Britain of the South. It can do even better than this country, because it wilna be repeating our mistakes. I believe we'll do verra weel there."

John repeated the arguments he had heard at the public meeting – arguments which had churned over and over in his mind. Arguments which had been practised on a doubting spouse.

"... it's a grand opportunity to do good business and at the same time live in a community built on Free Church principles."

David was not impressed by the religious justification, for, while he was a devout believer, it was the established Church of Scotland he supported. Unlike John, he had not come out for the Free Church in the big split of 1843. He did believe in business, however, and demanded to know what his brother had in mind.

"I'm thinkin' we'll set up as general merchants. Retailing is what we know best, and we'll take a consignment of goods with us.

"But that is just to start us off. I mean to own land over there, and go into farming."

John explained the land offer. "We will buy one of the New Zealand Company's special packages of land for £120 10s, and for that we'll get a quarter acre in the town, ten acres in a suburb, and a 50 acre farm further out.

"They say sheep can be bought for £1 a head in the town, and for much less if you bring them over from Australia. Those sheep should yield an annual profit of 2s. 6d. for the wool alone, and their number will increase by more than one-third every year.

"We will buy a coo, and that would cost us £12, but a deal o' money can be made from her. She'll cost nothing to keep, because she will get her own food off the land.

"The coo will have a cauf, and if we look after her, she'll have another cauf in a year's time and then we'll have three kyne worth £19. The coo cost £12, the year-old cauf is worth £5 and the new cauf will be worth £2. As well as that, we'll be sellin' her milk and butter for at least 12 shillings a week.

"An' we'll keep fowls, and sell the eggs."

"It doesna sound much better than a peasant farm tae

me. How can that be a step up in the world for ye?"

"I am told that further oot of Dunedin there is a great deal of waste land perfectly suited for larger scale sheep farming, and I have a mind to get into that eventually."

"It's nae doddle you're lettin' yourself in for, John. What d'ye ken aboot farmin'? You've never been closer to a coo than the butter ye sell. "

"There will be a muckle lot to learn, to be sure, but I intend to tak' advice. It may not be easy, but I am assured that the land is kind, and yields marvellously to attention."

David moved to his brother, refilled his glass from a crystal decanter, and shook his head.

"Weel then, ye seem determined to go ahead with this crazy venture. It's your decision of course, and I wish ye well wherever ye go, but it's not something I would be doin'. I like the idea of a Scots settlement though, and if it can start afresh without the mistakes that have been made here, it could be a good place to live. But before ye make a final commitment, I suggest ye look verra closely at the claims those promoters are puttin' aboot.

"Now tell me then, how are ye going to get there?"

"There are vessels leavin' for New Zealand every six weeks or so. More than ten have gone to Dunedin already. They're nearly all sailin' frae London, but I am told they'll be starting work at Dumbarton soon on a new ship that will be takin' emigrants frae the Clyde."

"How lang does it take to sail there?"

"About four months is the average. It's one of the longest voyages you can take anywhere, but the new ships are built for speed as well as comfort, and they dinna hae to stop anywhere for provisions."

"What will it cost ye?"

"We won't be going as assisted emigrants, and the cost will depend on what class we travel in. For all of us, it would be 153 guineas in the chief cabin, 83 guineas in the fore-cabin or 54 guineas below decks in steerage."

"Well ye wouldna be thinkin' of travellin' below decks, surely?"

"I hae a mind tae do just that. It will be less comfortable, but I'm sure we'll recover frae it verra quickly. Besides, they say this ship will have special cabins in steerage for folks who are payin' their own passage. That will suit us just fine."

"Well I'm not so sure I'd want to spend four months in such company, e'en if I had my own cabin."

"You might be too proud, David, but I'm more concerned with practicalities than appearances. We're nae wealthy, and for the difference in price between steerage and chief cabin, we could buy eight kyne, or more land. Or we could take more goods and gear to sell."

In a parallel conversation, Jessie was sympathising with her sister in law.

"Och, I'm sae sorry for ye Jane – havin' to follow that husband of yours and sail so far away frae hame. And with such a young wean to look after too. How will ye ever cope?

Will ye be safe on the long voyage? What do ye have to take on board the ship? Do ye know what it will be like when ye get o'er there? Where will ye live? What sort of society do they have in that Dunedin town? What do the bairns think aboot it all? Will there be schooling for them?"

The questions kept coming, and Jane did her best to answer them. By now she was fairly resigned to the idea of emigration, though it was a resignation that proceeded more from notions of obedience than anything else. John had patiently explained the whys and wherefores several times, and although she had begun to accept his analysis, her heart remained firmly fixed in Glasgow.

"...so that's it. We're going, and we have tae make the

FOR SALE

On the Farm of Douglas Hill, near Douglas, on Monday, 10th September, 1849.

The Public is respectfully informed that in consequence of Mr Creall having given up his lease of Douglas Mill to Lord Douglas, the WHOLE GROWING CROP, STOCKING, IMPLEMENTS OF HUSBANDRY, &c.,on said Farm, will be disposed by Public Sale, on Monday, 10th. September next, commencing at Eleven O'clock Forenoon, precisely.

The Crop and Stocking are as follows, viz :–

56   Acres of OATS.

2   Do. of BARLEY.

19   Do. of TURNIPS.

1   Do. of POTATOES.

1000 stones excellent RYE GRASS HAY, or thereby.

5   Ricks of Natural HAY.

A Quantity of STRAW.

29   Highland BULLOCKS, and 7 HEIFERS, all in excellent condition.

1   One year-old QUEY, and 1 CALF, both of the Ayrshire Breed.

13   EWES, 1 TUP AND 2 LAMBS of the Cheviot Breed.

3   SWINE and a number of PIGS.

4   Closebodied CARTS, 2 HAY FRAMES.

3   Two-Horse PLOUGHS, 1 Drill Plough., 2 Pair HARROWS.

1   Double Drill Turnip BARROW, 1 Rack GATHERER, 1 ROLLER.

1   Pair Circular HARROWS, 1 Pair FANNERS, 2 GRUBBERS, and a Number of other Farming Utensils, including Boilers, Smith's Bellows, Anvil and Vise, &c., &c.

4   Farm HORSES.

2   MARES in Foal, and 2 FOALS.

2   Three-year-old FILLIES.

4   Sets Cart HARNESS, and

3   Sets Plough HARNESS.

The crops are excellent in quality, and the Implements, Harness,&c. in good order and repair. The Whole will be put up in Lots to suit intending Purchasers, and Sold off without Reserve.

Three Months' Credit will be given on approved Bills for all Purchases above £5 and 3½ per cent discount will be allowed for Cash.

Douglas Mill, near Douglas
30 August, 1849.

(Glasgow Herald, 3/9/1849)

'Glencoe between Loch Long and Cairn Dhu', an engraving by G Richardson in William Beattie's Scotland Illustrated *(1838)*

best of it. What aboot you? I suppose everyone's all excited aboot goin' doon the watter next week?"

"Certainly. The children just can't wait to get on that steamer and sail doon the Clyde. Did I tell ye we've taken a new house in Dunoon this year? It's a big place, right on the water with a boat to sail in and we can promenade along the bay in the evenings.

"Oh Jane – ye should be coming with us! It would be grand for us all to spend time together afore ye gang awa'. But I suppose you really have to be minding the shop during Fair Week?"

"We really have no choice," Jane answered. "It's the busiest time of the year for us, being as we're right beside Glasgow Green and the Fair. Everyone else wants to be on holiday then, so it's nigh impossible to hire any extra help for the shop.

"There's naethin' I'd like better than to get oot a' Glasgow during the Fair. It's such a stramash, wi' all kinds of disgraceful things goin' on and ne'er do wells hangin' aboot. I worry for the bairns, too. I tell ye, it's one part of the Saltmarket I'll nae be missin' when we leave this place."

"Well Jane, I do insist that you bring the children to Dunoon and leave them wi' us for a few days. It would be nice if all the children could spend time thegither afore ye go."

"Thenk ye, Jessie. That's a right couthie offer – the bairns would love it, and it would keep them oot o' harm's way. I'll ask the guidman."

She broke into John's conversation to ask his permission, which was readily given. Just as he agreed,

Jessie's eldest daughter, Jessie Jr, came bouncing into the room. "Guess what, Mamma, our cousins are going on a great adventure! They're sailing to the South Seas!"

"Some adventure!" continued her brother Thomas, following behind. "They'll all be put in a big pot and boiled up for breakfast. My Sunday School teacher told us the Maori natives are cannibals! I bet they'd love to eat little Jeannie, but cousin Thomas should be safe – he looks a mite tough to chew on."

"That's enough Thomas!" shouted two mothers as the namesakes started a friendly jostle.

Jane McGibbon quickly cut in, "There are nae cannibals left since the missionaries brought Christianity to New Zealand. It's not something I have any worries aboot."

"They might not want to make a meal of you," said the Hamilton Crescent Thomas, "but they might still fight you – I bet they dinna like people pushing them off their land. Will ye be takin' some big guns wi' ye?"

John McGibbon, striding into the hallway to break up the sparring cousins, was quick to tell everyone that living in Otago would be perfectly safe. "Nearly all the Maoris live in the North Island, and that's many hundreds of miles away. All the reports say there are only a few natives in Dunedin, and they have shown nothing but kindness to the settlers."

"Well I think it sounds like wonderful fun, and I wish I were going too. I can't wait for you to come back to tell us all about living in the South Seas," cried Jessie Jr.

"That won't be as easy as you think, Jessie," said her mother. "New Zealand is such a long way from here. It

'The Head of Loch Lomond, looking South'. Engraving by H Jorden, in William Beattie's Scotland Illustrated.

takes four whole months to even sail there, and they're going to be very busy settling into a new life. It might be many years before we see them again."

"Then ye maist be sure to write to us every single day – I want to know *everything* that happens to you in that strange land."

"And ye maist send us letters aboot what's happening back here!"

Suddenly the reality of separation fell upon the two close families, and they fell silent with thoughts of parting, perhaps for ever. It was a common enough situation in Scotland, whose citizens had been emigrating in large numbers for the past 100 years or more. At least the McGibbon families would be able to keep in touch by letter. For illiterate people, emigration could be like a death in the family.

John and Jane could not foresee the future, and in spite of fervent promises to "be back hame afore very lang to see yez agin", they would never return. Nor would their two daughters. But baby John would visit Glasgow again, and his brother Thomas would call on his cousins several times in the years to come.

A world away from the comfortable life in Hamilton Crescent were the wynds and closes of the old city. This Thomas Annan photograph capures the gloomy existence of people who lived in a close off 80 High Street. This was not one of the jaunts recommended in Hugh McDonald's Rambles around Glasgow, *an extract from which is reproduced below.*

Society's dregs disport themselves on Glasgow Green

Old stairs at 28 Saltmarket Street. (David Small, 1887)

"The welcome sunshine, penetrating even into wynds and vennels with its golden invitation from on high, has called forth their wan and filthy inhabitants in swarms. In the vicinity of the Saltmarket, where we have made our *entrée*, the Green is alive with squalid groups, the children of misery and vice. Beguiled by the radiance of the summer noon, they have sneaked forth, for a brief interval, from their reekie and noisome haunts, to breathe for a time the comparatively 'caller air'. Unfortunate females, with faces of triple brass hiding hearts of unutterable woe – sleeping girls, who might be mistaken for lifeless bundles of rags – down-looking scoundrels, with felony stamped on every feature – owlish-looking knaves, minions of the moon, skulking, half-ashamed at their own appearance in the eye of the day; and alas! poor little tattered and hungry-looking children, with precocious lines of care upon their old-mannish features, tumbling about on the brown and sapless herbage. The veriest dregs of Glasgow society, indeed, seem congregated here. At one place, a band of juvenile pick-pockets are absorbed in a game of pitch-and-toss; at a short distance, a motley crew are engaged putting the stone, or endeavouring to outstrip each other in leaping about, while oaths and idiot laughter mark the progress of their play.

"You must not confound these parties with what are called the lower orders of our City. There is a deep within a deep in the social scale; to compare even the humblest working-man with such wretches would be in truth a wicked libel. The industrious poor are now at their various useful, and therefore honourable occupations, and the heterogeneous crowd before you are the idle, the vicious, and the miserable—the very vermin, in short, of our civilisation. Poor wretches! Let us not grudge them the limited portion of the Green where they invariably herd—let us not take from misery its few hours of sunshine."

(Hugh McDonald, Rambles Round Glasgow, 1854)

Saltmarket Street and the Glasgow Fair in 1825 – view from the roof of the Court House. The artist is unknown, but may be George Cruikshank. The McGibbon shop and residence was in the first building on the right of Saltmarket Street after the Fair constructions end. Glasgow Green is the open area to the right of the picture. The Tollbooth Steeple at Glasgow Cross can be seen on the left horizon. The artist is unknown.

All the fun o' the Fair

Walk up! Walk up! Ladies h'and gennelmen! Walk up and be on time for the next showing of the world's strangest creature...the Worsar! Never before seen in the British Isles, h'only discovered last month in the darkest Congo by the h'intrepid h'explorer and naturalist...Professor Morley Higginbotham! Ladies h'and gentlemen – the Worsar! Walk up! Walk up and view the Worsar! Only a penny and you can tell all your friends that you have truly seen the greatest wonder of the zoological age!

Inside the Worsar tent, sitting on a plank placed over a couple of old herring barrels, Thomas McGibbon was in a fever of anticipation, waiting for the show to begin.

At last the canvas door flap closed behind the grubby little freakshow barker who announced that *he* was the intrepid Morley Higginbotham, and the lecture would now begin! Stationing himself in front of a large box, he flung the end of it open and out trotted a large, well fed sow. 'Higginbotham' then proceeded to discourse at length on the animal's breeding, feeding habits and body structure.

"Loverley loins, 'eavenly 'hams – as foine as anything between John o' Groats and Land's End, would yer not say?" asked Higginbotham as he stroked the pig's back.

"Ay, certainly, nae doot aboot it," agreed the crowd, which was anxious to see the end of the animal so the real monster of the day could be revealed.

The showman banished the creature to its box, opened a second container and brought forth another sow. Again the animal's features and parentage were discussed at length, but this time everyone was compelled to admit that the second pig was not as good as the first. All agreed it was worse.

Having extracted this unanimous verdict from the increasingly restless audience, the pig was sent back to its box.

"H'and now, ladies h'and gentlemen, the moment you 'as all been waiting for!"

Higginbotham threw open the door of a third box, and out trotted a perfect skeleton-pig: a barely breathing bag of bones scarcely able to stand on its four spindly legs.

"Ladies h'and gentlemen! Today you 'as all seen a

good sow. And now you 'as seen a worse sow.

"But now all of you must agree that *this* creature – this representative of our blessed Creator's animal kingdom....is...is...a *worsar!*"

"Awww," groaned Thomas, turning to his companion. "That's a dirty cheat an' I want my money back!" A few others were reacting similarly, and angry words were spoken. But most were grinning, albeit in a wry fashion, as they recognised the show for what it was: a classic sideshow con. The joke was on them, but it was only a penny fraud, and aye, it was all part of the fair and they probably had their money's worth.

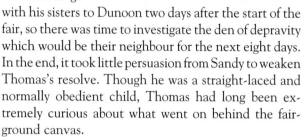

"Come on Thomas, we have a few mair pennies, let's see what else there is a' the Fair."

The speaker was Sandy Rowan, a school friend of Thomas who several days earlier had persuaded his classmate to investigate the annual Saturnalia at the foot of Saltmarket Street.

"But Father has always said I am never under any circumstances to go near the Fair," Thomas had protested.

"My Da' says the same," replied Sandy, "but everyone else goes if they're still in town during Fair Week. Look – we'll just gang doon there for a wee while and see a couple of things. Our fowks winna ken we've even been."

Thomas was due to go with his sisters to Dunoon two days after the start of the fair, so there was time to investigate the den of depravity which would be their neighbour for the next eight days. In the end, it took little persuasion from Sandy to weaken Thomas's resolve. Though he was a straight-laced and normally obedient child, Thomas had long been extremely curious about what went on behind the fairground canvas.

His interest was fuelled by what he *could* see, which was quite a lot. The tent village extended right up to the building the McGibbons lived in. Indeed, tacked directly onto the side of their building was a canvas lean-to theatre offering five acts of Richard II every twenty minutes for a penny. A scurvy little booth next door had the Wizard in Kilts showing magical feats for half that price.

Thomas could see the frolicsome holiday crowds in their thousands, read some of the garish canvas signs outside the theatres and freakshows, and hear the noise of the fair. He could almost taste the sweeties, nuts, biscuits, gingerbread, lemonade and gingerbeer displayed on tables and pushed around on barrows. But it had always been a case of "look but don't go anywhere near", and even looking was only allowed because you couldn't help it if you lived right next door.

But Thomas desperately wanted to know what was *inside* all those tents. He could see the showmen haranguing the crowd and there were some tantalising previews of the attractions within. "If it is so strange on the outside, what must it be like inside?" The mysteries had long churned about in the ten-year old's fevered imagination, and not just during Fair Week. Cheap, out-of-bounds theatres – the penny geggies – operated all year 'round at the foot of Saltmarket Street.

Now, only two months away from leaving for New Zealand, Thomas's

curiousity got the better of him and he found himself taking the back route to the Fair from Glasgow Green, avoiding Saltmarket Street where he might be spotted by parents who believed he was visiting a friend in a most respectable part of town.

Thomas and Sandy stepped out of the fraudster's tent and joined the jostle and cacophony of the festival. The air resounded to the strains of bagpipes, trumpets, trombones, cymbals, bass drums and touters' horns. The sideshow touters, dressed in threadbare stage clothes of many and soiled colours, were doing their shouting and cavorting best to attract people with pennies in their pockets.

Tumblers performed miraculous feats of gymnastics, bears danced, jugglers juggled and clowns wandered about with fixed smiles painted on tired faces, among the pressing crowds of eager urchins, grown-ups and the young men and women-about town.

"Losh, Sandy, take a look at that!" exclaimed Thomas, pointing to a sign showing an enormous boa constrictor to be viewed within for a half-penny.

"Hoots, that would be something to see, wouldn't it?"

"Shall we gang in?"

"Nah. I bet you if there's any snake at all in that tent, it will be a pitiful little thing rolled up in a blanket. I'm not going to be fooled twice in one day."

"Then look over yonder – there's a tent that has a black giantess *and* a pig-faced lady, and it's only a half-penny to see them both."

"Ugh! Who wants to gawp at a pig wumman?"

"I do, and I'm

ganging in. Are ye wi' me or no?"

The boys joined a crowd of fellow gullibles inside the tent and waited. After a short interval a statu-esque female wearing a bright yellow dress, yards of multi-coloured beads and a headdress of tall ostrich plumes walked onto the stage. "Hoot-toots – take a look at that! She really

is a muckle giant," exclaimed Sandy. "She maun be at least six feet tall and look at the size of her feet!"

"And see where she didna shave properly this mornin'," said Thomas, who had been looking out for such tell-tale evidence. The giantess fraud was well-known.

"Weel noo, an' when I take another gawp at her, I can see her face is nae quite sae black on the left as it is on the right," replied Sandy.

Throughout the tent, boys of all ages up to 60 had realised the giantess was a hoax, and were laughing and hurling insults. The burly poseur showed not the least bit of distress at being unmasked, and proceeded to announce the second part of the double act.

"Ladies and gentlemen – I give you the lady with the face of a pig!"

The giantess pulled on a cord, and a length of sacking fell aside to reveal a frightened bear with its head shaven, dressed as a woman and strapped to a sturdy chair.

This was too sick, even for the hardened and sceptical Glasgow audience, which filed out of the tent muttering darkly.

"That's the last freak show *I'll* be seein' the day," declared Thomas. Sandy agreed heartily, and for the rest of their visit they avoided all such establishments, thus losing the opportunity to see the Savages from Africa, the Armless Lady from Newfoundland who could sew and cut watch-papers using her toes, the Fire-Proof Lady who pranced about on a hot iron, the Hercules who

Not the Glasgow Fair, but something very similar: George Cruikshank's drawing of London's St Bartholemew Fair in 1835.

could bear tons of weight on his body and toss immense weights around like balls of wool, the Smallest Married Man in the World and sundry pairings of giants and dwarves.

They did enjoy the Punch and Judy show, but declined to visit the juggler who, they were hoarsely informed via a voice trumpet, swallowed knives and forks and vomited flames of fire and endless yards of silk ribbon.

They passed up several opportunities to win a thousand guineas. One of these challenges, crudely painted on a piece of fluttering calico, read:

CHALLENGE FOR 1000 GUNEUS. THE LION QUEEN
SHALL ENTER THE DEN WITH A THOUSAND
FEROSSIOUS BESTS. THE FOX DUCKS AND ALSO
ALL TO DANCE THE COMMON POLKA.
BOYS A HAPENNEY.

Seeking less tawdry amusement, the boys spent half-pennies on hobby-horses, merry-go-rounds and the exciting Waterloo-fly. They shot unsuccessfully for nuts at the Locomotive Targets, and enjoyed a game of rowley-powley. The boys both won cheap gee-gaws: Sandy on the Wheel of Fortune and Thomas at the Lucky Bag. Later, realising they could never take their prizes home, they gave them away to a beggar-boy.

Thomas indulged his fairfood fantasies at the lemonade and confections tables, and declared he'd never tasted anything better in his life.

By now the boys were running low on funds, and decided their last pennies should be spent on the wild beasts at Wombwell's Travelling Menagerie.

"The largest collection of these denizens of the forest and mates of the Red Man and Indian ever conveyed through the United Kingdom," read the Guide to Glasgow Fair.

"The menagerie is complete in all its departments, including beasts, birds and reptiles of every variety. Two ponderous elephants, said to be the finest specimens travelling ; and a huge Rhinoceros, weighing upwards of two tons, and the largest living one in Great Britain, (very likely the fabled unicorn of the ancients), are not the least attractive objects to be seen in this diversified

collection of wonders in natural history. Lions, Tigers, Panthers, Leopards, Bears, Hyaenas, rollicking about in their grated prisons, as if impatient of restraint, and panting to roam in their forest jungles.

"The menagerie is open during the entire day ; price of admission, One Shilling ; working classes and children, Sixpence."

Thomas and Sandy declared this to be the best part of the Fair, and although they doubted that the rhinoceros was really the unicorn of ancient times, they did agree that, by and large, the animals were far more real than anything else they had seen all afternoon.

What Thomas did not know was that he needn't have spent his precious sixpence to visit the zoo. The very next day he would be taken there again by his father. Having to see the animals once more was no hardship, though feigning surprise at each of them was not so easy.

Dealing with his conscience over the afternoon's deceit was a larger problem that would have to be treated with a heavy dose of prayer and private moral flagellation. But no-one could take away Thomas's new-found knowledge of what really happens at the Glasgow Fair.

GLASGOW FAIR

Long ere this the usual arena at the foot of the Saltmarket has been showing manifest signs of extensive preparations to allure the multitude during this festive week. Various erections, or wooden booths, have been placed upon the ground allotted for the purpose in that quarter, from the various stages of which all that is calculated to please the eye or ear, or engross the attention of sight-seers, has been brought into notice. Mountebanks, tumblers, and other personages of note, who create a noise in that part of the world, are busied in plying their usual avocations. Those who do not mind the freaks and fantastic gambols of the *fool*, may have their tastes gratified by an inspection of sundry denizens of the forest and the jungle, which have been transported hither for their inspection and gratification. The places of amusement are, we should say, more limited than in former days, although there is no lack of smaller enjoyments—such as "merry-go-rounds", "flys," &c. We believe the more reflecting part of the community, however, will betake themselves to the railway or the steamer. There they may inhale the country air and the sea-breeze, and be out of the reach of the din and clamour, and many undignified appearances which obtrude themselves upon the admirer of the picturesque or the rural scene.

Pocket-picking.— We would caution the visitors who, in all probability, will, during the present week, throng down to the foot of Saltmarket Street, to look sharply after the security of their pockets. Already a number of individuals have ben relieved of their watches, and handkerchiefs have disappeared in dozens. We have no doubt that the police will do their duty, and protect, so far as they can, the purses of the lieges, but, as they are not Argus-eyed, the citizens should take the hint, and look after their own property.
Glasgow Courier, 10/7/1849)

Glasgow Green, on the banks of the River Clyde, was a favourite recreation spot for Glasgow's citizens. The area in the foreground was evidently where the more genteel folk met. The barely mentionable classes described on page 40 congregated at the end of the Green nearest Saltmarket Street (in the centre of this 1838 engraving). The colonnaded building is the High Court, in Jailhouse Square at the foot of Saltmarket Street. This was also the area where the annual Glasgow Fair took place. (Author's collection)

Last days in Scotland

"D'ye think we'll ever stop thinkin' aboot this place when we're livin' the new life in New Zealand?" asked Jane as she adjusted her skirts and lowered herself to the grassy bank of the Clyde.

She continued, "It's all sae real to me the noo, but then so was Grannie Janet's hoose once, and I can scarce remember it any more. Och, it makes me richt sad tae be leavin', John."

She looked over her shoulder in the direction of their former house, her eyes brimming.

"You know, for all our complaints aboot it, I'll be leavin' the auld Saltmarket with fond memories. We've had happy times there, an' that's goin' back a lang time fer sure."

John glanced at his wife, saw the tears starting to form, and squeezed her hand.

"Ay, m'dear. I mind when ye were just a wee kimmer actin' shy when I went up the street to buy the bread frae your faither's bakery. That was aye a while back."

"I'm thinkin' ye never noticed me then."

"I did an aw! Well...perhaps it took a year or two."

John recalled walking home from church on a particular Sunday, and noticing that the child from McConachy's Bakery had become an interesting young woman. Still, he'd had neither the opportunity nor the gumption to do much about it for several years.

He increased the pressure on Jane's hand. "It's sae warm today, sittin' here watchin' the Clyde movin' doon tae the sea. It's hard to imagine it was this river that finally got us together. In a manner of speakin', that is."

"Ay, what a winter it was in 1837," said Jane. "I'll nae forget *that* in a hurry. Nor will I be forgettin' the young man who sent me sprawlin' on the ice."

"It was what ye micht term a maist fortuitous collision," recalled her husband.

"It maist certainly was! Och, but it was cauld that winter, John! Did ye ever see such frosts? Do you mind how the Clyde was frozen bank to bank for week after week? It's not been like that since."

"Ay I mind the time all richt. All the lads and lasses were havin' a gret time of it, laughin' and carrying on. They were slidin' aboot an' playing games frae mornin' tae nicht."

"And after ye picked me up frae the ice, we just kept on skatin' thegither, an' the next day we did the same agin. An' the day after that, as I recall."

"Skating the day lang wasna for us though, with wark to do in the businesses, but d'ye mind when I used to bring the lantern frae the front o' the shop so ye could do your pirouettes in the dark?"

"Ay, I mind it verra weel. Na, I'll not be forgettin' *that* in a hurry."

John and Jane were enjoying a Saturday walk in the sun on their own, the first time for ten years. With only four days left before their ship sailed for New Zealand, the shop had been sold, and the family had moved out of the upstairs apartment into David McGibbon's house. Today, Jessie had volunteered to look after the children while John and Jane went back to Saltmarket Street to wish the new shop owner well, and to say their goodbyes to former neighbours.

It had been an eventful few weeks as the family prepared to leave. John had paid the last instalments on the passage tickets and his land in Dunedin. In the end, he decided to compromise between cabin class and steerage, and travel in the fore-cabin.

"It will cost a deal more, but it's something we should be doin' when we're takin' such a young bairn," said John. "And going in a better class may put us in touch with people who could help us in business later on."

Jane had been extremely busy, coping with young baby John Junior, and getting clothing and other belongings ready for the voyage. There had been many a conversation about which furniture to keep, and what goods should be taken to New Zealand, for building their future home, and for selling in the general store they hoped to establish.

"We canna leave that sideboard behind, surely?" Jane had asked. "That's auld Grannie's, and it's almost as much a part of the family as the bairns."

John had also grown fond of the big carved mahogany piece. "Weel now," he said. "It is a fine piece o' furniture to be sure, but it's a muckle big thing, and it would use up nearly all o' our free allowance afore we start to tak' the things we really must have. They say furniture is being made in Dunedin, an' it's also bein' shipped in frae America."

In the end, all they could agree to take was a small chest of drawers, and a mahogany dining table which would still be in daily use in a descendant's home nearly 150 years later.

There were decisions to be made about clothing, although the choices were not too difficult, because the family did not have great social pretensions. Jane had brushed aside her sister-in-law's notions of what would be proper to wear in the new colony.

"You must keep up appearances that befit your station in life at all times, and you should never appear in public looking like working folks," Jessie had advised.

"Jessie, we're goin' tae a place where such notions are a deal less important than they are here. We'll tak' one set o' Sunday best, and everything else will be plain claithes that are strong and serviceable. That is the advice we have received, and it makes a gret deal o' sense tae me.

"Anyway, we're limited in the amount o' luggage we can take – we maun be sensible aboot it."

Jane had assembled a kit of clothes which was indeed serviceable, and well exceeded the New Zealand Company's minimum requirement, which for each emigrant was "Two complete sets of Outer Clothing, including two pairs of Shoes ; and one dozen changes of Under Clothing, including Stockings." She had packed extra shoes after reading about a shortage of bootmaking skills in Dunedin.

She had packed away best clothes, extra work clothes, bed linen, crockery, cutlery, cooking utensils and favourite ornaments in wooden boxes, to be stowed in the ship's hold. She bought two large canvas bags to contain the clothes they would need during the voyage. She also collected the bed linen, towels, cutlery, tin plates, drinking mugs and religious books they would need in their cabin, and packed a set of quoits for family members to amuse themselves with on deck during the voyage.

"Though how we're going tae pack all that and

ourselves as weel into that wee cubbyhole, I blessed if I know," commented Jane, after the family inspected their intended vessel, the barquentine Mooltan.

The family had been to see the ship twice: a week earlier when intending emigrants were invited to inspect the Mooltan at Greenock Docks, and the previous month, when John took the children to watch the ship being launched at Denny and Rankine's shipyard at Dumbarton.

The Dumbarton visit had been a great excitement. They had boarded a paddle-wheel steamer at the Broomielaw passenger wharves and cruised among the host of steamers and sailing ships which crowded the river all the way to the Firth of Clyde and the port of Dumbarton. They saw large ships under tow, and speculated on what exotic part of the world they had sailed from. Watching their very own ship being launched brought a sense of reality to the forthcoming voyage. It would be a very great adventure, the children declared.

A few days later another major event had taken place: the first royal visit to Glasgow of the young Queen Victoria and her husband Prince Albert. Jane and the children had found a vantage point at Jamaica Bridge where the royal party had swept into the city centre through a gigantic temporary gate.

John had been elsewhere on that day, standing self-importantly in Argyll Street with a large contingent from the Grocer Company – a benevolent society supported by Glasgow's 600-strong grocer fraternity. Dressed in bib and tucker and top hat, with a scarlet sash across his chest, John had enjoyed this last ceremonial outing with his peers in business.

"Wasnae today a graund occasion?" said Jane that evening. "And the auld city really turned on a wonderful day for it, after all the wet weather the royal party had at Loch Lomond."

"I've never seen so many people," said John. "There wasnae a spare inch to be found anywhere. In Argyll Street the streets were jam-packed. Every window was full o' people, an' there were others all o'er the roofs. They say it was the same everywhere her Highness went."

"If ye could only have seen it doon a' the bridge," said Jane. "That special gate they built is the biggest thing I ever saw, and it looked richt impressive carrying that enormous crown on top of it.

"The royal party came through the gate in a big open carriage with all those white horses, those men in uniforms, flags wavin' and miles and miles of red and blue calico hanging everywhere. All the cheers and cries of loyalty were the loudest ye ever heard.

"It's amazing to think it's only a hundred years since the English butchered us at Culloden, but naebodie seems tae be thinkin' of that any more. I was richt proud mysel' tae be a citizen of Britain theday."

"I felt the same," agreed her husband. "Queen Victoria has finally put things richt with Scotland, an' that's a blessing. Ay, but it is fortunate we were still here to see her.

Another month and we would have been on our way tae New Zealand."

Over the past few weeks, John had been preparing to sell the business, and he spent some time at warehouses in the Candleriggs and elsewhere, buying and crating up the goods he intended to set up shop with in Dunedin. The grocery items, including tea and coffee, four and oatmeal, were easy to select, because that was his business. He knew less about general goods, but gained an idea of what the colony needed from settlers'

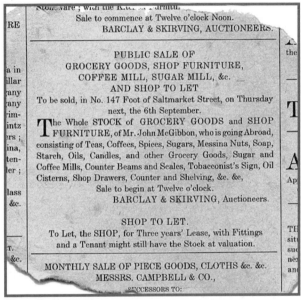

(Glasgow Herald, 3/9/1849)

(Glasgow Herald, 11/8/1849)

The Queen and Prince Albert arrive at the south side of Glasgow's Broomielaw docks in August 1849, at the start of the first royal visit to Glasgow since James VI in 1617. An eyewitness later described Victoria's landing: "...what a blazonry of preparation and turbulence of welcome awaited her! Ships were ablaze with bunting. Military, police, civic officials, and incalculable motley crowds were everywhere...There on the deck of the little steamer, stood the Queen of the British Isles, with Prince Albert near, and her little children gathered about her, including the little Prince of Wales in blue jacket and white trousers. She looked for all the world like an anxious young mother just returned from the seaside." (James Hedderwick in Backward Glances, *1891.)*

letters published by the New Zealand Company.

Through his brother's business, he bought a range of earthenware utensils including cups and saucers, cream jugs, egg cups, plates, covered dishes, gravy dishes and water jugs. Supplies of cutlery and sewing goods were added, and he stowed away iron goods which he expected home builders would need: hinges, bolts, nails and screws, locks, thumb latches, claw hammers, saws and joiners' axes. He added a small stock of implements for his own future agricultural pursuits – two spades, a mattock, a billhook and two American axes.

The oil paintings which had hung in the family parlour were too bulky to be kept, but John removed engravings from their frames, bought some additional engraved copies of famous British paintings, and packed these, along with small watercolour family portraits, into a slim case lined with tin and soldered to be moisture-proof.

Eventually, Jane's careful selection and packing of the family's personal luggage allowed it to fit within the free allowance of 20 cubic feet per adult, but John's 12 tons of business items, including the furniture, went as special cargo, for which the Company charged fifty shillings a ton.

"It is really costing us naethin' when ye consider we could hae spent that extra money and travelled in the chief cabins," said John.

"Then it would have cost naethin' tae send the sideboard either," replied Jane, still smarting from the loss of her family heirloom.

"Ne'er ye mind, we maun tak' what will make a living for us first, and I promise ye we'll replace that sideboard as soon as we can afford it," replied her husband, getting in the last word as always.

"We'd best be gettin' along then," said Jane. "It's been a right pleasure to be out on the Green agin wi' just you and me, but I maist be gettin' back to wee John Junior."

"Look at the time – Jessie and thre bairns will be wonderin' where we are," said John as he helped his wife to her feet.

"Only four days tae go."

"Ay, my love. This time Tuesday we'll be doon the watter for the verra last time." ∎

Separating fact from fiction

Was John McGibbon really hit over the head by a rioter in March 1848? Maybe, maybe not, but it makes a good story... The facts are that his shop existed, and that he would have been a tempting target for the rioters, who did rampage through Glasgow streets, looting food shops, jewellers and gunsmiths. Saltmarket Street was one of the main routes into the city from Glasgow Green, and the McGibbon grocery shop would have been an obvious target. At the very least, the family would have been well aware of the riot, and they would have been very frightened by it.

Sean O'Reagan is an imaginary character, but the broad events of the two days of rioting, and its aftermath in the courts, are historically accurate.

Saltmarket Street: The names of Saltmarket Street businesses, and information about numbers of grog shops, are taken directly from the 1849 Glasgow Post Office Directory. This directory, and directories for other years, also provided information about other McGibbon businesses. Incidentally, Saltmarket Street, which leads north from the River Clyde, is one of the oldest streets in Glasgow, and was originally the market for salt used in preserving salmon. The street was often known as simply 'the Saltmarket'.

McGibbon residence: We cannot be sure if the McGibbon family lived above their shop. The Post Office Directory gives no separate home address for John McGibbon, whereas it does for his brother David, and for many other businessmen. However it was also quite common for shopkeepers to live above their shops, and this may be why there was no separate residential address given.

The business: Details of the tea and coffee business were taken from an old cashbook, which exists today. The book is an example of the canny approach – some might say meanness – which characterised later MacGibbon retail businesses in New Zealand. The earliest entries are dated 1840, but the spine of the book says 'Cashbook, 1801'. Earlier pages were sliced out before it was recycled into John McGibbon's business.

Scottish dialect: The McGibbon family and their associates have been given lowland Scots accents and dialect. The basis for this is a published Southland pioneer reminiscence that John McGibbon spoke with a broad accent. A selected glossary of Scottish words and phrases is on page 34.

Attitudes to the poor: In the stories, John McGibbon and his associates are very dismissive toward the poor, particularly those of Irish origin. Their attitudes might not be politically correct today, but that is how Glas-

Watercolour portraits of John and Jane McGibbon, with their son Thomas, painted in Glasgow circa 1840

gow's emerging middle classes felt and spoke in 1849. They despised their poor brethren, and greatly feared the slums as dens of crime, disease and potential revolution. The working classes were scarcely seen as *brethren* – they were seen as almost a separate species of being, and justification for this was built into a Calvinist belief that the poor will always be poor, and should know their place. And if the poor should be afflicted by epidemics of typhus and cholera – well, that was God's punishment for a lifestyle that was sinful, irreligious and intemperate. (One difficulty with this thesis was that cholera, unlike typhus, didn't always distinguish between rich and poor. However, typhus was more discerning, and chose most of its victims from poorest areas.)

A distinction was also seen between the 'deserving' and 'undeserving' poor in Glasgow. The deserving poor were likely to have come from the native Glaswegian working class – and the men, and some of the women in the household probably actually had a job. This class also disliked the newcomers, who were mainly Scots refugees from highland clearances, or Irish escaping their potato famine.

Scots workers particularly hated the Irish, who were prepared to work longer hours, in worse conditions, for lower wages. Suspicion of Catholicism, fanned by the Protestant clergy, added to the problem.

Slum conditions: Descriptions of slum conditions in the story are not overdrawn. Thousands of people lived in situations as bad and even worse than those described. Glasgow had the most appalling housing and sanitary conditions in Europe – comparable to some of the worst Third World conditions today. Several official reports, dating from 1839, show how bad things really were.

In 1842, a government "Report on the Sanitary Condition of the Labouring Population of Scotland", was published. This describes conditions which were probably better than those in 1848-49, when the McGibbon story takes place.

Dr Neil Arnott, who investigated Glasgow's wynds (lanes leading to inner courtyards) for the 1842 report, described interlocking passageways and courtyards, which were "...occupied entirely as a dung receptacle of the most disgusting kind." The people who lived in these conditions were "...worse off than wild animals, which

withdraw to a distance and conceal their ordure."

Indeed, they hoarded their ordure in 'dunghills', which actually had economic value, being sold by landlords to local farmers once or twice a year as manure.

Dr Arnott reported: "The interiors of these houses and their inmates corresponded with the exteriors. We saw half-dressed wretches crowding together to be warm; and in one bed, although in the middle of the day, several women were imprisoned under a blanket, because as many others who had on their backs all the articles of dress that belonged to the party were then out of doors in the streets. This picture is so shocking that, without ocular proof, one would be disposed to doubt the possibility of the facts."

A year earlier, a report by the Commission on the Condition of Hand-loom Weavers had noted that: 'The wynds of Glasgow comprise a fluctuating population of from 15,000 to 20,000 persons. This quarter consists of a labyrinth of lanes, out of which numberless entrances lead into small courts, each with a dunghill reeking in the centre... In some of these lodging-rooms (visited at night) we found a whole lair of human beings littered along the floor – sometimes 15 and 20, some clothed, some naked – men, women and children huddled promiscuously together. Their bed consisted of a lair of rusty straw intermixed with rags. There was no furniture in these places. The sole article of comfort was a fire."

Cholera: Cholera reached epidemic proportions in Scotland in 1832, 1848/49, 1853 and 1866. The disease struck victims very suddenly, and often killed within a day; sometimes within a few hours. Initial symptoms were acute vomiting, followed by catastrophic diarrhoea, painful cramps and acute spasmodic vomiting. The death rate was about 60 per cent. The daily volume of stools could be four litres or more, resulting in very rapid dehydration, with life-threatening losses of water and essential electrolytes (salts) from the body. With water loss came a thickening in the blood and a slowing in blood circulation. The slowed circulation is what made victims' skin turn blue in colour. Shock would ensue, and the final result was death as the blood became too thick to circulate.

The Church: The McGibbons were communicant members of the Free Church, which had seceded from the established Presbyterian Church of Scotland in the

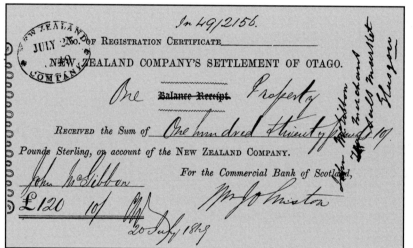

John McGibbon's receipt for purchasing one standard New Zealand Company property. Such a property included ¼ acre of town land, 10 acres of suburban land and 50 acres of rural land.

Disruption of 1843. Almost 40 per cent of the Church of Scotland ministers switched to the new church, which was more evangelical and severe in tone.

Descriptions of religious observance and the Scottish Sabbath are taken from contemporary accounts as well as more recent academic writings. Dr Murray Douglas of the divinity faculty at the University of Glasgow was particularly helpful in providing information on the form of service, and in reviewing the Sabbath section. Given the narrow, pious attitudes of the first two generations of McGibbons in New Zealand, it is reasonable to assume that they held similar attitudes before they emigrated.

Businesses and taverns: All businesses and taverns mentioned in stories actually existed, their names being taken from the 1849 Glasgow Post Office Directory.

Information for emigrants: Source materials for the section where the family learns about the Free Church settlement in Dunedin are contemporary newspaper advertisements, articles and publications.

While much of the material in support of emigration was reasonably factual, it *was* propaganda, and many of the claims were exaggerations or even lies. The most one-eyed of today's Otago boosters would pause before claiming their weather in winter is 'benign'! And to the best of the author's knowledge, no tropical cassowary birds have ever been found in Stewart Island. Overall though, the hype was a little more honest than that associated with earlier New Zealand Company emigration campaigns, such as for the Wellington settlement.

The systematic plan for interlocking nationality, creed, class, capital and labour was more theory than reality. Few wealthy capitalists took the bait, and most emigrants who wore the capitalist tag were people of moderate means such as the McGibbons. Indeed, the settlement suffered an acute shortage of capital until the gold boom of the 1860s. Of the 2,000 properties available for general purchase by settlers, only about 450 were sold after seven years, and only 3,600 acres were being cultivated. This was only 2.4 per cent of the 144,600 acres initially offered in the 400,000 acre Otago Block. (One acre = 0.405 hectare.)

Relatively few among Scotland's working classes saw emigration to New Zealand as an acceptable solution to their problems, even during the 1848 – 1850 period of economic depression: promoters struggled to fill their ships. *Selecting* emigrants, to choose the best type of (preferably Free Church) Scottish workers and their families, was just not possible, and the promoters even had to make up numbers with sassenachs from south of the border! Nevertheless, the early settlement

was overwhelmingly Scottish in character, and remained so for many years. Otago and Southland still have New Zealand's greatest concentration of people with Scottish ancestry.

Lay Association: Information about offices and staff of the Lay Association of Members of the Free Church of Scotland has come from the Association's account book, held at National Archives, Wellington. The Association promoted the Otago scheme and sold passages to, and land, in the new settlement. These activities were carried out on behalf of the New Zealand Company until July 1850, when the New Zealand Company's colonising charter was withdrawn by the British Government. The Edinburgh office, at 5 George Street, had two salaried officers: the secretary, John McGlashan, and a clerk, Thomas Atkinson. The Glasgow office, at 3 West Nile Street, had one clerk, a Mr Hutcheson. Dr Aldcorn was secretary of the Glasgow branch, but this was an unpaid, honorary position. McGlashan received what was in those days a substantial annual salary of £300, while his clerk was paid £65. Hutcheson's salary was £60. The account book also records substantial travelling expenses for McGlashan.

The ship Mooltan: The McGibbons travelled to New Zealand in the sailing ship Mooltan (which was sometimes, as in the Greenock Advertiser's advertisement, spelled Moultan). The New Zealand Company's embarkation list shows that they travelled in the intermediate 'fore-cabin' class. The Company's records show that John McGibbon shipped a substantial amount of freight, presumably to stock the store he advertised shortly after his arrival in Dunedin. Unfortunately the records do not say what was inside the 18 boxes, 1 bale, eight packages and eight casks. His freight bill of £30/15/8 was the highest of any passenger. The next biggest shipper, 'gentleman settler' Francis Pillans, paid £27/9/6. Most passengers paid no additional freight, and those who did, averaged around £3. Calculated on the published additional freight charge of £2/10/ - an imperial ton, John McGibbon would have shipped around 12 tons (12.2 metric tonnes). His freight bill was equivalent to around $2,890 in 1997 New Zealand dollars.

Glasgow Fair and other street activities: Descriptions of the Glasgow Fair and other entertainments in the Saltmarket Street area are taken from a variety of contemporary newspapers and other publications.

Lastly, John and Jane McGibbon's recollection of how they got together to become man and wife is presumed to be accurate: the story about the frozen Clyde comes from a speech John made on the occasion of their golden wedding anniversary in 1888. ∎

SPELLING OF THE FAMILY NAME

The family name used in the Glasgow stories is spelled McGibbon, as it had been since at least 1620 (to which date direct ancestors have been traced in Old Parochial Registers of Scotland.) The name began to be spelled MacGibbon in New Zealand around the late 1850s. When writing about the family before 1858, the 'Mc' spelling has generally been used. Just to complicate matters though, Dunedin newspapers spelled the name M'Gibbon during most of the 1850s.

Saltmarket Street today

In its heyday, Saltmarket Street was the place to be in Glasgow. It was well-known to novelist Sir Walter Scott, whose character in *Rob Roy*, the affluent city magistrate Bailie Nicol Jarvie, enjoyed "a' the comforts of the Sautmarket".

Saltmarket Street hosted some of the best people. Oliver Cromwell stayed there when he visited Glasgow. A famous 18th century mayor, Provost Bell, lived very close to the McGibbon shop site, and the future King James VII, while still the Prince of Wales, used to visit him.

As we have seen, the street and its immediate neighborhood moved to the opposite end of the fashion spectrum when the industrial revolution hit Glasgow and emigrants flooded in from the Scottish Highlands and Ireland.

Saltmarket Street. The newer building is on the site of John McGibbon's grocery shop.

Although the street was cleaned up from the late 1860s and none of the mid-century buildings remain, today's Saltmarket has not regained Bailie Jarvie's 'comforts'. It remains resolutely downmarket – a narrow street of four-story mostly late Victorian buildings containing upper floor apartments, and small shops and businesses at street level: bars, pawn shop, tobacconist, newsagent, delicatessen, shoeshop, golf and fishing equipment, chemist, fish and chips, fruit and vegetables, tailor, solicitor, bakery, Ladbrook's betting shop, hair salon, wine shop, coffee house, pet shop etc. A street where many businesses cover their windows with protective steel mesh outside opening hours.

At least two buildings have succeeded the former McGibbon building. The current occupant is a block of flats which were probably built in the 1960s.

The tired looking High Court building is still at the foot of the street, next to the bridge over the Clyde River. Opposite is the vast Glasgow Green, alas a sterile and tatty prospect in comparison with London's Hyde Park or Christchurch's Hagley Park. It requires a considerable leap of imagination to picture the rambunctious former Glasgow Fair.

At the other end of Saltmarket Street, Glasgow Cross and the Trongate have also been extensively rebuilt. But newer developments are themselves now old, and the area has never reclaimed its position as the hub of the city. The Tron Kirk Steeple, and Tollbooth Steeple remain.

Above: Glasgow Cross

Below: Debenhams in Argyle Street, site of David McGibbon's former business.

Argyle Street ranges from average to trendy, and in recent years it has been revitalised, with part of it transformed into a pedestrian mall. The mall includes the site of David McGibbon's business, these days occupied by the large Debenhams department store.

David McGibbon's imagined suggestion that his brother should move his business to the west end of downtown Glasgow was sound advice. After 150 years, Saltmarket Street is still depressed, while further west, addresses in George Square, St Vincents's Square, Buchanan Street and Sauciehall Street remain grand and fashionable. As do the impressive West End terraces such as Park Circus, toward and beyond Kelvingrove Park. ■

Photographs on this page were taken by Alastair MacGibbon and David Stevenson

Saltmarket Street looking toward Glasgow Cross.

GOING ABROAD
Part two: the Voyage

 # Contents

The Illustrated London News was an important chronicle of the Victorian era, and from time to time it looked at the subject of emigration from Britain. Most of the emigration illustrations published by the magazine between 1844 and 1853 are reproduced on the following pages.

The New Zealand Company's conditions, page 57

Advertising the voyage, page 59

Artist Andrew Devon's impression of the McGibbon family waiting to be rowed from Port Chalmers to Dunedin, a few days after their 26 December 1849 arrival on the Mooltan.

THE SAILING SHIP
MOOLTAN

The Mooltan, or *Moultan*, as she was usually called in Scottish advertising and newspaper articles, was a brand-new ship when she left for New Zealand in September 1849.

She had been launched only a month earlier, at the Dumbarton shipyard of Denny and Rankine. She was a barque rigged sailing ship of 610 tons (620 metric tonnes). Other dimensions were: length 128.4 feet (39.1m), beam 26.4 feet (8.0m), depth 18.4 feet (5.9m).

The Mooltan was listed in Lloyds Register as a 13 years A1 class vessel. She was sheathed below the waterline in yellow metal. This sheathing, which was 60 parts copper to 40 parts zinc, was to protect the hull against teredo worm.

In appearance, the Mooltan was probably very similar to the ship illustrated on this page. Unfortunately no drawing of the real Mooltan has been located, after a thorough international search.

The Mooltan probably had about 30 crew, and on the voyage to Otago, she was commanded by Captain William Chivas. Other officers included Mr Milligan (first mate) and Archibald Cook (3rd mate). The identity of the second mate is not known. The ship's surgeon-superintendent was Dr William Purdie, while the cook was James Eastman.

Company records show that The New Zealand Company paid £2,173/12/- to hire the Mooltan for the voyage, from her owners, Captain William Crawford and other townsmen of Greenock.

The following material from the Greenock Advertiser gives some idea of the process of fitting out the Mooltan. Warning: watch out for hyperbole!

"The duty of fitting [the Mooltan] up and provisioning her for the voyage has been entrusted by the New Zealand Company to Captain Reaves, a most active and attentive officer, who has had similar charge of all the previous ships despatched by them to the colony, and who has given equal satisfaction to the Company and the emigrants.

"Every part of the ship is fitted up with remarkable attention to the accommodation and comfort of the passengers...Steerage cabins have been provided for such steerage passengers as pay in full for their own conveyance, and very comfortable berths they are. Messrs A. Brown and Son have been employed by the New Zealand Company to fit up the between decks for the accommodation of the passengers, and their work is neat and very substantial. Great attention has been paid to the light-

ing and especially the ventilation of the ship; and we can safely say that we have seldom been on board a vessel where the space allotted to passengers was more roomy or commodious than in the *Mooltan*. The passage to the colony in this fine ship may be looked forward to as quite a summer cruise.

"The cordage, sails, awnings and windsails for ventilation have been supplied by Messrs Orr, Hunter and Co. The provisions &c., are furnished by Messrs Macfie, Graham and Co., and the bill of fare is altogether ample and of first-rate quality...

"Great attention has been paid to providing suitable medicines and medical comforts. Two commodious berths have been fitted up as hospitals for such males or females as may fall sick on the way, and the services of a medical gentleman of high character and great skill, who proposes to settle in the colony, have been secured.

"On the whole, no exertions have been spared to render the passengers every way comfortable, and we sincerely wish them a happy and prosperous voyage."

The Mooltan sailed for many years, mainly on the Australian and Indian runs. She dropped out of Lloyd's Register in 1870. ∎

"Ship from Clyde to Otago"

The Greenock Advertiser reports on the Mooltan's departure for Dunedin

"Numerous vessels have, within these few years, left different British ports under the auspices of the New Zealand Company, and the accounts which the immigrants have sent home, are of the most encouraging description. This applies in an especial manner to the settlement of Otago. To this interesting settlement the Moultan, with 158 emigrants has just departed. This fine ship was launched a few weeks ago from the building-yard of Denny and Rankine at Dumbarton, and is the property of Captain William Crawford and other townsmen. She is a 13 years A1 ship, with of course all the choice timbers and fastenings which vessels of that high class require, and is of 580 tons* register.

"Her dispatch on the very day for which, two months ago, she had been advertised to sail for New Zealand, is an instance of punctuality that well deserves to be recorded with due praise. The expedition is the more remarkable, as she was at sea filled with passengers and goods, on the twenty-third day after the launch.

"On Tuesday afternoon the vessel left the harbour, but came to at the Tail of the Bank till next forenoon, to allow the passengers to get themselves thoroughly in order for sea. In the evening the Rev. Mr. Bonar of this town and the Rev. Mr Morrison of Port-Glasgow, visited the ship, where the former delivered an admirable impressive address to those who were about to take up their abode in the distant colony of Otago, urging them to make diligent use of the means of religious instruction already provided there, and to bear ever on their minds the responsibility that attaches to those who form the probable founders of a great nation, and on whom its future character and success must greatly de-

*The vessel was actually 610 tons

pend. Mr Morrison concluded with a suitable prayer.

"The Moultan left the Tail of the Bank soon after mid-day on Wednesday, and was towed by the steamer considerably outside the Cumbraes,

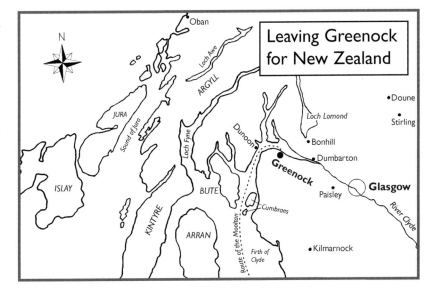

when a smart breeze of favourable wind springing up, she was left proceeding on her voyage, the passengers giving their friends who had escorted them so far, a hearty farewell cheer.

"No finer ship or more hopeful body of emigrants ever left the Clyde; nearly all of them persons moving in the middle rank, and inspired with the liveliest anticipation of improving their worldly circumstances, and that without depriving themselves of the associations connected with British society,—an advantage such colonies as Otago possess, and whose value it is impossible to over-estimate.

"Shortly before the tug left, the passengers were all mustered before the surgeon-superintendent, and Dr. Purdie, in signing the return, took the opportunity of expressing, in his own name, as well as that of his fellow-passengers, his deep sense of gratitude for the urbanity and attention they had met with, and for the

abundant provision made for their safety and comfort on the voyage.

"While the ship was fitting out, and especially on the last few days, she was visited by a large number of ladies and gentlemen from a distance, to see their friends in their ocean residence, and to view the preparations made on board for their accommodation. Among them were Charles Cowan, Esq., M.P. for Edinburgh, William Duncan, Esq., of that City, J. M'Glashan, Esq., Secretary of the Otago Association, and many others, some interested in the success of that promising colony, and not a few who have it in prospect also to proceed to it at an early day.

"The wisdom of the New Zealand Company in fitting up and despatching part of their vessels from the out-ports is very evident, as intending emigrants have thus the opportunity of satisfying themselves of the convenience of the ships, and are saved the trouble and expense of proceeding to the south of England to embark their families and goods, which is, in fact, to many as much as half of the whole labour of the voyage." ■

(Greenock Advertiser, September 1849; reproduced in the Otago Journal, November 1849)

Plan of typical 19th century emigrant sailing ship

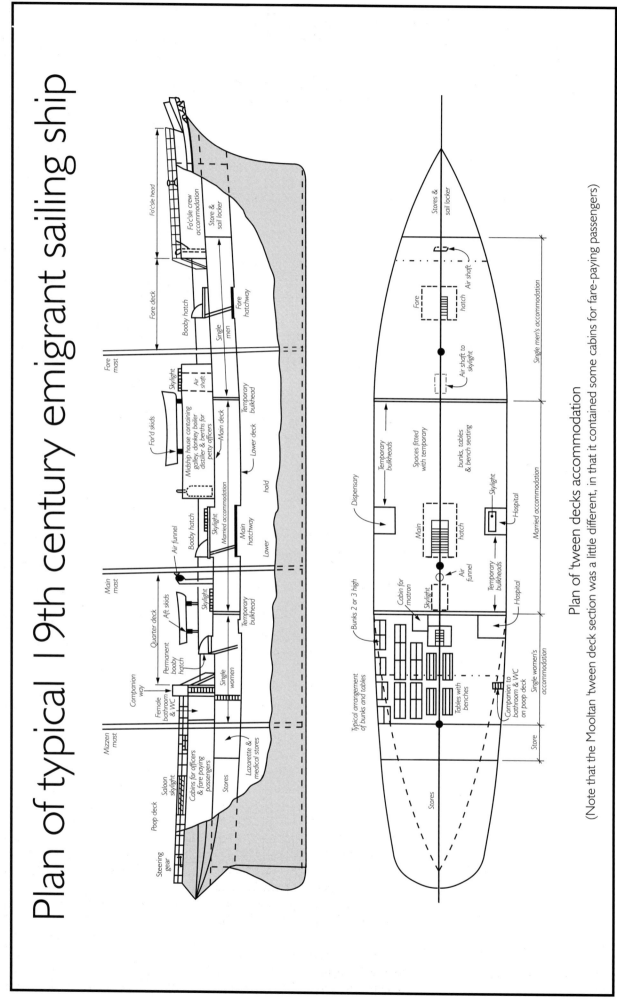

Poop deck

Quarter deck

Fore deck

Fo'c'sle head

Steering gear

Mizzen mast

Main mast

Fore mast

Saloon skylight

Cabins for officers & fare paying passengers

Stores

Lazarette & medical stores

Female bathroom & WC

Companion way

Permanent booby hatch

Single women

Air funnel

Booby hatch

Married accommodation

Skylight

Temporary bulkhead

Main hatchway

Aft skids

Skylight

For'd skids

Midship house containing galley, donkey boiler distiller & berths for petty officers

Skylight

Air shaft

Temporary bulkhead

Main deck

Lower deck

Fo'c'sle crew accommodation

Booby hatch

Single men

Fore hatchway

Store & sail locker

Lower

Lower

hold

Plan of 'tween decks accommodation

Dispensary

Temporary bulkheads

Spaces fitted with temporary

Main hatch

Air shaft to skylight

Stores & sail locker

Fore hatch

Single men's accommodation

bunks, tables & bench seating

Married accommodation

Skylight

Hospital

Hospital

Temporary bulkheads

Air funnel

Cabin for matron

Skylight

Bunks 2 or 3 high

Typical arrangement of bunks and tables

Tables with benches

Companion to bathroom & WC on poop deck

Single women's accommodation

Store

Stores

(Note that the Mooltan 'tween deck section was a little different, in that it contained some cabins for fare-paying passengers)

Emigrating with the New Zealand Company

The New Zealand Company had no ships of its own for taking people to its settlements in Wellington, New Plymouth, Nelson, Otago and Christchurch. It chartered ships as it needed them.

The Company published standard fares of passage, and rules and regulations relating to what people could take on the voyage and how they should conduct themselves on board.

Information in this article relates particularly to vessels which sailed to Otago under the auspices of the New Zealand Company in 1849, but similar conditions applied for other destinations in New Zealand and Australia around this period.

Getting to the Antipodes was expensive

New Zealand and Australia were probably the most expensive emigration destinations on the globe for British people. This was understandable, given that Australasia was as far from Britain as it was possible to be.

In 1849, five people could travel steerage to New York for the price of a single steerage passage to Otago.

For adults (14 years and over), the top rate of passage to Otago in a chief-cabin was 45 guineas. This might not seem a great deal of money, but 45 guineas is equivalent to roughly 4,440 New Zealand dollars in 1997 terms.*

The cheapest adult fare was 18 guineas in steerage, while a second class adult fare in the fore-cabin was 25 guineas. Children paid lesser amounts depending on their age.

Detailed rates are shown in the advertisement for the Mooltan sailing, reproduced on page 59.

To travel in relative style in a chief cabin (and it *was* only relative: today's traveller would consider the conditions primitive in the extreme), a family of two adults, one teenager, two children between seven and 14, and two children under seven, would have paid the 1997 equivalent of $22,200.

Small wonder that more than 90 per cent of British emigrants were content to swallow their pride and travel below decks. But even in steerage, this family of seven would have paid $8,880.

The McGibbon family's passage in the fore cabin for two adults and children aged nine, six, four and five months, would have cost the equivalent of today's $8,390.

Intending emigrants paid half their fare when booking the passage, and the balance the day before embarkation.

Some steerage passengers paid their fare in full, while others were subsidised or 'assisted'. More than two-thirds of the Mooltan steerage passengers were assisted, which probably meant they had skills which matched published shortages in the colony. They paid between one third and one half of the passage money, while the Company paid the balance.

About a quarter of them are listed in the Company records as being required to repay their assistance

---

*The Reserve Bank of New Zealand estimates that £1 (20 shillings) bought approximately as much in 1849 as NZ$94 does in 1997. A guinea was worth 21 shillings.

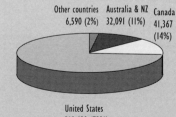

WEEKLY DIETARY.

ARTICLES	Chief-Cabin.	Fore-Cabin.	Steerage.
Prime India Beef, ...	2 lbs.	1½ lb.	1 lb.
Prime Mess Pork, ...	2 lbs.	1½ lb.	1 lb.
Preserved meat or fish,	2 lbs.	2¼ lbs.	1½ lb.
Fresh meat, ...	see below		
Biscuit, ...	4 lbs.	3½ lbs.	5¼ lbs.
Flour, ...	4 lbs.	3½ lbs.	1¾ lb.
Rice, ...	½ lb.	½ lb.	½ lb.
Sago, ...	½ lb.	..	..
Preserved Potatoes, if obtainable; if not, Rice, &c., to be substituted, ...	¾ lb.	¾ lb.	¾ lb.
Preserved Carrots, ...	½ lb.	½ lb.	..
Peas, ...	½ pint.	½ pint.	½ pint.
Oatmeal, ...	..	..	..
Milk, ...	see below		
Raisins, ...	16 oz.	12 oz.	8 oz.
Suet, ...	4 oz.	4 oz.	4 oz.
Butter, ...	8 oz.	8 oz.	8 oz.
Cheese, ...	8 oz.	..	..
Sugar, ...	20 oz.	16 oz.	16 oz.
Tea, ...	4 oz.	4 oz.	2 oz.
Coffee, ...	4 oz.	4 oz.	2 oz.
Salt, ...	2 oz.	2 oz.	2 oz.
Pepper, ...	¼ oz.	¼ oz.	¼ oz.
Mustard, ...	½ oz.	½ oz.	½ oz.
Vinegar or Pickles, ...	½ pint.	½ pint.	½ pint.
Water, ...	28 quarts.	24½ quarts.	21 quarts.

Children 7 years and under 14 receive each, of Water, 3 pints a day; of other articles, *Five-eighths* of the Ration of an Adult of the same Class. Children one year old and under 7 receive each, of Water 3 pints a day; of Preserved Milk, ¼ Pint a day; and of other articles, *Three-eighths* of an Adult's ration; or, if directed by the Surgeon, either 4 Ounces of Rice or 3 Ounces of Sago, in lieu of Salt Meat, three times a week. Infants under one year old do not receive any Ration; but the Surgeon is empowered to direct an Allowance of Water, for their use, to be issued to their Mothers.

A Milch-Cow is put on board, for Invalids if directed by the Surgeon, and for the Chief-Cabin; Live-Stock (for a supply of Fresh Meat), Fruit and other Extras, together with Yeast for converting a portion of the Flour into Bread, for the Chief-Cabin.

The several articles of Diet are varied from time to time, under the direction of the Surgeon, so as to promote the health and comfort of the Passengers, especially of Children. Every article is of the best quality, and examined by the Company's Inspector before shipment.

The Commander of the Vessel is allowed to lay in, at his own expense, and to supply to the Chief and Fore-Cabin Passengers, moderate quantities of Port and Sherry Wine at 3s. each per Bottle, and of Ale and Porter at 10d. per Bottle ; but no Spiritous Liquors are permitted to be sold on board, of any kind whatsoever.

(Otago Journal, November 1849)

after arriving in the colony. Presumably these individuals' skills were less in demand.

For the Otago settlement, assisted passages were advertised for people belonging to "...the Class of Manual Labourers working for Wages ; Farm Servants, Shepherds, Gardeners, Domestic Servants, or, in moderate numbers, Country Mechanics and Handicraftsmen."

No legal restrictions were placed on the employment or wages of assisted emigrants in the colony.

The most acceptable candidates for assistance were young married couples with no children. All applicants had to declare an intention to remain at their destination settlement and work for wages. They also had to produce certificates attesting to their good character, and competence in their trade or calling. On no account were references to be signed by publicans or dealers in beer or spirits!

A doctor's certificate was needed to confirm they had previously either had small-pox or been vaccinated against it, that they were neither seriously mutilated nor deformed and that they had had no previous diseases likely to shorten life or impair physical or mental energy.

It is interesting to note that the general requirements for assisted passages were almost identical to those published at the same time by the State of Victoria, Australia. But unlike New Zealand, the Victorian emigrants could be legally required to repay part of their assistance if they moved on within four years.

What you got for your fare:

Chief Cabin: Passengers in the chief cabin were expected to provide their own furniture, beds and bedding, while the Company provided everything needed for the 'table', such as plates, linen and glassware.

Food was provided by the Company, and for chief-cabin passengers, this was on a considerably more liberal scale than for lower-ranked passengers. They, along with fore cabin passengers, were also permitted to buy wine and beer.

Cabin class passengers were waited upon when dining, when they shared the saloon with the ship's captain: "...the Passengers are considered as his Guests ; and in deportment and dress they are expected to govern themselves accordingly."

Fore Cabin: Fore cabins, above deck at the forward end of the ship, had berths constructed in them, but the passengers had to supply their own bedding and everything for use at the table.

The Company provided mattresses, bolsters, food and cooking utensils. Each family maintained its own 'mess', assisted by a company-appointed cook and steward-boy. Groceries and 'small stores' were issued weekly, and other provisions daily.

The cabins, and an associated dining room, were extremely small.

Steerage: Bedding arrangements were similar to those for the fore-cabins, though the bunks were narrower and more crammed together. Passengers' food and cooking utensils were provided by the Company. Food was cooked by the ship's cook but mostly prepared by the passengers themselves.

Families were expected to provide, for each bunk, at least two blankets, six pairs of sheets and a coverlet. They also had to bring towels, soap, cutlery, tin or pewter plates, spoons and drinking mugs.

Clothing, luggage & provisions

No passengers could embark unless they brought a minimum of two complete sets of outer clothing, two pairs of shoes and a dozen changes of under clothing, including stockings. For males this was to include six shirts, six pairs of stockings, two pairs of shoes and two complete sets of exterior clothing. Females were to have at least six shifts, two flannel petticoats, six pairs of stockings, two pairs of shoes and two gowns.

The conditions said, "As a general rule, it may be stated, that the more abundant the stock of Clothing, the better for health and comfort. The usual length of the voyage to New Zealand is about four months,

or 120 days, and at whatever season it be made, the Emigrants have to pass through both very hot and very cold weather, and should therefore be equipped for both."

Families were asked to bring two canvas clothes bags for the cabin, as heavy boxes and chests were to be stowed in the hold and only made accessible every three to four weeks.

Free transport of luggage was limited to 20 cubic feet or half a ton per adult passenger; additional freight was 50 shillings per ton. The 20 cubic foot allowance was to be divided into two or three boxes no more than three feet (91 cm) long, 20 inches (51 cm) wide and 18 inches (46 cm) high.

The quality and quantity of provisions varied considerably among the three classes. Details are shown in the box on page 58. Ships were provisioned for a six-month voyage.

Passengers Act

In general, the dietary scale, minimum clothing requirements and on-board physical conditions were governed by the minimum standards set by the British Passengers Act of 1842, which was updated in 1848 and 1849. Although conditions on board the New Zealand Company ships of the late 1840s were far from comfortable, they were a great improvement on earlier standards. In the 1830s,

NEW ZEALAND COMPANY'S SHIP

The First-Class Passsenger Ship
MOULTAN,
580 tons,
will be despatched for the Company's Settlements, from *Greenock, on Tuesday the 11th of September next.*

Rates of Passage, Provisions included :—

For each person	Chief Cabin.	Fore Cabin.	Steerage.
14 Years old, and upwards	45	25	18
7 Years old, and under 14	27	15	10
1 Year old, and under 7	18	10	8
Under 1 year old	0	0	0

(Guineas / Guineas / Guineas)

An experienced Surgeon is appointed by the Company, and Medicines, Medical Comforts, and an ample Dietary provided for each Class of Passengers.

Steerage Cabins are provided for Persons paying in full for their own Passage in the Steerage.

For Freight, Passage, or further information, apply at the New Zealand House, London ; the Otago Office, 37, South Hanover Street, Edinburgh ; or to Messrs Roxburgh, Richardson and Co., Brokers, 1, Royal Bank Place, Glasgow.

By order of the Court,
THOMAS CUDBERT HARINGTON,
New Zealand House, 9, Broad Street Buildings.
London, 9th August, 1849.

(Greenock Advertiser, 17 August 1849)

PUBLICISING EMIGRATION TO NEW ZEALAND

High passage costs and isolation were reasons why New Zealand was one of Britain's least popular emigration destinations, and why the New Zealand Company was obliged to mount promotions which were among the more elaborate commercial hoopla seen in Britain up to the middle of the 19th century.

In the month before the Mooltan sailed to New Zealand, the Association of Lay Members of the Free Church of Scotland, which promoted the Otago Settlement on behalf of the New Zealand Company, placed 80 advertisements in 56 newspapers. These newspapers were spread throughout Scotland, plus Belfast, Dublin and Londonderry in Ireland. As well as this, the Association's secretary, John McGlashan, organised public meetings, and the Otago Scheme was promoted from Free Church of Scotland pulpits and in church magazines. McGlashan did his best to encourage newspapers to write favourable articles, and he certainly succeeded with the Greenock Advertiser, which produced paeans of praise for the Mooltan and the Otago Settlement, before and after the ship's sailing.

The New Zealand Company probably also advertised the voyage in England. Other means of promotion were posters, handbills and circulars, and the Association published several editions of the Otago Journal between 1848 and 1850. The New Zealand Company also had travelling exhibition material which included painted panoramas of New Zealand scenes.

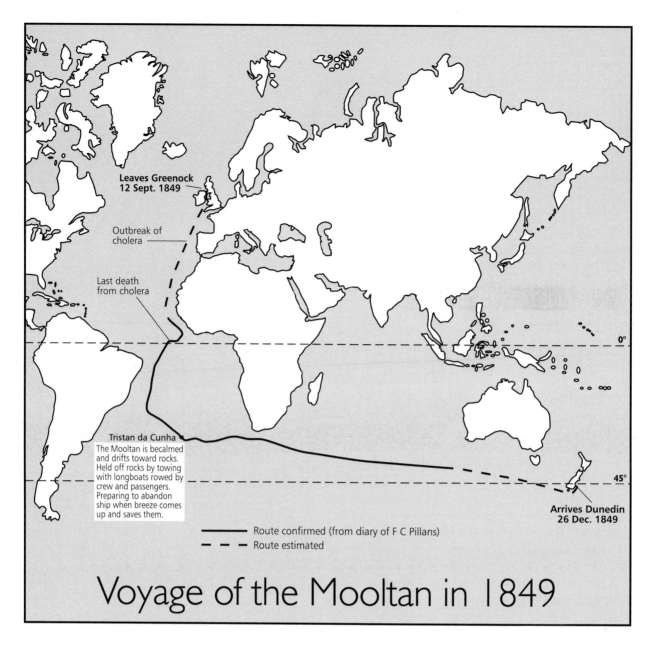

**Leaves Greenock
12 Sept. 1849**

Outbreak of
cholera

Last death
from cholera

Tristan da Cunha
The Mooltan is becalmed
and drifts toward rocks.
Held off rocks by towing
with longboats rowed by
crew and passengers.
Preparing to abandon
ship when breeze comes
up and saves them.

0°

45°

**Arrives Dunedin
26 Dec. 1849**

——— Route confirmed (from diary of F C Pillans)
- - - Route estimated

Voyage of the Mooltan in 1849

emigrant ships could be identified in Quebec at some distance by their foul stench.

The Passenger Acts greatly improved conditions – when their requirements were followed. (They weren't always.) Rules covered almost any exigency at sea, and guidelines specified the construction of vessels, their modifications for passenger use, the space needed per passenger and the amount and quality of rations.

Ships were to be first class vessels, rated A1 by Lloyds. The height of steerage cabins was to be at least six feet (183 cm), and deck flooring was to be at least an inch and a half (3.8 cm) thick. Bunks were to be built in no more than two tiers, and were to be at least six feet long and 18 inches (46 cm) wide.

Any ship carrying 100 passengers or more was to provide a cook and suitable cooking apparatus, which was to be on the upper deck to reduce the risk of fire.

Health

Part of the 'tweendecks was to be set aside as a hospital, and a "Physician, Surgeon, or Apothecary equipped with a Medicine Chest, Instruments and other Things" was to be on board the ship.

Every vessel was to be inspected before leaving port, to make sure it complied with the regulations. However inspectors were often underqualified or too busy to investigate properly, so not all ships which left Britain were up to scratch.

Before a ship could leave port, the assigned medical practitioner had to certify that the medicines were sufficient, and all passengers free from infectious diseases. People who failed the inspection were not permitted to sail.

Such inspections, even when scrupulously carried out, could not guarantee safety. Cholera came on board the Mooltan via infected bedding, and broke out ten days later, off the coast of Portugal.

The New Zealand Company claimed to liberally exceed the Passenger Act's minimum standards, but its advertised conditions were essentially the minimum level laid down in the Act. They were very similar to those advertised for emigration to Australia. ∎

"The Departure", Illustrated London News, 6 July, 1850. This illustration, and others from the Illustrated London News, is reproduced courtesy of the Alexander Turnbull Library, Wellington.

Quite a summer cruise...

Sailing to New Zealand on the Mooltan was something to be "...looked forward to as quite a summer cruise", advised the Greenock Advertiser in August 1849.

Anyone who booked a passage to New Zealand on the strength of that claim was in for a rude shock.

The Mooltan's voyage was one of the worst of its kind, and its passengers were to experience the terror of a cholera epidemic and a near-shipwreck. They would be miserably seasick, frightened out of their wits in dreadful storms, soaked, frozen and airlessly hot. They would eat rations of indifferent quality and limited variety and they would experience all these things while confined on a small ship for 105 days in crowded conditions.

At best, an emigrant voyage to New Zealand was a dubious pleasure, particularly for steerage passengers. An elderly woman immigrant of the early 1850s summed up the delights of her summer cruise in a poignant way. She said she hated Dunedin and would gladly return to Britain. But only if she could walk the entire distance!

Yet on board the Mariner, which anchored at Port Chalmers six months earlier than the Mooltan, young Catherine Orbell waxed lyrical about the joys of *her* voyage – admittedly in the relative comfort of cabin class: "Our voyage is over, and our thoughts must now turn from walks and talks on the Poop, lovely sunsets, and magnificent starlight nights to the hum drum monotony of every day life amid uninhabited Colonial wilds. Are we sorry to leave the world of waters? Ah! Yes! assuredly so....Many will be the sighs we shall give to her memory, and sadly, sadly will our eyes speak the last Adieu."

None of the written MacGibbon family reminiscences mention the Mooltan voyage. Did they consider it best forgotten?

Pillans diary

It would be nice to write specifically about how it felt to be an emigrant on the Mooltan, but unfortunately records of the voyage are fragmentary. The best source of information is the passenger diary of Francis Pillans. Though it is one of the more detailed accounts of any voyage to New Zealand, it still doesn't tell the whole story. One problem is that Pillans was a gentleman cabin passenger who was separated from the majority steerage passenger group by wide divides of accommodation conditions and class attitude. Another problem is that not all of his diary has survived – the first three weeks and last two weeks of the voyage are missing.

Readers of the Pillans diary, which follows these general articles, may well curl their lips in distaste at the author's personal arrogance. Indeed, 'Pillock' may be a more appropriate name for the man, but he does write a tale which fascinates, even as it infuriates.

Some information about the voyage is contained in New Zealand Company letters and reports written after the Mooltan arrived in New Zealand.

Still existing is a short second-hand account of the voyage written by R M McDowall for the 1912 book, *Reminiscences of the early settlement of Dunedin and South Otago.*

Because information about the Mooltan is incomplete, this article is written as a composite account of what it was like to travel on emigrant voyages to New Zealand and Australia around the middle of last century. The writings of Francis Pillans and diarists on several other ships, have been drawn on, as well as the work of three authors who have written on the subject. Of greatest value from the New Zealand point of view is Joy

Robertson's 1937 thesis, *The Otago Emigrant Ships*, which is partly based on passenger diaries.

Two excellent Australian books describe voyages which in most respects were the same as the New Zealand voyages. Not only was most of the route shared, but as emigration to both countries was controlled by the British Government, the rules and regulations and general conditions were very similar.

The Australian books are Florence Chuk's *The Somerset Years*, and Don Charlwood's *The Long Farewell*. The latter is a particularly good description of all aspects of emigrant voyages, and it includes extracts from three passenger diaries: John Fenwick (Lightning, 1854), Fanny Davis (Conway, 1858), and Henry Lightoller (Scottish Bard, 1878).

Passengers on most emigrant ships had three main pre-occupations: health, physical safety and food. Next to these came issues such as personal comfort and combating boredom. ■

HEALTH, AND OTHER CONCERNS OF THE SHIP'S SURGEON

Health was a worry for anyone who embarked on a four-month, 15,000 mile sea voyage. The greatest concern was always for young children, and women who gave birth during a voyage. It was not unusual for a family setting off from Britain with two children under five, to lose one child at sea.

Ships which visited Otago in the first few years of organised emigration had a much better record than that, and on the John Wycliffe and the Mariner, there were no deaths at all. The Mooltan had the distinction of recording the greatest number of deaths of any of the early voyages: 15 people died, nine of them from cholera.

Even the Mooltan's problems were minor compared with what happened on board the 'fever ships' which sailed to Australia in the early

Greenock, departure port for the sailing ship Mooltan. This engraving is believed to date from 1837. (Author's collection)

Illustrated London News, 13/4/1844

1850s. Strong demand for passages to Australia during the Victorian gold rushes had led the British Government to temporarily relax restrictions and allow double decker transports to carry emigrants. One of these, the Ticonderoga, carried 811 passengers, of whom 97 died on board and another 80 at the shore quarantine station at Point Nepean. The cause was a typhus epidemic.

In the middle of the 19th century, few medical treatments were effective, and some frequently used drugs, such as calomel (mercurous chloride), were dangerous to health. Prevention was the more effective branch of medicine on board ships, and here, much had been learned from the experiences of explorers such as James Cook, and from the transport of convicts to Australia.

Emigration to Australasia was government-controlled, and less of a free-for-all than the North American emigration voyages. Surgeon-superintendents, which the ships' doctors were called, had to be qualified and in theory were officially monitored. But they were not always fit for the job, either physically or psychologically.

Most surgeons understood the importance of good diet, cleanliness, keeping dry, exercise, fresh air and keeping VD-ridden sailors away from female passengers. It was one thing to *know* all these things, but quite another to apply them in real life.

Some areas of preventative medicine simply did not exist or were too new to be applied. Until 1909, no-one understood that typhus was spread by body lice, which were very common on the ships. The link between cholera and contaminated drinking water was established in 1848, but ships' water continued to be drawn from rivers at British ports for some years. On-board desalination facilities were rare, and not compulsory until later in the century. It was not understood that tuberculosis was communicable, and sufferers were not rejected at pre-embarkation medical inspections. Carriers were free to cough and splutter over fellow passengers.

The first health problem for most emigrants was simple sea-sickness.

This was a great cause of misery on board sailing ships, and some passengers were miserable for much of the voyage.

CHOLERA

But far worse than seasickness lay in wait for passengers on the Mooltan. On the morning of the 21st day of September, 1849, ten days into the voyage, 24-year old Mary McNeil was struck down with cholera. By 2pm she was dead.

Dr Purdie's medical report (see page 219) is a horror story. His worst day was October 3: "Mr Geo. Perkins...was seized with the Cholera at 3 A.M. and died after 6 P.M.

"Mr Peter Harrison was seized shortly after Mr. Perkins and died about 10 p.m. Mrs. Harrison, wife of the last named, was seized about an hour after her husband and died an hour before him.

"After the death of these three individuals, I visited the rest who were ill and returned to my cabin to see my own dying infant whom I had scarcely seen since morning."

Cholera stalked the cabins of the

Mooltan for 28 days, and during that time, according to Purdie, almost everyone on board showed symptoms of it. The crew were not immune, and two died, including the popular boatswain. Even the captain and chief officer were affected.

Fifteen children were made orphans on one day.

Given lack of knowledge of the causes and treatment of the disease in those days, it could be said that Purdie did remarkably well to contain the deaths to only nine people. This was the retrospective view of the Dunedin medical establishment.

Dr Purdie

Purdie certainly did not enjoy the confidence of his fellow passengers on the Mooltan, where the general fear and loathing was well captured by the Francis Pillans diary. Pillans was highly critical of the doctor's approach, and he was not alone in this. Terrified passengers threatened Purdie with violence on a number of occasions, and he was forced to carry a revolver for his personal safety.

The surviving portion of the Pillans diary began three days after cholera struck the ship, and the first entry read: "The calm of yesterday, and the hopes we had allowed to be raised within our breasts that the dreadful scourge that had been raging amongst us had in some degrees abated, was but an idle dream and a vain hope, for this morning Mrs Proudfoot, one of the most respectable and good looking young women

on board, was suddenly attacked with vomiting and purging and in the course of 2 or 3 hours the cramps were on her and before sundown she will be in all probability another meal to the sharks.

"As soon as she was attacked, she was carried into the temporary bath house rigged out close to the cabin door and placed in a cot there. Everything was done for her that could be expected from such a doctor – her hair was cut off, hot and mustard baths tried as well as large quantities of laudanum administered, but the case is a hopeless one."

Indeed it was, and Mrs Proudfoot breathed her last during the night. Wrote Pillans, "…as usual, the breath was barely out of her body when she was overboard, casting a gloom over the whole ship that continued all night long – men, women and children looking at one another in perfect despair."

The Mooltan officers did not stand on ceremony when disposing of cholera victims. Mrs Proudfoot was given short shrift, and a week later, during a church service, "…the doctor was called away by the first mate sotto voce to be informed that the poor little child that was so ill last night had just expired. In order not to cause needless alarm, the thing was kept quiet, the first mate heaving the body of the poor little thing overboard and returning to the forecastle in a few minutes after, as if nothing had happened."

Earlier the boatswain's corpse had been secretly smuggled over the bulwarks.

Pillans commented: "We have all heard and read of the solemnity of a burial at sea. This may be the case when it occurs seldom, and in the usual way, but when human carcasses come to be thrown over the ship's side like dead dogs, the case is very different."

One victim spared the instant heave-ho was the surgeon's own child, whose burial was delayed until a shark stopped following the ship.

The atmosphere on board must have been appalling. Said Pillans six days after the epidemic began: "It is hardly possible to conceive a more

> *In the course of 2 or 3 hours the cramps were on her and before sundown she will in all probability be another meal to the sharks.*

melancholy spectacle than to look down from our poop deck and see the unfortunate husband(s) who have been bereaved of their wives, the former great strong young country men nursing their poor little infants months old.

"In another instance, you may see the women of 75 and upwards now obliged in this hot latitude to attend to 6 young children, the eldest of whom is only about 9 years, and the youngest at the breast. In short, the future consequences of these deaths that have occurred on board are truly heart rending, but our humane Captain is doing what he can to get some of the young women not having children of their own to assist the poor orphans."

Later he writes of the women passengers: "When things were at their worst you saw them lying about the deck just as they got up, with their hair all undressed and otherwise looking most untidy."

Judging Purdie

It is impossible from this remove to say whether the cholera outbreak was quelled through the actions of Dr Purdie, or in spite of his efforts. Pillans said the man was incompetent, and claimed support for that view from the ship's officers and cabin passengers.

After the ship arrived in New Zealand, officials closed ranks behind Purdie. On 5 February 1850, William Fox, the New Zealand Company's Principal Agent in Wellington, wrote to Captain William Cargill, Agent at the Otago colony, saying, "In reference to the case of Dr. Purdie's remuneration as Surgeon Superintendent of the "Mooltan", I beg to express my entire concurrence in your opinion of the propriety of not making any deduction on account of the deaths which occurred under the very trying and distressing circumstances described in the enclosure to your despatch No. 10/50.

"I have also to request that you will convey to Dr. Purdie the expression of my approbation of the manner in which he performed the arduous duties, which it thus fell to his lot to discharge, as well as my sympathy for his domestic loss on the occasion."

The deduction referred to was an arrangement whereby surgeons on board New Zealand Company ships received gratuities at the end of a voyage of £25, less a deduction of £1 for each death that had occurred. They also received bonuses of for every live birth on board ship, and 10/- for every adult landed alive.

The previous day, Fox issued a certificate which included the words: "That the Passengers, and Emigrants [on the Mooltan] appear to have been well treated during the voyage, and the terms of the Charter Party properly complied with. And further that the conduct of Capt Chivas especially, and of the officers of the ship generally, under the awful visitation of the Cholera, which broke out on board the ship, was most exemplary and praiseworthy."

The Wellington office also recommended to the Company's Court of Directors in Edinburgh that the cholera outbreak be taken into account when considering a 339 lb discrepancy between butter loaded in Greenock and what was finally accounted for, saying the ship had been "...in such confusion during the time the Cholera was on board that no accurate account of the provisions expenses could be kept."

William Purdie remained in Dunedin after the voyage, and built a thriving medical practice. Highly regarded in his profession, he is remembered for having introduced immunisation to Otago, and for probably having been the first doctor in New Zealand to use chloroform as an anaesthetic. He was also active in local body politics, electoral administration and as a Justice of the Peace.

THE SURGEON'S ROLE

The surgeon-superintendent on emigrant ships was much more than a medical man. He was responsible for both the physical and moral welfare of the passengers, and had many duties. A good idea of the range of these duties is given in the journal of Henry Wells, who sailed as surgeon on board the Blundell, which reached Otago in September 1848. Here are the activities – mostly daily – he recorded:

• Made up lists of names and ages of passengers at the beginning of the voyage.

'decks' even when down below) to be holystoned (rubbing with blocks of soft sandstone) and sprinkled with chloride of lime (a disinfecting agent), several times a week.

• Encouraged passengers to spend every day on deck, weather permitting. ("I find that in consequence of there being so many infants and nursing mothers on board that it is impossible to have all on deck at seven in the morning, but the rule is strictly adhered to by the male emigrants.")

• Ordered bedding to be brought on deck and aired every day, weather permitting.

The muster (roll call) was carried out on deck every day, weather permitting. This was an important responsibility for the ship's surgeon-superintendent. (Illustrated London News, 6/7/1850)

• Worked out quantities of rations to be served out, in conjunction with the Captain.

• Appointed committees of passengers to oversee cooking arrangements.

• Held a muster on deck at 9:30am every day, weather and sea conditions permitting. When the muster wasn't possible, he checked passengers in their cabins.

• Made sure the cisterns of water for flushing toilets were full.

• Checked the quality of salt beef whenever casks were opened.

• Toured the decks at 7am and 10pm to check that everything was in order. He made sure lights were out at 10pm, except for lamps in hatchways.

• Ordered cabin floors (known as

• Read the Sunday Service.

• Organised entertainments.

• Maintained discipline among the passengers – this included dealing with a deranged passenger who stole money, chased people with a knife, and threatened to throw himself overboard.

• Called a meeting to establish a ship's paper.

• Distributed lime juice to all passengers, and porter (stout) to nursing mothers.

• Supervised special rations for children and unwell passengers from his store of 'medical comforts'. (The nature of these 'comforts' is not given in Wells' journal, but those shipped on the Mooltan included one barrel of oatmeal, one keg of arrowroot, one keg of barley, one barrel of sago, 34 one pound cases of preserved beef and 26 of mutton; 66 gallons of lemon juice, two barrels of sugar, one cask of port wine, 108 gallons of stout in casks and 16 dozen bottles of stout, 12 gallons of brandy, one cask of rum, 14 gallons of vinegar, seven casks and 1,300 cases of preserved milk.)

• Ordered a studding sail to be rigged as a bath for females.

• Appointed Samuel Perry to take charge of the cow.

Some of Henry Wells's early entries are quite detailed. By the time the ship had passed the Cape of Good Hope and was travelling along the Roaring Forties, the daily log was often a short summary like: "Went round as usual, decks scraped, cleaned and sprinkled no beds up as it is wet, nothing particular happened went around at 10p.m. all right."

Or a Sunday entry which hints at a fair degree of foul weather misery behind its matter of fact summary: "Went round as usual, did not muster but saw all at quarters, had no prayers, it is a wet, dull uncomfortable day. Cabins leaky etc etc decks were cleaned as well as possible. Went round at 10p.m. found all right."

Other activities not detailed by Wells, but which would have been an important part of his job, included encouraging personal hygiene and maintaining a high moral tone, especially among the young ladies. He would have been responsible for children's education (although he himself would not have taught), and would have organised and encour-

aged sports and recreation. He would have appointed 'constables' from among the married men to help maintain good order, honesty and modesty.

KEEPING CLEAN

Keeping clean on board these ships was not easy, especially for female passengers. Usually the problem was Victorian modesty, but for many there was another cultural difficulty: the notion of regular overall bathing was quite foreign to many of the Highland Scots and Irish, and the English lower classes.

Men could at least strip to the waist and have buckets of water thrown over them, or, on windless days in the tropics, be rowed out of sight of the ship for a swim in the sea.

Even cabin class women were rather dirtier than one might imagine. Don Charlwood quotes an incident from the diary of William Thompson, a passenger on the Meteor bound from Glasgow to Australia in 1854. Through an open cabin window, an acquaintance had seen a woman lying on her bunk, wearing what he thought was a pair of shoes. Not so: "…low and behold the Black things turned out to be a pair of veritable feet & Covered with a thick coat of filth. Quite enough to turn a Man's Belly upside down, such a sight meeting his eye in the morning. The Capt. Certainly ought to erect a Temporary Bath a place covered in so they can wash themselves from the Clew to the Earing."

Some passengers required con-

siderable encouragement to use the primitive flush toilets. They preferred to use chamber pots, which were hardly desirable on a pitching ship.

The flush toilets had a chute which led to the outside of the ship, where the opening was covered by a flap of leather to prevent seawater coming back up the tube and turning the toilet into a bidet. The toilets were flushed with seawater held in overhead tanks.

Because of the reluctance of a few passengers to operate the water valve to flush the toilets, some surgeons allowed a constant stream of water to flow from the tanks above. That could lead to unhygienic leaks into the 'tween deck cabin, where food was stored under tables.

Another problem surgeons had to deal with was the inclination of some countrywomen to wash clothes, and their hands, in urine.

MEDICAL TREATMENT

The most common approach to passenger maladies was to prescribe a purgative such as Calomel, Jalap, Ricini (castor oil) or Sulphate of Magnesia. These drugs were prescribed for constipation, which was by far the most common ailment listed in the surgeon's journal on the Blundell. On board this ship, Dr Wells treated 51 people for constipation – almost one quarter of the patient entries. But purgatives were also used for non specific illnesses where 'a good purge' was considered beneficial. Examples included rheumatism, headaches, anxiety and general debility.

The extraordinary number of constipation cases during the first few weeks of the voyage may well have been a side-effect of passengers dosing themselves with their own supplies of laudanum (an opium based mixture), to help them sleep.

As the voyage wore on and food supplies deteriorated, surgeons treated a good deal of diarrhoea in various forms. They liked to gum up the works with Cretae Prep (prepared chalk), or aromatic chalk powder. Dr Wells also gave diarrhoea sufferers opium drugs and the all-purpose Jalap and Ricini. (The later

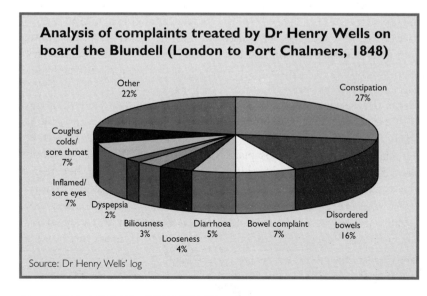

Analysis of complaints treated by Dr Henry Wells on board the Blundell (London to Port Chalmers, 1848)

Other 22%
Constipation 27%
Coughs/colds/sore throat 7%
Inflamed/sore eyes 7%
Dyspepsia 2%
Biliousness 3%
Looseness 4%
Diarrhoea 5%
Bowel complaint 7%
Disordered bowels 16%

Source: Dr Henry Wells' log

drugs were akin to throwing petrol at a fire to put it out. The theory was probably that the patient had something he needed to get rid of, so let's purge him again...)

For relieving pain, the only available drug was opium. Analgesics and sedatives had not been yet been developed.

A fourth main group of drugs was those prescribed for colds and coughs: cod-liver oil, creosote and oil of peppermint.

Various digestion ailments accounted for two-thirds of all cases treated by Dr Wells.

Eye irritations were common on the Blundell, and were treated with solutions of magnesium sulphate and zinc sulphate. Wells considered one case to be caused by cold and exposure. The bright light on deck could have been quite a shock to eyes more accustomed to gloomy slum surroundings. Some of the irritation may also have been caused by the liberal sprinklings of chloride of lime.

Many passengers on emigrant ships carried personal stocks of patent medicines which were probably no better or worse than supplies in the surgeon's medicine chest.

HORMONAL CHALLENGES

Four months of enforced separation from the opposite sex could be a hormonal challenge for both single men and single women. (No doubt there were also frustrations for married people in their communal cabin on a three foot (914mm) wide double mattresses, but no-one seems to have written about that.)

Keeping sex beyond arm's length was a particular responsibility of the ship's surgeon, assisted by a dragon-lady ship's matron, and constables appointed from among the married male passengers.

Strict segregation applied, with the single men and women's quarters at either ends of the 'tween decks, separated by the married quarters. Single people of opposite sexes were barely, if at all, allowed to speak to each other, and dancing together,

except occasionally on the upper deck, was strictly forbidden. The women had to resort to all-girl 'balls' in their own cabin. Single females were not allowed to collect their own rations from the ship's galley in case they came into contact with males. Married men, those ships' eunuchs, were deputed to deliver food and hot water to the young women.

But boys will be boys and girls will be girls, and couplings did take place,

though more often involving the crew and officers than single male emigrants. Indeed, one daring attempt by some of the latter led to ignominious failure. Two single men on an Australian-bound vessel once sneaked along the deck and insinuated themselves into the female quarters via a ventilation shaft. The would-be lotharios' hope turned to chagrin as they were stripped, tied to a bunk and whipped, before being turned over to the captain for further punishment.

Affairs between the crew (usually officers; sometimes even the surgeon) and single women were not uncommon, and might come about through the women exchanging favours for extra rations. On one ship, the captain conducted an affair with a woman from steerage. The lusty lass had an upper bunk that was just inches below the captain's cabin, and a hole was cut in the floor that separated them, allegedly to allow the captain to pass down items of food and drink...

Liaisons more often took place in cabins, and even in the ship's hospital, if it had no patients.

Fanny Davis, a single woman who traveled steerage on the Conway to Melbourne in 1858, describes punishments for fraternisation. A "girl" was or-

dered below for a week for speaking with a sailor. For a similar crime, a sailor was banished aloft for a day. A "boy" was "locked up" for carrying messages from sailors to the young women.

Not all young women were innocent or exploited. As a passenger on the Scotia, which sailed to Australia in 1849, pointed out: "...some of the single females have been detected cohabiting with the sailors – which cannot be a matter of surprise to anyone as most of them have seen *life* in London or been sent out by their friends for delinquencies at home."

One of the worst stories, which may or may not be apocryphal, is of a shipload of domestic servants bound for Nelson. The ship took a somewhat roundabout route, and by the time she berthed, most of the women were pregnant.

Hormones were even surging in cabin class. Catherine Orbell, a 22 year old single woman traveling on the Mariner to Otago in 1849, made much comment about the ship's officers and crew. She had a particular fetish for sou'westers, and wrote: "...a sailor in the midst of a squall, and in the midst of his appropriate costume, is my beau ideal of things pleasant to the eyes, and refreshing to the soul. So much for sou'westers – if I say more after this, I shall go beyond the mark of decorum."

She is particularly enamoured of the ship's officers and declares, "What a detestable plan it is the mates are not allowed to converse while on watch with the passengers, except in the most cursory way."

Catherine ignored the "detestable" rule, conversed with a mate, and said she would continue to do so:
"...if I feel disposed (which I certainly do) to speak to them, **shall do it.**" (The diarist emphasises, stamping her feet in pique. Whether middle class decorum preserved Miss Orbell's virtue throughout the voyage, we'll never know.) ■

Dining, but hardly cordon bleu

The quantity and quality of provisions varied considerably, depending on the passenger class. Cabin passengers had the best food, and this is clear from the victualling report for the Mooltan. The voyage allowance per steerage passenger was £5/-/-. Intermediate 'fore cabin' passengers got one-third more, at £6/13/4 per head, while cabin passengers got 141 per cent more, at £12/6/8 per head.

Although a dietary scale was published (see page 58), the quantity of provisions varied from ship to ship. On some voyages food was short and passengers did not get their full entitlement, while on others there was so much food that passengers were able to hoard enough supplies to last them for up to three weeks after they arrived at Otago.

It was commonly said that ships which left from Scotland were less well provisioned than those which left from London.

Among the many advantages of being in cabin class was that meals were cooked for you, and, until the sheep, pigs and fowls were all dead, you ate fresh meat. The Mooltan left Greenock with nine sheep, ten pigs and an unknown quantity of poultry. There may also have been a cow.

The surgeon on board the Pekin, which arrived at Otago a few weeks before the Mooltan, made a formal complaint about the food: "Fresh provisions were of a very inferior description and passengers were obliged to live principally on salt meats. Consequence was a number of cases of diarrhoea and other complaints arising from lack of fresh meats and vegetables such as cabbage, turnips etc. which I consider absolutely necessary. In consequence of there being less suet, butter and oatmeal than was stated in the list of provisions sent on board, the passengers have been without same for several weeks, which has caused great dissatisfaction, they declaring that the New Zealand Company has not kept faith with them."

The official report about the Pekin, from the resident agent in Dunedin, was a New Zealand Company cover-up. "...all emigrants had been well treated and the Charter complied with in all respects," wrote Captain Cargill, hand on heart. As we have already seen, a similarly misleading statement was made by the Company about the Mooltan.

A separate report noted that the Mooltan stores had been "...abundant and of the best description"(!) It conceded that some of the soup was sour (without noting the large number of cases concerned, which almost certainly caused a shortage). No mention was made of the salt beef which Dr Purdie had condemned. There was mention of a lack of poultry, which presumably was the result of the hen coop being washed off the deck during a storm. Only the cabin passengers would have been inconvenienced.

With the evident exception of those on the Pekin, all classes enjoyed fresh vegetables for a while at the beginning of a voyage. For some of the poorer emigrants, the food was undoubtedly better than they had known on shore. Cabin class passengers also had real bread in the early days. As the options narrowed, passengers, particularly those in steerage, faced several months of extremely limited variety. Principal among their rations were salted or preserved meat (optimistically called 'Prime India Beef' and 'Prime Mess Pork' in the published Dietary), ship's biscuits and soup.

Dining at the long table in the centre of the married steerage quarters on an emigrant ship. Note that the artist's perspective is rather strange, and the amount of headroom is greatly exaggerated. (Illustrated London News, 13/4/1844)

Salted meat, which was mostly beef, had been the standard meat ration on board ships since the days of Henry VIII. It was known to sailors as salt horse or salt junk, and was preserved for months on end in brine and stored in casks. Salt horse was said to look like a coloured chunk of wood and some claimed it had a similar consistency.

It also varied in quality. Dr Purdie condemned 560 pounds of salt beef on board the Mooltan, certifying that "… several of the casks of Salt Beef contained large bones with scarcely a bit of beef on them, and which I found it necessary to condemn. After the quantity for a whole mess [six adults] was boiled there was not as much meat as one man could eat."

'Preserved meats' were meats preserved by pickling and heavy salting. Presumably they were less wooden than salt junk, because they were more likely to be spoiled.

Ship's biscuits, which were meant to substitute for bread, were something no-one could get excited about – least of all anyone whose teeth were not in good order. Biscuits were 100mm square and over 25mm thick, and were unleavened bread, baked very hard. Even cabin class passengers saw a great deal of ship's biscuit before the voyage was over. People would soften their biscuits by dunking them in tea, coffee and soup.

Soup, or 'boullion', could vary in quality. Dr Purdie again: "There were also 92 cases of Preserved Soup sour, so that I had to condemn them. I generally found that those cases which had turnips in them were quite sour."

Many passengers, from all classes, brought additional food which might include ham, pickles, jams, sugar and preserved eggs.

Water was a problem for everyone. Stored in barrels, the water emerged dark in colour (black and dirty, said Pillans), heavily tainted and sometimes accompanied by gases which could be ignited with a naked flame. It was usually boiled before being drunk, and even then, it was best disguised by tea, coffee, lime juice or sugar. Collecting fresh water during storms was popular. Even tasting of old sailcloth, it was a great improvement over the ship's ration. ■

The steerage meal routine

Breakfast in steerage was at 8am. It usually consisted of ship's biscuit with tea or coffee, although sometimes the women would prepare a dish called 'stirabout', which probably included leftovers from the previous day.

Dinner, at 2pm, included meat, one or two vegetables and some kind of pudding. The meal was largely prepared by the emigrant women. Single men did their own preparation, and for many of them, this was a major learning experience.

One of the vegetables might be preserved potato, which was reconstituted from dark slate coloured crumbs into an foul concoction children preferred to ignore. Children's propensity for rejecting food that was allegedly good for them was one reason why the ship's surgeon kept a stock of 'medical comforts' which were allegedly more child-friendly. (One wonders how tempting sago and arrowroot would be to today's children.)

The evening meal, at five o'clock, consisted of tea or coffee, ship's biscuit, salt butter, meat and leftovers from the midday meal. It often included soup, prepared in copper boilers by the ship's cook.

Messes

Steerage and fore-cabin passengers were organised into messes by the surgeon at the beginning of the voyage. Messes contained about six adults or adult equivalents, chosen as family units or including people from compatible backgrounds. Each mess had a captain, and this position would rotate among each male member during the journey. The mess

captain was responsible for collecting food and distributing it among members of his mess. Each mess would have a card listing provision entitlements, and the card would be presented to the steward when food was being distributed. Messes also had metal identity tickets which they

Dinner time for steerage passengers in the forecastle. (Illustrated London News, 20/1/1849)

attached to beef and potatoes which were cooked in the communal boilers, using seawater.

Serving out of daily rations took place after breakfast. It was usually presided over by a purser or one of the mates, but sometimes by a passenger appointed by his fellows.

Other provisions such as tea, coffee, sugar and butter were distributed on Saturdays. When the weather was fine, this 'market' would be held on the main deck. The supervisor would sit on a cask with his notebook and call out mess numbers, while his assistant served out the allocations.

The eating arrangements worked reasonably well in fine weather, but could be disastrous in storm condi-

The popular call of "Hot water!" brought passengers up from 'tween decks with their tea and coffee pots. (Illustrated London News, 20/1/1849)

Soup time on a calm evening. Many an emigrant went hungry when her soup hit the deck in rough weather. (Illustrated London News, 20/1/1849)

tions. Many a passenger went hungry after he or she parted company with a soup ration.

The situation was graphically described by William Johnstone, who watched from the relative comfort of his cabin accommodation on board the Arab, sailing for Hobart: "The cook [was] dealing out pea-soup to those of the Emigrants who were well enough to fetch. The heavy seas broke over the side, occasionally extinguishing the fire, or pouring into the coppers by way of seasoning the soup…In endeavouring to walk from the galley to the hatchway with their bowls in their hands, three out of five were thrown down, by which they not only gained a complete ducking, but lost their dinner as well…"

The popular call of "Hot water!" would see a stream of emigrants emerging from hatchways and heading for the big cast iron stove on the deck, to fill their tea and coffee pots. Again, this was an exercise fraught with danger in rough weather.

Steerage passengers would often eat on deck, or at the long communal table in their cabin. ∎

Dining in class

Breakfast for the cabin class passengers was prepared by the steward and served in the saloon at 9am. The fare was more varied than in steerage class. Tripe fried in butter was a staple which might not have appealed to everyone, especially on a lurching day, but there could also be ham, ship's biscuit, salt butter, and coffee with preserved milk. Occasionally the steward might produce a rather sour baked mixture of oatmeal and flour. Disguised leftovers might also be served.

Dinner, at 3pm, was based on a set menu for each day of the week. The menu was fixed for the entire voyage, and Miss McGlashan, who sailed to Dunedin on the Rajah in 1853, copied it into her diary:

Monday: Pea soup, roast fowls, suet pudding, cheese.
Tuesday: Preserved salmon, roast pork, rice pudding.
Wednesday: Bouilli soup, preserved meat, curried fowl, fritters.
Thursday: Rice soup, boiled fowls and bacon, potatoes, plum pudding.

Friday: Pea soup, salt fish, boiled meat, potatoes, rice pudding.
Saturday: Tripe, salt beef, suet pudding.
Sunday: Soup, roast pork, preserved potatoes, preserved fruit tart, cheese.

Commenting on the menu, Miss McGlashan wrote: "…this sounds very well, but our fowls, a bad selection at first we are told, have not improved in their confined coops. They are skin and bone, and tough as leather. Our dinner then consisted of one spoonful of soup to each person, a couple of fowls, with a small supply of bacon, to be divided among fourteen, and a pudding, very good, but not over large, to end with. If we could only have our food well cooked and cleanly prepared, it would be a comfort."

The evening meal for saloon passengers was at 6pm, and invariably consisted of the ubiquitous ship's biscuit or the steward's sour bread, with salt butter and tea.

Some ships served supper for the cabin class at 9pm. ∎

Day in and day out

Steerage passengers would rise between 6am and 7am, when the men would often go on deck for a wash. After breakfast the muster, or roll-call, would take place, and from then on, most of the morning would be taken up by chores. Receiving and organising rations occupied a good part of the morning. The cabin had to be tidied out, bedding rolled up, and brought up on deck to be aired if the weather was suitable.

Compulsory duties assigned to the male steerage passengers included keeping watch through the night as constables, cleaning floors between decks and drawing water from the hold. Most passengers were glad of something to do, but some objected. George Hepburn, who arrived in Dunedin on the Poictiers in 1850, said a man who refused to do duties assigned to him was sent to coventry on the poop for a day. Single women in steerage did compulsory sewing under the control of the matron.

Every fine Monday, wives and sometimes their husbands did the family washing on deck in tubs and barrels filled with hot seawater. Clothes were dried on the rigging.

Children had to attend school twice a day, for hour-long sessions at 11am and 4pm.

After lunch, and in the evenings, steerage passengers were free to do as they liked. The cabin passengers, of course had been free all day. Some cabin wives did a little housekeeping, but most had servants to do this for them.

Passengers spent much of their spare time on deck when weather permitted, and conditions were quite cramped. A favourite occupation for women of all classes was sewing, knitting and crocheting. Often one of their number might read aloud to them, on topics which could include religion, vocal music and celebrated monuments.

Ships had their own libraries, and reading was a popular activity. However several diarists noted that it was difficult to concentrate on subjects of a serious nature because of the distraction of the continual noise on board: orders shouted to sailors, children running about, and sounds made by livestock.

Francis Pillans read his book in bed, to escape the distraction of "... the thousand children roaring and rolling about in every direction..."

A few passengers worked at 'self improvement' during the voyage, and some illiterates learned to read and write. Other solitary diversions included model-making, writing diaries and writing letters.

Games of all kinds were popular. They included cards, chess, backgammon, draughts and quoits.

Francis Pillans on the Mooltan, showing his usual contempt for the ship's surgeon, describes how he and his cabin friends took up backgammon: "Mr Todd, Ferguson and hon. moi have managed to get hold of a backgammon board, and we now have regular battles at it. We only thought of this recourse on account of the Dr. trying to prevent the people below playing, which was the signal for our introducing the

"Spinning a yarn" "Draughts"

Passing the time on the sailing ship Duke of Portland

In 1851, John Pearse sailed on the Duke of Portland to Lyttleton. During the voyage he drew many tiny sketches of his fellow passengers, the crew and ship activities. The original sketches are held at the Alexander Turnbull Library, Wellington.

"Russian Step practiced on board because they had nothing else to do!" (John Pearse)

game into the Cabin – which no doubt shocks his imbecile ideas on the subject of religion. Had he said a word to us on the subject, I would have been the first to pull his nose for it and no mistake."

John Tyler, cabin passenger on the Mariner, described a game of 'deck billiards', which the captain organised. Four persons played, each armed with pieces of wood 150mm in diameter and 25mm thick. A grid of ten numbered squares was chalked on the deck. The objective was to slide your piece of wood along the deck and end up in one of the higher numbers. "If one person gets in five, his opponent tries to knock him out, which he sometimes does, leaving his own in, or only aids his adversary by shifting him into the 8 or 10. 50 or 100 generally is the game."

Catherine Orbell was not the only passenger who enjoyed watching sailors at work. Diarists showed particular interest in sea-shanties sung as the sailors hauled on ropes and secured sails. Young male passengers might help sailors trim the lower sails when the vessel was tacking, and in times of peril they would pitch in to help save the ship.

Climbing to the top of the mainmast in fine weather was another young men's activity. It was traditional to pay a fine for the privilege, and for this reason sailors encouraged the activity. Presumably the fines went into a sailors' fund. Some sailors would take part in amusements, and display their own skills in rope climbing and somersaulting.

It is not clear how female children generally amused themselves, but they did participate in a bobbing for raisins activity sketched by John Pearse, who traveled to Lyttelton on

John Pearse, Duke of Portland

"Juvenile passengers (Steerage)"

the Duke of Portland in 1851.

There are some recorded activities for small boys. They would beg to be allowed up on deck when the ship was pitching and tossing around. The trick was being able to walk around without falling over, and one boy claimed it was just like waltzing.

Lessons on deck (John Pearse)

Paddling was a popular pastime. When the vessel was heeled over in a good breeze, the lee scuppers were always awash. In warm weather this was a great place to wade – a sea beach out on the ocean!

Practical jokes helped combat boredom, and boys could be involved. Pearse related how pupils took revenge on an unpopular schoolmaster. They screwed his cabin door shut one night when he was asleep, covered the screw heads with putty and painted them over. They also played fun and games with the schoolmaster's cap.

But not only small boys played practical jokes. Don Charlwood quotes James Robertson, a passenger for Melbourne in 1852, saying the passengers' enthusiasm for the voyage had waned by the time they rounded the Cape of Good Hope: "By this time, two months at sea, salt junk and idleness had so deteriorated the bearing and mental character of the passengers that they had sunk into milksops, and found languid amusement in small practical jokes that a child would be ashamed to be diverted at."

Physical activities were encouraged by the ships' surgeons, and these included such things as foot races, leapfrog, skipping and ball games. Dancing came into this category too, although a fine moral line had to be tread at times. Dances included polkas, quadrilles, waltzes, galops, reels and schottisches. Tropical moonlight balls were recalled in later years with particular nostalgia.

Music was a good way of passing the time, and passengers played instruments such as accordions, violins, flutes and penny whistles. Concerts would usually end with a general singalong.

Some concerts were organised affairs, while others were impromptu. Singing and dancing often took place below decks on evenings when it was too cold to be on deck. Reading below was impossible unless you were

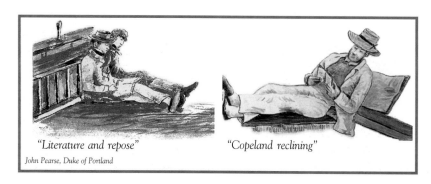

"Literature and repose"

John Pearse, Duke of Portland

"Copeland reclining"

John Pearse, Duke of Portland

directly underneath the lamp.

Music could also be a good way of bucking up morale, and it was used to good purpose after the cholera epidemic on board the Mooltan. R M McDowall wrote of people making encouraging speeches, after which "...all available musicians were posted near the cabins, the decks cleared, and a gay throng was speedily joining in the merry mazes of the dance. In these and other pastimes devised from time to time to keep up the spirits of the passengers, the sailors were the leading actors, and their comical antics did much to divert anxious and troubled hearts from dwelling on possible danger."

During what turned out to be a temporary lull in the cholera epidemic, Pillans wrote that, "Last night, for the first time after a long pause, the people on the main deck began again to make themselves heard a little in the singing way, and after giving us half a dozen psalms, they proceeded to more cheerful music which continued until the hour of 'out lights below there', which is at 10 o'clock."

One imagines that on the Mooltan, frivolity below decks took place in spite of Dr Purdie, whose wowserish attitude even had him railing against backgammon.

Pillans took another swipe at his bête noir on the subject of music and dancing: "...the fiddler was upon deck and all the sailors dancing like possessed ones. The doctor will be saying again that it is by indulging in this wickedness that the wrath of God is brought upon the ship – a piece of cant for which I would like to pitch him overboard."

A common way to pass the hours was just sitting around yarning. Or as Pillans described it, "...building or

perhaps only finishing the Otago castle in the air which they probably laid the foundation of in Scotland."

Just taking one's ease in the evening and watching the young folk dance and play games, was enough amusement for many. The beauty of the skies must have been a

Dan at Wheel.

sensation for many. What person, brought up in grey tenement surrounds, could fail to be thrilled by a spectacle such as that described by John Tyler: "This evening was one of those beautiful sunsets to be seen only at sea. First the whole of the sky was tinged with red, the reflection of

which on the blue waters gave the whole sea the appearance of a shot silk dress. Then the sky became dark and the spot where the sun sank was a bright blood red, above which was the most beautiful bright primrose streaked with black."

A favourite meeting place for older passengers was in the forecastle just in front of the capstan. They would sit on barrels, light their pipes and shoot the breeze.

Sabbath

Sundays were days of sanctity and a degree of dressing up. Services were held on deck once or twice during the day, but they were nearly always cancelled in bad weather. Some services were held 'tween decks if it was only raining, but if the ship was pitching violently it was impossible to stand upright, let alone maintain a solemn stance. Francis Pillans explained: "...it being impossible for the Parson and congregation to stand on their feet, and perhaps it would not be decent to do so on our heads."

His attitude would have been considered wimpish by the indefatigable Reverend Thomas Burns who sailed on the Philip Laing. Burns insisted on preaching in all weathers, sometimes with his son holding him upright as he read the lesson. And his performances were numerous: two every weekday and three on Sunday.

On most ships no minister was available, and the service was conducted by the surgeon, who might be assisted by a passenger. Cabin class ladies liked to contribute worthy sermons for the men to read.

Pillans described the seventh day with his customary cynicism: "The afternoon of yesterday spent quietly

"Juvenile chess players"   "Morrison"   "Sam"
John Pearse, Duke of Portland

and decently in a Sabbath day way – that is, going to church in the morning and talking scandal and gossiping the remainder of it."

John Tyler described one divine service as a "...perfect mockery. Foolish sermon with the word Mariner repeated 2 or 3 times in every 20 words. I believe it was written by one of the young ladies on board, who was to treat the Doctor to a bottle of wine to read it."

On another Sunday, a homesick Tyler contrasted the ship environment unfavourably with Bath, where there were "...clean streets, bright sun shining on the decent people, and church bells ringing. All these things make us think of our homes and friends, and lead us to say: 'Absent friends, God bless them.'"

Blood sports

Many male cabin passenger diarists wrote about blood sports carried out from the poop deck. Oblivious to Coleridge's Ancient

"Dry or comfortable side of the cabin" (John Pearse)

Mariner warnings, they happily blazed away at albatrosses, as well as Mother Carey's Chickens and Cape Pigeons. William Ferguson had beginner's luck with the Mooltan's first albatross visitor, downing it with No 4 shot. But albatrosses were usually associated with pitching seas and impaired aim. A great deal of shot and powder was expended without harming the birdlife.

Whales, sharks, porpoises and dolphins were also targets. Passengers and crew caught sharks and albatrosses with hook and line.

Opening boxes in the hold

Every three to four weeks, passengers were permitted to open up boxes they had stored in the hold. This could be a time of great disappointment, because goods were often damaged by damp or leaking containers of food. John Tyler noted on one occasion that, "...the shawls, fancy waistcoats etc., were mildew spotted and spoiled. All is confusion and lamentation."

Amusements and diversions which happened less frequently included whale watching in the Southern Ocean, Halloween frivolities and the Crossing the Line ceremony at the Equator.

Francis Pillans described Halloween on board the Mooltan: "...there were lots of capers going on. For want of apples to dive for and nuts to burn, some of the crew and passengers rigged

themselves out in character and sang comical songs, while others amused themselves with dancing, crowning the nights entertainment with a lot of jovial songs."

Not everyone approved of amusements such as these on board – not even Pillans' fellow first class passengers: "On these occasions, with the exception of the Todds, our stupid bigots of cabin passengers shut them-

selves up in their cabins and, thinking to honour the Lord, abstain from all such iniquity and may the Devil seize them for their pains!"

Sailors were not supposed to involve passengers in the Line ceremony, but they often did. Pillans saw sailors on the Mooltan having "...their usual fun about getting Neptune dressed up and allowing him to exercise his rights as to shaving and heaving buckets of salt water on all those of the passengers, and all the crew who had not crossed the line."

An emigrant on another ship recalled that when the ceremony ended, everyone let their hair down and let rip with a water throwing battle which included the rout of an unpopular cabin passenger.

Class

Such disrespectful contact between steerage passengers and their 'betters' on the poop deck was rare and no doubt considered scandalous. Class distinctions were rigid. No matter that everyone was moving to a new country: only steerage people were called emigrants. Only people travelling cabin class were passengers. George Hepburn wrote, "...cabin or poop passengers are gentry, and have no intercourse with any other – the second cabin [fore cabin] passengers are also would-be gentlemen, and wish no communication with its steerage passengers, though only separated by a sparred partition."

Most diarists travelled cabin class, so we tend to get a one-sided view which was nearly always superior and frequently sneering. Pillans is one of the worst, complaining about having to share the Mooltan with "...as poor a lot of bigoted humanity as could be well brought together."

Meeting ships

Surrounded as the passengers were by a monotonous blue marine desert, the occasional appearance of other ships was cause for great excitement. It was customary to make contact with passing ships, by signal flags, writing messages on blackboards, hailing with voice trumpets and visits by longboat. Ships heading back to Europe would report details to Lloyds Register, which published lists of ship meetings.

Letters could also be dispatched on homeward bound ships, so sightings were often the signal for feverish bursts of letter writing.

Not all letters could be delivered, and Francis Pillans described a par-

Tyler. Their ship, was shadowed for most of one day by a small, but faster vessel. The captain spent a great deal of time observing the visitor through a telescope before announcing that she was "up to no good".

The mystery ship disappeared later in the afternoon, and then, said Tyler "...soon after 7 p.m. she was

a time it was an eventful night. All women and children, (chief cabin passengers excepted) were ordered below. "Grog-oh, there forward" was sung out. The male Emigrants had also grog served to them to give them Dutch courage. Wine and Brandy and water was served to all the Chief Cabin passengers. All lights were put out fore and aft, even the binnacle light was covered up. [The emphasis is Tyler's.]

"Those men who had arms were requested to load and prepare themselves. The ship's muskets, pistols and blunderbusses were loaded with ball cartridges and slugs. The cutlasses (3 doz) were put on the skylights, and a large can of Powder was fixed to one Binnacle. The men were all ordered to remain on deck, and every stitch of canvas being spread, we did our best to keep a good distance between us, which we fortunately succeeded in doing. In the dead of the night we altered our course and completely gave her the slip.

"I have since learned on good authority that she was a Spanish Cruiser about 120 tons. She had a very long gun amidships on a swivel; had she attacked us we stood no chance."

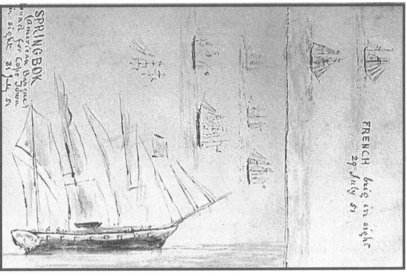

Ship sightings from the Duke of Portland (John Pearse)

ticularly cruel incident when they met the brig Fortitude, 27 days out from Rio with a cargo of coffee for Falmouth. The Fortitude sent a boat to the Mooltan, seeking food supplies. This "...was readily given along with a dozen of beer, on the understanding that as soon as she reached England she was to report us "all well". This was done in order not to alarm our friends with hurried and garbled statements of the miseries we have gone thro.

"As the boat however was in the act of packing off, a lot of the Emigrants made a rush to the ship's side and threw into the boat a great many letters begging them to deliver them as soon as arrived in England. The Captain, however, requested the boat's crew to throw them all overboard, which they appeared to do. But who knows but some stray letter may yet find its way, telling our tale. The poor Doctor was sadly down in the mouth, for he well knew these letters would contain many complaints against him..."

A sinister ocean meeting was described by Catherine Orbell and John

discovered again, running down upon us like lightning. Then the ship was put about to keep her from throwing grappling irons on us. She could run around us like a cooper would a barrel, but as she shot under our bows we tried to run her down, but she was too quick for us.

"Lights were now put at the ports, and she, supposing we were getting the guns ready, edged off again. For

Cowman's boy with the ship's cow (John Pearse)

Miss Orbell's account was similar, but she added an interesting postscript. Next day the loaded guns had to be discharged, and "...some would not obey their master's hand for some minutes – some were overcharged, others undercharged – altogether, 'twas very clear we were fortunate in our expectations of the previous night being deceived, for little service would such remarkable guns have done."

Storms

The Spanish cruiser episode was potentially disastrous, but it was only one of many dangers faced by all ships. Storms and high seas were very frightening – particularly for steerage passengers below decks.

The Mooltan sailed through stormy seas in the southern latitudes, and her situation was made worse because of Captain Chivas's tendency to add canvas rather than subtract it, for the sake of speed. He had a brand new ship to make a name for, and indeed, apart from the

"Sportsmen on board. Albatross, Mollymawks and Cape Pigeons rather shy." (John Pearse)

John Wickliffe voyage in 1848, the Mooltan's 105 days to Otago was the fastest passage of any of the ships chartered by the New Zealand Company.

One storm description by Pillans actually included a rare good word for the men in steerage: "When the gale came on and all the sails let go, there was a dreadful panic took place amongst all the people below, as from the noise of the sails flapping and the wind and sea roaring, they at first thought it was all over with the ship. On rushing on deck however they (the men), behaved very well, having joined at once in assisting the sailors to haul upon the ropes – in this way doing right good service."

On another occasion he noted how high seas during the night were "...breaking over the ship every now and then with fearful fury, making her stagger as if she had gone bump up against a rock. At half past 11, the 2nd mate, whose watch it was, was standing on the poop. The ship giving a roll that nearly laid her on her beam ends, one of the hencoops broke loose and came rattling down to the lee side upon the mate, and nearly broke his leg."

Another entry read: "A young girl trying to cross the deck with a child in her arms was thrown down this morning, with a thundering crash which sent the child spinning to the lee side of the ship as if it had been shot out of a gun. But strange to say,

it escaped with little injury, as also did the girl, barring her bones pretty well bruised. Considering how tender our ship is, causing her at times to be nearly on her beam ends, it is wonderful how we all have hitherto escaped broken bones, for verily the number that has kissed the decks since we left, has not been trifling."

Fanny Davis, on board the Conway to Melbourne, wrote vivid descriptions of storms from the point of view of a steerage passenger. Her first bad experience was only two days out from Liverpool:

"...the ship rolled and creaked and every mentionable article in the shape of water kegs, cans, teapots, buckets, with innumerable other things all pitched off the shelves and the tables into the other side of the ship and then in a minute after, the ship would roll to the other side and all our things come back joined by all the articles from the other side of the ship with the most horrid noise as most of them were made of tin. We had to hold on to the sides of our berths to keep from joining the other articles on the floor. The people were all very much frightened..."

Later in the voyage she wrote: "It has been a most terrific night, such a one as makes young people old in one night, for it was a regular night of horrors. The wind blew a perfect hurricane and every now and then the ship seemed perfectly under water and it poured down the hatchway in a perfect deluge. It is at such times as we feel the comfort of having a top berth, for the people in the bottom ones get washed out of their beds. The screams of the people as each wave comes down the hatchway was enough to make the stoutest heart to tremble..." Even cabin passengers did not escape dousings: huge waves would crash through skylights and smash stern windows.

Keeping dry under these conditions was obviously impossible. Late in her voyage, Fanny Davis said she had "...a severe cold again and no wonder, for we go to bed with the beds wet through and it still keeps very cold."

The usual way to dry out cabins

Centre: "On the yardarm"; bottom: "Reefing – study of legs" (John Pearse)

was to light hanging stoves, and to spread sand which had been heated in the ship's oven.

On some parts of the voyage, bitter cold accompanied the unwanted water. In warmer climes, water shipped into cabins exacerbated what was already a damp and foetid atmosphere. One can only imagine the effect of adding a hot stove and heated sand to the tropical mix. Because of the need to keep cabins dry, cleaning floors with water was not permitted.

Shipwrecks

Ships could be swamped so badly that they would sink, but none of the early Otago ships met such a fate. All vessels arrived safely, though two almost foundered on rocks. The Mariner nearly drifted ashore at Cape Ortegal in north-west Spain, while the Mooltan nearly ran ashore in the Irish Channel during a fog, and narrowly escaped shipwreck at Tristan da Cunha, a small island in mid-Atlantic, south-west of Capetown.

The Mooltan arrived at Tristan da Cunha unexpectedly, on a calm, foggy night. She began drifting shorewards, where, as Pillans wrote, there was "...no place within sight where even a seal could land, the face of the rock being as steep as the north side of Edinburgh Castle and many times higher."

With only sail to provide motive power, and no wind, Captain Chivas seemed unable to save his ship. In the morning, in an attempt to drag her out of danger, he sent emigrants and sailors out with longboats and towropes. The men pulled on their oars in relays for about eight hours, but at best they could only slow the drift of the ship to shore. Stores were brought on deck and rafts began to be constructed. (The Mooltan only had enough boats for one-third of the passengers.) Then, just as all seemed lost, a series of small wind gusts from shore blew the Mooltan out of danger.

It wasn't the last time the Mooltan nearly foundered. At the end of the voyage, only an hour's sailing from the Otago Heads, she grazed a rock.

Relief

When the Mooltan dropped anchor at Port Chalmers on Boxing Day, 1849, relief would have been uppermost in the emigrants' minds. But at least one person left the ship with some regret. In a later reminiscence, possibly filtered through rose-tinted glasses of time, John McLay, a steerage passenger on the Mooltan wrote:

"And now on this second day of January we are in our new home and it is a lovely morning – I stand and look in every direction – but I can't see the dear Mooltan – That I had spent so many happy days on this fine ship – that I feel so sad and lost like – that the teares roll down my cheeks in streames – Oh but I must try to forget – but I don't think I ever will forget all the nice men that brought this ship safely to Otago – and the dear familiar faces of the Passengers – that I may never see again." ■

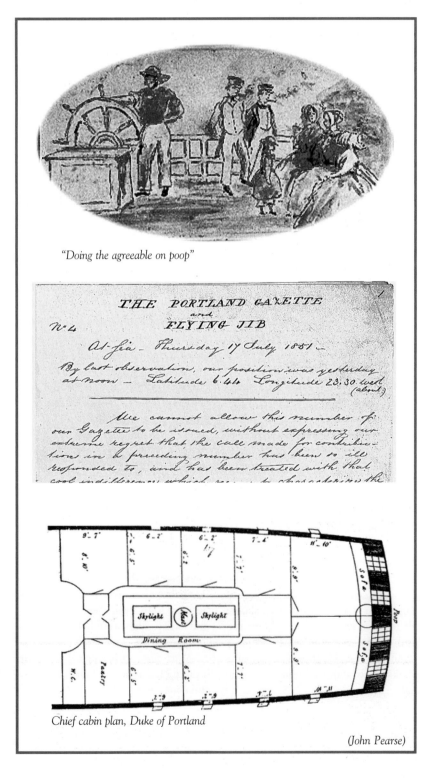

"*Doing the agreeable on poop*"

Chief cabin plan, Duke of Portland

(John Pearse)

Port Chalmers in 1849 (Alexander Turnbull Library)

On the new home run

How did the Mooltan passengers react when they first sighted New Zealand, and when they first set foot on the strange shore? Unfortunately we know very little, and probably never will, unless the missing pages of Francis Pillans' diary turn up.

In brief reminiscences, Mooltan passenger Elspeth Duncan said Dunedin was in a condition of primitive simplicity when she arrived, but the residents were very welcoming. On the day they landed at Dunedin, they were invited to the double marriage of Mrs and Mrs Andrew Mercer and Mrs and Mrs John Healey – followed by a dance.

Elspeth's brother-in-law, John Duncan, was engaged by Captain Chivas to help discharge the ship. There were no lighters or steamers to carry the cargo from Port Chalmers to Dunedin, so it had to be done with the ship's own boats. Duncan wrote later: "It took us nine weeks to discharge and ballast the ship, when we had some very rough times of it on sand banks, as we did not know the channels.

"I was paid 30/- a week and found, which all helped to give me a start; after that I was engaged with a man as boatman to do work upon the river –

anything we could get to do – but I found this all very rough work, there being no jetties to land cargo. We had to wade up to the armpits in water to load and anchor the boat, so I soon gave that job up."

Dunedin was evidently not what some Mooltan passengers expected it to be. Fourteen people who originally embarked for the colony, decided to carry on with the ship to Wellington. On the other hand, Plumpton Clemison, who was originally bound for Wellington, fell in love with fellow passenger Mary Peterson and stayed in Dunedin to marry her.

Other ships

We can also get an idea of how the Mooltan passengers might have felt, from passengers on other early ships.

The first sight of New Zealand came at the end of a long and turbulent passage along the Roaring Forties. Stewart Island was the first sighting, and sweepstakes were held to predict its appearance.

With Stewart Island sighted, John Tyler joined a further Mariner sweepstake for 2/6, and drew a ticket for the day of arrival at Port Chalmers. Tyler later described the ship being cleaned and painted ready for entering port, but showed little emotion – on paper at

least – about the actual sighting of land.

On the same ship, Catherine Orbell was her usual gushing self:

"At length we sighted the shores of our adopted home – New Zealand. The sailors' charming songs and the chorus of Land Oh!, Land Oh!! bursting forth as it did during the midnight watch sometimes, fascinated us beyond all bounds. In fact we admired it to folly. Land Oh! Land Oh!! After a four month voyage, how pleasant doth it sound. Land Oh! Land Oh!! After a thousand perils on the deep and a thousand anticipations of a new and untried Country, how eagerly, how joyously did we hearken to it."

One imagines the passengers from Scotland were more taciturn.

As the Mariner sailed north up the Otago coast, Orbell noted, "A line of wild majestic mountains extends throughout the whole eastern coast of New Zealand. One rising after the other and so alike, it needs an experienced eye to perceive any difference at all."

The Mariner had problems getting into Otago Harbour, where she had to double back in a south-westerly direction after arriving at Otago Heads. This was a common difficulty for sailing ships in the days before the port had a steam tug. George Whitby, captain of the Pekin, which arrived in December 1849, noted in his log that "This is certainly a very awkward port for getting in and out, as you can only get in with one wind and get out with the wind at the adverse point. The winds are very local here, owing to the high land on each side."

The Mariner waited several days for the wind to blow in the right direction. A year earlier, Dr Wells on the Blundell described the same problem. The Blundell remained off Taiaroa Head for five days, during which time she was actually visited by small boats from the settlement.

When ships finally dropped anchor at Port Chalmers, they were still a goodly distance from the Dunedin settlement. Another ten years would pass before a dredged passage in the upper harbour would allow large ships to tie up at Dunedin.

The emigrant visitors were nearly all impressed with the natural environment, but far less impressed with the actual settlements of Dunedin and Port Chalmers.

Reverend Thomas Burns, within a few days of his arrival on the Philip Laing, had inspected Otago Harbour, and described it as "…one uninterrupted series of the most romantic beauty… [the hills] densely clothed from the water up to their very summits with evergreen woods, presenting an unrivalled scene of the richest sylvan green and alpine beauty."

Catherine Orbell arrived in June 1849, and wrote of the "…silvery rays of the full moon lighting up the glorious prospects around into a scene of perfect beauty. The waters have not a ripple, and we gaze in admiration long, on the wild hills enclosing us."

The spell was broken when she finally went ashore: "During the succeeding month we visited and were disgusted with Dunedin, a wretched condemned looking hole – too bad for convicts, and without one redeeming quality. Port Chalmers, with its half dozen hovels is preferable even… Disappointment is expressed by almost all on landing, each one having been more or less deceived."

Six months later, Captain George Whitby described Dunedin as "…a small village containing about 20 wooden houses and the persons who live there not of the 'most respectable class'." [There were actually many more

than 20 houses at that time – the town's population was approaching 800 people. In April 1850, just a few months later, there were 202 houses, of which 80 were of weatherboard construction.]

Whitby described Port Chalmers as a village with one or two stores, about half a dozen wooden huts and three or four public houses. There was also a collector of customs with whom Whitby had an extended argument. "…[he] refused my clearance for some time for no other purpose, in my opinion, but to get some remuneration (alias bribe)." The reception was better in Dunedin, where from the Resident Agent, Captain Cargill, and the Emigration Agent, William Cutten, he "…received great hospitality during my long and arduous detention at such a place…"

John Tyler inspected Port Chalm-

ers one day after the Mariner anchored, and the following day, he and several other "decent cabin passengers" were rowed to Dunedin. They ran aground four or five times going there and once coming back. His last description of Dunedin before heading for Wellington was reasonably favourable:

"It being dark soon after we arrived at Dunedin, we could not see much, but it seemed a succession of moun-

Artist Andrew Devon's impression of the McGibbon family waiting to be rowed from Port Chalmers to Dunedin, a few days after their 26 December 1849 arrival on the Mooltan.

tains covered with immense trees. At Dunedin we dined together at the Hotel. We had a very good dinner of boiled leg of mutton, roast quarter of pork, ribs of beef, puddings, vegetables, bread, cheese, wine, ale and spirits for which we paid 5/- a head."

Dr Henry Wells arrived at Port Chalmers rather pre-occupied with a dangerously ill woman who was suffering complications after the birth of twins. He was less impressed than

Coming ashore at Dunedin on New Year's Eve, 1849

Captain Tyler with the Resident Agent. Following is the last week of his diary, beginning two days after the Blundell anchored at Port Chalmers.

Monday September 25th. 1848: Went rounds – people busy packing. Expected to have been boarded by the Colonial Surgeon, who has not made his appearance. Alison Rodgers has been going on favourably and I am happy to state that I have had the able assistance of Dr. Manning in conducting her case since our arrival.

Tuesday September 26th. 1848: Went rounds as usual – A Rodgers going very well, but as it is impossible she can have attention and quiet here, I sent her up to Captain Cargill's to the Charge of the Colonial Surgeon, in proper charge, with plenty of blankets and her mother with her, and in the evening I received an official letter from Captain Cargill of rather a sharper tenor than I like, and which I do not intend to take any notice of.

Wednesday September 27th. 1848: Today busy in disembarking and knocking down berths. I cannot but express my surprise that no Official person should have been sent down to superintend, as I do not see that I have anything to do with it. They appear to let every thing take its own way here.

Thursday Sept. 28th. 1848: A good many people were sent off this morning for Dunedin. The accommodations are, I understand, wretched. We are very anxious about the Long Boat, as a heavy gale has come on. Young Mr. Cargill came on board and told me to order what vegetables and meat we might want. At Port Chalmers, exceedingly rough weather and bitterly cold with hail and rain.

Friday September 29th. 1848: The Longboat returned about 8 a.m. with all the people and luggage. They had to bush it, and the poor children were all shivering with cold. It has been a most bitterly cold day and the stoves had to be lighted below.

Saturday September 30th. 1848: Discharging all day. The Coxwain of the Company's cutter came on board intoxicated and one of his men very much so. He ran his boat on a shoal, and we had to send a boat to bring them off. Wrote to Captain Cargill on the subject.

Sunday October 1st. 1848: Nothing occurred today worth mentioning. [Diary ends.] ∎

The Philip Laing sails into Port Chalmers on 15 April 1848, joining the John Wickliffe, which had arrived on 23 March. (1898 painting by Captain D O Robertson)

John Wickliffe and Philip Laing were the first two ships

The first two ships for Otago were the John Wickliffe and the Philip Laing. The John Wickliffe, an older ship of 662 tonnes, had a reputation for speed, and indeed her 100 day passage was the fastest of any of the New Zealand Company ships. She was the supply ship for the advance guard of settlers, and carried only 90 passengers. She departed from Gravesend on 24 November, 1847, but was damaged by rough weather in the English channel and finally set sail on 14 December, after repairs at Portsmouth. Captain William Cargill, leader of the Otago settlement, was a passenger. The Philip Laing, 547 tonnes, left the Firth of Clyde on 27 November, 1847. She carried the spiritual leader of the settlement, Dr Thomas Burns, as well as the first schoolmaster, James Blackie.

Emigrant ship arrivals at Port Chalmers, 1848-1851:

	Ship	Arrival date	Passengers
1.	John Wickliffe	23 March, 1848	90
2.	Philip Laing	15 April, 1848	243
3.	Victory	8 July, 1848	4
4.	Blundell	21 September, 1848	145
5.	Bernicia	12 December, 1848	58
6.	Ajax	8 January, 1849	101
7.	Mary	11 April, 1849	2
8.	Mariner	5 June, 1849	100
9.	Larkins	11 September, 1849	79
10.	Cornwall	23 September, 1849	59
11.	Kelso	28 November, 1849	13
12.	Pekin	5 December, 1849	116
13.	Mooltan	26 December, 1849	140
14.	Berkshire	12 March, 1850	6
15.	Lady Nugent	26 March, 1850	26
16.	Mariner	6 August, 1850	171
17.	Poictiers	4 September, 1850	34
18.	Phoebe Dunbar	24 October, 1850	29
19.	Eden	27 December, 1850	14
20.	Titan	17 January, 1851	18
21.	Stately	7 August, 1851	8
22.	Dominion	28 September, 1851	13
23.	Clara	16 November, 1851	9
24.	Simlah	23 November, 1851	33

The prime source for these figures is Joy Robertson's 1937 MA thesis, The Otago Emigrant Ships. Ms Robertson took her figures from Dunedin newspaper ship arrival notices. These figures can only be regarded as approximate. There is little agreement among historians as to passenger arrival numbers, and some of the New Zealand Company records are confusing. Interpretation problems include adjusting for deaths on board, people who carried on to other ports in New Zealand, and mistakes made by the newspapers. The figure given above for the Philip Laing, 243, compares with 197 from Tom Brooking and 247 from A H McLintock and Dr Hocken. Robertson says 90 people arrived on the John Wickliffe; Brooking, McLintock and Hocken say 97. The Mooltan figures above are somewhat higher than those reported in the ship arrival notice, but have been adjusted by the author, based on separate research.

Diary of Francis Pillans, a chief cabin passenger on the Mooltan

Francis Pillans, born in Fifeshire, Scotland, emigrated to New Zealand on the sailing ship Mooltan. Describing himself as a 'gentleman settler', he took up land at Inch Clutha. A member of the Legislative Council between 1863 and 1873, he died in 1889, aged 80. This diary, the original of which is held in the Hocken Library, Dunedin, does not cover the beginning or end of the voyage. The Mooltan left the Greenock docks on 11 September 1849, anchored overnight at the Tail of the Bank, and set sail for New Zealand on 12 September 1849. She arrived at Port Chalmers on 26 December 1849.

The diary text has been slightly edited to improve readability. Editing consisted mainly of inserting commas in the lengthy sentences (commas were almost non-existent in the original diary!), and breaking up some of the longer sentences and paragraphs. Pillans' spelling and grammar remains essentially 'as is'.

Saturday 6 October 1849; Latitude 9°; Longitude 20.7°; Thermometer 29° Centigrade; Distance travelled 53 miles

The calm of yesterday, and the hopes we had allowed to be raised within our breasts that the dreadful [cholera] scourge that had been raging amongst us had in some degrees abated, was but an idle dream and a vain hope, for this morning Mrs Proudfoot, one of the most respectable and good looking young women on board, was suddenly attacked with vomiting and purging and in the course of 2 or 3 hours the cramps were on her and before sundown she will in all probability be another meal to the sharks.

As soon as she was attacked, she was carried into the temporary bath house rigged out close to the cabin door and placed in a cot there. Everything was done for her that could be expected from such a doctor – her hair was cut off, hot and mustard baths

tried, as well as large quantities of laudanum administered, but the case is a hopeless one.

There are some most affecting circumstances connected with the fate of this young woman. Her husband left Scotland some 6 months ago for Otago, leaving his wife to follow him as soon as she got thru the confinement of her 2nd child. It was destined however that neither she nor her children were ever to meet with him again, for both her children died shortly after her husband left and now she is about to follow them under circumstances that border on the horrible. We will arrive in New Zealand to carry out the news to the poor husband that he stands alone again in the world.

The Captain and mate are recovering, and the sail maker also is perhaps nearly free of immediate danger – but after the shake he has got, it will be months ere he is fit for work again.

The reason the doctor's child was kept so long yesterday was that just as they were going to lower the coffin down at midday, the Purdies heard from their cabin the people on deck call out that a shark was astern and not to throw it into its mouth. As it were, it was held up in the hope that a breeze would spring up to enable the ship to get away from the monster.

The state of feelings of us on board are in the extreme, and I believe there is hardly a man on board that would not give all he had, if he could be freed from this charnel house. But there is nothing now but standing to our fate.

Sunday 7 October; Lat. 8.32°; Long. 20.11°; Ther. 28°C; 52 miles   Death of Mrs Proudfoot

As anticipated, poor Mrs Proudfoot breathed her last about 5 o'clock last night, and as usual, the breath was barely out of her body when she was overboard, casting a gloom over the whole ship that continued all night long – men, women and children looking at one another in perfect despair. As however no new case had as yet broken out today again, we begin to hope that the worst is over – such is the sanguine nature of man.

At eleven piped to prayers, but our poor Dr. was so affected at the scenes passing around him that he was unfit to go thro' the whole service. Even this very weakness adds a thousandfold to the consequences his ignorance has occasioned, as it tends to increase a power which if not checked will lead us all to destruction. This is the fourth Sunday we have been at sea, and you hear everyone around you complaining to one another that the month we have just passed appears to them an eternity.

The Captain continuing to place more confidence in me than anyone in the ship, takes me into all his counsels, and, together with the 1st mate, an old High School fellow of mine, we three form the committee of safety. The Dr., except in saying long graces and prayer at table, has become a complete cypher.

Monday 8 October; Lat. 7.17°; Long. –; Ther. 28°C; 75 miles; Strong country woman attacked and dying. Boatswain attacked and dying child dead. Talk with the Doctor. Worst day we have had.

Worse and worse. Last night a country woman we all fixed upon as the strongest creature on board, was attacked at 11 o'clock at night with cholera in its worst form, along with a child of 6 years belonging to another woman. After the usual sufferings, they were numbered with the dead and overboard this morn by 11 o'clock.

To add to the horror, the Boatswain was attacked while the dead were being cast overboard and he too may be considered as numbered. Another child also is at the point of death, but we have arrived at that stage now that children are hardly considered. The Captain and Mate looking fagged to death attending to the sick.

Having agreed at the request of all the cabin passengers to call the Doctor aft and openly accuse him of ignorance and imbecility imperilling the lives of all on board, I did so as quietly and in as moderate language as I could. I told him he had much to answer for, in having assumed a duty he was totally unfit to perform, and that from interested motives or others equally bad, he had deceived the New Zealand Company and placed in jeopardy the lives of every human being on board. I accused him on his confession of being a follower of Homeopathy, a believer in spirits and mesmerism and in short an enthusiast in everything save in common sense and knowledge of the duties he had assumed. The poor man tried to prove that in every case, although against his conviction, he did not fail to administer all the medicaments most approved of, but upon being at once refuted by both the captain and mate and the other cabin passengers standing around, he was compelled to strike under upon this. I told him if he were a conscientious man and wished to stay the havoc going on amongst us, he had better resign at once. But like all, or at least a great many of your canting and psalm singing set, he thinks twice before giving up his passage money, which under such circumstances he would have to do, and here the discussion ended for the present.

An hour or two afterwards, the Doctor came up to me along and said that if I would agree to round and visit with him the patients, he would gladly take me into his councils and act according to the general wishes. On this, I told him that my life was as precious to me as anyone else, and that I did not see why I should risk it to cover his ignorance. If he resigned, I should, with the Capt and mate, not flinch from taking a share in the sad duties that someone must perform.

In the meantime, from the books on board, I have collected a new system to be adopted in the new cases that may occur and if the Dr. says a word, we will confine him to his cabin, which I told to his face would be done if he shewed anything like [...]

Tuesday 9 October; Lat. 6.55°; Long. 18.80°; Ther. 28°C; 23 miles Boatswain buried this morning. William looking very ill. Sun's altitude 77'

After midday yesterday, no new cases of cholera had occurred, but the poor Boatswain gave it up this morning and was smuggled overboard in order not to let the people know. But the poor sail maker, who could see everything from his berth in the forecastle, was so shocked at the sight that altho we looked upon him as a saved man, down he went like a shot and was a dead man in two hours afterwards, raving mad, thus making our twelfth death since we sailed.

Women, men emigrants, children, sailors – shewing a mortality that bad as cholera is never occurred before. Every case that has occurred has ended fatally, with the exception of a child, which however is still lingering at the threshold of the other world.

It is hardly possible to conceive a more melancholy spectacle than to look down from our poop deck and see the unfortunate husbands who have been bereaved of their wives, the former great strong young country men nursing their poor little infants months old. In another instance, you may see the women of 75 and upwards now obliged in this hot latitude to attend to 6 young children, the eldest of whom is only about 9 years, and the youngest at the breast. In short, the future consequences of these deaths that have occurred on board are truly heart rending, but our humane Captain is doing what he can to get some of the young women not having children of their own to assist the poor orphans.

The Captain does not seem over anxious to attempt catching sharks, as he says something might be found in them which would not be pleasing to the eye in the agitated state we are still in. But as yet they will not take the bait and if we do take any of them we will merely cut their heads off and let them go again.

Willie, after the sharp dose of physic I have given him, is getting quite sound again. Ferguson is also now all right, and in fact all on board for the moment, save the poor child, are on foot and well, but trembling for what may yet come.

The weather during the last two or three days has been nearly the same as it was ever since our splendid run out of the English Channel. The prevailing winds have been westerly and north west and very light, with a line of long rolling swells, which every now and then caused our women to get sick again. Had these winds not been so prevalent, in all probability our Captain would have at this season of the year attempted to have kept to the westward of the Cape de Verd Islands, in which, had he succeeded, in all probability we should have had a better chance of falling in with the N East trades – which have humbugged us altogether.

Standing in so close upon the African coast the winds come off light and what we have of them are muggy, hot and unhealthy. We are now dodging about the coast of Sierra Leone, and on Monday last, there were some serious wishes expressed by the people to the Captain that he should run his ship into this hotbed of sickness rather than die like rotten sheep out at sea. I joined some others in combatting this mad scheme and as things for the moment look better on board, the people have been pacified. But should they again grow worse, the Captain may be expected to be forced to run his ship into Rio de Jana or some other port on the Brazil Coast.

Heat continuing but not increasing. Notwithstanding we are daily increasing the sun's altitude, in a few days will pass perpendicularly below her. The only particularly new feature I have observed in the weather in these low latitudes is that up to about the 9th and 10th parallel North, the sky remains clear and brilliant, as we used to have it in Italy and Greece. But on approaching the Equator, the meeting of the South and North East trades or rather the vacuum that is formed between those two prevailing winds, causes such a general convulsion that the sky is almost always clouded, and squalls and dreadful thunderstorms are of nearly daily occurrence.

Wednesday 10 October; Lat. 6.45°; Long. 18.7°; Ther. 28°C; 6 miles of southing

Up to the hour I write, all has passed off well – no new cases of cholera during the night and the poor child is supposed to be rallying a little, leaving some hopes to the father of its ultimate recovery. The consequence of all this is that you see brighter faces all around you, and the poor women are beginning to deck themselves out and put on their good looks again. When things were at their worst you saw them lying about the deck just as they got up, with their hair all undressed and otherwise looking most untidy.

A northwest bit of a breeze too is about sprung up, leading us to hope that we may do a little better during the next 24 hours, cheering us up with the thought that we will be so much sooner across the line and the sooner falling in with the S.E. trades, which are sure of carrying us into cold weather – the only thing we hope will check the further breaking out of our dread enemy the cholera.

And the remarkable fact is that we have seen no more sharks following the vessel for the last 24 hours, which is taken up by our superstitious people as a happy omen. It was one of the poor women who died a few days back – the one I mentioned who had lost her children before leaving and was now going out to join her husband at Otago – who while perfectly hale at breakfast time, received such a shock to her nerves on hearing that there was a shark astern, that she immediately exclaimed in her excitement that it was waiting for her, altho then in perfect health. The words were hardly out of her mouth when she was seized with the dreadful malady, and the shark she so much dreaded, was not cheated out of his prey.

We have all heard and read of the solemnity of a burial at sea. This may be the case when it occurs seldom, and in the usual way, but when the human carcases come to be thrown over the ship's side like dead dogs, the case is very different.

Emigrants on deck. (Illustrated London News, 20/1/1849)

All these disasters which have been occurring on board have quite driven out of my head the idea of studying navigation, and it is even as much as I can do to jot down these few notes, fancying sometimes that they are likely never to reach my dear friends at home.

What different animals sailors under affliction are from what we see of them when on a spree on shore! Keeping up my old habit of not turning in until late, I generally every evening have a long quiet gossip with the officer of the watch and at times also with the man at the wheel. Strange as it may appear, the most dispirited on board the ship are the seamen. Not only do they see almost daily one or two of the emigrants expiring before their eyes, but they have lost two of their best hands – one of them the Boatswain, the jolliest and merry hand on board. Let us be thankful however for the mercies we are now enjoying – 48 hours having now passed without fresh disasters.

Thursday 11 October; Lat. 5.45°; Long. 17.13°; Ther 27°C; 60 miles

The N-West breeze which sprung up at 12 o'clock yesterday continued pretty steady until 10 at night, when a regular squall with violent thunder and lightening came on. It was just all we could do to get in sails in time to save our spars being carried away. Until twelve, it blew a regular sneezer and we were running before it with reefed topsails at a tremendous rate, but at midnight it died away to a complete calm. But towards 11 o'clock this morning, the N-West breeze again sprang up and we hope it may carry us along a bit until sundown at least. On account of having made a good deal of easting during the last 24 hours, we made only an advance of 60 miles towards the equator.

So far all going on well – no new cases of cholera and the child continuing to recover. Our Humbug of a doctor is reading some books and pamphlets we have given him on the cholera, and we are going to force him to follow one of the cures therein recommended, under the surveillance of myself and someone else. He is now in the cabin making up opium pills and medium he looked upon as poison when he came on board. He was also a teetotaller but now both he and his toad of a wife drink away at the Captain's brandy and beer at no allowance. They don't do this with impunity however, for I roast them during dinner every day in a way that they don't much fancy.

As soon as I see them shake into their proper places and give themselves less pretensions, they will fare better, but not till then. They are people who require to be snubbed and kept down, or they would otherwise render themselves so unbearable as would lead to something worse than mere words.

Friday 12 October; Lat. 4.54°; Long. – Ther. 27°C

The breeze of yesterday still continuing, but unable to keep our course by 3 or 4 points, tho our progress thru [...] this [...] has been increased. Still, from our making so much easting, we are making but little progress on our journey. During the last two days a large ship on the same course as ourselves has been working away ahead of us, but as yet all our efforts to make up with her have proved in vain. Our only chance of doing so will be for the breeze to freshen with us, and die away a little with her.

Our ship getting very tender owing to the quantity of water taken out under the forecastle and to keep her more on an even keel, they talk of filling up our casks and tanks again with salt water.

The wind getting round a little to the south, altho very light. We are half in hopes that we are gradually getting hold of the south-east trades and which we trust will prove more favourable to us than the N.E. did, which in fact failed us altogether.

Since Monday, on which day the poor boatswain and sailmaker were thrown overboard, no fresh sickness had occurred on board. But, to our horror, this morning our chief mate was reported ill, which caused a sensation on board beyond all description. Even the Captain, altho a man of otherwise strong nerve, was so taken aback that we even now begin to fear for him. The anxiety shown in his face is so evident, that if anything happens to our first mate, Mr Milligan, I should not be surprised to see him also attacked with some illness or other – and then what will become of us?

As I take such a deep interest in Mr Milligan, whose attendance on the sick was truly beautiful, and the fatigue of which must be the cause of his present illness, I go down constantly between decks to keep him company and assist in seeing him properly attended to. So far I don't think there are any symptoms of cholera – his illness rather arising from getting wet after having taken a dose of 30 grains of Calomel – a dose enough to kill a horse.

In other respects, the health of the ship improving, but with a treacherous disease like the cholera, we must not be too sanguine in having as yet escaped our fearful enemy. To shew the nervous state we are now all in, even the stout-hearted seaman Mr Milligan, who had the middle watch, turned in at 4 o'clock and was then perfectly well, but owing to an alarm of fire having been sung out from between decks, the poor man, who was then

Canterbury Association ships Bangalore, Duke of Portland, Lady Nugent, Midlothian and Canterbury in the East India Docks. (Illustrated London News, 17/5/1851)

probably in a sound sleep, received such a shock that immediately after, he was seized with sickness and vomiting and now remains in this critical state.

The alarm of fire was occasioned by a stupid woman screaming out that she smelt fire, which at once being taken up by others, of course soon created a panic. The whole affair turned out to be only the smell arising from some of the women ironing clothes with too hot irons. The Captain, however, to prevent the recurrence of any such mishap again, has prohibited all further ironing of clothes below. A very wise precaution I should say, when one contemplates the horror of an emigrant ship taking fire, with boats only sufficient to save about 1/3 of our number.

We are all much disappointed, but myself in particular, that we have as yet had no fishing of any kind. It appears the sharks that were keeping about the vessel for so many days while we were feeding them with cholera patients, would not take the baited hooks – and right fools they would have been had they done so – for all we intended to do with them was to cut off their heads and pitch them into the sea again.

Saturday 13th October;
Lat., Long – no sun taken;
Ther. 27°C

The South E. trades, which we fancied we had got hold of yesterday, died away again this morning, returning now and then in slight puffs. The chances are, however, that we are on the verge of them and may expect a spanking breeze from one day to another, which ought to carry us a long way south of the Line.

While writing, the heat which for the last two days owing to the breeze we had was diminished, is now again intolerable, being in a dead calm with the sun nearly perpendicular over our heads. The first thing I did this morning was to go down and pay a visit to my

good friend the 1st mate, and to my joy, found him much better and I hope out of all danger. He is however much reduced from the sore sweating he was put thro. He refused, at my suggestion, to take any of our Doctor's stupid medicine stuffs, which never being sufficiently strong to work off the stom-

NEW ZEALAND COMPANY, EMIGRATION.

THE COURT OF DIRECTORS
NEW ZEALAND COMPANY

Are prepared to assist in Immigrating to their Settlements in New Zealand

AGRICULTURAL
MECHANICS,
FARM LABORERS,
Domestic Servants

Of good character, who will assist themselves by defraying a portion of the cost of their passage

The Directors will receive Applications accordingly, until

WEDNESDAY, the 9th AUGUST,
From persons of the above description, desirous of proceeding on these terms by the Ship

AJAX

Appointed to Sail from the London Docks on

Monday, the 4th September next.

Further Particulars and Forms of Application may be obtained at New Zealand House

By Order of the Court.

Thomas Cudbert Harington.

New Zealand House, 9, Bread Street Buildings, London,
14th July, 1848.

Poster seeking emigrants for the voyage of the Ajax, which arrived at Port Chalmers on 8 January, 1849, about a year earlier than the Mooltan. It had been intended to populate the settlement with people of Scottish stock, but in the event, not enough Scots applied. Numbers had to be topped up with people from other countries, mainly England, where this poster was distributed. No publicity posters have been found for the Mooltan sailing. (Alexander Turnbull Library)

ach, remain on it merely to cause nausea, and, predisposed as we all are for cholera, to render us more likely to be seized with the malady.

The Doctor and I had another fearful tug today in the cabin, on which occasion, before all the passengers, I openly accused him of being the cause of the mate's illness from the former's [...] in attending to the sick, which ought all along to have been his duty

had he been fit for it. He appealed to the passengers to save him from my accusations but no one raised a voice to defend him. Having no one on board particularly interesting me beyond Willie and the Stewarts, it was perhaps more the duty of another to be spokesman, but as I told the Doctor, it was not for myself that I spoke out, but for the sake of relations of mine who may follow me hereafter from Scotland. It was for their sakes that I wished that the New Zealand Company should take greater care to appoint such surgeons to their ships as might be fit for any emergency.

The day being cloudy, the Captain could not get the sun properly, so we cannot tell what speed we have come during the last 24 hours. But in all probability, we have not made more southing than 20 miles.

Last night, for the first time after a long pause, the people on the main deck began again to make themselves heard a little in the singing way, and after giving us half a dozen psalms, they proceeded to more cheerful music which continued until the hour of "out lights below there", which is at 10 o'clock.

The ship keeping company with us still ahead, with some symptoms of our having gained a little upon her during the night. A child sick, infant daughter of the last woman who died.

Sunday 14 October; Lat. 3.53°; Long. 16.15°; Ther. 26°C

South E. Trades fairly begun, but as at their commencement they generally have too much southing in them, it does not enable us to lay our exact course south as it would otherwise do. Our proper course south 10 by south, instead of which we are now steering west 1/4 south, thus taking too direct in for the American coast.

Chief mate fairly thro his dangerous illness, to the joy of all on board. A merciful Providence alone has saved him. At 11 as must all hands [...] to prayers, and our Doctor gave us his usual dose. On this occasion he returned thanks to God for saving the mate's life, which of a verity went to the heart of all on board. It is probably the only popular thing he has done since he came on board.

While a second service was going on the forecastle today, performed by one of the sailor apprentices – a gentleman scapegrace son and a young man of very considerable ability – the doctor was called away by the first mate sotto voce to be informed that the poor little child that was so ill last night had just expired. In order not to cause needless alarm, the thing was kept quiet, the first mate heaving the body of the poor little thing overboard and returning to the forecastle in a few minutes after as if nothing had happened.

This makes our 13th death we may say within the month – only one recovery having taken place – that of the child. Perhaps in the annals of children, there never was such mortality in the same number of cases. Notwithstanding however, all we have gone thro, the lull that has taken place in the breaking out of fresh cases has merely restored us to our former and comparative quiet state of spirits, and in a Sunday's morn if all went well, it will even be forgotten that Death had been sweeping us down on board, and that within so short a time back, death had been striding triumphantly amongst us.

Today we had great fun in setting all sail to overtake a vessel ahead of us and are gaining fast upon her, but we fear it will be night before we come up with her; thus leaving us again to pass our ship in the dark. So far we have passed every sail we have seen, running them out of sight within the 24 hours.

Temperature now quite cool – our fishing not a bit too warm for comfort. The trades increasing as we approach the line, and as we advance proving more favourable for us .

Monday 15th October; *Lat. 2.52°; Long. –; Ther. 26°C*

Yesterday I expressed a hope that all might now commence to go better with us as regards the cholera, but it was only a vain delusion. This morning when we came on deck, a little girl of

7 years old belonging to Mrs Peterson, now become a chief cabin inmate, was reported vomiting and purging and now altho only four hours have elapsed since she was first attacked, she is now in the throes of death.

Our doctor is going about like a madman, not knowing what to do, what to say or where to go. In short, the creature is nearly out of the little mind he ever had.

I am again beginning to be much alarmed about Willie – he complains of headache, want of appetite and occasional pain at the pit of the stomach, and looks [...]. As I am determined the ship's butcher shall not kill him, I have taken him in hand myself alone, with the Captain and 1st mate – my intention to give him tonight 5gr. of calomel and work it off tomorrow with 30 or 50grs of Jalop. His illness may have nothing to do with anything like cholera, but in such moments, when our little finger aches we tremble.

Since this fresh outbreak of cholera, we are again all in the dumps, and long faces are in abundance. In every corner you hear a sign with a "Oh, if we were only safe at Otago or at home".

South east trades gradually increasing; the ship carrying all sail except [...] sails of [...] being close hauled and steering S west by south. Amused myself this morning making a line with a small hook on it, to catch some of Mother Carey's chickens, which keep constantly following in the wake of the vessel. The illness of the little Peterson however will make me put off my attempt until tomorrow, and who knows what tomorrow may bring forth?

A lot of a fish called by the sailors Bonetti were seen playing about the bows of the vessel. They weigh from 8 to 10 lbs, and altho dry eating, are much liked by the sailors. On some occasions, ships catch them in such quantity that they salt them and lay them by for storing. As yet we have not taken any, the 3 mates [...] having as yet failed in striking any of them with the grain [...]. Nor will they as yet look at the hook. We are now going too fast thro the water to see sharks, so the chances are that they have had more of us than we of them.

Tuesday 16th October; *Lat. 1.29°; Long. 20.13°; Ther. 26.5°C*

It is not yet God's will that we shall escape our enemy, the cholera. The

little girl reported attacked yesterday, breathed her last at 2 o'clock, having only been 6 hours ill. Her case was rather a peculiar one – for instead of being seized with the usual cramps and other symptoms of the disease, she seemed to feel no pain whatever and seemed to die in a state of lethargy as if poisoned.

The poor thing with its bedding was thrown overboard in the same way as the others uncoffined and unhallowed. The mother, having 7 other children on board, takes her loss with great fortitude, for I dare say she has the keeping [...] of making face against all she may yet have to undergo. Other poor children are kind of ways threatened, but I hope their cases are not to turn out cholera.

No change in wind or weather, except that the temperature is much cooler and pleasanter to the feeling. Still alarmed about Willie, as he looks ill and cannot exert himself to anything. As long as he is fit for it by taking his post at the cabin work, he gets cabin fare, so that he has had his share of the best food going. Last night gave him 5gr of Calomel and this morning a strong dose of Jalop to work it off and so far it seems to have done him good. On the whole I continue well enough, altho have to watch my stomach and otherwise keep as good a look out to windward as we poor mortals can.

Wednesday 17th October; *Lat. 18 miles from the equator; Long. 21.46°; Ther. 26°C*

Against all hopes, and notwithstanding the warning of yesterday, the health of the ship again on the mend. Apparently the children who were ill, and suspected cases of cholera yesterday, are recovering. God grant we may know another week of quiet, for no one but those who have experienced it, can imagine the gloom which is thrown over a ship by deaths occurring at every turn.

Willie I think also getting round, altho he has a very different look from what he had when he was at home. However it may only be a general change coming over his whole system in consequence of his new mode of life, and not yet being accustomed to it.

Amused myself fishing a couple of hours for Mother Carey's chickens, taking a small trout hook with a little bit of bacon on it, but did not succeed catching any. The Captain promised to eat any I caught, with all the feathers on. No more fish coming about the vessel.

Being now so near the line, the sailors are getting ready to play off their jokes upon some of the passengers. We have had great fun drawing upon the ignorance of some of the people, making them believe that the line consists of a high wall of water about 10 feet, over which the vessel has to mount, causing a fearful shock. In conse-

home, it would be better that we had no communication with any ship, as it would only tend to alarm you all for our future fate, with this dread pestilence on board of us.

Had a long talk with the mother of the child that died yesterday, and not all I could say to her could remove the feeling from her mind that her child had been poisoned by an overdose of opium – a circumstance I fully believe myself, but of course I tried to comfort the poor mother with a different view

part of the ship in such a manner that altho all hands searched every corner of the ship for him they could think of, it was no go. So the cunning Parson saved his soul as well as the shaving, the salt water, and the after polishing off with tar with a [...].

We now begin to hope that the comparatively cool temperature we have had during the last 10 days has begun to tell [...] in clearing the ship of cholera, as, with the exception of Mrs Peterson's poor little child which was

Steerage quarters on an emigrant ship. (Illustrated London News, 10/5/1851)

quence, many last night wedged themselves well in their berths in order that they should not hurt themselves by being pitched against the sides.

So much for the boasted intelligence and education of the Scotch peasantry. In short, with the exception of some half dozen out of the 60 or 80 working men on board, they are about as poor a specimen of Scotia's sons as could well be seen. Nor are they even the hardy, strong looking people such as would be supposed to be good only for the spade and the plough.

Being now in the exact track for outward and homeward bound vessels, we are all on the outlook, but with the breeze now blowing, it is doubtful whether we may board any of them. However if we do, there will be letters ready to send on board. From the account however which will be sent

of the case, as being more likely to calm her than an opposite supposition.

Thursday 18th October; *Lat. 1.39°; Long. 23.11°; Ther. 26°C*

South E. trades freshening every 24 hours and proving more favourable for us – ship steering South W by South – staggering under a fearful load of canvas. Passed the equator yesterday evening about 5 o'clock PM, thus making exactly 5 weeks from Greenock.

As usual, the sailors took their usual fun about getting Neptune dressed up and allowing him to exercise his rights as to shaving and heaving buckets of salt water on all those of the passengers, and all those crew who had not crossed the line. The Parson sailor was of course a marked man, but like a true saint, stowed himself away in some

attacked and died on the morning of the 15th, things decidedly begin to look better. But as already said, with such a strange mysterious and capricious disease, who knows but this is only the prelude to another storm. Let us however not forbode any evil. Sufficient is the day &c. &c.

This morning at daylight, a homeward bound ship was seen but a long way to windward of us. As we are now exactly in the track of both the homeward and outward bound vessels, am surprised at not meeting with more of our brothers of the deep.

Last night the fiddles were to be set and agoing again, but on the musicians taking up their instruments which had been so long abandoned, they were found to have become all unglued and unfit for work. The joiner therefore will have to put them to rights, which

I dare say will be done for this evening if all goes well.

Doctor Purdie's 2nd youngest child rather complaining, and altho there appear to be latent symptoms of the old enemy, we still hope nothing serious is to happen. Madame takes the sickness of her child with an apathy that may be peculiar to a (hypocritical) saint, but it savours not of humanity. Even the brute beasts show more feeling and might put her to blush. The theory is, if it is ordained that it should die, there is no need attempting to save it. In this way, the poor little thing is left to the care of the Doctor, and the mother remains all day on deck apparently as indifferent as an old sow. At the sound of a bell, she rushes down to her victuals and stuffs herself with salt beef and pork as well as the sturdiest of them. This too, is the woman who, a few days ago, gave out she was ill because she could not eat the provisions served out on board.

sail which was showing us that she also wished to pass a communication perhaps to ourselves, by the trouble she was taking. When about a mile off, with our glasses we saw her lowering a boat and in half an hour afterwards her boat, with the 1st Officer and 4 men, were alongside of us.

This brig proved to be the *Fortitude*, 27 days out from Rio with a cargo of coffee for Falmouth. Her bread having got bad, she applied to us for a few

creature is totally helpless, I begin to have pity on him – but not so his wife, who is a bitch and will die a bitch.

A kind of row was got up at dinner by Miss McAdam, the aged spinster alias an old maid, who in a very angry tone abused us gentlemen right round for our insolence and want of gallantry to the ladies. The circumstances arose thus: when the 1st officer from the Brig yesterday came on the poop deck to pay us cabin gentry a visit, Mr Oates remarked to him, "You see Sir, we have plenty of women on board (the latter from the between decks having also crowded round us in all directions). If you like, we can spare you a few." This of course went off – or was intended to go off – as a mere joke, but our captious spinster, along with another of the same tribe from below, thought otherwise and kicked up a hully baloo about it. Poor creatures – they might have felt certain there was little fear of being molested under any circumstances – not even if they were the last two women left to dwell in the world.

TO EMIGRANTS, CAPTAINS, SHIPPERS, &c.

No one should leave England without providing himself with a stock of Gutta Percha Soles and Solution. The ease with which these soles can be applied in countries where no shoemaker can be found—their power of keeping the feet perfectly dry, thus preserving the body from coughs, colds, &c., in lands where medical advice cannot be had; and their great durability and cheapness, render them invaluable to all who propose sailing to distant countries. Gutta Percha Wash Basins, Chamber Bowls, Sou'-Westers, Bottles, Flasks, &c., are admirably suited for shipboard and emigrants, as they *can so readily be converted into life-buoys in the event of a shipwreck*. The Gutta Percha Life-Buoys and Portmanteau are valuable for Emigrants. Any person taking a stock of Gutta Percha across the seas will find it afford profitable speculation.

Manufactured by the Gutta Percha Company, patentees, Wharf-road, City-road, London; and sold by their wholesale dealers in town and country.

Friday 19th October; Lat. 4.4°; Long. 24.53°; Ther. 26°C

The Trades have freshened into almost a gale of a wind during the night. Were obliged to haul down Jenny Lind jib, Cock of the North [the yard...] name given by Captain Chivas to some new stay sails he has set, and for most of the night were obliged to furl the royals. At daylight the royals were set again, and the ship is heeling to it in a way to prevent you standing on deck without a hold on.

At four o'clock yesterday, saw a homeward bound brig bearing right down upon us, right before the wind on our weather bow backed over [...] our main and mizzen topsails, and lay to, in order to show the brig we wanted to speak to her. Shortly after this, we observed her taking in her studding

bags which was readily given along with a dozen of beer, on the understanding that as soon as she reached England she was to report us "all well". This was done in order not to alarm our friends with hurried and garbled statements of the miseries we have gone thro. As the boat however was in the act of packing off, a lot of the Emigrants made a rush to the ship's side and threw into the boat a great many letters begging them to deliver them as soon as arrived in England. The Captain, however, requested the boat's crew to throw them all overboard, which they appeared to do. But who knows but some stray letter may yet find its way, telling our tale.

The poor Doctor was sadly down in the mouth, for he well knew these letters would contain many complaints against him, and really now, seeing the

der any circumstances – not even if they were the last two women left to dwell in the world.

Dr's child still dangerously ill, now said to be a gastric fever. At all events, it can't be cholera, from her having survived so many days. In other respects, the hopes of the mysterious scourge having in so great degree left the ship, or at least become dormant for the moment, are fast reviving us, altho every day there is a kind of an alarm got up of some one being attacked. So far it only ends in a little sickness or dysentery, but so scared are people, that an extra wink of the eye is cause for alarm. Willie and Ferguson keeping well.

Not a bit too warm, altho within 7 & 8 degrees of the Line. Week or ten days more, we will be putting on over clothing at night. The thermometer, from which I have noted down each day's heat at noon, stands in the cuddy in the Capt's cabin. But below between decks, where the emigrants are, it is always 2 & 3 degrees higher. Thus when we had it at 29, they were above 32.

Sunday 21st October; Lat. 10.5°; Long. 28.36°; Ther. 26°C; 186 miles

The fine spanking breeze still carries us along at the rate of 9 & 10 knots an hour, with the ship's sails square a point or two easier, astern souwest by south, right on for the Brazil coast. All well on board, barring the exceptions of yesterday. Doctor's child reported worse, but with such imbeciles to attend to it, who knows in what state it is in – for lies these Saints tell bigger than their neighbours.

One circumstance I may mention thereby the Doctors skill was, that in those cases of cholera to which he did attend, he was of course often asked by the anxious people around how his patient felt and it was invariable observed that just as the last crisis came on, previous to dissolution, he came out saying "Oh thank God my patient I now consider now doing well, and blessed be the Lord, she or he is enjoying a gentle refreshing repose". Well in two minutes, a messenger ascended from below to say his patient was gone – when a groan with "God's will be done" and echoed by us with a "but he does not approve of wholesale murder".

Did not get up our game at cards last night, as the fiddler was upon deck and all the sailors dancing like possessed ones. The doctor will be saying again that it is by indulging in this wickedness that the wrath of God is brought upon the ship – a piece of cant for which I would like to pitch him overboard. The dancing was kept up until the usual hour, when all hands were piped down below and Ferguson, the Capt, a Mr Clemison and myself were left alone in all our glory – then came the night

[Missing text.]…pipe of baccy, with half an hour of yarning when we too turned in, leaving the deck in undisputed possession of the officer for the middle watch. Had service today as usual on deck, the Doctor reading a sermon on sanctification and on this occasion there was more than numerous congregation, most of the sailors and a few of our Free Kirkers being the only exceptions.

Monday 22nd October; Lat. 13.11°; Long. 30.18°; Ther 26°C; No sun

No change in the weather, the S.E. trades having rather increased if anything. Still the ship is enabled to carry all sail, and a pretty lot of it she has on her. I sometimes wonder how the masts can bear the pressure of so much canvas bearing down upon them from one side causing the ship to keel over on her beam ends. But our Capt says we have leeway to make up, and if anything be carried away, we have more spars and sails on board with which to repair the damage.

The afternoon of yesterday spent

George Cruikshank

quietly and decently in a Sabbath day way – that is, going to church in the morning and talking scandal and gossiping the remainder of it.

During the night, it having proved rather puffy, were obliged to take in royals and staysails, setting them again this morning at daylight. Killed our second pig yesterday, part of which was gobbled up at dinner – the liver portion falling to the Doctor's wife, who is a devil for pork. Two of our sheep are also in the land of their forefathers, thus leaving still for mastication 2/3rd of our livestock.

Ship's health keeping good, and no further symptoms of fresh cases of cholera. The Doctor's child reported no better this morning – but none of us can make out how things stand in the

Purdie den, where none but savage beasts do dwell.

Tuesday 23rd October; Lat. 16.6°; Long. 30.39°; Ther. 26°C

Since 12 o'clock yesterday, we have had some severe squalls of wind and rain when it was stand by the mizen and fore royals halyard. Then as the gale increased, let go the main royal and stand by to let go the shroud &c. These orders being bellowed forth while one is in a deep sleep below, wakens you up in double quick time, and I confess until our senses are all collected and we know where we are, it is not over pleasant. These squalls are not common when the S. East Trades are prevailing but in the present instance we have just been passing across […] the sun's […] which generally occasions unsteady and squally weather. During the blanks between the squalls however, the stars last night shone out with a splendour far beyond what we see in the Northern Hemisphere.

Ever since we got hold of the Trades, our good ship must have managed from 8 to 8.5 perhaps even 9 knots an hour, sometimes in the squalls going 10 knots, which, with a tight bowline, is considered first rate sailing and promises us at least 12 and perhaps even 15 knots when we round the Cape and get hold of the westerly winds.

Calculate that we passed the parallel of St. Helena yesterday or during the night the latter lying in the South Lat. If we hold our present course, hope to sight the Island of Trinidada, which lies directly in the usual track. But if the Trades do not enable us to bear up a little more than we are now doing, fear we shall pass too much to the westward. It is, I believe, a small and uninhabited Island except by pigs, of which there are an immense quantity and it is said that ships when passing near in fine weather often send a boat on shore and fill her with pigs and deer they find there in such quantities.

Quietness and peace thanks to God now reign throughout the whole ship and every man, woman and child in it seem now happy and contented – such are the blessings of health. The salt junk and black dirty water, the sight of which yesterday as it were turned every man's stomach, now appears to them the most delicious food. The sea that was rough yesterday in their imagination, is like a lake today, altho in reality the swell and pitching of the ship is greater than usual. In short, all for the present is couleur de rose, and many of those who a short time ago would have given all they had to return to their native shore, are now at work again building or perhaps only finishing the Otago castle in the air which they probably laid the foundation of in Scotland.

The Doctor's child said to be passed all point of danger and we therefore hope soon to see the little thing on deck again for of a verity it was the nicest little thing in the ship – in this case the fruit has fallen very far from the tree.

Wednesday 24th October; Lat. 18.55°; Long. 30.29°; Ther. 26°C

It now appears we are gradually drawing to the outside of the S.E. trades, as the wind for the last 24 hours has been very irregular, blowing at one time from the South, at another drawing round to the East, and so on. Add to this, the winds have got lighter, which is I believe a sure sign some change is taking place.

Nothing new today of any kind to narrate, save and excepting that Mr Clemison popped the question to Miss Mary Peterson and was refused ipso facto – upon which the lovesick swain straightaway went down to his cabin and fired his fist thro his looking glass, sending it to slivers of course. He is now going on like a mad man for fool he was before and no mistake.

All hands well, except myself, as I am suffering much from headache and can find no quiet place to lay down in – but as I can't hold up my head, I must now descend to my cabin and make the most of it. The noise and screaming of children is bad to bear when one is well, but it is the devil to pay when one is ill.

Thursday, 25th October; Lat. 20.32°; Long. 29.6°; Ther. 27°C

Turned in yesterday at noon with headache and remained in bed until 10

"Here and There – or Emigration a Remedy". (Punch, 15/7/1848)

at night, when I went on deck for half an hour to get the fresh air about me, but still suffering. The night was fine and quite cool enough for enjoyment. The want of sleep, however, prevented me getting round sufficiently to enjoy the cool air, so after a sniff round away, I turned in again. This morning I rose at six most refreshed and with very slight remains of my headache.

On coming on deck, I was hailed with the grateful announcement that the Island of Trinidada was in sight, and right ahead on our larboard bow, the Island appearing some twenty miles off. Holding our present course, we are likely to come as close to it as would be prudent. A description of a closer view of the Island falls to tomorrow's notes.

The wind and weather during the night has been very moderate, but we have been enabled to steer a much better course, owing to the wind shifting a little round to the N & W, hence our coming upon Trinidada, which yesterday morning we were a long way to leeward of. It is now getting so cool that during the morning and evenings I must wear my warmer clothes again.

When passing the Equator, having secured a good deal of rain water, small quantities were given off to the passengers for washing, so giving mine to Mrs Stewart. She washed up all the dirty linen which had accumulated since I left. As no ironing is allowed on board after the alarm of fire which was given, my things have been merely washed in the rough. But altho I can't wear them in their present state, it enables me to lay them by in a clean dry state, and which

will also serve to preserve them from mildew.

Everything in one's cabin gets the sea damp in a fearful way about it, which makes me fear for the seeds sometimes. But I am recommended by the Capt not to unpack them, as it would only increase the danger of them being further affected by the sea air. Let us hope therefore that all is right.

We are now nearly getting abreast of the Island, and a dead calm seems coming on, the sails beginning to flap against the masts of the ship as if they were sick of holding the wind any longer. The heat this morning, in consequence, is greater than we have had since leaving the immediate vicinity of the Equator.

Friday, 26th October; Lat. 21.14°; Long. 28.58°; Ther. 23°C

All yesterday was a day of much rejoicing on board, as much interest was taken in the splendid views we got of the Island of Trinidada, which is one of the most barren rocks ever beheld. At a distance it has the general appearance and shape of Edinburgh Castle, but on nearing it, you are soon forced to form another idea of it, for desolation itself would think shame to dwell there. The highest point of it is about 1600 feet, and from the sea it only represents a mass of rough and ragged rocks, all thrown pell mell on top of each other. It is not inhabited of course, altho, strange as it may appear, two or three shipwrecked Portuguese managed to live upon it for some time and survived to tell the tale. It lies very much completely on the track of outward bound ships, which may approach the Island in safety within a mile or two – altho from the great surf running towards the shores, boats never or very rarely think of landing unless driven to do so for want of water.

Our first Mate, Mr Milligan, told us today at dinner of his having once been on it for water and which they got off with the greatest difficulty. He says he saw a lot of wild pigs and marks of goats' feet but did not see any of the latter. A few wild dogs, however, they made chase of and succeeded in capturing one which he took to Calcutta with him. It was quite young, and seemed to be something of the Scotch Terrier breed.

Some of the different views of the Island we had were so beautiful that I was tempted to take a couple of sketches of it, which will at least serve to preserve la memoria dal passato.

On turning out this morning, the Island was still in sight, bearing NN West, but very far distant. On leaving the Island, we observed a heavy swell setting in from the South W, which was soon followed by a heavy shower of rain and then a stiff gale from the South East, forcing us to take in all our royals, mizen and fore top gallant sails for our ship's being so very tender, there is no carrying canvas on her when close hauled, and with a heavy head sea to plough thro.

A great many of the people, especially the women, seasick again, but otherwise all symptoms of cholera or other disease appear to have left the ship for the present at least. The Doctor's child is also recovering fast, but the poor little thing has had a dreadful shake.

Before it came on to blow, Ferguson and I had some fun with an albatross, the first we have seen, and rarely met, it is said, so far to the north. He came flying about the ship very close, and I got out a line with a hook baited with a piece of pork as large as the palm of your hand, which I no sooner lowered down into the water, than over it went into his voracious maw, hook and all. But my line not being strong, he snapt it in two as if it had been a thread, taking away the hook and a yard or two of line attached, as if nothing particular had happened. On gorging it, he flew to

some distance, probably tickled with the feather in his throat, but after a short interval he returned, evidently prepared for some more pork. But not being prepared yet with a new and stronger line, altho his gun was only loaded with no. 4 shot, Ferguson shot him as he sailed past within 15 yards of the ship and down he dropt into the water a dead man, thus making an end of the first albatross we saw. As we get nearer the Cape, the Captain assures us we will have lots of them flying about the ship, so that I expect to have some good sport both with

Embarkation at Liverpool. (Illustrated London News, 6/7/1850)

my line and rifle. Weather getting quite cool, and at nights even cold.

Saturday, 27th October; Lat. 22.13°; Long. 29.2°; Ther. 22°C

The South E breeze still continues, and during the past night, the ship tossed and plunged into it – to a greater extent than has occurred since we left. The Captain regrets not having had another 100 tons of ballast in the ship, as in heeling over so much as she does, there is considerable danger of our masts being carried away. However when we come to run before it, as we are likely or rather certain to do when we round the Cape, she ought to fly and perhaps make over 12 knots an hour.

Nothing new going on today, as from the pitching of the vessel, most of the people are below, and those on deck far from comfortable. As, however, this South E wind is quite unusual in these lati-

tudes, it is expected that the wind will soon gradually draw round to the west, enabling us to steer our true course with the wind on our quarter.

All I did today was to get the joiner to make me up a kind of temporary writing table in my cabin, as with such a noisy crew we have of men, women and children, it is quite impossible to find a moment's quiet anywhere else.

Sunday, 28th October; Lat. 24.24°; Long. 29.33°; Ther. 21°C

Blowing still fresh from the South E, but the sea rather tapers off. In consequence of the ship pitching less, got our topgallant sails set again, and by and by, the royals will follow and in their turn all the small tribe of the junerush [...] sails.

At eleven, all hands piped to church, when Pills, as usual, did the needful. The service was curtailed of the sermon however, owing to the congregation not being very steady on their feet. In the afternoon, however, the sailor parson gave us another of his yarns, but he had hardly commenced when a squall came with rain and it was all hands to take in sail and the congregation flew in all directions.

Getting very cold to the feel, notwithstanding the thermometer still stands at 21 and we are within 2 or 3 degrees of the equator. When we sat down to tea last evening about half past 5, there was a disagreement amongst some of the Glasgow bodies about the degree of coldness, some affirming that it was colder than in Scotland, and it was only settled by my taking the thermometer up on deck and shewing them the true state of things. The fact is however, if you have a strong breeze blowing, you can never, in any latitude, be incommoded with heat, and especially when luxuriating in the trade winds which blow with the same strength nearly for six months on end.

Monday, 29th October; *Lat. 27.10°; Long. 29.52°; Ther. 21°C; 170 Miles*

Since 12 o'clock yesterday the wind has continued to blow steadily from the same quarter – namely South E, which prevents us holding as good a course as we would like. Had we gone 'Iwall [?] of the pit [?]' we would hold the ship's nose South E by E – instead of steering SW by West, thus swinging too far down upon

Charting the voyage at night. (Illustrated London News, 20/1/1849)

the American coast. But we must be contented, and right reason we have for being so. Here we are with nearly half our journey done, and since we left, not a reef has been taken in our topsails and even our topgallants have only been twice taken in – and that for a short time only.

The heavy sickness we had on board has been our worst lot, but thank God that cause of complaint now seems also removed from us. The period when we left Scotland, when we look back upon it, certainly does seem very long but somehow or other [...] admit that the Sundays come round upon us very fast. As it is generally said that the last half of a sea voyage seems always the shortest, we must hope that the worst of our trials are over. I do not by this mean to say that the voyage to New Zealand,

"taken as a voyage", as a friend of mine always says, is a disagreeable one – or such as ought to deter the most timid from undertaking it. On the contrary, as far as the weather and the ailing part of it is concerned, it is really little worse than a pleasure excursion, but then this presupposes you to be in a well-found ship with a limited number of pleasant fellow passengers, an agreeable Captain and 1st Mate, and in fact all the other necessary qualifications. Very far different, however, is the comfort on board an

emigrant ship, and that emigrant ship too laden with as poor a lot of bigoted humanity as could be well brought together.

Tuesday, 30th October; *Lat. 29.58°; Long. 29.12°; Ther. 20°C; 180 miles*

South east gale still continuing but having drawn somewhat round to the North East; with symptoms of its veering still more round and getting into the North, we are holding a better course and are now with our nose nearly straight on for Tristan d'Acunha. Last night at times it actually blew half a gale, but our Captain having such confidence in his ship; he carries on to the last, at same time always ready at a moment's notice to take in sail when actual danger approaches. Since 12 o'clock yesterday, we have passed a rather uncomfortable

24 hours, as from the ship being nearly on her beam ends, we can't move about with any comfort or without in fact rolling into the lee scuppers. All we do therefore in such circumstances is to huddle together into the corners and pass the time as best we can.

Temperature now getting quite cold, and at night a blanket, and even a couple of them in bed is not to be sneezed at. Have had occasional beautiful moonlight nights but the sky for the most part has been very clouded and having much the appearance of our own skies at home.

Today a great hulla baloo kicked up on account of it having been discovered that a regular system of petty theft has been carrying on below between decks amongst the emigrants. A poor fellow who had left his trousers by his bed found them lightened of all the change that was in them, consisting of 18/- or 19/-. One or two black sheep have certainly got into the fold, but it is to be hoped they will yet be detected and duly punished. Two sentries are posted a night to keep watch over the others and on one of those gentry suspicion for the moment seems to have fallen.

Wednesday, 31st October; *Lat. 32.15°; Long. 26.57°; Ther. 20°C; 185 miles*

As was expected, the wind after sundown yesterday got round to the east and by north, enabling us now to hold our course well and full for Tristan d'Acunha. The sea too, which was running pretty high yesterday, has much gone down, and the ship, I found on coming on deck this morning, was cutting thro it with main top gallant sails and royals set. Now we are getting every studding sail in the ship set, the wind being on our quarter and not too strong for carrying all we have.

Got my new line ready for the albatrosses and also my rifle, and expect today to have a little fun with them, as being now nearly on the same parallel of the Cape, we may consider ourselves now fairly in their regions. The past two days were too stormy, altho Ferguson "with his bow & arrow" shot an albatross with no. 5 shot as it sailed past within 20 or 30 yards of the ship.

Last night the Captain invited for the first time one or two of the intermediate passengers into the cabin, and treated us all with some grog. Ferguson & I treated them out at no small allowance and altogether had a good deal of fun with them. Tonight being Halloween, there is to be lots of jollity, the mate having promised to get up a bag of apples from the stores if there is one. Weather getting colder and colder with generally a cloudy sky.

Thursday, 1st November; Lat. 33.32°; Long. 23.09°; Ther. 20°C; 210 miles

Yesterday, completed the seventh week since we left Greenock, and, looking back upon it, it certainly feels as if it had been an age, but this of course is more owing to the grievous trials we had undergone and the extraneous circumstances of our position than real discomfort attending the voyage itself – which in a good ship and pleasant company ought to be one of the most unexceptionable long voyages that there is.

Wind and weather for the last 24 hours have been both most passable for us and as we are continuing to steer E.S.E. and right on our course for Tristan d'Acunha Islands, which we hope to make on Sunday or before, if this fine breeze continues, enabling us to set a power of sail and going very free.

Expecting every day to come up with some sail, having hitherto been most unfortunate in doing so. Our skipper is burning to try some of Greens crack ships, or in fact anything that sails us near in such light trim and with such lots of canvas on board that he fancies he could beat all the world.

At 11 o'clock this morning a shout was made of a sperm whale being close alongside, when all hands made a rush to the sails to have a view of the monster, which rose and spouted within 15 yards of the ship's side. Had any of us been prepared with a rifle, we might have tickled him a little with some lead, but before we were ready he was away ahead of us, a mile or two. Another was seen shortly after a long way to windward but he did not dain to pay us a closer visit. The American whaling vessels are sometimes met cruising about in this locality but as yet we have seen none of them.

Albatrosses and Cape pigeons getting a little thicker, but as yet are rather shy in approaching very near us. It is only when there are a great many of them that they take courage to approach very close to us. In squabbling with one another, they seem to forget the enemy is so near.

Friday, 2 November; Lat. 34.26°; Long. 19.42°; Ther. 20°C; 190 miles

Today we arrived within a few miles on the exact parallel of the Cape, and are continuing to steer South E by E, with the wind nearly right at, all sail set, with smooth water and a steady breeze.

Last night being Halloween, there were lots of capers going on. For want of apples to dive for and nuts to burn, some of the crew and passengers rigged themselves out in character and sang comical songs, while others amused themselves with dancing, crowning the nights entertainment with a lot of jovial songs. On these occasions, with the exception of the Todds, our stupid bigots of cabin passengers shut themselves up in their cabins and, thinking to honour the Lord, abstain from all such iniquity and may the Devil seize them for their pains!

Dancing 'tween decks. (London Illustrated News, 6/7/1850)

In the morning Ferguson and I had some firing at the Cape pigeons, a very pretty bird about the size of our own pigeon and in many respects resembling it in its flight as well as in the shape. They are difficult to shoot, at least I found so, having missed the first four shots I fired at them and thereby losing as many glasses of grog in a bet with Mr Clemison. Tomorrow however, I expect to do better things, now that my hand is probably a little more in. One or two albatrosses kept following the ship but not having rigged my rifle, did not fire at them. Ferguson however blazed away at them

but did nothing, at least as far as killing them. Frighten them he might have done, but that was his gun's doing, not his. My fishing attempts to catch both the Cape pigeon and the albatross have as yet proved fruitless, but this is owing to the ship going too fast thro the water than anything else.

Of the health of the ship I have said little of late, as thank God, since we have got into the cooler weather all is going well, there now being nothing ill on board of the ship but the Doctor's goat, which has eaten nothing I believe since he left Scotland, and is now reduced to a complete piece of living anatomy.

Saturday, 3 November; Ther. 19°C

Since 12 o'clock yesterday the wind has continued steady from the same quarter. Ship going on an average 7 to 8 knots an hour. Smooth sea but very cloudy sky to shewing symptoms of rain – a sign that the wind is likely to shift to the north, which in these latitudes corresponds with our rainy South wind at home.

Ferguson and I amused ourselves all afternoon yesterday, and this morning, taking our quarters in the stern boat, he at one end and I at the other, firing away at the Cape pigeons and the albatrosses, but as yet have done little damage. The motion of the vessel I find renders firing very easy, but hitting most difficult. It is, however, good practice and serves to pass away the time. To be upsides with our winged visitors, we have our rifles and fowling pieces close by our hand – using the former for the albatrosses and the latter for the pigeons. Saw another whale today, but it was a small one and did not come within 500 yards of the ship.

By the observations taken at noon today, which however were not quite the thing, owing to an imperfect view of the sun, we calculate that we are about 180 miles from the Tristan d'Acunha Islands – which probably will heave in sight some time tomorrow morning.

All well on board and the emigrants in good spirits. The poet Laureate of the ship put into my hand this morning one of his effusions addressed to myself, in which he was pleased to sing my praises in a way I little deserved and still less expected. In return I am now attempting to give him a reply in some doggerel of my own, which however I shall suppress from these pages for reasons that will be easily understood.

perhaps ever occurred in a mans life, he living to narrate it. The thick weather and rain, which continued without a moment's cessation throughout all Saturday and Sunday with a stiffish breeze from the North West, ended as far as the wind went in nearly a calm towards 10 o'clock last night – the ship then under double reefer topsails.

At that hour I was sitting with the Captain in his cabin spinning a yarn and smoking a pipe with him in order to pass away an hour, he intending to remain on deck all night on account of our doubtful position. At 12 o'clock at night I left him and turned in, the ship

Departing on the Artemsia. (Illustrated London News, 1848)

tack and set the royals, top gallant sails and any sail that could be got up in the hurry of the moment, in the hope of still working the ship off the land. The next order given was to lower the boats and undo the lashing of the long boat on deck, and [...] up the stream cable to carry ashore to [...]. Then came the preparations of getting the anchor all clear to let go, should we be taken aback or struck.

The boats were then manned by some of the passengers to tow the vessel ahead. All this took place from the half past 12 to 1 o'clock, and managed in the most seaman like manner – notwithstanding there was not a soul on board who for one moment hoped that we should be saved from destruction – there being no place within sight where even a seal could land, the face of the rock being as steep as the north side of Edinburgh Castle and many times higher. In short, it was a sight which few have ever before or will live to narrate.

About half past 12, a good deal of sail was got upon the vessel, and altho we were then probably within 2 or 300 yards of the breakers, and the spume of the cataract falling over the precipice now astern of us was almost falling upon us, an occasional puff or two from the land drove us a few yards from the danger. Then came the fearful lull when the roll of the sea gradually laid hold of us again, carrying the vessel bodily on to destruction – the breakers roaring, closing behind for their prey.

Once more the breeze comes gently down from the rocks, when every advantage was taken of it to get out of the vortex, the boats ahead pulling like mad. Again comes the lull once more, and this was the most critical moment of the fearful danger we were in.

The breeze which came and went every 3 or 4 minutes on this occasion, left us for a minute or two longer than usual when, with the indraft of the sea towards the land, the ship gradually began to broach to, which being seen

***Sunday, 4 November**; Lat., Long. – no Sun; Ther. 17°C*

Shortly after 12 o'clock yesterday, the clouds, which had been gathering all morning, began to shower down rain in torrents, and which still continues without the least appearance of its fairing. The thick fog which has accompanied it too, prevents us seeing 20 yards ahead of the ship. In consequence of not having seen the sun, stars or moon for two days, Captain a little uneasy as to the bearing of the Tristan d'Acunha Islands and in consequence in the hope of giving them a wide berth is steering due South, expecting thus from his dead reckoning to pass them well to the westward.

On account of the rain, all hands are below and the church service was performed between decks for the emigrants.

Monday, 5 November

I come now to detail one of the most fearful and appalling events which

with so little sail set, and the wind very light, going very slowly thro the water. In getting into bed, being Sunday night, I took that little favourite book of my dear mother and which she gave me before I left, and read from it some of the prayers and amongst others the one calling upon God to guard us from danger while undertaking a journey.

I had hardly closed the book and put out my lamp, when the fearful cry of breakers close ahead broke upon my ears, making me shudder from head to foot. My first impulse of course was to leap out of bed, only drawing on me a pair of trousers and with nothing else on, to rush on deck. The first object I beheld thro the mist was a great mass of black perpendicular rock, which appeared to rise to the very clouds high standing right under our bows, with the roar of the breakers enough to appall the stoutest heart.

The first order given by the Captain was to put the ship on the other by the Captain, he wrung his hands and said all was over. This however was only muttered to himself, for it was only my happening to be close to him at the moment that I alone heard him. Immediately recovering himself, he bellowed out what might have been heard by the people on shore, had there been any, "be ready there ahead to drop the anchor, drop the lead there. Captain Blackie astern, what water we have?" "6 fathoms, Sir." "Great God, she will be striking if I don't let go."

When just giving this order, which might have saved some of our lives but irretrievably lost the ship, down comes another gentle breeze from the precipice above us. When round go the yards, and again the sails fill which, bringing her head up again, takes us a few yards on. Another lull, but it lasts but a moment, and again the sails gently feel the breeze and the boats ahead, feeling they were no longer being dragged in shore by the ship, redouble their exertions and tug away at her like madmen.

Wreck of the Strathmore on the Crozets, 1875

At this time, near two, we were probably not a yard further than half a mile from the rocks. But it was something in this hour to have gained even 400 yards. Towards two, the wind freshened a little more still mercifully, right off the land, and then by taking advantage of every breath that came, we by 4 o'clock had increased our distance to about 3 miles from the breakers.

Day now began to dawn, when all the horrors of our position were more clearly shewn to us, but as a merciful God had saved us when all hope was gone, we began now to think ourselves comparatively safe. The great danger to be feared being the wind shifting round and blowing in shore when our position would be worse than ever. But also from this danger we were saved, for by six o'clock we had got probably something like 6 miles from the land, which was giving us nearly sufficient offing to clear the rocks, even had the wind shifted.

By ten and eleven all was out of danger, and, a stiff breeze springing up from the sea, the ship was laid into it, and closehauled, we were well clear of the land, which by 12 o'clock was no longer visible in the fog which became denser as the wind increased.

The rain fell in torrents all the night, but who thought of wet skins in such appalling moments.

The women were kept down below, but all were ready dressed to come up on deck at a moment's notice, and I must say they behaved very well.

The Doctor and his wife were the two most frightened creatures in the ship – the former rushing about the deck like a madman, and to shew the calculation of such holy people, they were heard consulting amongst themselves which of their children they intended to save if possible. The Doctor had his life preserver all ready in his berth, to save the most useless life in the ship, I should believe.

The behaviour of the Captain and other officers and crew of the ship was beyond all praise. The calm and cool way in which they worked the ship off the rocks was a piece of seamanship I should say hardly, if ever, excelled. Mrs Purdie was consulting about which of their children they were to save with their life preserver.

***Tuesday, 6 November**; Lat. 38.27°; Long. ; Ther. 17°C*

As might be expected, every one of us arose this morning much refreshed with a night's sleep after the fearful one we had passed the night before – and I hope with a feeling of eternal gratitude towards his maker that would be far more acceptable to Him than the humming of eternal psalm singing

and all such humbugging cant.

The weather now taking up and rain ceasing, the wind having shifted round to the North West, which enables us to steer right before it. Our course now E by South, having passed the Islands some 30 miles to the Northwest. Saw several whales close to the ship, and during the day shot several albatrosses and cape pigeons.

***Wednesday, 7 November**; Lat. 36.30° South; Long. 9.44° West; Ther. 16°C*

A beautiful calm day and, while the sun is out, warm. Sea as smooth as a lake and the ship since seven o'clock this morning has been laying like a log in the water. At eleven, one of the quarter boats was lowered, and the Captain gave us in different parties, a sail round the ship which was much enjoyed by all those who were lucky enough to be of the number.

Whales in considerable numbers continuing to shew themselves not far off from the ship, at times spouting within 50 or 80 yards of us. Shot one of the largest kind of albatrosses, which was picked up by the boat. It measured 10 feet from wing to wing, and was one of the most beautiful birds I ever saw – nearly white with a splendid plumage. Had one been on board, would have had it stuffed, of which it was well worthy.

One second mate taken seriously ill with a rheumatic fever and suffering such pain as to make his bellowing from below to be heard on deck. There seem to be no other bad symptoms however attending his illness, which was entirely brought on by his almost superhuman exertions pulling in one of the boats on the memorable night of Sunday. Weather getting very cold, and top coats and comforters the order of the day, with as many blankets as you will in bed at night.

***Thursday, 8 November**; Lat. 36.50°; Long. 7.52°; Ther. 17°C; 90 miles*

The calm, which commenced yesterday at seven in the morning, continued until this morning at eight, when a slight breeze from the North E sprang up. The ship holding her course East

South East, which ought gradually to bring us down on the parallel and close to New Zealand in the course of six weeks, provided the wind and weather favour us.

Cold gradually increasing, with a feeling in the air as if at times it would snow, notwithstanding that we are now in the summer seasons of these regions and the thermometer at 17. The sea however, being very smooth and the wind not strong, we are enjoying it on deck very comfortably. The nights in general – and in fact have been so for the last ten days – always thick and cloudy, with seldom a star to be seen. The barometer, which has seldom been under 29 since we left the channel, has risen to 30 3/8. We are again in hope of fine clear weather to repay us for the past. All well on board except the 2nd mate who however is recovering fast.

Friday, 9 November; *Lat. 37.25°; Long. 4° South West; Ther. 17°C; 150 miles*

Towards 4 o'clock yesterday it set in very thick weather, as much like a Scotch November fog as could well be, wetting you to the skin in a very short time, altho no rain fell. Towards midnight, the stars shone out overhead, but all round the horizon, the fog kept as thick as ever until six o'clock this morning, when it cleared away, giving us the promise of as splendid a day as we have had on this side of the equator. Sea as smooth as a lake and a nice gentle breeze sufficient to take a light ship thro the water at the rate of 7 & 8 knots an hour. The wind blowing north north east; ship steering South E by East.

F & I amused ourselves as usual in the afternoon yesterday, shooting albatrosses and cape pigeons – when some not very bad shots with ball were made, by I shall not say whom. As far as myself is concerned, I am beginning to get quite reconciled to the ship, as I find what with a little drawing, read-

ing, yarning and smoking, the time slips away. Ferguson employs his idle hours making a model of the Mooltan, and right well he is doing it. He is as neat a workman as you could see come out of any engineers shop.

At daylight a sail was seen a long way to windward, but as the sun got up and weather cleared, she had disappeared – from which we infer she must have been going to the Cape – or perhaps some of the whalers dodging about for their prey.

Saturday, 10 November; *Lat. 37.4°; Long. 2.42°; Ther. 18°C; Bar. 30 3/10*

Weather beautiful, but hardly to

Cutaway view of single women's quarters at the beginning of a voyage. Note that the ceiling of the cabin is drawn to look much higher than it would have been in reality. (Illustrated London News, 17/8/1850)

be called so for us, as since daylight we have been nearly becalmed, and what little wind there is, is causing us to steer 3 points off our course. During the day while the sun is over our heads, it is almost uncomfortably warm, but the evenings are sufficiently chilly to cause you to button up coats.

Nothing going on today of interest on board ship, as every man, woman and child has now so settled themselves down into their right places that our present domicile has become more like a snug little village than a floating prison.

Today I have commenced marking out our track on the little chart CG gave me and by my having taken down every day's reckoning since we left, I expect to make a job of it.

All the sea folks on board say they never recollect to have seen or heard of such calm weather and smooth water

in these regions as we have now been experiencing since we left the memorable Tristan d'Acunha Islands. In general, in these latitudes strong westerly winds prevail, causing ships running to the Eastward to send away before it with reefs, and even double reefs, in their topsails. And here we are with our royals flapping against the masts as if we were sailing in a pond.

Second mate nearly all right again and expecting to do duty by tomorrow or next day. A Mrs Beatie and a Miss Dick below in the between decks have been ailing the last two days. The former, having a presentiment that she is to die, seems to be getting worse. She is an old lady not far off seventy, and is the mother of poor Mrs [blank] who died of the cholera. Her complaint is indigestion, or rather an incapability of digesting anything she eats. Miss Dick is suffering from a slight attack of bilious fever. In neither case there being the slightest appearance of cholera, thank God. As usual, F and I partook of our usual couple of hours pigeon and albatross shooting, which however have not been about the ship in such numbers as usual.

Sunday, 11 November; *Lat. 38.11°; Long. 2.4°*

Voila another Sunday come around upon us, making within a few days the 9th week since we left, and still we have some 7 or 8000 miles of our journey to make. The calms still continuing lead us to fear we may yet be in for a long voyage, altho the Captain hopes that with the new moon which takes place on the [blank] we will have some change, so as to enable us to be upsticks and away.

Church service performed on deck today, when our poor body of a doctor tried to be as impressive as possible when dwelling on the events which took place last Sunday. But I hope every living creature on board needed no such prompting to feel more than gratitude to his maker for his helping hand in that awful hour of need.

Immediately after church was over, the doleful tiding was brought to us of the Doctor's goat having died, on which occasion Mother Purdie thought proper to weep, altho when her child died and the other one was at death's door for a week, not a tear fell. Nor did she seem to care a button for them – a more heartless bitch I never saw, as never since she has been on board has she been seen speaking to or taking interest in any of the poor women below with a lot of children to attend to and suffering all the discomforts of a steerage passage. On the other hand, never a day passes that Mrs Todd does not go down below and chats and gives comfort to all around her – so much for Baptists.

Monday, 12 November; Lat. 38.38°; Long. 1.40°; Ther. 17°C; Bar. 30 4/10

Another 24 hours of nearly dead calm, having made little more than 40 miles since 12 o'clock yesterday. Weather during the day hot in the sun, but the air is cold or at least bracing, while at night it is no longer comfortable to be on deck after 9 or 10 o'clock.

During an hour in the day when a slight puff came up, sent up the kite I made and F and I at 80 yards had some pipping at her – in 12 shots however, we only put 4 balls thro her. The fine weather keeping away all kinds of birds from the ship, except now and then when a stray albatross comes sailing past us, on which occasions we are always ready to give him a salute as he passes. Whales seen every day within a mile of the ship, but still no whalers heave in sight or ships of any kind. All our patients recovering; the 2nd again on duty.

Tuesday, 13 November; Ther. 17°C; Bar. 30 5/10

This completes our 9 weeks of ploughing the deep, and as things now

are going, another 9 weeks may pass over our heads 'ere we see New Zealand. Since 12 o'clock the ship has been actually laying like a log in the water, with the exception now and then a cats paw of a breeze, which lasts but an hour and drives us on a few miles. The whole distance made being 30 miles. At seven o'clock this morning when they were bracing up the yards, the main top gallant yard gave a crack and when examined was found to have sprung just at the slings and in consequence it was obliged to be taken down. The carpenter and all hands are now at work at one of our spare spars, getting another yard made which

Searching for stowaways, (Illustrated London News, 6/7/1850.)

is expected to be ready by six o'clock this evening. Had this happened during a breeze of wind, we should run the risk of losing the sail and perhaps causing other damage, besides endangering the lives of some of the crew, had they happened to be on or near the yard at the time.

Had another piece of poetry dedicated to me by our Poet Laureate in answer to the piece of doggerel I tipped him a few days ago. A decided piece of flirtation is being carried on by the Captn Stewart and Miss Pills, which accords much amusement to us all.

Wednesday 14 November; Ther. 16°C; Bar. 30 4/10

Breeze somewhat increased but still very light and baffling. Appearances of making a long voyage every day increasing and in consequence all hopes of

arriving at Otago by New Years Day nearly given up. Being nearly unable to hold a pen in my hand, owing to a bad cut in my fore finger which is now festering and giving me fearful pain. A week or ten days of my log will be necessarily cut very short. But as all things on board are going quite smooth, there is little chance that in this interval there would be much for me to say.

Thursday 15 November; Ther. 15°C; Bar. 30 4/10

Winds still light and making but little way. Smooth sea and clear sky, with beautiful nights. Great many whales seen during the day. Weather cold and chilly.

Friday 16 November; Ther. 14°C; Bar. 30 4/10

No change in the weather except that it seems to be getting colder and colder. All sail set, but making very little way owing to our steering as close to the wind as possible to keep to the south – the wind being from the East S East. Few birds seen about the ship for some days past.

Friday 16 November; Ther. 15°C; Bar. 30 4/10

Rather a better breeze today, but still doing little good. The atmosphere pleasant and general in the sun, but cold at nights. A heavy sea running and ship rolling a great deal, and most of the folk sick again.

Saturday 17 November; Lat. 36.12°; Long. 13.29°; Ther. 16°C; Bar. 20.4

Breeze rather freshening, but being from the South East and by East, we have to sail as close to the wind as we can, to run our course East and by South. Fell in with several outward bounders at last and passed them all in first rate style. One large ship astern a long way seemed to be doing her utmost to get up with us, but we run her hull down before the 24 hours were out. Wind fresh but carrying all sail – heavy sea still running.

Sunday 18 November; *Lat. 36.42°; Long. 17.21°; Ther. 17°C; Bar. 20.3*

Made a fair run of it during the last 24 hours, altho close hauled and with heavy head sea. Atmosphere getting warmer again, but still far from being the least oppressive. Barometer inclined to fall, which betokens either a change of wind or a gale or both. Finger very very bad.

Monday 19 November; *Lat. 37°; Long. 20.54°; Ther. 18°C; Bar. 30.2*

As the skipper expected, the wind has chopped round to the North West and is blowing half a gale if not more, and the Bar. still showing indication of falling. We are getting the ship snug, ready to meet it. Made a fair run of it during the last 24 hours, and our hopes of getting on now increased. Considerable sea running but the wind being now abaft or on our quarter, we feel it less. Nearly going mad with the pain occasioned by my festered finger.

Tuesday 20 November; *Lat. –; Long.– Ther. 19°C; Bar. 29.3*

Last night about 5 o'clock it began to thicken all around us and every moment the wind was increasing into a regular gale. By 7 o'clock it almost blew a hurricane, with a fearful sea running and the ship rolling most tre-

mendously. Shortly after having reduced our canvas to double reefed topsails, the sheet of the mizen topmast gave way and down the yard hurled upon the poop, luckily doing no damage to any one. This was the first mishap we had met with in the way of tackle giving way, but in a little time, all was repaired and so we continued to scud before the gale, pretty snug, but ship rolling more than ever as the sea increased.

About midnight a heavy sea came right over the poop, knocking down to the ground our first mate like a bullock who narrowly escaped being washed overboard.

The gale kept on until towards daylight, when it moderated a little, this enabling us to shake a reef out of our main topsail. The ship began to go a little steadier, but still rolling much. Towards 8 o'clock, the sky began to clear and the wind fall every minute until towards midday, when it died away into nearly a calm but still leaving a heavy sea running.

This is the first real gale of wind we have had since we left Scotland. On the whole our good ship weathered it right well. As might be expected, no one on board managed to get much sleep during the past night but this was soon forgotten when morning shewed we were well out of the storm. As this gale has proved a fresh incident in this monotonous journal of mine, I have with the greatest difficulty owing to my festered finger managed to enter the

particulars of it, hoping there may not be another of the same quality to mention. In taking our midday observations today the Capt was surprised that notwithstanding the strong gale of last night, he found the ship had only run some 200 miles during the last 24 hours, which he could only account for by there being a strong current against us, which also accounted for the heavy sea met with.

Wednesday 21 November; *Ther. 17°C; Bar. 19.5*

The calm which I mentioned having set in after the gale of the preceding night, lasted until about 2 o'clock when a steady breeze from the west sprung up, enabling us to set all sail again, with every prospect of our having at last fallen in with the right kind of wind for us – the current also setting in from the west.

Shortly after midday, observed a sail a long way ahead of us which was the signal for our skipper setting every rag of canvas he could on the ship, in order to come up with our friend ahead. Before it got dark, came within signalling distance, when we experienced some very neat work performed between the two vessels in this marine style of telegraphing. We ascertained by signals that the vessel's name was the *Recorder*, 74 days out from Liverpool and bound for Calcutta. We being in our 69th day, thus beating her by only 5 days. By half past 4 o'clock this morning, we came right up with her and got so close as to carry on a conversation without the aid of a speaking trumpet. All we had made out the previous evening by signals was confirmed to us, thus shewing how accurately this kind of work can be managed. As 12 o'clock struck, she was 5 or 6 miles astern of us, and I have bet with 2nd mate a glass of grog that by tomorrow at 6 o'clock she is nowhere, he asserting that she will be visible. Time will shew. Weather now fine but blowing an 8 and 9 knots breeze – cold but not disagreeably so. A good look out ahead is being kept at night now in case of falling in with icebergs, altho we are hardly in the season for such customers.

Thursday 22 November; *238 miles*

Continuing to have my hand next to disabled, it is with the greatest difficulty and pain that I can keep up my daily notes of what occurs on board.

Steerage passengers having a rather disturbed cup of tea. Although this scene was drawn much later in the century, the situation is timeless. (Illustrated London News, 12/2/1887)

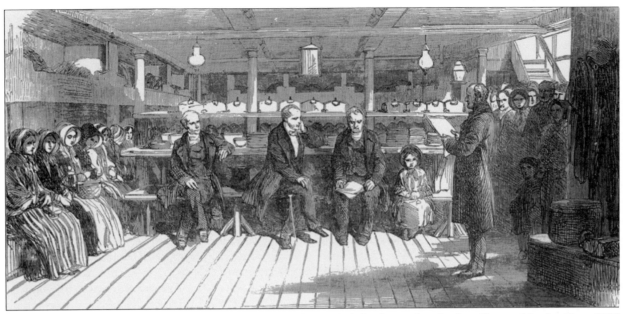

Single women on the Madagascar being lectured, probably on moral rectitude, before leaving from London. (Illustrated London News, 1853)

After the fine morning we had, up to 12 o'clock, a thick drizzling rain commenced and with it came fresher the breeze. Before four, had to take in a little sail, but still cracking with our top gallant sails unreefed. Towards midnight it blew in gusts most fearfully again, snapping in two our new main top gallant yard – which, happening while we were in bed, created much alarm amongst the passengers – the sail flapping in the wind like thunder. Getting the broken yard down and sails secured was very neatly managed, and by daylight all was found pretty snug, barring the want of the wing we lost.

Won my bet with the 2nd mate about not seeing the vessel this morning, the gale of the preceding night having much assisted us. We are now running down for the Island of St Pauls, which, being direct in our course, we are likely to sight – hope we shan't do as we did with Tristan d'Acunha. Run since 12 o'clock 220 miles – very heavy sea was running all night – cold wind from the south.

Friday 23 November; Ther. 17°C; 246 miles

Fine weather again, but breeze sufficiently stiff, and altho in our favour, prevents our setting royals or studding sails. Sea much gone down and in consequence the ship has made the best run we have had since we left.

At daylight this morning a sail was seen ahead on our larboard bow, and by the aid of our telescope made her out to be a Dutchman bound probably for Batavia.

Busy getting a new top gallant yard made – until it is made, we cannot hope to gain much upon our friends ahead. It is not likely we shall be ready with it until tomorrow.

Weather again mild and very pleasant, the wind having shipped round from the freezing South to the balmy north – so much for change of hemispheres. All hands on board in good health except one 2nd cabin lady passenger, a Miss Bell, who is threatened with a very serious complaint on account of its having carried several of her family, something wrong with her liver. She is an old spinster, so if she does go, there [...].

Saturday 24 November; Ther. 18°C; 170 miles

Magnificent weather, and warm enough to be on deck without greatcoats. Wind all light, and carrying all sail, having just got up our new main topgallant yard. The Dutchman ahead of us nearly out of sight, having gained much upon us during the night as we were obliged to shorten sail on account of our mishap.

A great many birds kept flying about the ship when we took some of the usual sport with the rifle – a shoal of bottle nose whales this morning passed close to us, but not having our rifles ready, we lost a fine chance of giving one that came right under our stern a shot in the eye.

Doctor getting more unpopular every day and hardly anyone now paying him the common civility of speaking to either him or any of his family – his

conduct to the poor people below too, disgusts all hands.

Sunday 25 November; Lat. 38.52°; Long. 44.50°; Ther. 18°C; Bar. 30; 171 miles

From 12 o'clock yesterday to about 8 in the evening, very light winds ending nearly in a dead calm, the latter lasting about an hour. About 9 however, the wind went round to the N West and shortly after it freshened up into a nice 7 and 8 knots breeze and continued so throughout the night, freshening in the morning as the sun rose into a stiff breeze or half a gale – causing us to lower our royals and take in our studding sails.

On getting on deck this morning, the Dutchman was seen on our weather bow not far ahead and by twelve we were abreast and passing her fast. When bearing down upon us a little, we backed topsails in order to let him come up and hear what he had to say. From his having no signals on board, he put out a board ahead with his longitude, which showed us he wanted to compare notes with. Doing the same thing by him. He hoisted his ensign to shew that he was obliged to us. We then hoisted our flag with the Mooltan on it, and on a board wrote in large letters with chalk, "Report us", which he led us to understand he would do by hoisting and lowering his ensign 3 times – which act of politeness we returned. And then each held on their course again the Dutchman going fast astern. She was a very fine vessel, but did not carry one half of the sail we did, otherwise I suspect we might have had a tough job to keep company with her. To shew the difference, she is now merely under topsails and courses, while we have our topsails, topgallant sails and royals, with studding sails set – which however keeps our ship nearly on our beam ends, making it very uncomfortable for moving about on deck.

No church today, owing to it being impossible for the Parson and congregation to stand on their feet and perhaps it would not be decent to do so on our heads.

Monday 26 November; *Lat., Long. – No Sun; Ther. 18ºC; Bar. 29.9; 242 miles*

Been blowing hard and squally for the last 24 hours. Ship running under double reefed topsails – but no great sea on. Weather thick and hazy with occasional showers as the squalls came on. Been running 10 knots fully since 12 yesterday, and as the glass is going down, every appearance of this gale continuing.

Fell in this morning with two other ships besides our old friend the Dutchman who had made with us during the night – but he is now going astern. The other two ships, from the thickness of the weather, we cannot well enough make out except that one of them is also a Dutchman, probably going to the same destination as the other one. These two new craft however seem to be fully our match in the sailing way, as thro the haze we made out they were both rather going ahead of us. For the first time meeting anything that could keep company with us – our Capt rather down in the mouth at the event.

Not getting the sun today, no exact bearings could be taken but by dead reckoning we must have run fully 250 miles – wind being from the north and ship steering nearly due south course. No sickness on board except the spinster with the bilious fever, but she is as yet in no great danger.

Tuesday 27 November; *Lat. 39.56º; Long. 55º; Ther. 18ºC; Bar. 29.7; 243 miles*

The gale of yesterday still continuing, having blown great guns during the night. Ship on her beam ends nearly, but sea comparatively smooth with a nasty drizzling rain obscuring the sky in toto, and a falling barometer.

This morning, nothing was seen of the three vessels we were in company with yesterday, but when the weather clears up it is not unlikely we may see them again, as they are evidently steering the same course as ourselves, probably to make the Island of St. Pauls which ought to be some 7 or 800 miles right ahead of us.

When in bed last night, a sea came right over the poop and, not having the outer port closed, the water came slosh into my window which is not a very close one and gave me a jolly good wetting. Got up and managed to get my port closed but the mischief being done, I had a most uncomfortable night of it.

William no longer in the cabin, as having taken offence at something the Captain said in joke while waiting at table, he took offence and like a fool has asked for his steerage rations which he will find a bad change after his having had the pickings of the cabin fair. Green horns however must pay the penalty of having a little experience of the world. Run during the last 48 hours, 487 miles, which is not bad going.

Wednesday 28 November; *Lat., Long., – No sun; Ther. 17ºC; Bar. 29.5; 268 miles*

The strong gale of the two preceding days still blowing, accompanied with rain and thick heavy weather. From 11 to 12 last night, it blew so strong that we [...] it was the next thing to double reefing the

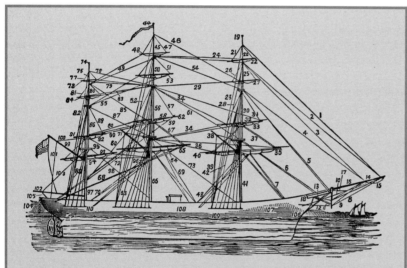

Sailing ship rigging and spars

1 fore royal stay; 2 flying jib stay; 3 fore topgallant stay; 4 jib stay; 5 fore topmast stays; 6 fore stays; 7 fore tacks; 8 flying martingale; 9 martingale stay, shackled to dolphin striker; 10 jib guys; 11 jumper guys; 12 back ropes; 13 bobstays; 14 flying jib boom; 15 flying jib footropes; 16 jib boom; 17 job footropes; 18 bowsprit; 19 fore truck; 20 fore royal mast; 21 fore royal lift; 22 fore royal yard; 23 fore royal backstays; 24 fore royal braces; 25 fore topgallant yard; 26 foretopgallant lift; 27 fore-topgallant yard; 28 fore topgallant backstays; 29 fore topgallant braces; 30 fore topmast and rigging; 31 fore topsail lift; 32 fore topsail yard; 33 fore topsail footropes; 34 fore topsail braces; 35 fore yard; 36 fore brace; 37 fore lift; 38 fore gaff; 39 fore trysail vangs; 40 fore topmast studding-sail boom; 41 foremast and rigging; 42 fore topmast backstays; 43 fore sheets; 44 main truck and pennant; 45 main royal mast and backstay; 46 main royal stay; 47 main royal lift; 48 main royal yard; 49 main royal braces; 50 main topgallant mast and rigging; 51 main topgallant lift; 52 main topgallant backstays; 53 main topgallant yard; 54 main topgallant stay; 55 main topgallant braces; 56 main topmast and rigging; 57 topsail lift; 58 topsail yard; 59 topsail footropes; 60 topsail braces; 61 topmast stays; 62 main topgallant studding-sail boom; 63 main topmast backstay; 64 main yard; 65 main footropes; 66 mainmast and rigging; 67 main lift; 68 main braces; 69 main tacks; 70 main sheets; 71 main trysail gaff; 72 main trysail vangs; main stays; 74 mizzen truck; 75 mizzen royal mast and rigging; 76 mizzen royal stay; 77 mizzen royal lift; 78 mizzen royal yard; 79 mizzen royal braces; 80 mizzen topgallant mast and rigging; 81 mizzen topgallant lift; 82 mizzen topgallant backstays; 83 mizzen topgallant braces; 84 mizzen topgallant yard; 85 mizzen topgalland stay; 87 mizzen topmast and rigging; 87 mizzen topmast stay; 88 mizzen topsail lift; 89 mizzen topmast backstays; 90 mizzen topsail braces; 91 mizzen topsail yard; 92 mizzen topsail footropes; 93 crossjack yard; 94 crossjack footropes; 95 crossjack lift; 96 crossjack braces; 97 mizzenmast and rigging; 98 mizzen stay; 99 spanker gaff; 100 peak halyards; 101 spanker vangs; 102 spanker boom; 103 spanker boom topping lift; 104 jacob's ladder, or stern ladder; 105 spanker sheet; 106 cutwater; 107 starboard bow; 108 starboard beam; 109 water line; 110 starboard quarter; 111 rudder.

tiller sail we had set, but our skipper who was on deck all night, let her drive thro it at all hazards.

Altogether it was the most uncomfortable night I have passed since I came on board for, being on the weather side, and having shipped several tremendous seas, the water poured into my cabin like a mill dam thro a badly made port and wet thro my bed and bedding in such a manner that I had to get up and dress and lay myself down on top of my trunks and thus pass the night. To make matters worse – with every roll of the vessel, down I went on the wet floor, and lay there till I had courage to rise again. In the morning got a brazier into my cabin and heating it till it was nearly red hot; managed to get my things all dried again.

Nothing more seen of the ships we were in company with the preceding days. Nor are we now likely to see them again. Towards midday, the rain came down in torrents, and with it a sudden change of wind from the west north west. But as the glass is not yet rising, this may be only a lull. It is not impossible the gale may recommence again as strong as ever from the old quarter, say from the north. South winds in these latitudes bringing with them always clear cold weather with a high barometer – neither of which there is as yet the slightest indication.

Nothing occurring on board, as from its having been impossible to keep your feet on the decks, all the people kept quietly below. The fastest sailing we have yet got out of our ship was last night at the height of the gale which was 12 knots an hour. Wind on the beam, with merely reefed topsails and mainsail set. Atmosphere cold and damp owing to the

rain, altho the thermometer still keeps up at 17 and 18 more or less with little variation night or day. All chance of sighting St. Pauls now completely gone as we are nearly 3 degrees to the south of it. By dead reckoning, the Capt makes out that the ship must have run at least 270 miles during the last 24 hours.

Thursday 29 November; Ther. 16°C; Bar. 29.5; 143 miles

From 12 o'clock to midnight yesterday, very light winds from the north west and north, when it freshened into a six knot breeze and has continued so until now. Weather cold, thick and hazy, with occasional rain, and from the glass still going down, we are looking out for another gale.

Sea much smoother however than we have had it for a week past. In consequence we all passed a very pleasant night except perhaps myself, as my bed I found was still damp from the preceding night's wet work.

Our sick spinster got up today for the first time since her illness, and is now "as well as can be expected" – meaning no offence to her virtue.

A sail seen from the mast head far to windward, but being so distant, can't make out if she is one of our friends we were in company with a couple of days back. A whale today came within nearly rifle shot of the ship and spouted his dirty water almost in our faces. A few yards nearer, and F and I would have tickled his spare fat with a couple of leaden bullets with which we were ready to serve him.

Friday 30 November; Lat. 41.10°; Long. 63.48°; Ther. 16°C; 180 miles

As expected, about 3 o'clock yesterday, observed some ugly looking black clouds gathering on the horizon right astern of us and not many minutes after, we saw the white foam of the sea rolling along after us at a tremendous pace. Bar. down to 20.4 – the word was hardly given for letting go the halyards of the royals, topgallant sails, when it was right down upon us. In the course of quarter of an hour, we were running before it under bare poles, but not before our main royal was blown to shivers. Altogether this was the severest gale while it lasted which we have had, and had it come in the night, some of our topsails must have gone. In the course of an hour it seemed to have done its worst. When the double-reefed fore and main topsails were set and away, she ran before it like lightning.

About 5, the sky began to clear and the gale settled down into a steady 9 and 10 knot breeze from the south west, which is the best wind we could have – all sail was got upon the ship by seven, and we then had one of the most beautiful clear moonlight nights I ever beheld; the air however cold and bracing. The moon having commenced her 3rd quarter last night, we are in hopes this breeze will last us for a week at least, when please God we may expect to shew another long line upon our chart again.

When the gale came on and all the sails let go, there was a dreadful panic took place amongst all the people below, as from the noise of the sails flapping and the wind and sea roaring, they at first thought it was all over with the ship. On rushing on deck however they (the men), behaved

(Illustrated London News, 19/7/1852)

very well, having joined at once in assisting the sailors to haul upon the ropes – in this way doing right good service.

Sea today much gone down, and the barometer commenced rising immediately after the gale was over. A good barometer to a sailor is the best friend he has after his compass.

During the last 8 days we have run no less than 1721 miles, which averages 215 miles a day. Weather being now beautifully clear and bracing. It was all hands to get up the luggage and a pretty work there, with all the people diving into the hidden recesses of their trunks, lugging out the goods and chattels they wanted.

To our sorrow and amazement, the first mate informed us that the ship's stock of brandy was clean run out, as also the oil, or the latter nearly so. The Capt has therefore asked if I would

Saturday 1 December; *Lat. 41.39°; Long. 72.3°; Ther. 18°C; Bar. 30.1; 203 miles*

Splendid weather continuing. Wind from the north west and all sail set, ship having been running over 8 knots an hour since 12 yesterday. The three last days have been perhaps, taken them all in all, the finest we have had since leaving Scotland – the air being clear bracing, and in the sun sufficiently warm for comfort.

By today's calculations and the present wind continuing, we make out that by Monday morning we will be abreast of the Island of St. Pauls, and to the southward of it about 180 miles. The Capt. now wishing to sight Van Dieman's land, for the sake of his chronometer. We are now steering nearly a due east course, being not far off the parallel of latitude of that Island. If all goes well we ought to make land by the

The second mate and doctor today had a regular blow up between them, the former giving his mind to him in a way that could not have been very palatable. But the poor Devil is so badgered by every one on board, that by this time he ought to be well used to it. To shew the hypocrisy of this Santa famiglia, as the Doctor's family have been dubbed by me, we have discovered that to make up for the water they drink before us at dinner, they have a regular supply of wine sent into their private cabins, of which they must partake right cheerily, by the steward's account of it. The Doctor and I have never spoken since the row we had during the cholera panic and I am only waiting for his giving me a chance of pulling his nose, which he takes good care not to do by never opening his mouth while I am present, except perhaps in a very sotto voce tone to his nearest neighbour at the dinner table.

Shot an albatross today with ball, after however missing a good many shots.

Sunday 2 December; *Lat. 41.57°; Long. 75.26°; Ther. 18°C; Bar. 30.1; 145 miles; differ from Greenwich time 5 hours 5 mins*

Another beautiful day and another Sunday round. Wind however has been rather lighter, and in consequence have not made up our daily 200 miles. Still we are, or ought to be, well satisfied our run from the Cape – on the chart shewing a track as if it had been drawn with a ruler. As usual in fine weather, Church service performed on deck, the Doctor reading a sermon, luckily not of his own composition.

Monday 3 December; *Lat. 41.55°; Long. 79.46°; Ther. 17°C; Bar. 29.8; 191 miles*

Shortly after 12 o'clock yesterday, until 6, the wind seemed inclined to die away altogether but towards 6 it sprang up again from the Northwest, and blew a nice stiff 8 and 9 knot breeze, increasing towards night into as much as we wanted. Ship going all night 10 knots to 10 and a half knots.

The glass shewing symptom of falling – an eye is kept to windward in order to shorten sail if too much for us. This morning was colder than we have had it for some time back, but still the air is bracing and on the whole very agreeable. A finer run from the Cape

Emigrant ship at Port Lincoln, South Australia. (Illustrated London News, 1848)

dispose of a part of the Wilson dips to them at my own price, which of course I am ready to do, thus bringing part of the dips to an early and good market.

The brandy affair is not so easily remedied, but we must just do the best we can without it. During the cholera, a greater quantity of the ship's brandy was consumed than of course could have been calculated upon, owing to our stupid homeopathic idiot of a doctor not supplying the people with what was shipped as medical stores.

17 or 18 of the month, which would leave us 12 or 13 days to run on to New Zealand, thus be there by new year's day – the great aim of our ambition.

No sickness of any consequence now on board with the exception of the Cabin Cook who is in a very sickly state, but at best was always a poor weak kind of creature. My sore finger on the mend, but I have suffered dreadfully from it and at one time was so much alarmed by a curious kind of swelling in both my hands and arms as well as feet. But this too is now taking off again.

perhaps no ship ever had than ours, which fully makes up for the calms and baffling winds we had between the Cape de Verde Islands and the Line.

Passed the island of St Pauls during the night – now considerably to the Eastwards of it. A great many of the whale birds (a description of bird that is said to follow and feed upon what the whales spout up) were flying about in all directions, but no whales have been observed. Albatrosses are not so plentiful as they were, but Cape hens are still in abundance, and some days also the Cape pigeon. Nothing new going on on board except some more thefts taking place between decks amongst the emigrants – but the man that does it is well known, altho as yet he has not been fairly detected in the act.

Tuesday 4 December; Lat. 42.13°; Long. 85.14°; Ther. 18°C; Bar. 29.3; 247 miles

The barometer after midday yesterday, continued falling and falling until it reached 29.3 at the same hour today, which was 8/10 since Sunday. In consequence, as night approached, the ship was put under courses and topsails, from having a few hours before been carrying every stitch of canvas that could be clapped on her. By ten it was blowing a strong gale of wind, the scud flying over the moon like wildfire. The sea too kept increasing fast, and during the night shipped some very heavy seas, some of which tried hard to break in at my cabin window, but having taken the precaution to have the outer port well secured and caulked, no water got in. The wind being right aft, managed to keep a fair quantum of sail on the ship all night, which kept her running before it at the rate of ten knots an hour throughout the 24 hours. But occasionally she gave some tremendous rolls, nearly pitching us right out of our berths.

The glass seems now to have become stationary, so we are in hopes of having seen the worst of the gale. Weather thick and hazy, with occasional heavy squalls accompanied with rain, which, with the seas every now and then breaking over us, keeps the decks almost floating.

In weather of this kind I generally take to my bed and pass the time in reading, as to attempt doing so in the cabin with the thousand children roaring and rolling about in every direction,

would be a most endless task. A young girl trying to cross the deck with a child in her arms was thrown down this morning, with a thundering crash which sent the child spinning to the lee side of the ship as if it had been shot out of a gun. But strange to say, it escaped with little injury, as also did the girl, barring her bones pretty well bruised. Considering how tender our ship is, causing her at times to be nearly on her beam ends, it is wonderful how we all have hitherto escaped

the 2nd mate, whose watch it was, was standing on the poop. The ship giving a roll that nearly laid her on her beam ends, one of the hencoops broke loose and came rattling down to the lee side upon the mate, and nearly broke his leg. By a miracle, however, he escaped with a very severe bruising – the effects he is now feeling not a little.

The sea now rather going down, and we are in hopes the worst is over. But the rain falls fast, and altogether it is a most

Double decker ship taking emigrants from Skye to America. Double decker ships did not carry emigrants to New Zealand, but they did take emigrants to Australia in the early 1850s. Some of these vessels were badly hit by disease, and were known as 'fever ships'. The worst case was the Tichonderoga, which carried 811 passengers, of whom 97 died on board, and another 80 in the shore quarantine station at Port Nepean, Victoria. The disease was typhus. Most of the early vessels to Otago carried less than 140 people. (Illustrated London News, 15/1/1853)

broken bones, for a verity the number that has kissed the decks since we left, has not been trifling.

Wednesday 5 December; Lat., Long. – No sun; Ther. 17°C; Bar. 29.6

Immediately after 12 o'clock yesterday, the glass began to rise gently, or at least it shewed no symptom of falling further until 11 last night, when it was 29.5 and now stands at 29.6. The gale however did not begin to take off until 7 or 8 this morning, and even then, it was as much as we could to carry our topsails unreefed.

During the night, the sea ran tremendously high, breaking over the ship every now and then with fearful fury, making her stagger as if she had gone bump up against a rock. At half past 11,

disagreeable day. Very cold and damp, and so hazy that no observation could be taken. By the log however, we must have run some 240 miles, or not far off it – are now beginning to calculate that we may sight Van Diemen's land some 12 days or 14 days hence, leaving other 10 or 11 days to get into Otago. The distance being some 2600 from the former and 3800 from the latter place.

We have now been kept pretty much within doors for the last 4 days, which is rather trying, accustomed as we have been hitherto to be all day on deck. Mr Todd, Ferguson and hon. moi have managed to get hold of a backgammon board, and we have now regular battles at it. We only thought of this recourse on account of the Dr trying to prevent the people below playing, which was the signal for our introducing the game into the Cabin – which no doubt shocks his imbecile ideas on the subject of religion. Had he said a word to us on the subject, I would have been the first to pull his nose for it and no mistake.

Thursday 6 December; *Lat. 42.44°; Long. 95.11°; Ther. 16°C; Bar. 29.6; 455 miles during the last 2 days*

After midday yesterday, the sea gradually continued falling, as also the wind into a 8 knot breeze, but the weather continuing still thick and hazy, and the Capt., fearing a sudden change of wind, little sail was kept on the ship all night. It was only this morning at daylight that we began to crack on sail upon her again, when it became beautifully clear, but still blowing a stiff breeze from the west north west. Ship making 8 to 9 knots.

For the last 2 days, lost sight of the Cape pigeons, and the albatrosses are also getting very scarce. Hard work going on at the backgammon board every day between Ferguson Todd and myself, which has become our new chief amusement.

Today at dinner we were thinking how cold and uncomfortable the weather must be in old Scotland, and I con-

fess I thought much how perhaps my dear mother might be suffering from the cold easterly winds prevailing with you at this season. May God grant, however, she may have escaped her acute cold, and that you may have an early and favourable spring.

Nothing been going on in the ship today worth noticing further than that we are all well, except the cook still ailing very much, and looking forward with hope that our voyage after all is to be a sufficiently speedy one.

Willie occupies himself in his spare hours casting me a lot of balls, to have a stock on hand for New Zealand, if it pleases God that we arrive there in safety. All this comes from our skipper cracking on too much in his anxiety to make a quick run of it, to get up the name of his new ship.

Today we felt it colder than perhaps any day since we have been on board. Cook getting around again and everyone else in good health. Capt expressed his regret to me today in having given offence to Willie, but I told him the boy was a fool and he punishes himself enough for his folly, in having to live upon the

steerage fare instead of the Cabin down.

Sunday 9 December; *Lat. 43.44°; Long. 108.58°; Ther. 14°C; Bar. 29.3; 407 miles in two days; diff. of Greenwich time 7 hours & 3/4*

The breeze of yesterday still continuing and at times blowing half a gale from the North West. Bar. down to 3/10 and still falling, with rain and thick weather. The sun however luckily breaking thro the clouds at twelve, were enable to take an observation, shewing that we had run 407 miles during the last 48 hours.

Ship under double reefed topsails, and all snug for worse weather, should it still come. In these latitudes, the prevailing winds are from the west, drawing occasionally round to the north and northwest bringing wet and squally weather. After blowing hard from this quarter a day or two, it almost invariably chops round to the south and south west, when the atmosphere becomes clear and bracing – exactly as it does at home, reversing the case. The southwest wind corresponding with the north wind at home.

No church on deck but down below, after which the Doctor has his extra psalm singing in his own cabin with his baptist friends.

■

Emigrants setting sail from England, (Illustrated London News, 19/7/1852)

List of passengers who sailed on the Mooltan

CHIEF CABIN

Ferguson, William, gentleman (25) [gentleman settler, Molyneux; m. Miss Rattray]

McAdam, Caroline, spinster (39) [Anderson's Bay]

Oatts, Henry*, gentleman (30), Ann*, wife (25), Ann* (4), Maurice* (10 months)

Pillans, Francis S, gentleman (38) [gentleman settler, Molyneux]

Purdie, William, surgeon (52) [doctor, local government involvement, Dunedin], Elizabeth, wife (36), Margaret (15) [d.], Jessie D (9) [d.], William (7), Henry (6), Jane (3) [m. – Gibron; Ashley Downs], David (1) [bank clerk], Elizabeth† (2 months)

Todd, Alexander, accountant (46) [ag.; Anderson's Bay; E. Taieri], his wife (37), Cornelius (16) [ag.; Cave Valley], James (14) [ag.; Cave Valley], Jessie (8) [m.], Archibald (6), Alexander (3), William (2)

FORE-CABIN

Bell, Alison H, spinster (36) [dressmaker d.]

Blackie, William, shipmaster (45) [ag. Caversham and Taieri], Jane, wife (36) [Second marriage to James Forrest, ag. E. Taieri], William (11) [Caversham], John (9) [m. Miss McLeod; Caversham], Mary Jane (6), Jessie (4) [m. Johnson; farmer; Taieri], Catherine (2 months)

Clemison, Plumpton, gentleman, (29) [Sawyer's Bay, m. Mary Peterson, Mooltan] (Clemison was originally to travel on to Wellington, but instead stayed in Dunedin.)

Doig, Andrew, farmer (21) [Green Island, d.]

McDougall, Thomas, farmer (26)

McGibbon, John, grocer (40) [grocer; ag. Mataura; d. 1892], Jane, wife (30) [Mataura], Thomas (9) [storekeeper; ag. Mataura], Jessie (6) [Mataura], Jeannie (3) [d. 1886], John (5 months) [storekeeper; ag. Gore]

McGibbon, Marg.+, spinster (24)

STEERAGE (FULL FARE)

Beattie, Margaret, widow (67)

Beattie, Mary, niece of Margaret (12) [m. John Duncan; Corner Bush]

Gilchrist, Isabella, widow (34) [dressmaker; m. R Miller]

Hall, Margaret, spinster (30) [m. Daniel Macandrew; went to Aberdeen]

Harrison, Peter†, gentleman (45); Martha†, wife (25), Harriet (6) [m. Joseph Martin, bootmaker], Joseph (5), Edward (4), William (2), Clorinda† (6 months)

McGregor, Daniel, joiner (21), Magdalen, wife (21)

Perkins, George†, gentleman (42), Catherine, wife (40), William (16) [ag.; Mataura; m. Mrs Reid (Pekin)], John H (13) [ag. Mataura; m. Miss Johnson], James (11) [d.], Charles (9) [d.], Catherine (6) [m. – Perkins; West Coast, Clorinda (4 months) [m. – McGregor]

Perkins, Mrs Snr, widow (70)

Peterson, Mrs Mary (42), [Anderson's Bay], Mary (18) [m. Plumpton Clemison (Mooltan); Sawyer's Bay], Rosanna (14); Jessie (12), Mina (9) [m. Frank Laing], Peter (7), Agnes† (5), Edward (3), Florence (6 months) [m. Frank Laing]

Proudfoot†, Mrs Jane, (25)

Smellie, William, gentleman (42)

STEERAGE (ASSISTED EMIGRANTS)

Aitcheson, William, groom (16) [grocer ag. Kaitangata]

Barr, Jean, servant (22) [d]

Barr, John, mason (47) [Wellington], Mrs Barr†, wife (48)

Beaton, Malcolm*, ploughman (25)

Bennie, Janet, servant (24)

Bissett, William, mason (22) [Molyneux], Agnes, wife (17)

Boyd, Alan, shepherd (29) [Runholder; Deep Stream]

Boyd, John, shepherd (35) [Deep Stream]

Cameron, Duncan, ploughman (24) [Halfway Bush]

The Mooltan passenger list is based mainly on the New Zealand Company's embarkation list, compiled at the beginning of the voyage and signed by the Mooltan's surgeon and captain. This was cross-referenced against a list of arrivals published in 1898 by Dr Hocken. There are discrepancies between the two lists, and in most cases the New Zealand Company version has been deferred to. Amendments have also been made based Dr Purdie's voyage report, and information from descendants of some Mooltan passengers (Bissett, Blackie, Boyd, Curle, Duncan, Kirkland, MacGibbon McNeil).

Hocken gave additional information about what some individuals did between their arrival in New Zealand, and 1898, when the book was printed. This information is included within square brackets. Hocken's occupations are included only if they have changed from those in the embarkation list. His abbreviations are: m. married; d. died;

ag. engaged in agricultural pursuits whether as a farm labourer, small farmer, or general labourer.

Individuals marked † died on the voyage. The total of 13 is two less than the figure published by other historians, but is considered to be accurate, as it is based directly on contemporary reports by Dr Purdie and New Zealand Company officials.

Two passengers mentioned in the Pillans voyage diary are absent. They include Captain Stewart and Miss Pills, who had been carrying on "...a decided piece of flirtation." These names may well be pseudonyms. Also absent from the list is a Mr R M McDowall, whose descriptions of aspects of the Mooltan voyage were published in the 1912 publication, Reminiscences of the early settlers of Dunedin and South Otago. Although McDowall's descriptions are couched partly in the first person, it seems he was actually passing on second-hand information.

Curle, John, labourer (27) [tinsmith; Mornington, d.], Elizabeth, wife (28), James (3) [m. Jane Matthews; Lookout Point]
Dick, Mary, servant (18)
Duncan, Agnes, servant (14)
Duncan, George, shepherd (23) [butcher, M.P.C.; San Francisco], Elspeth, wife (20)
Duncan, John Jr, labourer (20) [butcher, ag.; Corner Bush]
Duncan, John Snr, gardener (39) [labourer; N.E. Valley; d.], Mrs Duncan, wife (37), Henry (8) [goldminer; Waikouaiti], John (6) [brickmaker; N.E. Valley], William (2) [d.]
Ferguson, Donald, shepherd (32)
Gebbie, Alexander, agriculturalist (46) [teacher; East Taieri; ag. Saddle Hill; d.], Isabella, wife (38) [d.]
Gebbie, James, gardener (32) [N.E. Valley; St David St.], Mrs Gebbie, wife (33), James (3) [gardener; Oamaru], Jeannie† (1), John (three months) [Greymouth]
Grant, Alexander*, shepherd (28)
Kirkland, John, ploughman (34) [E. Taieri], Margaret†, wife (26), William (2), Agnes† (5 months)
Lumsden, Andrew, blacksmith (26) [Wellington]; Jane, wife (30)
McDonald, John, ploughman (24) [Wellington]
McIndoe, Ann, servant (17) [m. W Stevenson, Taieri]
McLachlan, Donald*, shepherd (32), Catherine*, wife (20)
McLachlan, Duncan, ship's carpenter (26)
McLay, Thomas, ploughman (29) [Waikouaiti; d.], Margaret, wife (28), John (8) [Waikouaiti], James (6) [Waikouaiti], Janet (4) [Waikouaiti], Mary (2) [Waikouaiti]

McMaster, Allan, ploughman (22) [labourer, farmer; Saddle Hill]; Jane, wife (22)
McMillan, Angus, ploughman (31) [shoemaker; Halfway Bush], Margaret, wife (19)
McMillan, Janet, servant (33)
McNeil, Alexander, blacksmith (26) [York Place; ag. Balclutha], Mary†, wife (24), Ann† (5), James (2), Mary (4 months)
McNeil, James, ploughman (46) [ferryman; ag. Balclutha]; Ann, wife (48), James Jr (22) [ag. Port Molyneux; m. Mary Chalmers (Stately)], George (18) [ag. Kaihiku; m. Jane McMaster], John (13) [ag.; mayor; Balclutha; m. Margaret Ayson, then H. Bannerman], Robert (11) m. Margaret McDonald [d. 1865]
McNeil, Margaret, servant (34)
Miller, David, millwright (18) [carpenter; Halfway Bush; Melbourne]
Nicholson, John*, shepherd (29)
Nicholson, Donald*, ploughman (23)
Sinclair, Georgiana, servant (28) [d.]
Sinclair, Grace (25) [m. W Miller, blacksmith; Invercargill]
Smith, Alexander, labourer (31) [farmer; Mosgiel; d.]; Jean, wife (27) [d.]
Steven, John Snr* (20), joiner
Steven, John Jnr*, flesher (20); Mary*, his wife (18)
Stewart, Alexander*, labourer (36) [Wellington], Isabella*, wife (38)
Torrance, Isabella, servant (14) [m. W Thomson; Maungatua]
Torrance, Margaret, servant (21) [m. – Culling; Mataura]
Wright, James, labourer (23), Mary, wife (33)

---

* Originally embarked for Dunedin, but carried on in the Mooltan to Wellington.   †Died during the voyage.
⁺It is not known if Margaret McGibbon was related to John and Jane McGibbon. She is listed in Reverend Burns' visitation book in 1850 as living in Rattray Street, married to Thos Matthew (probably Thomas Matthews, a fellmonger who arrived on the Blundell in July 1848), and living in Rattray Street. In 1856, Burns' book shows her living at the same address, but having left her husband. She had a child named Mary.

Category	Chief cabin		Fore-cabin		Steerage		Total	
	Male	Female	Male	Female	Male	Female	Male	Female
Married adults	3	3	2	2	22	23	27	28
Unmarried adults	4	2	3	2	18	18	25	22
Children 7 and under 14	1	2	3	0	8	3	12	5
Children 1 and under 7	5	2	0	4	11	7	16	13
Children under 1 year	1	1	1	1	1	5	3	7
Totals	14	10	9	9	60	56	83	74
	24		18		116		158	

Occupations given in the embarkation list include: ploughman 9, servant 9, shepherd 7, gentleman 6, labourer 5, blacksmith 2, farmer 2, gardener 2, mason 2; and one each for accountant, agriculturalist, flesher, grocer, groom, joiner, surgeon, joiner, millwright, ship's carpenter and shipmaster. Apart from the servants, all people who declared occupations were men. Most occupations were connected with farming.

Passenger deaths included two adult men, five adult women, two five year olds and four babies aged between three months and one year. Nine of the deaths were from cholera, two from 'Stomach and Bowels' and one each from 'Decline' and 'Hooping Cough'. The person who died of 'decline' was Agnes Kirkland, aged six months. Dr Purdie attributed her decline to a "change of diet" following the death (by cholera) of her mother, six days earlier.

GOING ABROAD
Part three: Otago

 # Contents

The early Otago newspapers were a valuable source of information about the early colony. They also yielded much information about the McGibbon family. Included are facsimile reproductions of many advertisements and editorial items, which chronicle local events and impart local flavour.

THE inhabitants of Dunedin and suburbs are respectfully informed that the subscriber has opened that Store corner of Princes and Rattray Streets, opposite the Royal Hotel, for the purpose of selling Tea, Earthenware, Ironmongery, Lamp Cotton, &c.
   The stock is warranted as very superior in quality, and requires only to be tested so as to insure future sales.
                    JOHN McGIBBON
Dunedin, 10th January, 1850.

Dunedin in 1849 – a view from Stafford Street painted by Charles Kettle, Chief Surveyor.

The McGibbon home farm, hacked out of the bush at Caversham.

Flesh on the bones of an ancestor

Placing flesh on the bones of an ancestor can be a difficult task, particularly if there are few bones to start with.

Before this investigation started, all that the McGibbon descendants knew about the family's early Dunedin period was:
• [Fact] The family arrived on the sailing ship Mooltan in 1849, and they lived in Caversham suburb.
• [Fact] They left Dunedin in a covered bullock wagon and moved south to Mataura at the end of 1858.
• [Fact] John and Jane McGibbon had existed as stolid images in a portrait gallery on the walls of the Otago Settlers Museum.

• [Legend] John had owned valuable land in Dunedin. He had been a business partner with the town's celebrated and sometimes notorious entrepreneur and politician, James Macandrew. Macandrew got into financial difficulties; McGibbon, as a loyal business partner, sold his land to raise funds to bail out Macandrew. Then, with his circumstances considerably reduced, McGibbon moved south to seek a new fortune.

It is hard to dig out much information about early pioneer ancestors unless they were major public figures. Even well-known people may have left little other than a series of public highlights. James Macandrew himself is a good example. His descendants have discovered huge information holes while trying to flesh out his life.

For lesser lights, the problem is greater. Determined investigation may add much to our knowledge, but there will still be many gaps. One way to close the gaps is to link known facts to knowledge of how others lived in the new colony. The aim is to get a feel for what life may have been like for the family – a broad picture that hopefully is not far from the truth.

To a degree, even this truth may be suspect, depending on your ancestor's social class. Most of the information that has come down to us about early colonial life originated with people from the educated and land-owning middle and upper classes. Such people, particularly if they were male, were more likely to have left traces of their lives beyond births, deaths, marriages, occupations and addresses. They may have left personal reminiscences, been written about by contemporaries and historians, have land records, been on electoral and jurors rolls, and been mentioned in newspapers.

Fortunately for McGibbon posterity, the family was of the land-owning middle classes, and it proved relatively easy – though very time consuming – to add greatly to the stock of knowledge of their early Dunedin life. Unfortunately, some of the new information begs further questions that will probably never be answered.

The family left no reminiscences of its Dunedin period. Their life in the town was briefly described in the 50th jubilee edition of the Otago Witness in 1898, and they are given fleeting mention by several historians. They feature in a number of inscrutable land records held by the National Archives. They show up in Reverend Burns' visitation book. The sum total of that information wouldn't add flesh to the bones of one leg.

Dunedin's newspapers of the 1850s. The Otago News began publication in December 1848, appearing once a fortnight, then once a week. The size was similar to a modern tabloid, and it was usually four pages long. The Otago Witness, a paper in the same format, took over in February 1851. Initially a weekly, it lasted until June 1932. The Otago Colonist first appeared in December 1856 and ceased publication in January 1863. Originally the same size as the Otago Witness, it later changed to broadsheet format.

Searching old newspapers

There was only one thing for it – see if there was anything in the newspapers of the time. There was no easy way to do this. Every newspaper published over the period had to be read for any mention of McGibbons. It was well worth the effort. After many, many hours in the Otago Settlers Museum and Alexander Turnbull Library, reading the Otago News, Otago Witness and Otago Colonist, the stock of knowledge on the subject expanded greatly, so that we now know that:

• The Mooltan's arrival was covered by the Otago News in some detail, and that the ship had been stricken with cholera during the voyage.

• John McGibbon was probably upset because the Otago News did not include his family in the Mooltan's cabin passenger list, and so, by inference, lumped them in with the anonymous "102 emigrants". Not a promising start when you paid extra to sail among the better classes!

• He set up in retail business almost immediately, on the corner of Princes and Rattray streets. From newspaper advertisements we get a good idea of the nature of his business.

• He later sold the business and became a wholesaler/importer of starch, and probably other household goods.

• He had a wife called 'Mrs John McGibbon', who gave birth to unnamed sons at the family home, 'Ambresbeg', in Caversham Vale.

• He was involved in his local Caversham community – repairing roads and agitating for a school.

• He was on committees which helped regulate and oversee use of public farmland surrounding Dunedin.

• He was a prime mover in setting up a public market in Dunedin.

• He was involved in politics, though apparently not as a candidate. He publicly supported candidates from the Free Church Establishment faction – including heavyweights like Cargill and Macandrew.

• His home in Caversham was a centre for political activity in Dunedin's Eastern District. It was a polling place for several elections, and used for at least one major political dinner.

• He sold land and livestock.

• He was inclined to lose animals and had to advertise for their return.

• He was a moderate public figure – undoubtedly one of the town's gentlemen, though his place was in the background, compared with Dunedin's big names. But he did rub shoulders with those 'names'.

• He was associated with James Macandrew in some political and business situations.

• No direct business partnership with Macandrew showed up (and nor was it evident from any other information source). The family legend could neither be proved nor disproved.

Facsimiles

Another reason for scouring the old newspapers was to get a feel for what the community in general was reading, talking about and doing. A selection of this material is reproduced on the following pages, in facsimile form.

The facsimile section captures the flavour of the times more vividly than after-the-event descriptions by historians, but readers should note that it is an unreliable record. There is not enough space in this book to include all significant events of the eight year period, and in any case, newspapers did not report everything of importance. In particular, they were very lax about 'following up' stories. The newspapers showed a great deal of editorial

bias, and they catered mostly for the activities and interests of the wealthier part of the community.

It could be argued that day-to-day life in the community was better represented by advertisements than editorial columns. The humblest ploughman and his family had to feed and clothe themselves and buy utensils and implements. But the advertising record doesn't tell everything, because of the high proportion of barter trade which went on in the early years. After a year or two, people

Images of John and Jane McGibbon, from the Otago Settlers' Museum portrait gallery. As with other early settlers in the Otago section of this book, these portraits were taken much later in life. During the 1850s, most Dunedin settlers were in their 20s and 30s. John and Jane McGibbon were a little older than average: when they arrived in Dunedin, John was 40 and Jane was 30. These portraits were probably taken in the late 1860s.

grew most of their own food, and the life of clothes they brought on the emigration voyage was greatly extended by darning, patching, re-making and handing-me-down.

The facsimiles contain notices and news items which represent notable Otago 'firsts' and significant events. They are marked by the symbol 'F'. Examples are the first boat built in Dunedin, establishment of various societies and committees, the first Burns Night, first veterinarian, first Town Board, first bank, first industrial enterprise – and, of course, John McGibbon's announcement that he was open for business!

While the facsimile section aims to be reasonably representative of what people were reading in the papers, inevitably there are exceptions and gaps.

John McGibbon gets more than his

1849

SHIPPING NEWS

ARRIVED.

December 26, ship *Mooltan*, 580 tons, from Greenock. Passengers—chief cabin, Mr. and Mrs. Todd and 6 children, Miss Macaddam, Mr. and Mrs. Purdie and 6 children, Mr Pillans, Mr. W. Ferguson, Mr. and Mrs Oatts and 2 children. Fore-cabin, Miss Bell, Mr. and Mrs. Blackie and 5 children, Mr. F. McDougall, Mr. A. McJames Doig, Mr P. Clemison, and 102 emigrants.

Same day, schooner Amazon, from California, via Sandwich Islands.

December 27, barque *Lady Clarke*, from Sydney, with cattle.

December 29, schooner *Scotia*, Ward, from Wellington.

SAILED.

None.

IN PORT.

Ship *Mooltan*, barque *Lady Clarke*, and schooners *Otago*, *Amazon*, and *Scotia*.

(Otago News, 29/12/1849) (The report omitted to mention that the McGibbon family was also in the Fore-cabin, as shown in the New Zealand Company passenger list.)

The news of the cholera having appeared on board the ' Mooltan' during her passage out created no little alarm amongst our small community, as one of her boats had been allowed to land at Dunedin, and some of the passengers had visited the Port. Mr Strode, the Police Magistrate, having had the subject notified to him, instantly left Dunedin with a medical gentleman to visit the ship and see if there were any grounds to justify his placing her under quarantine; but, we are glad to say, that such is not the case, and the passengers will therefore be immediately landed.

(Otago News, 29/12/1849)

STORE TO LET

Tʜᴀᴛ Sᴛᴏʀᴇ lately occupied by Mr. Mᴇʀ-ᴄᴇʀ, opposite Royal Hotel,

For particulars apply to

A. ANDERSON

Dunedin, 4th Nov., 1849

(Otago News, 29/12/1849) (This is the store which John McGibbon set up business in.)

HOUSE TO LET

That HOUSE opposite the Royal Hotel, presently occupied by Mr. Anderson.

For particulars apply on the premises.

Dunedin 27th Dec., 1849

(Otago News, 29/12/1849) (The McGibbon family moved into this house.)

FOR SALE,

A good, substantial self-containing Cʟᴀʏ Hᴏᴜsᴇ, with two apartments, shingled and lofted, with a good chimney ; situated near the Cricket Ground, leading to the North-East Valley. Immediate possession can be had, and will be sold cheap for cash.

Apply to A. Mercer, General Store and Commission Warehouse, Brick Building, Princes Street.

(Otago News, 29/12/1849)

To be Sold, below cost price, the following new and useful articles:—

Box Churn and Milk Pans.
Corn Mill.
Peck and Bushel Measures.
Shower Bath.
Filter.
Copper and Furnace.
Apply to the Printer.

(Otago News, 29/12/1849)

EX " KELSO."

A large and useful assortment of Plain and Fancy Sᴛᴀᴛɪᴏɴᴇʀʏ, on Sale, at the *Otago News Office*, consisting of—

Ledgers, Day and Cash Books
Sporting, Racing, and other Prints
Letter Books and Metallic Pens
Manuscript Music Books
Manifold Letter Writers
Blotting Books and Lock Blotters
Printing and Direction Cards
Bristol Boards and Bonnet Boards
French Tracing Paper
Daily Indicator
Portable Brass, Cocoa, Fountain, Patent Hydraulic and other Inkstands.
Letter Clips, and Patent Screw Pencils
Merdan's Lead and Pencil Cases
Music Dotters, and Penholders
Rulers, Ivory and Bone Folders
Wax and Wafer Seals
University Writing Desk Complete
Bill Cases and Letter Weights
Tortoiseshell and other Penknives
Patent Document Bands
Letter Stampers and Bronze Taper Lights
Ivory and Morocco Tablets
Colored and White Tissue Paper
Curling Paper
Royal Cartridge and superior Demy
Copying Ink and Common Ink
Slate Pencils
Self-acting and Adhesive Envelopes
Multam in Parvo Cards and Cases
Copying Press with necessary Material
Turkey Sponge
Wafers, Wax, India-rubber
Cloth for Binding
Children's Books and Pictures at London Prices
Copy Books and Slates

(Otago News, 29/12/1849)

---

fair share of mentions. His name did appear more frequently than most townsmen, but community leaders such as Cargill, Cutten, Macandrew, Reynolds, Valpy, McGlashan and Chetham Strode were given vastly greater prominence.

The facsimiles are light on coverage of local politics, national and international affairs. It was impractical to include much of this material, because it is so long-winded, and is fairly incomprehensible without considerable explanation and analysis. Readers interested in the complicated politics of the period should read A H McLintock, A H Reed, Tom Brooking or Eric Olssen.

Or they can arm themselves with a magnifying glass and a packet of aspirins, peruse the original newspapers and try to figure it all out! ■

Newspapers of the 1850s

Readers will find the old newspapers quite unlike those published today. There was no news on the front page, which was reserved for advertisements and public notices. There were no large headlines. Every story received equal weighting in that respect, with headlines being only the capital letters of the same size type used for body copy.

Letters to the editor often dominated editions. Individual letters could be thousands of words long, and one can imagine the herculean task the editors and compositors faced as deadlines approached while they struggled to decipher handwriting and set the type by hand. The longest letters were on constitutional, political and legal matters, and the same names came up time and time again. The letters contained a great deal of robust comment and personal abuse, on a level that would be considered libellous today. The abuse usually followed initial protestations that the subject was really a very fine fellow.

The longer articles

William Cutten, editor of the Otago Witness, businessman, politician and William Cargill's son-in-law.

ON SALE,

AT the General Stationery Store, Princes-street, a choice selection of BOOKS, from the best authors, at English prices.

(Otago News, 29/12/1849)

GARDEN CALENDAR

BY DAVID BOWER, GARDENER, DUNEDIN

JANUARY.

Plant out cauliflowers, lettuce, savoys, greens, and cabbages of all sorts; sow kidney beans and turnips. For a general crop sow broccoli, lettuce, radish, and pea. Gather herbs for drying.

(Otago News, 29/12/1849)

 ROYAL HOTEL.

ALEXANDER McDONALD, in returning his best thanks to his friends and the public for the very liberal support which he has met with since opening the above Hotel, begs to inform them that he has, for their better accommodation, recently made several alterations and additions to his House, and laid in a stock of Wines and Spirits of the very best quality, recently imported from England and Scotland.

AN ORDINARY AT 2 O'CLOCK DAILY, AS USUAL.
Dunedin, 20th Nov.

(Otago News, 12/1/1850)

ENGLISH FOWLS FOR SALE

A FEW Couples of English Fowls for Sale, Game and Barn Door, apply to Mr. DEWE, Dunedin.

(Otago News, 20/4/1850)

and letters are hard to read. For a start, the type was tiny, and might become progressively tinier in an effort to fit material into the space available. Sentences were long and involved, and paragraphs even longer. Subheadings were unheard of.

While cutting copy to make it fit was evidently a no-no, the editors sometimes had spaces that needed filling, and they liked to fill them with pithy little stories and moral homilies, mainly lifted from overseas publications. Local verse was also a useful space-filler.

Local news made up only a small portion of the papers. What news there was (and in a tiny community there would not have been much), was often squeezed out by letters to the editor. This undoubtedly made life easier for the editors, who had limited assistance and were personally involved in other

EX " MOOLTAN."

JUST received, Ladies', Gentlemens' and Children's Boot and Shoes.
Also, Cloth Caps of various descriptions.

J.R. JOHNSTON, & CO.
Dunedin, 3rd Jan., 1850.
(Otago News, 12/1/1850)

THE inhabitants of Dunedin and suburbs are respectfully informed that the subscriber has opened that Store corner of Princes and Rattray Streets, opposite the Royal Hotel, for the purpose of selling Tea, Earthenware, Ironmongery, Lamp Cotton, &c. Ⓕ

The stock is warranted as very superior in quality, and requires only to be tested so as to insure future sales.

JOHN McGIBBON
Dunedin, 10th January, 1850.
(Otago News, 26/1/1850) (First advertisement for John McGibbon's shop.)

JUST PUBLISHED,
THE " New Zealand Magazine,"
No. 1, containing—
  The Address
  The Whale and Whaling
  Maguerite, a Tale of Brittany
  Geological Observations on the Book of
  Genesis.
  An Agreeable Rencontre
  Sweethearts and Wives
  Reminiscences of Early Life
  A Visit to Roto-Mahana
  The Geology of the Middle Island of New
    Zealand
  Native Waiata or Song
  A Glance at the History of New Zealand as
    a British Colony
  The Debutante
  Lines to——
  Wakefield's Art of Colonization Reviewed.
The " New Zealand Magazine" is published Quarterly, terms 21s. per annum, one-half to be paid in advance ; single Numbers 5s. 6d. each. Agent for Otago, H. B. Graham, " News" Office.

(Otago News, 26/1/1850)

JUST ARRIVED.

A Mercer begs to inform his customers and friends that he has just received a new supply of
  Best Black Tea.
  30 Kegs superior Salt Butter, from 1s.
    4d. to 1s. 8d. per lb.
  Fresh Butter from the Country every
Tuesday and Saturday.
  Mould and Dip Candles.
  2 Cases Confectionery.
  1 Case Jams.
    ALSO, DIRECT FROM GLASGOW
  4 Cases, containing the real Navvie
    Water-tight Boots.
  Ladies' and Gent's. fine Boots and
    Shoes.
  Ladies' House Shoes.
  Children's Boots and shoes, very
cheap.
  Also, on hand, for sale, a quantity of

Camp Ovens, Frying Pans, and Kettles, very cheap.
  2 Pack Saddles and Mounting.
  1 Set of Cart Harness.
  A quantity of Head-Stall Bridles.
    BRICK BUILDINGS,
      Princes Street.
(Otago News, 26/2/1850)

TEETOTAL SOCIETY

A Society for the supression of Intemperance is now forming in Dunedin, and parties desirous of promoting this object and becoming members, will receive every information on application to P. CREW. This society is intended to exist, as a trial scheme, for twelvemonths, and needs not any particularization to point out the many benefits which will result from its establishment among the inhabitants of Dunedin and the neighborhood. Let every well-wisher to human happiness come forward and take the pledge. Several members have already joined the cause, whose names may be seen by applying as above.

(Otago News, 2/3/1850) (Few Dunedinites took the pledge, and a good deal of serious drinking went on in the young colony.)

TO BE EXCHANGED.

THE holder of Two Rural Choices will be happy to exchange them for Suburban Choices, and an equivalent in money.
For further particulars apply at the Office of this Paper.

(Otago News, 2/3/1850)

ON Sale, for Cash, at the STORE of the Undersigned, corner of Princes and Rattray-streets, Dunedin —
  Black and Green Teas, Raw and Roasted Coffee, Raw and Loaf Sugar, Rice, Flour, Soap, Candles, Writing Paper. Also an assortment of Earthenware, Ironmongery, Tobacco-pipes, and Lamp Cotton ; with a limited supply of excellent Fresh Butter.
  N.B. — Farmers having Butter to dispose of will find immediate sale for the same by applying at the above premises.

JOHN McGIBBON
March 7, April 6, 1850
(Otago Witness, 9/3/1850)

ONE HUNDRED POUNDS FOR ONE!

TO BE RAFFLED for in One Hundred Chances at ONE POUND each, a Suburban Section, with a substantial DWELLING HOUSE thereon, situate at the Green Island Bush, in a beautiful situation. About Four Acres of the ground is fenced and under cultivation ; the Section is finely timbered, with an unfailing stream of water running through it.
  Possession of the House at the end of October, 1850, and the Land transferred and entered upon, if desired, immediately.
  Further particulars of MR. H. B. GRAHAM.

(Otago News 1/6/1850)

business activities. William Cutten, who owned and edited the Otago Witness for several years, had considerable additional business and political interests. He prosecuted those interests vigorously in his own newspaper.

Editors were unconcerned about copyright in the 1850s, and couldn't wait to get their hands on newspapers and magazines from elsewhere in New Zealand and overseas. They regurgitated many column inches of news and articles from home and abroad, usually without attribution.

Editors and correspondents were able to besmirch character without worrying about libel or contempt of court. An example of what today would be considered serious contempt of court was in an 1852 Cutten editorial which included the words: "Well, if ever there were a body pre-eminently distinguished for their vacillation, vanity, absurdity, cowardice and deceit, it is that illustrious body – the Otago Bench, or rather a Majority of it."

The majority referred to were the English/Anglican opponents of the Cargill Free Church clique, which Cutten then supported. (Arguments between the Anglican 'Little Enemy' (as it was called) and the Scottish class settlement establishment were common and extremely bitter, and only faded after the provincial self government was achieved in 1853.)

Old news new again

News from outside Otago was always months old, even if it came from other parts of New Zealand. But old news still seemed like new news. For example, when word arrived on 9 January 1856 that Allies had won the Crimean War's Battle of Sebastopol, the event itself was already four months old. Yet, reported the Otago Witness, "Flags were immediately hoisted, the bell set ringing, the services of our one gun, an eight-pounder, called into requisition, and a salute of (we do not know how many guns) fired – the latter an ebullition of loyalty and enthusiasm which will be fully appreciated when we state that the powder cost 4s. 6d. per pound."

As well as bringing news, ship arrivals started new cycles of advertising: *Direct from Glasgow, ex "Pioneer," the undersigned has for sale...*

In what was probably an accurate reflection of the colony, the newspapers were a man's world. Advertisements were one of the few items which addressed themselves to women as well as men. There were almost no reports of women's activities, except indirectly through descriptions of events such as post-harvest celebrations ('harvest homes'). Even at these events, which celebrated female as much as male endeavour, women were unable to speak for themselves – at least not publicly. At a Halfway Bush harvest home in 1854, Mr Paterson toasted 'The Ladies', giving a "...highly humorous and diverting speech." The ladies could not reply – Mr Hood did it for them, in another "amusing" speech.

'Filler' paragraphs were often directed at the ladies, sometimes reminding them of their place in the scheme of things. (See 'Golden Rules for Married Wives' on page 119.) ∎

Predecessors

The McGibbons were early settlers in Dunedin, but they were far from being the earliest. Their ship dropped anchor in December 1849, in the second year of organised European settlement, but people had been living in the area for upwards of 900 years.

The first occupants were Maori, who lived mainly near the entrance to Otago Harbour, particularly at the kaika (village) of Otakou, southwest of Taiaroa Head.

Until European settlers provided jobs and a permanent local market for fish and garden produce, few Maori lived permanently in the Dunedin region. Most would have been semi-nomadic, living in different places depending on when particular foods became available. They were also influenced by the availability of the moa, New Zealand's now extinct giant flightless bird. In later years, a number of Maori quarried greenstone, and traded it with tribes living in the north.

The identity of the earliest tribes in Otago is unclear, though they may have been Te Rupuwai and Katikura. About five centuries ago, the Waitaha established themselves, and in the 1500s, they were joined by the North Island Ngati Mamoe tribe. Then around the end of the 17th century, the Ngai Tahu tribe moved south from Hawke's Bay to became the dominant tribe in Otago, and in the South Island generally.

When the Europeans arrived, it seems there were no permanent kaika at the head of the harbour, where Dunedin would be situated. This area, known by the Maori as Otepoti, may have contained some semi-permanent kaika in the 17th and 18th centuries.

The Maori preferred the outer harbour which was better placed for their coastal food gathering lifestyle, and contained enough cultivable land to grow crops for a relatively small population. It was also a better defensive situation.

An early whaler, E S Haberfield, estimated that when the first whalers and sealers landed in the area, there were 2,000 or more Maori living in various settlements in the vicinity of Otago Heads. Most later scholars be-

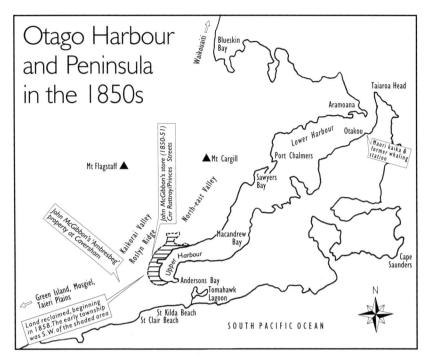

Otago Harbour and Peninsula in the 1850s

lieve the population was considerably lower. Maarire Goodall and George Griffith, in their book, *Maori Dunedin*, suggest that in 1830, about 1,500 people lived in the coastal area between Karitane and Taieri Mouth, and "Several hundred lived on various bays and beaches around the Otago Heads..." The writers believed that the total Maori population of Otago and Southland at this time would have been several thousand – possibly as high as 5,000.

Maori numbers were decimated by diseases brought by the early whalers and sealers. Measles was the greatest killer, and there was a particularly bad epidemic in 1835-36. Influenza and smallpox also caused many deaths, and alcohol abuse contributed to ill-health.

The rapid decline of the Maori population was evident in the first European census, taken in the 1840s. This showed the Maori population of Otago as a whole had fallen to a little over 400. Of these, 110 were living at Otago Heads.

Europeans

The first Europeans to see the general Dunedin locality were on board Captain Cook's Endeavour, which sailed down the coast in February 1770.

Sealers and whalers entered Otago Harbour from at least 1817, and the first European landing at the head of

the harbour took place in 1826. In that year, a Captain Herd brought the *Rosanna* and a shipload of intending colonists into Otago Harbour. One of the officers, a Mr T Shepherd, took a small boat 24 kilometres up the narrow harbour to the site of present day Dunedin. Though they thought the soils had agricultural potential and liked the harbour, on balance they rejected the site and sailed on northward.

In 1831, the Weller brothers established a whaling station alongside the Maori kaika at Otakou. Later, as whales became less plentiful, the Wellers developed a strong sideline trade in potatoes and flax. Produce was bought from the local Maori and exported to Sydney.

The French navigator Dumont D'Urville visited Otakou in March 1840, and sailed on, apparently unimpressed.

(One resident whaler he could have met was John McGibbon – but not the John McGibbon featured in this book. It was probably the same person as the John 'Tiger' McGibbon who at other times lived at the Bluff whaling settlement in the far south, near Invercargill.)

Another visitor in 1840 was the Catholic Bishop Pompallier, while the Anglican Bishop Selwyn dropped by in 1844. From earlier years, the settlement had been visited periodically by

James Watkin, a Methodist missionary based at Waikouaiti, a coastal settlement a short distance to the north. Waikouaiti was a base for whaling and farming operations, and about 100 Europeans were living there in 1844.

The Waikouaiti settlement, particularly its leader, John Jones, would later give considerable support to the fledgling Dunedin.

In 1842, Colonel Wakefield of the New Zealand Company sent Captain Mein Smith from Wellington to investigate South Island harbours which had potential for future settlements. Otago Harbour was investigated, but did not find favour.

A visit by Crown representatives followed in 1843. One of them, Edward Shortland (Protector of Aborigines), with a botanist named Earle, and three Maori, took a small boat right up the harbour, and explored some of the surrounding land, including present-day St Kilda and St Clair beaches, Green Island, the Taieri Mouth, Saddle Hill, Caversham and Kaikorai Valley.

By this time the whaling station at the Heads had closed, though about 20 Maori and Europeans still lived at Otakou.

The next significant visitor was Frederick Tuckett, principal surveyor for the New Zealand Company. With an assistant, David Monro, his principal brief was to look for a site in Banks Peninsula for a future Scottish settlement to be called New Edinburgh. Tuckett was not satisfied with Banks Peninsula and carried on south.

The party proceeded up Otago Harbour, and Monro wrote enthusiastically of the experience: "The sky was without a cloud, and not a breeze ruffled the surface of the water, which reflected the surrounded wooded slopes, and every seabird that floated on it, with mirror-like accuracy. For some hours after sunrise the woods resounded with the rich and infinitely varied notes of thousands of tuis and other songsters. I never heard anything like it in any part of New Zealand."

On 29 April, 1844, they landed on the beach below the present junction of Princes and High streets.

Tuckett's explorations continued southward along the east and southern coast. On the way back, he checked out the Otago Harbour again, to con-firm his feeling that this was the best place to establish the future New Edinburgh.

Three months later, Colonel Wakefield, as agent for the Crown, arrived from Wellington to buy the land required.On 31 July, he met 150 Maori men, women and children assembled at Koputai (later called Port Chalmers), and formally purchased the Otago Block for £2,500 in cash. The block extended from Otago Peninsula south to Nuggett Point near the mouth of the Matau River. (The Matau was also known as Molyneux, and today is called the Clutha.) The 400,000 acre (162,000 hectare) block was around 100 kilometres from north to south, and extended inland for an average of around twelve kilometres.

Tuckett's 1844 map of the Otago Block is on page 21 of this book.

The deed of sale included the setting aside of native reserves within the boundaries of the Otago Block.

The New Zealand Company also had a stated policy of setting aside one-tenth of all land purchases for the benefit of the Maori. In practice, this did not happen, and contributed to later resentment and compensation claims. During the 1840s there were disagreements between the Company and the Government over how the 'tenths' policy should be applied. The problem was effectively consigned to the 'too hard' basket, and never resolved.

Tuckett now set out to survey the new township site, but he had hardly started when news came that the New Zealand Company had financial problems. Expenses were to be cut to a minimum and no fresh obligations were to be entered into in respect of New Edinburgh. Survey work ended.

However news of the mooted Scottish settlement had spread, and two families moved down immediately, from Nelson. Although their occupation was informal rather than officially sanctioned, they were effectively the first settlers in the planned settlement. James Anderson, with his son John and daughter-in-law Isabella, explored the locality and decided on land in a small bay opposite the future city centre. Today the bay still bears their name. The other family, Alexander and Janet McKay, settled at Port Chalmers and established a hotel.

In February 1846, the New Zealand Company turned its attention once again to the head of Otago Harbour, and the new chief surveyor, Charles Kettle, arrived to begin laying out the new town. By then the Company had decided to call it Dunedin, the former Gaelic name for Edinburgh.

Two years later, on 23 March 1848, the *John Wycliffe* arrived with the first group of new settlers from Britain. ∎

Early days in Dunedin

When the McGibbon family arrived in December 1849, conditions in the small town were primitive. But the situation was better than it was in March 1848, when the first settlers landed from the John Wickliffe.

Even then, conditions could have been much worse. The ship's arrival coincided with a spell of excellent weather, and for several weeks the beauty and novelty of the new situation more than compensated for the lack of accommodation and amenities.

One passenger recalled how Dunedin looked from the harbour: "To the left, lay a long range of sandhills shining in the sun and disguising the ocean beyond. Directly in front towered the high range of Whakeri, or Flagstaff as it is now known, which descended by many a spur and many an intervening gully to the shores of the harbour. On a nearer approach it became evident that there was no possibility of landing except at the point where the little creek, the Kaituna, found outlet to the harbour amid fern, flax and swampy ground, for extensive mudflats stretched in front of the deeply indented low-lying shores. Two or three hundred yards from the shoreline began an irregular fringe of native bush, veronica, fuschia, broadleaf, supplejack, and lawyer, while beyond this rose the majestic forest giants."

The first settlers had been shown maps of Dunedin before leaving Britain, and expected to find streets and houses. All they saw in the main town area were two buildings – Watson's

Hotel on the beach and the chief surveyor's home. Princes Street, the main street, was wilderness apart from two survey lines 20 metres apart and about three kilometres long. The pegged off area was covered with flax, grass, stumps, creeks and bogs.

In those days before harbour reclamation, the beach was close to Princes Street. (See the map on page 117).

Women and children remained on board the John Wickliffe while the menfolk erected a temporary barracks. It was very primitive, made of mapau posts, crossmembers tied with flax and walls and roof thatched with grass and rushes.

When the second group of settlers arrived on the Philip Laing on 15 April, a larger barracks was constructed. The building mirrored shipboard steerage accommodation, with single men at one end, families in the centre and single women at the other end. It had bunks along the walls, a single door and no windows.

Conditions were tolerable while the Indian summer lasted, but in early May,

wet weather set in with a vengeance. Cooking, which had to be done outdoors, became miserable drudgery. Wives struggled to keep fires burning and pots boiling, while their husbands held an umbrella overhead.

Umbrellas were also needed *inside* the barracks. One settler described a "...long windowless room in almost total darkness, the rain pouring through the roof, the floor in a miserable condition and women with young children on their knees and mid-leg deep in mire and puddle, huddled in many instances under an open umbrella."

By now the environment had lost its romantic charm and presented a depressing aspect. A recollection published in the 1898 jubilee edition of the Otago Witness described "...dark sombre forests reeking with misty vapours hung on the steep hillsides right down to the water's edge while dripping mist rested like a pall overhead, shutting out the sun and landscape alike."

Gradually the occupants were able to move to town sections and build their own houses. Few were as fortu-

nate as the two leaders of the settlement, Captain Cargill and Reverend Thomas Burns, who brought prefabricated wooden houses with them. Other settlers had to do their best with local materials from bush and swamp.

There was little sawn timber available and most early homes were of wattle and daub construction. They were small, being no more than five metres long by three metres wide, with two rooms.

Building a grass house

James Adam described the building of his grass house on the corner of Princes and High Streets: "I engaged two natives at 3/- a day to help me build a house, and sent them at once to the swamp for a boatload of grass to thatch the roof and sides.

"On my leasehold there was a clump of Mapau trees, but before cutting them down, I stretched a line through them for the ground floor of the house. Trees which coincided with this line I left standing, merely cutting off the tops, and those which were out of line were

MILK COW AMISSING

DISAPPEARED, on or about Wednesday the 19 March, a low-set MILK COW, having the following marks:— General colour of Body, Light Brown ; Head Black Brown : Horns rather drooping ; dewlap Black Brown, with a few White Spots; Back Hollow ; Belly Large ; both Hind Thighs White from rump downwards; on top of Right Thigh has brand

JJ
IH

Whoever returns the animal to JOHN McGIBBON, Ambresbeg, will be suitably rewarded.

(Otago Witness 4/4/1851)

LIME! LIME! LIME!

CAPTAIN BLACKIE respectfully requests Builders, Farmers, and others to inspect the Lime turned out from his kiln at Pleasant Villa, Caversham Vale, which he confidently recommends, and feels certain only requires a trial to ensure it that success and extensive use its superior qualities entitle it to.

Present Prices: — at the Kiln, 9d. per Bushel ; and 1s. per bushel at the Store of

ANGUS MATHIESON

(Otago Witness, 19/4/1851)

Dunedin markets

Retail prices current, April 19, 1851

First Flour, per 200 lbs., £2 4s. ; Bread, per 4 lb loaf, 11d. ; Beef, 6d to 6½d. ; Pork, 6d. to 6½d. ; Fresh Butter, 1s. 6d. ; Salt do., 1s. 3d. to 1s. 4d. ; Ground Coffee, 1s. 4d. ; Tea, 1s 8d. ; Raw Sugar, 3½d. to 4d. ; Loaf do., 7½d. to 8d. ; Mould Candles, 7d. ; Cheese, 1s. ; Milk, 3d. to 4d. per quart; Potatoes, 4s. to 5s. 0d. per cwt. ; Firewood, per cord, 10s. to 12s. ; Sawn Timber, 10s. to 11s. per 100ft. ; Shingles, 12s. per 1,000 ; Bricks, £2 5s. per 1,000.

(Otago Witness,19/4/1851)

TO CAPITALISTS

TO BE SOLD by Private Contract, a capital SECTION OF SUBURBAN LAND, situate at Sawyers Bay, partly Fenced and Cultivated. Also a good and substantial Fern-built House erected thereon, late in the occupation of the Messrs. Carter.

For further particulars and terms of purchase, apply to MR. HARRIS, Stafford Street, Dunedin.

(Otago Witness, 1851)

ON Tuesday, the 11th ultimo. W. H. Valpy, Esq., wound up the festivities of the season at the Forbury by feasting the young members of the community. About 90 children sat down to dinner, and did ample justice to the good cheer provided for them... The wants of the little party were kindly ministered to by the Misses Valpy and their young friends, who appeared highly amused by the merry laugh and joyous countenances of their little guests, who strenuously exerted themselves to realise Punch's description of 'something like a holiday.' After dinner the party adjourned to the Ocean Beach, to enjoy a ramble and frolic on the sands; the anticipated enjoyment of which had been the subject of conversation amongst the children for some weeks past.

(Otago Witness, 3/5/1851)

THE 'Wellington' schooner sails this day for Port Cooper and Wellington, and as a vessel is laid on at Wellington to sail direct for England, an opportunity is thus presented of sending letters home. The 'Wellington' takes with her a cargo, the produce of Otago, consisting of lime, machine-made shingles, and potatoes ; of the latter we have not too much to spare. If our settlers would only bestir themselves and set to work vigorously with the plough, another year would not only give us sufficient flour for our own consumption, but allow us to export some to the neighbouring rising settlements of Canterbury. What is coming in from Mr. Valpy's mill is of good quality, and proves that our climate is admirably adapted to the raising of wheat. Let it be remembered, that until our exports are greater than our imports, we cannot be said to be in a healthy condition.

(Otago Witness, 3/5/1851)

THE EMIGRANT'S SONG.

My barque is afloat !—I'm afloat on the wave,
The sky shines above me, below frowns the grave;
My heart beats in sadness, but my hopes are still bright,
As I'm wafted along 'neath the moon's gentle light.
    Then weep not, dear Mary, Oh! weep not for
      me,
    I'm sailing away to the land of the free ;
    My heart shall be with thee wherever I roam,
    And with good Old England, my own dearest home.

My barque is afloat !— 'tis the frail barque of life,
And wildly I'm tossed on the waters of strife ;
But the haven appears o'er the far distant wave,
And welcomes the stranger from the land of the brave.
    Then weep not, dear Mary, Oh! weep not for
      me,
    I'm sailing away to the land of the free, &c.

When Fortune has smiled on the work of my hands,
I'll wander no more in those far distant lands ;
But again o'er the waves of the oceans I'll ride,
And then, dearest Mary, I'll make thee my bride.
    Then weep not, dear Mary, Oh! weep not for
      me,
    I'm sailing away to the land of the free ;
    My heart shall be with thee wherever I roam,
    And with good Old England, my own dearest home.

          L. A. M.

Dunedin, May 29th., 1851
(Otago Witness 21/6/1851)

cut down and put in line by digging holes. By this novel plan the walls were made strong and substantial in one day. The natives then put small wands or wattles across the uprights, about 12 inches apart, fastening them firmly with strips of flax, and over all they laced the long grass to the wattles; did the same over the roof and at the end of four days my home was habitable.

"I have owned good houses since, but never have I been able to evoke the pleasure and happiness felt on the night my home was habitable. I couldn't refrain from going out after dark to contemplate its proportions, architecture and site."

True wattle and daub houses were built in a similar way, but with the wattles closer together. The insides of the walls were plastered with a mixture of clay and chopped grass. Houses were also built with walls of sun-dried mud bricks and tree fern trunks.

Windows in these rude dwellings were usually strips of calico, and fireplaces would occupy an entire end wall. Floors were bare earth, levelled and stamped hard.

Women, and sometimes their children, worked as hard as husbands to build their homes. The story is told of one young woman in the Taieri Plain who set herself the task of making mud bricks. She dug clay from the property, mixed it with water and chopped tussock, and packed it into moulds. When the mixture was set, it would be turned out to dry in the sun. Her goal was to produce more bricks each day, and she made as many as 80.

One type of rough shelter was the grass whare, a hut made of saplings and grass, that was usually only about two metres square. It had no chimney, and all cooking was done in the open. It gave little protection in wet weather, and the trusty umbrella was again needed inside the hut. Dirt floors turned into quagmires.

Furnishings began with rough bunks, probably constructed out of packing cases, and softened with fern if no mattresses were available. Logs and whale vertebrae served as chairs.

Cooking, whether in or out of the house, was done over open fires rather than with stoves, which for most people came much later. A basic kitchen item was the camp oven. This was a round iron container which could sit among the ashes or hang from the chimney bar. Hot embers could also be placed on top of the lid. Pots were made of iron and had to be shifted about on their bars and hooks while their contents were cooked. Later – luxury of luxuries – came the oblong shaped colonial ovens.

From time to time there were shortages of processed food like flour, salt and rice, and in the first two years, most of these items were imported from Sydney by John Jones. Tea sometimes ran short, and the bitter leaves of the manuka tree would be used as substitutes. Wheat was roasted and ground as a substitute for coffee. When tobacco ran out, the men were sometimes forced to smoke manuka bark and tea leaves. For a time, milk and butter were scarce.

But the settlers would never starve. Before they were able to grow their own vegetables, they could buy potatoes produced in Maori gardens and from John Jones' farm at Waikouaiti. There was plenty of fish and wild game to eat. Quail, native pigeons and kaka parrots were popular, and wild pigs, descended from animals released eighty years earlier by Captain Cook, were plentiful. Cattle running loose in the bush were considered fair game, and a settler might shoot one and share it with his neighbours. ∎

Arriving at the end of 1849

When the McGibbons arrived in town 21 months later, they fell on their feet, relatively speaking. We have some information about the circumstances from an 1898 Otago Witness article by Jane Bannerman about early pioneer women.

Mrs Bannerman, who came on the Philip Laing as the 13 year old daughter of Reverend Burns, wrote: "It was very difficult in those days to get accommodation of any kind, and when an immigrant ship arrived, the barracks provided for the immigrants and every other available place was filled up. The lady [Jane McGibbon] and her family were fortunate enough to secure a wooden building of exceed-

ingly limited accommodation at the corner of Princes and Rattray Streets, where the new Government Insurance Offices now stand."

The McGibbon family was much better off than the Harrison family. Mr and Mrs Harrison had died of cholera on the voyage, and as the ship had passed Van Diemen's Land on 17 December, Clarinda Harrison died of whooping cough. Four Harrison orphans aged between two and five years ended up in the Dunedin barracks. One of the children died shortly afterwards of whooping cough. The survivors were placed in the care of Dr Burns and Captain Cargill, and put in a foster home.

The house rented by John

McGibbon appears to have been the same building, or at least on the same block of land, as a small shop. Both were advertised to let by Archibald Anderson in the 29 December edition of the Otago News. As this was only three days after the Mooltan anchored at Port Chalmers. McGibbon must have read the paper and moved fast.

The location, now occupied by the Department of Social Welfare in Philip Laing House, is among the more valuable pieces of Dunedin real estate. In 1850 it was much less desirable – a dank hollow, well below today's Princes Street frontage. Still, it was better than the immigrants' barracks or a wattle and daub hut.

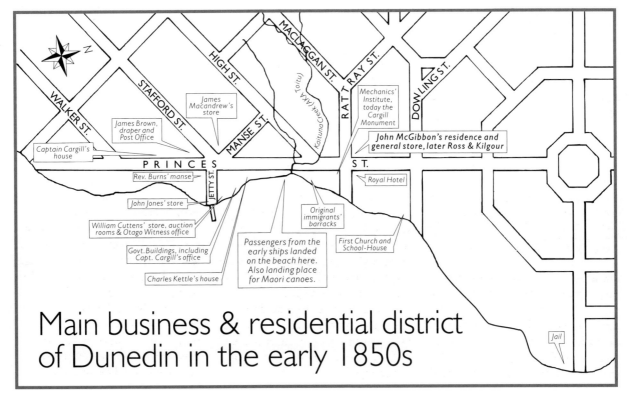

Main business & residential district of Dunedin in the early 1850s

Less than two weeks later, John McGibbon respectfully informed the inhabitants of Dunedin and suburbs that he had "...opened that Store corner of Princes and Rattray Streets, opposite the Royal Hotel, for the purpose of selling Tea, Earthenware, Ironmongery, Lamp Cotton, &c. The stock is warranted as very superior in quality, and requires only to be tested so as to insure future sales."

John McGibbon had brought several tons of goods from Scotland and a background in professional shopkeeping. There were certainly others with retail experience, but at this time, small-time shopkeeping was a popular semi-amateur occupation, and many small businesses operated from homes. Dunedin was 'over-shopped'.

John Jones, Dunedin's preeminent trader and businessman in the earliest days of the colony. Jones provided a good deal of food from his farm up the coast at Waikouaiti, and he had a substantial store on Dunedin's waterfront. (Otago Punch)

James Barr, author of the delightful *Old Identities*, published in 1879, recalled that in 1850, Dunedin had "...one real merchant of colonial training [John Jones, who by then had a substantial store in Dunedin] and quite a sufficiency of storekeepers." He noted that "...one or two brought experience, ready made, coming in very handy, from sundry neuks o' Fife, Auld Reekie, and the "Sautmarket." The last reference was probably to John McGibbon.

Barr described the atmosphere inside these general stores. They typically dispensed complimentary liquid hospitality, and "...a wonderful number of people were familiar with the way to it."

"Even the settler's wife, when she had trudged to town from the Taieri or Green Island, with her butter and eggs, getting in exchange some "grey wursit," or perhaps a blue shirt, or a pair of mole trousers for the gude man, or some ribbons for the lasses, was treated to a nobbler.

"There was an air of constant bustle and stir about, and the foundations for some very substantial fortunes were laid, by hard grubbing in these crowded little places where there was hardly any room to turn."

McGibbon did build a significant retailing fortune in later years, but it was in the Mataura Valley rather than Dunedin. After 21 months in the Rattray Street shop, he sold his stock and temporarily retired from the retail trade.

Still a wretched prospect

Dunedin in December 1849 was home to around 800 souls, but it was still no entrancing prospect. Mid-way through the year, Catherine Orbell had described it as "...a wretched condemned looking hole," and in December, Captain Whitby was equally critical and observed that the townspeople were not of the "most respectable class."

By now Princes Street and a few other streets were roughly formed. The bush still dominated, although it had largely disappeared from the very edge of Princes Street. In March 1850, it was reported that some streets were even passible by bullock wagon when the weather was fine. Sledges were generally more practical, because they were less easily bogged.

Robert Fulton, in his 1922 book, *Medical Practice in Otago and Southland in the Early Days*, described the appearance of streets leading to Princes Street around 1850: "A few whares and wattle and daub huts dotted the lower slopes of the hill, which is now cut into High and Stafford streets. These dwellings were surrounded by thick manuka, tarata and mapau, and from their windows, or open shutters which took the place of windows, the settlers shot kakas and pigeons at their leisure, for the birds were at that time exceedingly plentiful."

"Wild pigs frequented the fern and manuka and the thick pine bush spreading up the hill in Rattray Street..."

Fulton said that for several years, Princes Street was "...a mass of mud, and Kaituna [a stream close to the McGibbon shop which was originally known by Maori as the Toitu] meandered across and under an old rickety wooden bridge made of logs, far too frail for the bullock sledge traffic...It was no uncommon thing for pedestrians to be bogged up to their waists in the main street in the middle of winter." ∎

NOTICE

Whereas on Sunday last, the 7th instant, a furious Bullock was driven through the town of Dunedin, and there slaughtered by discharging firearms, to the great disturbance of the quiet solemnity which should exist on the Sabbath day, and whereby the lives of Her Majesty's liege subjects were endangered. — This is to give notice, that any person offending in the above manner after this warning will, without fail, be prosecuted with the utmost rigour of the Law.

A. CHETHAM STRODE,
Resident Magistrate

Resident Magistrate's Court
Dunedin, 11th. Sept. 1851.

MR. MATHESON is favoured with instructions from MR. McGIBBON to Sell by Public Auction at his store in Princes St., on Wednesday first, October 1, the whole STOCK IN TRADE, consisting of earthenware, Whale Oil, Lamp Wick, &c., &c.
Sale to commence at 2 o'Clock

(Otago Witness, September 1851)

WANTED

A SERVANT who can undertake plain Cooking, or a Girl who will be anxious to learn it.
Apply to
MRS. JAMES MACANDREW
Stafford Street

(Otago Witness, 4/10/1851)

GOLDEN RULES FOR MARRIED WIVES— Resolve every morning to be cheerful that day; and should any thing occur to break your resolution, suffer it not to put you out of temper with your husband. Dispute not with him, be the occasion what it may ; but much rather deny yourself the satisfaction of having your own way, or gaining the better of an argument, than risk a quarrel, or create a heart burning, which it is impossible to see the end of. Implicit submission in a man to his wife is ever disgraceful to both in the eyes of neighbours; but implicit submission in a wife to the just will of her husband is what she promised at the altar — what the good and sensible will revere her for ; and what is, in fact, the greatest honour she can receive. Be assured, a woman's power, as well as her happiness, has no other foundation than her husband's esteem and love, which it is her interest, by all possible means, to preserve and increase, to share and soothe his cares, and with the utmost assiduity conceal his errors.

(Otago Witness, 18/10/1851)

MR. W. H. CUTTEN will Sell by Auction at his SALE OF STOCK, to be held on Saturday, the 8th November next—
A very superior RIDING HORSE, 16 hands high, warranted sound.

(Otago Witness, 25/10/1851)

NOTICE

ALL Persons indebted to MR. JOHN McGIBBON, Storekeeper, Princes St., are requested to pay their accounts to MR. JAMES BROWN, Post Office, who is authorised to receive same.

(Otago Witness, 18/10/1851, 1/11/1851)

ALEXANDER M'NIEL respectfully intimates to the Settlers of Otago, that he has commenced business in Dunedin as a BLACKSMITH and FARRIER in all its departments, and trusts to merit a share of patronage by moderate charges and punctuality to orders.

Workshop near the new Court-house.

(Otago Witness, 25/10/1851)

PUBLIC LECTURE

DUNEDIN MECHANICS' INSTITUTION

THE Rev. Mr. BURNS will deliver a lecture in the School-Room on Thursday Evening, the 13th November, at 7 o'clock on the

"Pleasures and Advantages connected with the Pursuits of Literature and Science ; or the value of Intellectual Self-Culture to the Working Man."

Ladies are respectfully invited.

(Otago Witness, 8/11/1851)

Captain Cargill, Dunedin Resident Agent for the New Zealand Company. He was later elected as Otago's first Provincial Superintendent, when self-government was attained in 1853. The drawing below is by cartoonist James Brown.

TO WOOL SHIPPERS

FIRST SHIP THIS SEASON

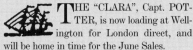 THE "CLARA", Capt. POTTER, is now loading at Wellington for London direct, and will be home in time for the June Sales.

Should a sufficient cargo offer before the "Henrietta" returns from the Southward, she will be despatched for Wellington, so as to arrive there in time for the "CLARA". If not, she will proceed to Nelson, for which Port a cargo is already engaged.

Those who are desirous of sending their wool home per "Clara" are requested to apply at once to
JAMES MACANDREW & Co.

(Otago Witness, 3/1/1852)

FOR SALE

EX " COLUMBUS"

GLENFIELD'S Powdered Starch
Tobacco Pipes.
Wrought Single Nails.
Cut   do   do
Table Knives — Pen Knives.
Britannia Metal Tea Spoons.
Gimlets Assorted.
Scotch Reaping Hooks.
Bath Bricks.
Epsom Salts.
Senna.
Flour Sulphur.
Calcines Magnesia.
Cream of Tartar.
Nitre.
Roll Sulphur.
Blacking.
Bell's Patent Matches.
Ladies' Combs.
Worsted.
Moleskin.

JOHN McGIBBON

Orders for any of the above to be left with Mr. BROWN, Post Office, or Mr. DUNCAN, Butcher, Princes Street.

(Otago Witness, 14/2/1852, 21/2/1852)

ORIGINAL CORRESPONDENCE

To the Editor of the OTAGO WITNESS

Sir, I am delighted to observe that your correspondent — "The Man in the Moon" — has at last come forward with his real name ; for I have always felt convinced that no-one but a *lunatic* could possibly be the author of much of the original correspondence that weekly *dis*graces the columns of the "Otago Witness."

SOL.

(Otago Witness, 14/2/1852)

Dunedin in April 1850

By 1850 the town was looking a little less make-shift. One of the more obvious signs was that new houses were being built with wooden weatherboards rather than wattle and daub.

Progress in the settlement was detailed in the 6 April edition of the Otago News. The town's population had reached 1,182, and consisted of: married males, 212; married females, 197; single males, 458 and single females, 315.

The religious mix was: Church of Scotland, 36 per cent; Church of England, 26 per cent; Free Church of Scotland, 26 per cent; other Dissenters, 9 per cent; others, 3 per cent. The 'others' included a grand total of 13 Catholics – this was *not* an Irish settlement! (In practice, many of the Church of Scotland adherents and some of the Anglicans worshipped in the Free Church.

Rosalind McClean, in her thesis, *Class, Family and Church*, calculated from the Reverend Burns visitation book that in 1850, 45 per cent of heads of households were Free Church communicant members. Episcopalians (Anglicans) made up 17 per cent, other denominations 7 per cent, and non-committal 31 per cent.)

Houses in April 1850 were made of: stone, 5; brick, 5; weatherboard, 83; poles or logs, 14; grass and poles, 10; clay etc, 85; total, 202.

Cultivated acreage totalled 219.75 acres, comprised of: potatoes, 92.5; garden ground, 49; oats, 27.75; wheat, 20.75; grass, 19.5; barley, 10.25. The total fenced area was 316.75 acres. (1 acre = 0.405 hectare.)

Livestock comprised: cattle, 921; sheep, 3,408; pigs, 732; goats, 169; horses, 45. ∎

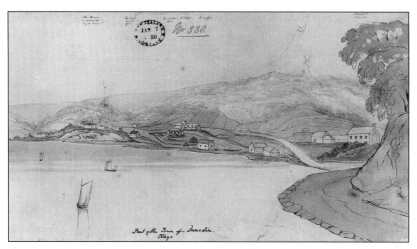

Two views of Dunedin in 1849 by the New Zealand Company surveyor, Charles Kettle. Top: looking toward 'downtown' Princes Street from the shoreline near the site of the original jail (see the map on page 117). Above: Looking toward the harbour from Stafford Street. (Alexander Turnbull Library)

The McGibbon environs

John McLay, a fellow passenger from the Mooltan, wrote a description of the immediate neighbourhood of the McGibbon dwelling. McLay was only eight years old when he arrived, and, looking back after fifty years, his memories may not have been entirely accurate. Following, slightly edited to improve comprehension, is what he had to say about his family's first Dunedin home, which was across the 'street' from the McGibbon family:

"The place we are living in is called Rattery (sic) Street – although I don't see any street formed at present. The house that we are living in for a short time is the third house up from the shop on the corner on the left side go-ing up. Down by the end of this shop, held by Smith and Allen, you have to cross a small blind creek on a plank, and a few yards over the plank into the left was the bake house.

Archibald Anderson, who let a store and dwelling in Rattray Street to John McGibbon in January 1850.

"When they had flour they baked, but when we lived at this place, they were out of flour. We lived on Biskits from the ship, and Maori potatoes. They were a small round kind of potato streaked all through with black streaks like marble, but they were very nice to eat. We had plenty of fish brought up to Dunedin by the Maori boats. We did not do so bad. The fish was mostly barracuta, and hapuka, called groper by the white people.

"These Boats came from a long way along the coast: Otago Heads, Waikouiati and Moeraka [Moeraki] in the North, and from the Taieri Mouth in the South, making over 40 miles.

"When the Maori boats got up at big tides, they sailed into a big creek [Kaituna Stream] that came along the foot of the big hill on the left side of Rattery Street. When they got into this creek and got the fish unloaded onto mats, they pulled the boats up on to a nice dry Gravel beach.

"They turned the boats bottom up, and then put all their mats, blankets and fish under them away from the sun. Men, women and children also slept under their boats, and you could buy four of the barracuta for a shilling, three foot long and more. Hapuka is a thick fine heavy fish weighing from 20 lb up to 40lb. You could buy one for one and sixpence, and often for less.

"Up the little glen that Rattrey Street is in – out in front of the house we was living in – was a high hill, covered with flax, Toi Toi, Tutu, fern and all kinds of scrub. Wild pigs was often got in this rough scrub."

Maori neighbours

John McLay recalled his uncom-fortable first exposure to the local Maori:

"While we lived in Rattrey Street, we had to go up to the bush to get firewood. On the way up there was a Maori Camp on the left side... When we got near the Maori camp, us boys and Girls was terrible afraid of the wild Maoris dancing their war dances. It was terrible to see the frightful faces they made as they danced, leaped and jumped about – with fierce, blood-curdling yells. We trembled with fear.

"There was a row of men on one side with long spears in their hands, and 20 feet away was a row of women that these men seemed to be quarrel-ling about. These poor women were supposed to have been taken in some of their tribal fights.

"All the people about here was very much afraid of them. After a lot of complaints, the Superintendent (Cap-tain Cargill), Rev. Doctor Burns, and the magistrate, Mr Stroud [Chetham Strode], got them to shift down to Otago Heads. All was very pleased they had left this place for ever."

It is hard to know just what was going on at the Maori camp, if indeed it existed where McLay described it. The women would probably not have been prisoners, and the occupants could have been indulging in normal ceremonial activities – with an enthu-siasm possibly amplified by the white man's firewater. Activities like chal-lenges and haka would be very alien and frightening to a young immigrant from a very different culture. ∎

Maori in the media

Local Maori received little mention in the early newspapers. There were a few small advertisements in the Maori language, which would have meant nothing to the Scots and English.

In November 1852, the Otago Witness reprinted a long article from the Taranaki Herald titled 'The Amalgamation of the Anglo-Saxon and Maori Races'. No doubt it was read in Dunedin with great interest, albeit with a degree of detachment, given that the settlers shared their colony with relatively few Maori, and were separated by a considerable distance from the tensions of northern settlements. The article is reproduced on page 123.

The Witness commented in May 1853 that local Maori were becoming commercially sharp, in placing the best quality potatoes at the top of their sale baskets.

In October 1853 a short article described an assembly of Maori chiefs in Dunedin to sign a deed of sale to the Crown for the Murihiku Block (later known as Southland), for £2,600. This was only £200 more than the New Zealand Company had paid ten years earlier for the Otago Block, while the Murihiku land area was considerably greater.

Pawns

In 1853, Maori became pawns in local political intrigue. The 'Little Enemy' attempted to enlist Maori support against the Scottish class settlement establishment, in the first Provincial Council elections. Ultimately the attorney general ruled that Maori, as communal landowners, could not meet individual property qualifications for registration as voters. Donations toward the costs of "...preparing Claims and lodging Objections against the Maories" were later requested in a notice published by the Otago Witness.

Details of disturbances between Maori and Europeans in the North Island were published from time to time. In November 1855, settlers read that the arrival of 200 soldiers from Wellington and several field pieces had had a "very salutary effect" on Taranaki natives.

The Rattray Street camp described by McLay may have been removed by the new authorities, but Maori continued to camp on the beach for several years, in a situation which reflected poorly on civic authorities. The problem was bound up with arguments about whether a special Maori reserve should be created on the Dunedin foreshore, and the need for a Maori shelter in the town.

By June 1857, inaction had caused the Otago Colonist to thunder: "It is positively harrowing to the feelings of humanity to see a number of women being huddled together cold and shivering upon the open beach, with the thermometer below freezing point, exposed to the rain and snow; and yet such a spectacle might have been seen any night during the past week in the Christian town of Dunedin. An aged respectable native told us the other day that they desired a house as much for the purpose of keeping out Europeans, and spending the night in quietness, as anything else. We are almost ashamed to repeat his complaint that they are frequently forcibly roused up at mid-night by vagabonds who are a disgrace to their own community, and by them plied with intoxicating drink for the most debasing and foul purposes."

The newspaper stirred discussion, but no concrete action, and nothing was done about a town shelter and little about Maori welfare for the next two years. Then, in July 1858, the Colonist railed forth again: "...we can contribute freely towards the missions to India, to the New Hebrides and elsewhere, and yet can stand calmly for years and see the residue of the race we have supplanted dying out, and going down in the grave under our very eyes as it were, like the beasts that perish – surely we say there must be something radically out of joint."

Officials finally provided a town shelter in 1859 or 1860, and the churches stepped up pastoral activities among Maori living at Otago Heads, after forming the Society for the Elevation of the Physical, Moral and Social Conditions of the Maoris.

The Maori reserve, which would have been on the harbour side of Princes Street, was never granted, and remained a focus for grievance and claims for compensation.

While the coming of the Europeans was a mixed blessing at best for Otago Maori, relations between the two groups were generally excellent – much better than in New Zealand's northern settlements.

Maori played an important part in establishing the young settlement – guiding newcomers around the locality, growing food for them, showing which bush plants were edible and supplying them with fish and pigmeat. They demonstrated the use of local building materials and worked for the Europeans in a number of areas, making particular use of their skills in building and boating. ■

During the 1853 Provincial Council election campaign, the English 'Little Enemy' opposition to the Cargill Free Church establishment sought voting support from Maori. Here James Brown's cartoon shows blandishments being offered by Mantell (right) and Carnegie.

THE Inhabitants of Dunedin and Neighbourhood are respectfully requested to make a trial of the GLENFIELD PATENT STARCH, which is unequalled for purity.

Sold wholesale by 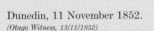 John M'Gibbon.
Retail by Mr. Healey, Baker,
        Mr. Summers, do.
        Mr. Allan, Storekeeper.

(Otago Witness, 6/11/1852)

Public Market of Otago in Dunedin

SEVERAL Individuals in the Agricultural Line having met, and taken into their serious consideration the benefit that would arise to the whole Community by the Establishment of a QUARTERLY MARKET for the exposing for Sale of Horses, Cattle, Pigs, &c., and all other Farm Produce, at a place to be agreed upon by the Voice of a Public Meeting, Do hereby call upon all persons interested in the Establishing of a Public Market, to assemble together on Thursday the 25th November 1852, at 6 o'clock p.m., in the School-House, to consider and decide upon the above proposition.

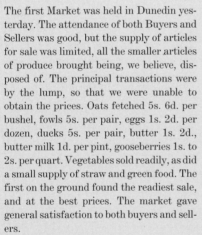

J. McGibbon.	Captain Blackie.
D. Calder.	D. London.

Dunedin, 11 November 1852. Ⓕ
(Otago Witness, 13/11/1852)

The first Market was held in Dunedin yesterday. The attendance of both Buyers and Sellers was good, but the supply of articles for sale was limited, all the smaller articles of produce brought being, we believe, disposed of. The principal transactions were by the lump, so that we were unable to obtain the prices. Oats fetched 5s. 6d. per bushel, fowls 5s. per pair, eggs 1s. 2d. per dozen, ducks 5s. per pair, butter 1s. 2d., butter milk 1d. per pint, gooseberries 1s. to 2s. per quart. Vegetables sold readily, as did a small supply of straw and green food. The first on the ground found the readiest sale, and at the best prices. The market gave general satisfaction to both buyers and sellers.

(Otago Witness, 4/12/52)

AMALGAMATION OF THE ANGLO-SAXON AND MAORI RACES

We have extracted from the " Taranaki Herald" the following article on the admission by the proposed Constitution of the natives to the electoral franchise, which, from the density of the native population in New Ulster, and the opportunities there afforded of judging of the native habits, our contemporary's opinion is of the more value:–

The political rights and privileges of the Natives in New Zealand as British subjects have never, till recently, been distinctly recognised by our legislators, whether at home or in the colony.

Now, for the first time, mention is made in decided terms of the amalgamation of the Anglo-Saxon and Maori races ; the claims of the latter to equal political rights with the former under the new Constitution being fully admitted. Sir J. Pakington takes credit for having conceived the project; nor is it likely to be rejected, for it is a subject of congratulation from Sir E. W. Buxton and the party he represents, and no objection seems to have been raised in any part of the House.

Under these circumstances it is absolutely necessary that the settlers should seriously consider the character and qualities, mental and social, of the nation with whom they are to regard hereafter as "fellow subjects" and who may any day become an influential body of electors, and even elected. The Secretary for the Colonies, in his speech in the House of Commons, quoted the following passage from a despatch of the New Zealand Aborigines :–

"It would appear that a race such as has been described could easily be incorporated into any British settlement, with mutual advantages to both races. * * * Such a class of settlements might easily grow into prosperous communities, into which the natives, with characters softened by Christianity, civilization, and a taste for previously unknown luxuries would readily be absorbed. This process of the incorporation of the native population into the European settlements has, accordingly, for the last few years, been taking place with a rapidity unexampled in history. Unless some sudden and unforeseen cause of interruption should occur, it will still proceed, and a very few years of continued peace and prosperity would suffice for the entire fusion of the two races into one nation."

He also set apart £7000 out of the revenues of the colony for "native purposes ;" among others, for the establishment of schools in those parts of New Zealand which shall be out of the Provinces ; looking forward, of course, to the time when a large portion of those districts shall become the property of Europeans, its native inhabitants really British subjects, and consequently entitled to exercise political rights.

Three questions arise in the mind on viewing the new position the natives are to take in relation to the Europeans. 1st, their numbers? 2nd, how far their social habits and physical condition favour the idea of amalgamation? 3rd, will their mental qualities fit them for the right use of the powers about to be conferred on them?

It is probable that New Zealand contains 100,000 natives, of whom by far the larger portion dwell dispersedly in the northern island. This number is daily diminishing. A respected missionary, who has dwelt among them for many years, and who now resides at Waimate, assures us it is so with sorrow. Dr. Thomson of the 58th regt. confirms this statement, and enumerates four principal reasons of this decay : "A considerable sterility among the women ; infanticide, chiefly from neglect ; neglect of the sick, more particularly the sick children ; and a great prevalence of scrofulous diathesis, which produces a large amount of sickness among men, women, and children"—(dangerous subjects for amalgamation!)

Dr. Thomson's statement is quite sufficient to make any sane European, man or woman, pause, at least, before they unite their lot to any member of a nation so afflicted. Of course lawful marriage is the social amalgamation contemplated by the Legislature ; any other being disgraceful to the European and degrading to the Maori ; but there are fewer legitimate unions now than 15 or 20 years ago, when only whalers and people from Sydney frequented these islands, and found none but Maori women to marry.

The great excess of males over females among the native tribes will of itself prevent, in a great measure, intermarriages between white men and native women ; in addition to which, it may be mentioned, that, until lately at least, the missionaries encouraged marriages among the natives at an injuriously premature age of the females to prevent their being sold to white men for illicit purposes, a practice now suppressed by the tone of society which exists in this colony. These early marriages have become habitual among the natives ; and it is painful to witness its result upon the diseased and feeble generation which is now growing up.

An educated European, who marries a native woman, must give up all idea of peace and domestic comfort. His wife can never be his friend and companion ; she may be his servant, for to serve somebody she has always believed to be her destiny in life. The natives are worse than the Scotch for tracing kindred ; and his wife's relations are in his house morning, noon and night, eating, smoking, talking, and sleeping at his expense ; angry if he attempt to turn them out, and seriously draining his pocket ; for he can scarcely refuse them anything with safety, or at least, with any prospect of peace.

A Maori will never marry a white woman, because he feels her superiority, and he cannot make a slave of her as a native woman. A white woman, not even the most degraded, could be induced to unite herself with a Maori—to herd native fashion in a PA, surrounded by vermin, filth, disease, and discomfort in every conceivable form— to carry enormous burdens, such as faggots of firewood, heavy kits of potatoes, maize, or wheat, weighing generally 50 and 60 lbs.— and to perform other laborious work exacted from their women by barbarous races wherever they may exist.

Another obstacle in the amalgamation which our home legislators hope to effect is the apparently indomitable preference of the natives for their pas. This was unfortunately fostered in former times for purposes we need not here allude to. It seems an utter impossibility to persuade the natives to live in separate families after the European fashion. They like to herd together at night to talk. Their fear of evil spirits, who are then abroad, as they think, deters many from stirring beyond the precincts of their pas. They like the stifling heat of their huts impervious to air ; and as long as their tobacco, or a bit of wood ember remains,

there they will squat on their haunches and smoke and prate about–Land– their eternal topic. Let any one who has been in the pas at night give an insight into what an Englishwoman would suffer if condemned to take part in these nightly conclaves. Let him describe the nude figures of dirty, fetid, unwashed men, women, and children, of all ages, squatting or lying about, accompanied by pigs and dogs ; some perhaps wrapped in filthy blankets or ragged mats, augmenting the unwholesome effluvia of the place. Let him paint the natives at home, and our readers will perceive that one means of amalgamation is impossible.
(Otago Witness, 6/11/1852)

GLENFIELD PATENT STARCH,
NOW USED IN THE ROYAL LAUNDRY,
And awarded "Honourable Mention" at the Great Exhibition.

The following very flattering Testimonial from upwards of Fifty of the principal grocers in Glasgow, where the Starch has been long Sold, is the best proof of its great superiority :—
"We, the Undersigned, have been selling the GLENFIELD PATENT STARCH for some time, and find that it pleases our customers

BETTER THAN ANY WE HAVE HAD."

The Ladies are therefore respectfully solicited to make a trial of the GLENFIELD PATENT DOUBLE-REFINED POWDER STARCH, which, for Domestic Use, now stands unrivalled.

Copy of testimonial from the Laundress of Her Majesty's Royal Laundry, Richmond, Surrey.

Mr. WOTHERSPOON, 40 Dunlop St., Glasgow
The Glenfield Patent Powder Starch has now been used for some time in that Department of the Royal Laundry where all the Finest Goods are finished for her Majesty, Prince Albert and the Royal Family, and I have much pleasure in informing you that it has given the highest satisfaction.
M. WEIGH, Laundress to Her Majesty.
Royal Laundry,
Richmond, near London, 15th May 1851.

Sold wholesale by JOHN McGIBBON. Retail by Mr. HEALEY, Mr. ALLAN, and Mr. SUMMERS.
(Otago Witness, 11/12/1852)

Holloway's Pills for Bowel Complaints, Diarrhoea, and Disordered Stomachs.—Persons subject to these complaints cannot use a finer medicine than these invaluable Pills, and if taken in moderate doses, and the diet attended to, a certain cure will be effected. Their strengthening nature speedily renovates the impaired tone of the stomach, and renders the digestive organs more powerful. Bile and disorders of the liver may be infallibly cured by their use, and those who are suffering from a long residence in hot climates cannot adopt a more effectual remedy than Holloway's Pills. They are also the best family medicine extant.
(Otago Witness, 25/12/1852) (Holloway's pills and ointments were advertised regularly for many years, usually in larger and more elaborate advertisements than this example.)

SOIREE.

MECHANICS' INSTITUTION

THE above Building will be opened by a SOIREE on Monday the 3rd January, at half-past 6 o'Clock p.m.
Several Gentlemen will address the Meeting ; and the entertainment of the Evening will be varied by Songs and Duetts.
Tickets of Admission 2s. 6d, to be had of Messrs Adam, Scott and Rennie. The proceeds to go towards liquidating the debt on the building.
(Otago Witness, 1/1/1853)

HOME-SPUN WEAVING

THE Undersigned having got his WEAVING and WARPING LOOM completed, begs to inform the public that after harvest he will commence the Weaving of Shepherd Tartan, Blankets, Plaiding, &c. ; and parties having Spun Yarn will have an opportunity of getting it manufactured into cloth at Moderate charges.
JOHN BARR
Mavis Bank, Little Paisley
22nd January, 1853
(Otago Witness, 22/1/1853) (First industry in Dunedin)

We have much pleasure in calling the attention of the public to the announcement of Mr. Barr that he will be prepared to commence weaving immediately after harvest ; and we trust there will be no want of yarn. Spinning wheels have been manufactured in the colony, and can be obtained in Dunedin. We are informed that a purchase of wool at 1s. 3d. per lb. has been made for the purpose of manufacturing in the colony ; at any rate there can be no difficulty in obtaining wool ; and why should we be paying long prices for many imported items manufactured for sale, and not for use, when we can make a better and cheaper article for ourselves. In the few instances in which we have seen yarn made in the settlement from colonial wool, it has been of superior quality, and when woven into the coarser kinds of clothing would command a ready sale. There is a large number of our population who have all their lives been accustomed to spin; they should not neglect so useful an employment here, so that " once again we may hear the burr of Scotland's spinning-wheel."
(Otago Witness, 22/1/1853)

THE Undersigned begs to inform his Friends and the Public that he has opened a BUTCHER'S STALL in High Street, Dunedin, where he intends to sell Meat of the best quality at Reduced Prices.
JOHN SIDEY.
January 1st, 1853
(Otago Witness, 29/1/1853)

Public Market

AS business of importance is to be considered, a full attendance of Members of the Committee is requested on Friday, the 25th instant, at 12 o'clock noon, in the Royal Hotel.
JOHN MCGIBBON, Convenor
(Otago Witness, 12/2/1853)

Anniversary Fair for Live Stock

AT a Meeting of the Market Committee held on the 25th ultimo, Mr. Calder in the Chair, it was resolved to hold a Market for the sale of Horses, Cattle, and other Live Stock, on Friday, the 26th instant, at Mr. Cutten's Stockyard, in the vicinity of the Court-House, the Market to commence at 11 A.M.
The Committee would suggest the propriety of parties having grain for sale coming provided with samples, and that purchasers of grain should attend.
(Otago Witness, 5/3/1853)

For Sale or to Let,

A WELL-BUILT Fern-Tree House, floored and lofted, situated in Princes Street. A quarter of an acre of land is attached, which is held on lease.
For particulars apply to
WM. WHITE, Princes Street.
(Otago Witness, 5/3/1853)

REAPERS WANTED IMMEDIATELY at Grant's Braes.
Reapers are requested to bring their own Hooks (not Sickles) and Sharpening Stones.
Apply to A. BURNS or to J. RITCHIE.
(Otago Witness, 5/3/1853)

DUNEDIN PROPERTY INVESTMENT COMPANY.

A PUBLIC MEETING will be held in the School-Room, Dunedin, on Tuesday, the 15th instant, at half-past 6 o'clock p.m., for the purpose of commencing the above Society, Submitting the Rules, Enrolling of Shareholders, and the election of Office-Bearers.
By order of the Interim Committee,
THOMAS BAIN.
(Otago Witness, 5/3/1853)

THE " Royal Albert," from London direct, arrived at the Heads on Saturday night, the 5th inst. She sailed from London on the 1st November, and from the Downs on the 9th. She brings 120 passengers, about 50 of whom are for this place. Owing to some difficulty which we are unable at present to explain, she is still lying off the native village, inside the heads.
(Otago Witness, 12/3/1853)

Moving to Caversham

Some time during 1850, the McGibbon family relocated to its ten acre suburban section at Caversham. They had bought this section, along with a quarter acre in town and 50 acres in the country, as part of their standard New Zealand Company land package.

While at Caversham, they added another 20 acres and developed a small farm which included dairy cows and poultry. Possibly John McGibbon intended from the outset to move into agriculture, even though it was a 180 degree career switch for a Glasgow storekeeper. But such a switch was not unusual. Many New Zealand immigrants exchanged shopkeepers' aprons or steel pens for a life on the land.

The decision to get out of retailing may also have been influenced by the prevailing economic conditions. Dunedin was anything but a boom town, and, as we have seen, it had more shops than it needed.

Land sales had been well below expectation, and as a result, New Zealand Company activities were grinding to a halt. Captain Cargill had been told in April 1850 to stop road development, and keep labour costs to a minimum. In October, word came that the Company had been wound up. The colony now had to rely on its own resources, though it was under the administrative control of the British Crown, in the person of Governor George Grey in Auckland.

Stagnation

Stagnation was inevitable. There was no longer an effective campaign in the home country to sell Otago land and sign up emigrants, though the Lay Association of the Free Church of Scotland would continue rather ineffectual promotions for another two years.

Back in Dunedin, the requirements for development were sadly lacking. There was no properly constituted bank and no land transfer system which could award legal titles, register and transfer property. There was no regular shipping communication with other ports in New Zealand. Most serious of all, there was almost no money to develop the town infrastructure – the roads, bridges and other public works.

The only form of community income was customs duty on goods coming into Dunedin. The Crown kept a firm grip on that income, and spent most of it on government officials, most of whom were little more than seat-warmers. As well as this, most were English and formed the nucleus of the 'Little Enemy' opposition to the Scottish clique.

The largest single drain on community funds was the Supreme Court, presided over by Justice Sidney Stephen. During his two years in this remarkably law-abiding community, the judge had no cases to try. Yet he was paid the princely salary of £800 a year – 60 per cent higher than the Otago Superintendent's £500.

As a gazetted juror, John McGibbon would have been among the 36 men summoned to the pointless twice-yearly Supreme Court sittings.

There was also a surprisingly large police force and a resident magistrate who, with the help of a large number of local justices of the peace, dealt with run of the mill offences. These consisted mainly of drunkenness and fighting, usually involving ships' crews.

The Otago Witness, complaining about Governor Grey and his "despotic schemes", noted that the resident magistrate and the armed police cost £600 a year, yet "...dirt and filth are cast into the streets, bridges are taken away for firewood, holes are dug for sand and clay in the middle of the streets, bullock carts are driven in the drain, and every species of the destruction of public property goes on without restraint."

Small wonder there was continual

Certificate of selection for John McGibbon's first ten acre suburban block at Caversham. He added a further 20 acres to the property. (National Archives)

A SPECIAL GENERAL MEETING of the Otago Settlers' Association will be held in the School-Room on Monday Evening next, at Six o'clock precisely, for the purpose of receiving several Communications from Home, and other important Business.

By Order of Committee,
P. PROUDFOOT.
(Otago Witness, 12/3/1853)

WE learn with satisfaction that the Wool shipped from this Port last year, and sold in London at the last October Wool Sales, fetched as high as 1s. 8½ and 1s. 9d. per lb.
(Otago Witness, 12/3/1853)

ON the 25th ultimo the Rev. Charles Jeffreys delivered the Opening Lecture at the Mechanics' Institution, the subject being "A remarkable lately discovered Experiment for establishing, by means of a Pendulum, the fact of the rotation of the Earth about its Axis." The attendance was numerous, many persons coming from a considerable distance to be present. Many were, however, unable to obtain admission. The lecture gave universal satisfaction.
(Otago Witness, 12/3/1853)

BY the arrival of the "Scotia" from Wellington, we have received our files of colonial papers, from which we have given several extracts. Very little of importance has occurred since our last advices, not withstanding our not having received a mail direct from that Settlement for nearly four months...

We learn from the Government Gazette" of the 19th Nov., that three more Magistrates have been added to the already notorious Otago Bench—addition of which will not raise the dignity, or increase the respect in which it is held by the public...

One of the new J.P.s has been most actively engaged in making preparations, and has avowed his intention of enfranchising the Natives wholesale, without reference to the qualifications required for Europeans.

There are now 19 Magistrates appointed to Otago, or about 1¼ per cent. upon the population, or 1 J.P. to every 20 male adults, or 1 to every 13 electors.
(Otago Witness, 12/3/1853)

FOR SALE

A POWERFUL CHEESE PRESS
An American Churn
Superior Scotch Cart Harness
Bullock Chains
Large Iron Milk Dish, with Valve
Small quantity of Sheet Lead
Lamp Black
Cotton Wick
Gutta Percha Soles
Apply to MR. CUTTEN
(Otago Witness, 2/4/1853)

ONE THOUSAND POUNDS AND DAMAGES can be recovered by the manufacturer of the Glenfield Double Refined Patent Starch from any party attempting to introduce to the market any article in Starch, bearing a similar name or similar packages to the above. Reference is made to the case recently tried in Chancery (see "Times," &c., of 29th and 30th July), in which the Advertisers obtained a Writ prohibiting S. J. Milne and others, from selling Starch in similar packages, or bearing a similar name to the Glenfield Starch, under the above penalty !

The Master of the Rolls said there could be "but one opinion of the conduct of the "Defendant, which was shrewdly devised to " deceive the Public and promote the sale of "Defendant's article under false pretences."— Vide "Morning Herald" of 29th July.

Considering the high reputation which the Glenfield Starch has acquired from its intrinsic merit, the Proprietor will justly consider it a Fraud against the Public and himself, on the part of anyone bringing himself, under the penalty contained in the "Writ of Chancery" before referred to, and will consider it his duty to proceed against such parties according to Law.

The Ladies

are respectfully requested to observe that the Glenfield Starch has been specially recommended on account of its Superior Strength and Purity by the Laundress to Her Majesty ; the Laundress to Her Excellency the Countess of Eglinton ; the Marchioness of Breadalbane ; the Countess of Dartmouth ; the Lady Mayoress of London; the Lady of W. Chambers, Esq., of Glenormiston, &c. ; and if anxious to secure their laces and other fine articles of the Toilet " well dressed," are solicited to make a trial of the Glenfield Patent Starch, which is sold by all respectable Grocers, Druggists, &c., in the United Kingdom.

Sold wholesale by R. Wotherspoon & Co., 40, Dunlop St., Glasgow, and John McGibbon, Dunedin, Otago ; Retail by John Healey and Andrew Summers, Bakers, Princes Street.
(Otago Witness, 7/5/1853)

Civilization certainly seems to have had the effect of sharpening the Wits of the Maories, if not of fostering the bump of conscientiousness, inasmuch as they have learned to pack their baskets in such a manner that good potatoes are visible, while the centre contains rubbish. The shortness of supply in the town may be accounted for by the vile state of the roads, which render us dependent upon those places having water carriage; hence the ready sale for native grown crops.
(Otago Witness, 14/5/1853)

---

agitation for self-government, which was finally achieved with the passing of the Constitution Act in 1852. News of the Act triggered the biggest party yet seen in the colony, but it would be another year before the first Otago Provincial Council would sit. From that time though, Dunedin's fortunes would begin to improve.

One indication of the slowdown in the young colony is the fall-off in the numbers of ships visiting the port. Between March 1848 and December 1849, 13 ships arrived. Only 15 came between 1850 and 1853, and then around ten ships arrived each year between 1854 and 1860. After 1860, ship arrivals – and economic and population growth generally – increased greatly under the stimulus of the Central Otago goldrush.

Incentive

Given the business stagnation, there was every incentive for John McGibbon to do something other than retailing.

When the family moved to its suburban selection at Caversham is not clear, but they were certainly living in their new home, Ambresbeg, in early January 1851 when the Reverend Burns listed family members in his visitation book.

Burns noted that the family included John and his wife Jane, plus Thomas (11), Jessie (8), Jeannie (6) and John (1). Living with them, probably as a maid, was Margaret McNeil. McNeil had sailed with the McGibbons in the Mooltan as a 34 year old, giving her occupation as servant.

Three more McGibbon children would be born at Ambresbeg: David in 1851, Ebenezer in 1854 and Archibald in 1856. David died in 1858 and was the first occupant of the Presbyterian section of Dunedin's new Southern Cemetery.

Jane Bannerman's article on Jane McGibbon says the family built a "comfortable and commodious" house at Caversham, and adds, "...it was here that the brave lady began colonial life in earnest, and very laborious it must often have been. Besides the cares of her house and family there were the fowls and the garden, and the labours of a considerable dairy early and late, but she brought in brave spirit to the work and it prospered in her hands."

We get some idea of the property from its eventual sale notice: "A VERY DESIRABLE PROPERTY, consisting

FRUIT TREES FOR SALE

THE Undersigned has for Sale the following collection of Fruit Trees, &c. :— Apples 1s. each or 10s. per doz. ; Pears 1s. each or 10s. per doz. ; Plums, Purple Gage, 1s. 6d. to 2s. 6d. each ; Damsons 1s. each or 10s. per doz. ; Moa's Egg 1s. to 1s. 6d. each ; Cherries 1s. to 2s. 6d. each ; Figs 1s. each; Gooseberries 4s. to 6s. per doz. ; Red Currants 4s. to 5s. per doz. ; Black Currants 6s per doz. ; Raspberry Canes 2s. per doz. ; Strawberries, Large Red Alpine, 2s. 6d. per 100. Honeysuckle Plants 1s. each ; Fuschias and Roses of sorts 6d. each. A collection of Flowers too numerous to mention, and very moderate.

Parties wishing to send home native seeds can be supplied by the Undersigned, and orders may be left at Messrs. Jones & Grey's store, Princes Street.

DAVID BOWER, Gardener, Pelichet's Bay.

(Otago Witness, 21/5/1853)

To the Electors of Otago

CONSIDERABLE expense having been incurred in preparing Claims and in lodging Objections against the Maories, it is hoped that the Electors will provide the necessary funds. Upwards of £30 have been expended.

Subscriptions will be received by the Treasurer, Mr. Macandrew, or any member of the Committee.

By Order of Committee,
PET. PROUDFOOT.

(Otago Witness, 16/7/1853)

To Stand this Season,

From the 15th October, 1853,
AT THE STABLES OF THE ROYAL HOTEL,
THE THOROUGH-BRED HORSE
IL BARBIERE, or THE BARBER.

THIS Horse was got by *Figaro* out of a thorough-bred Mare imported from England by the late H. A. Thompson, Esq., of Nelson. This Mare was by *Emilius*, (winner of the Derby) out of *Sal*, own sister to *Sam*, (also a derby winner) by *Scud*.

Figaro, a thorough-bred Horse, was foaled in New South Wales in 1837, by *Operator* out of *Adelaide* by *Theorem*. *Operator* was foaled in 1832 by *Emilius*, dam *Worthless* by *Walton* out of *Altisidora* by Dick Andrews.

Adelaide was by *Theorem* out of *Manso*, a thorough-bred Mare imported into New South Wales, by T. Icely, Esq. *Vide* Stud Book.

On Monday, the 3rd instant, the whole of the principal Chiefs, and a large number of the native population, assembled at Port Chalmers, for the purpose of completing the sale of the lands Southward of Otago, when the necessary documents were signed and witnessed, and the first instalment of the purchase money paid over to the natives. There was the usual amount of speechmaking, and the arrangements passed off without dispute. We cannot refrain from again expressing our satisfaction at the settlements of this transaction, adding as it does to the province of Otago, as large and fine a district, both for agriculture and pasturage purposes as any in New Zealand. It is impossible to over-estimate

the advantages it will be to the setters of Otago.

(Otago Witness, 8/10/1853)

THERE is no news which will be received with a greater degree of satisfaction by our country settlers than the intimation given from the pulpit last Sabbath, that the Rev. Mr. Will, a Minister of the Free Church, recently ordained, is expected to arrive in the Province by a vessel which was to sail in the month of September. To us, as a Free Church Settlement, this is an essentially desirable addition, and it must have been a constant source of regret that we have not been able to accomplish this before. It must have been felt by every one that it was impossible to carry out and maintain our character as a Christian People, with but one Minister, to whom the constant increase and dispersion of our settlers must have been a source of continued anxiety, from the utter impossibility of his overtaking his increased and increasing labours.

(Otago Witness, 15/10/1853)

TO LET ON LEASE

THAT Desirable Piece of Ground, adapted for a STORE, situated in Princes Street, between the Stores of Mr. McGlashan and Mr. Robertson.

For terms, apply to John M'Gibbon, Caversham.

(Otago Witness, 19/11/1853.)

NOTICE

TO BE LET ON LEASE,

ALL that old-established Hotel known by the name of the " Commercial Inn," situate Dunedin.

For particulars as to Rent, &c., apply to William Stevenson, Builder, Dunedin, acting trustee of the late T. S. Watson, deceased.

Dunedin, 2nd Nov., 1853

(Otago Witness, 19/11/1853)

Watercolour of Caversham Valley painted by Juliet Valpy in May 1852. Miss Valpy identified houses on the hillside as belonging to Messrs McGibbon, Blackie, Nicolson and Peterson. (Otago Settlers' Museum)

THE reception with which Mr. John McGlashan met on Friday last is a most significant fact in itself, as showing how completely unfounded are the charges against the scheme of the settlement, and as a manifestation of how highly the great body of the settlers appreciate that gentleman's labours, and the blessings attended upon a systematic style of colonization. It is true that our progress has been somewhat slow; but as trees of the slowest growth are the most durable timber, so, no doubt, it will be with Otago. Colonies in the gold country grow with astonishing rapidity ; but the start is the most vigorous part of their existence. With us our population is of a picked class—every stone forming the edifice has been quarried and hewn to fit its station ; and the foundation being sound, the superstructure will be secure.
(Otago Witness, 29/10/1853.)

VACCINATION

PARTIES requiring their Children Vaccinated are requested to call at Stonehenge, Dunedin, every Saturday, at 11 o'clock in the forenoon.

HENRY MANNING,
SURGEON, &c.
(Otago Witness, 17/12/1853.) (First vaccinations in Dunedin.)

NOTICE is hereby given, that the Master of the Ship, "CARNATIC" will not be answerable for any Debts contracted by the Crew.

Otago, 13th Dec., 1853
(Otago Witness, 17/12/1853.)

THE past week has been one of holiday making, the New Year having been kept with various sports—near Dunedin, and in the Taieri especially. We have no space for details, but shooting at a mark appears to have been much approved of ; and we are happy to state that no accident occurred. Out-door sports are certainly a much more preferable method of welcoming in the New Year than are some of the practices in the old country. The weather may there be pleaded as an excuse, but we trust that our colonists will take advantage of the change of season on this side of the globe to enjoy themselves in future—as they have done on the late occasion—in a more rational way.
(Otago Witness, 7/1/1854)

ADDITIONAL Subscriptions received towards defraying the expenses of Outfit and Passage of two Ministers to this Colony:-

Subscriptions already advertised	£106 13 0
John McGibbon	0 10 0
John Salmond	1 0 0
Peter Lindsay	1 0 0

Subscriptions will be received by Mr. James Adam, Princes St.

(Otago Witness, 18/3/1854)

CHEESE FOR SALE

EX "ENDEAVOUR," from the Clutha, a quantity of very Superior Ripe Cheese, of Redpath's well-known brand.
J. MACANDREW & Co.
(Otago Witness, 18/3/1854)

---

of 30 acres of LAND, all fenced round, with a large DWELLING HOUSE, Barn, Stockyard, and abundance of timber and good water for domestic purposes. A considerable quantity of the ground is under grass, nearly 8 acres ploughed and ready for seed. Persons connected with Dunedin by business, will find the said property exceedingly useful."

A lifestyle block?

The advertisement gives a clue as to how the Caversham property fitted into John McGibbon's scheme of things. If it would "...particularly suit persons connected with Dunedin by business", he may have seen it as a sideline activity. Was Ambresbeg the Victorian equivalent of today's lifestyle block?

Most of the work on the farm could have been done by Jane and the children, with help from the maid. (The maid was likely to have been paid £19 a year – almost double the going rate in Scotland.)

McGibbon kept his Rattray Street store going for a year or more after moving to Caversham, and it would have been very difficult to combine the two operations. While cutting down bush and developing the house and farm, he was walking the four kilometres into town each day. In the winter particularly, slogging through the bogs and bush would have been an arduous start to the day. It is not surprising that he would want to put a stop to the daily trek as soon as he could develop other ways of making money.

Captain William Blackie and his wife Jane, who were shipmates of McGibbon family, and also their neighbours in Dunedin.

The Otago News and Otago Witness give us fragments of other business activities. In July 1850, McGibbon was appointed to a committee which was to investigate the possibilities of setting up a run near Kaikorai where butchers could run sheep to provide meat for the town. Other members of the committee included the town's wealthiest man, William Valpy, and a Mooltan shipmate and Caversham neighbour, Captain Blackie.

In February 1852, after he had left the shop, McGibbon advertised a variety of goods he had imported via the ship *Columbus*. They included Glenfield's Powdered Starch, tobacco pipes, wrought single nails, table knives, Britannia metal teaspoons, assorted gimlets, Scotch reaping hooks, bath bricks, epsom salts, senna, flour sulphur, roll sulphur, calcines magnesia, cream of tartar, nitre, blacking, Bell's Patent Matches, ladies' combs, worsted and moleskin.

Later in the year, and again in 1853, he described himself as a wholesaler in long-winded advertisements for Glenfield's Patent Starch.

McGibbon and Blackie were among four signatories to a November 1852 notice inviting people to attend a meeting aimed at establishing a public market for farm produce: "Several Individuals in the Agricultural Line having met, and taken into their serious consideration the benefit that would arise to the whole Community by the establishment of a QUARTERLY MARKET for the exposing for Sale of Horses, Cattle, Pigs, &c., and all other Farm Produce..."

FOR SALE,

A SET of the most approved Scotch Barn Fanners, or winnowing machines, made by M'Cartney and Drummond.—Apply to

J MACANDREW & CO.

(Otago Witness, 25/3/1854)

DUNEDIN SCHOOL.

The Annual Examination of the School in Dunedin taught by Mr. Robert McDowall took place on Wednesday last in presence of the office-bearers of the Church, and of a respectable number of the heads of families and other inhabitants of the place. The number of pupils in attendance during the season amounted to 60, or thereby. The branches taught were English reading and writing, English grammar, geography, arithmetic and Latin ; the children, with hardly any exceptions, being under 11 or 12 years of age, and the great majority of them under 8 or 9. The different branches taught were mostly elementary ; at the same time, the proficiency displayed, and the progress made in each, was highly creditable to both teacher and pupils, more especially in the department of geography. In arithmetic and English grammar, in English reading and writing, the examination was very sat-

isfactory. The great disappointment was that the numbers of children in attendance should not bear a larger proportion to the extent of the population in Dunedin and the surrounding neighborhood. Between the two schools n Dunedin there does not seem to be much above 100 children at school. There must be, we think, about 50 more running about idle, to their own serious loss as well as to the great reproach of the parents. We feel it to be a duty incumbent on us to call attention to this.

(Otago Witness, 1/4/1854)

At an early hour on Tuesday last, the Court-house was surrounded by applicants for the unoccupied sections, the private estate of the New Zealand Company. The sections appeared to be in good request, there being in one instance no fewer than 189 applications put in, each applicant being more eager than his neighbour to ascertain how far fortune would favour him, and ready, at a moment's notice to avail himself of the minute afforded to complete the purchase, in case his name should be called. Mr. Commissioner Mantell's balloting arrangements were highly satisfactory, and the public were satisfied that no preference was given to one individual over another.

Otago Witness, 22/4/1854:

R ESTORATION and completion of the Line of Poles from " Half-Way Bush" to the " Clump of Trees."

LIST OF CONTRIBUTORS.

	£	s.	D.
John Jones	1	0	0
J Macandrew & Co.	1	0	0
A. Chetham Strode	0	10	0
Walter Mantell	0	10	0
H. C. Hertslett	0	10	0
Fredk. Richardson	0	10	0
George Duncan	0	10	0
W. G. Filleul	0	10	0
Messrs Harris and Gillies	0	10	0
George Smith	0	10	0
G. B. Wright	0	10	0
John Sutton	0	5	0

(Otago Witness, 14/4/1854)

BIRTHS

At Ambresbeg, Caversham Vale, on the 9th inst., Mrs John M'Gibbon, of a Son.

At the Forbury Hill, on the 11th inst., Mrs John Anderson, of a Son.

(Otago Witness, 22/4/1854. The McGibbon child was Ebenezer.)

FOR SALE,

A Few very superior Cows and Heifers. To be seen at Mr. Barrs, Mavis Bank. Apply to George Duncan or James Reid, Princes Street.

(Otago Witness, 8/4/1854)

Part of Caversham Vale in the late 1850s, showing what is believed to be the McGibbon family's 30 acre Ambresbeg property (in the central to upper left part of the photograph). A wooden house with a verandah, and outbuildings, can be seen. Although no animals are visible, it is known that the property had dairy cows, bullocks, horses and poultry. Ambresbeg was the political centre for Dunedin's Eastern District between 1855 and 1858. It was advertised as the place where people could inspect the rolls and later cast their vote. It was also used for at least one political dinner in support of Dunedin's Scottish faction. On the upper far right side of the photograph can be seen Captain Blackie's wattle and daub cottage, near the Blackie limeworks. The photograph gives a good idea of the original bush cover in this valley, and shows how early fences were constructed.

THE ancient custom of " Harvest Home" was celebrated by the settlers of the East Taieri on Thursday se'nnight past. The festival was a simultaneous one, the assembly meeting at Mr. Todd's, who kindly gave the use of his premises for the purpose, and rendered every assistance to promote the comfort and happiness of his fellow settlers and their guests. The arrangements did great credit to Mr. Oughton, and Messrs. Todd, Shands and Allans, junrs. Mr. Todd's large barn was tastefully fitted up and decorated for the occasion with devices, exhibiting the wild fern, flax, and tutu of New Zealand, superseded by the products of European cultivation. Nearly 100 sat down to a sumptuous dinner at 6½ o'clock, after which and the usual adjuncts, the floor was cleared for the dance,—music, song, and dance, alternating until an early hour in the morning, when the party separated for their respective homes, highly pleased with their evening's enjoyment.
(Otago Witness, 29/4/1854)

OTAGO PROPERTY INVESTMENT COMPANY.

The Quarterly Meeting of this Society was held in the School-Room on Tuesday evening, 2nd instant. Mr. Wm. Stevenson in the Chair.

The Secretary read the Minutes of the Company since last quarterly meeting, and reported a balance in the Treasurer's hands of £212 17s. ½d., which was then put up to auction, and realised the following premiums, which are higher than those of any previous occasions :—

1st lot of £160,	premium at per £20	£8	7
2nd " £80,	"	8	10
3rd " £80,	"	8	1
4th " £20,	"	8	5
5th " £20,	"	7	3

The amount advanced amounted to £360, and the premiums to £148 8s.,- making a total sum out at interest of £1500 at the close of the first year of the Society.
(Otago Witness, 6/5/1854)

To the Editor of the OTAGO WITNESS

SIR:– In the *Witness* of 15th inst. Mr. Peter Proudfoot, in reporting on the various districts of public road repaired by the voluntary efforts of the settlers, has made use of language in reference to the work done in Caversham Vale calculated to impress on the public the idea that the funds collected were not judiciously expended. The public must understand first, that out of twenty-one settlers invited to attend a meeting to arrange about repairing the road, only four appeared, and on these lay the burden of doing the work. Compare the indifference manifested by several in the Caversham Vale, to whom good roads must be an advantage, with the hearty and almost unanimous turn-out of settlers in the other districts, and say is the work well or ill done. Secondly, keep in remembrance the shocking bad state of the road previous to the temporary improvement (and all the improvements in this and other districts are temporary), and the improvement effected by going direct into the bad parts. We had not power, be it observed, to deviate from the old line of the road like our neighbours in Green Island district, who thereby gave the slip to a great deal of dirty work. The dray and cart reposing-holes were more numerous here than in the other districts, yet these by our efforts are removed. In short, the road is as comfortable as elsewhere, and yet Mr. Proudfoot is pleased to say it is "*not well done* ; there is not obtained for the public value equal to the money expended." Verily, had he been two days nearly to his knees in mud giving us a helping hand he would "hae ken't better aboot it."—I am, &c.,

JOHN M'GIBBON.

N.B.—Your insertion of this will be but justice to the Caversham folk.—J. M'G.
(Otago Witness, 29/5/1854)

This was the second attempt to set up such a market in Dunedin. It was never very successful, partly because individual farmers rarely had much surplus to sell. John McGibbon became convenor of the market, which seems to have petered out after the October 1853 session, where "Transactions were few and prices were high. Milk Cows sold for £18. Holders did not appear anxious to part with their stock...it is quite evident there is a great need of importations."

Earlier in the year, the Otago Witness had commented that the Market Committee and the Committee of the Mechanics' Institution were important local bodies, but that lately, both committees had been asleep.

The Dunedin Hundred

One of John McGibbon's more public activities was in connection with the Dunedin Hundred. The system of hundreds was a short-lived arrangement to administer closer settlement of land for agricultural purposes. The actual working of the system in Dunedin is something of a mystery, but it seems to have been used mainly to administer grazing of cattle on land not already taken up for agriculture.

A system of hundreds for the Otago Block was mooted in May 1852, but nothing more appeared in the newspapers until October 1854, when the British Crown proclaimed three hundreds in the Otago Block. One of them, the Dunedin Hundred, was to include lands in the Taieri and Dunedin districts.

These hundreds were apparently never set up, because in September 1856, we see a new proclamation of hundreds within the Otago Block, this time eight of them. 'Depasturing' licences would cost 10/-, and licence holders would be charged 1/- per head for small cattle and 5/- per head for 'great cattle'.

In February 1857, the Witness named 75 initial licensees for the Dunedin Hundred. They included John McGibbon, along with many of the town's notables including Cargill, McGlashan and Macandrew.

Seven wardens were elected to administer the Hundred. One of them was John McGibbon, who would be appointed secretary two months later. Over the next few months, until November 1857, McGibbon signed notices regarding meetings, and a warning that dogs worrying cattle would be shot.

There were no more newspaper references to the Dunedin Hundred until June 1858, when a Witness correspondent asked what had been done with the £50 paid by licensees the previous year. This money was supposed to have been spent on improvements to benefit the licence holders.

The editor replied that the wardens had pursued an "extraordinary course" with the funds, and in some cases, licence fees had been returned to those who had paid them. No accounts had ever been published, so "...we are, like our correspondent, in ignorance of what was done with the whole sum." The editor noted that no-one had turned up to a meeting held to elect new wardens. This showed the licensees were "...indifferent upon the subject and do not appreciate the advantages and privileges of the system of Hundreds, – an indifference which, we believe, they will some day regret."

Presumably one of John McGibbon's commercial activities was running his own cattle on the Dunedin Hundred.

He would also have owned a separate 50 acre rural block that came with the original land package. This block may well have been on the Taieri Plains. His name also appears in National

INAUGURATION OF THE PRESBYTERY OF OTAGO, NEW ZEALAND Ⓕ

The inauguration of the Presbytery of Otago, in accordance with the public notification to that effect, took place in the church of Dunedin on the 27th ult. Present—the Rev Thomas Burns, Minister, and His Honour the Superintendent of Otago, elder of the Church of Dunedin. The Reverend William Will, Minister; and Mr. John Allan, elder of the church in the Taieri and Waihola districts. And the Rev. William Bannerman, Minister of the church in the Tokomairiro and Clutha districts.

Besides the members of the Presbytery, there were from 200 to 300 elders and members of the Church of Otago, including several from the rural districts. [Much more.]
(Otago Witness, 8/7/1854.)

By the *Thomas and Henry*, which arrived here on the 17th inst. from Sydney, *via* Wellington, we received our colonial papers to late date, containing English intelligence to 4th April. War against Russia had been formally declared, both in England and France—(see 4th page.) The markets in consequence upon this announcement had gone up.
(Otago Witness, 29/7/1854)

HARVEST HOME
(Communicated)

On Friday evening the 14th inst. the settlers resident in the Half-way Bush district met together in the commodious barn of Mr. James Marshall, to celebrate for the first time their Harvest Home. The evening being fine, about 70 persons assembled, and at 6½ o'clock sat down to an excellent and substantial dinner. The arrangements on the occasion were in every way complete, and did great credit to the young gentlemen who took charge of the entertainment. The apartment was very tastefully decorated with evergreens, flowers, and flags, the Royal Standard of Great Britain being displayed at one end of the room, and the Union Jack at the other.

Mr. G. Hepburn occupied the Chair, supported by the Rev. R. Hood, and Mr. A. Chalmers. Messrs. Gillies and Williamson acted as croupiers. After the usual loyal and patriotic toasts, which were duly honored and accompanied respectively by the " Queen's Anthem," and " Rule Britannia," (led by Mr. James Adam) the Chairman rose to propose the toast of the evening, namely, " The Agricultural and Pastoral Interests of Otago, and particularly of this District....

....Mr. Paterson, in a highly humorous and diverting speech, gave, " The Ladies."

Mr. D. Hood, in the name of the Ladies, very amusingly replied....

....On the suggestion of the Chairman, the company retired to the house of Mr. Marshall's (where tea was in readiness for the ladies) till the tables should be removed preparatory to dancing, which was kept up with much spirit till an early hour.
(Otago Witness, 29 July, 1854)

WORKING BULLOCKS

FOR SALE, Four Bullocks, two Rung and partly Broke in. Apply to

A. ANDERSON, Belle Vue
(Otago Witness, 26/8/1854)

NOTICE

THE Undersigned begs to caution the Public against Trespassing on any part of the land enclosed at Cherry Farm, and passing through such enclosure without his authority.

J. JONES

Waikouaiti, 1st August 1854
(Otago Witness, 9/9/1854)

Archives land records of 1855-58, in connection with 50 and 100 acre blocks in East Taieri, Tokomairiro and Clutha. His original land package gave him a quarter acre section in town, and his selection was in McLaggan Street. He bought one more section in that street, and one in Princes Street. The Princes Street section, believed to be near the corner of High Street, was bought from Edward McGlashan for £25 in 1851, and sold in early 1854 for £35. ∎

View of Dunedin in 1858 by photographer John Tensfield. Possibly the earliest existing landscape photograph of the young settlement, it shows the extensive mudflats which existed east of Princes Street before the area was reclaimed. Landmarks identified are: 1: John Jones' store; 2: Rev Burns' manse; 3: Cutten's auction rooms, store and Otago Witness printing office; 4: Government Buildings, including Captain Cargill's office; 5: Charles Kettle's house; 6: James Brown's drapery; 7: James Macandrew's store; 8: Maori landing place known as Otepoti, where the early settlers were carried ashore, at the mouth of Kaituna Creek (also known as the Toitu); 9: NZ Company survey office. The former McGibbon shop and residence, at the corner of Princes and Rattray streets, is just off the right hand edge of the photograph. (Otago Settlers' Museum)

James Macandrew the "coming man"

On 17 January, 1851 the schooner Titan arrived at Port Chalmers. It was an important event for the new settlers, and particularly for the McGibbon family, if their legend is to be believed. On board the Titan was James Macandrew, and in view of his impact on the colony, it is worth summarising some of the man's activities during the 1850s.

Originally from Aberdeen, he had been on the London committee of the Lay Association and had played an important role in negotiations between the New Zealand Company and the Colonial Office. He was a man of means with an optimistic and entrepreneurial nature. He was a scheme a minute man, and not all the schemes came off – to the detriment of himself, the community and perhaps John McGibbon. But on balance, he was a shot in the arm for the new colony.

He opened a store on the corner of Manse and Stafford Streets, announcing it in the Otago Witness of 8 March, 1851. The store soon grew to rival John Jones' large establishment. He acted as banker for the settlers before there was a formal bank. Macandrew became a substantial landowner, and was involved in all manner of community boards and committees. He erected a flour mill and initiated a local ship-ping industry with a small lighter, the Bon Accord, and then a 50 ton schooner, the Star, which was important for coastal trade, and was Dunedin's main link with Tokomairiro and Clutha districts before there were roads. He brought the first steam vessel to Dunedin and was instrumental in establishing steamer links with other New Zealand ports, Australia and later the UK. He chartered a ship to carry the first cargo of Otago wool to Britain.

In 1853 he was elected to represent country districts in the first Otago Provincial Council. He was also Speaker of the Council. He was elected to the first Dunedin Town Board in 1855, and in 1860 he succeeded Captain Cargill as Superintendent of Otago. He was jailed and dismissed from the position, in what was one of the most colourful scandals in New Zealand's political history. (Details of this and other Macandrew controversies are described at length in several other histories of the Otago settlement.)

He later served a further term as Superintendent, and was a member of the New Zealand House of Representatives, and was associated with the development of the University of Otago. ■

*From James Brown's cartoon,
"The Coming Man".*

CAPTAIN BELLAIRS will, on Friday, the 10th November, at 6 o'clock evening, give to such of the public as may do him the honor to attend in the School-house, an account of what he heard, saw, and did in relation to political affairs during his recent absence from this Settlement.

(Otago Witness, 4/11/1854)

A DINNER

WILL take place at the Royal Hotel, Dunedin, on Thursday, 25 January 1855, to celebrate the Anniversary of

ROBERT BURNS,

whose manly integrity of character, and his warm and true heart, should elevate him in the conception of every Briton ; and almost as much as the native force and beauty of his POETRY!

Tickets may be had of the following
stewards:—

Messrs. John Barr, Craigie Lee.
   "   Fisher, Dunedin.
   "   Kilgour,   do.
   "   Birch,   do.
   "   Wilson   do.

And at the bar of the Royal Hotel.
Price 5s. 6d.

Dinner on the Table at 7 o'clock precisely.

As the number of Tickets are limited, early application is necessary.

(Otago Witness, 20/1/1855)

DAGUERREOTYPE PORTRAITS AND MINIATURES ON IVORY.

MR G. B. SHAW will be prepared, on or after Wednesday next, to take sittings for Portraits in either of the above Branches of Art, at Captain Broadfoot's house, Caversham, daily between the hours of 10 and 4, until further notice.

Mr. Shaw thinks it as well to state that portraits in Daguerreotype can only be taken in fine weather, the clearer and drier the atmosphere is the better ; and that all children, without distinction, under three years of age are quite ineligible.

In order that such an opportunity as the present may not be overlooked, Mr Shaw has determined upon a scale of prices as shall bring this interesting Art within the reach of all classes. His prices for single portraits in Daguerreotype range from £1 5s. to £4 4s., according to size ; and for highly finished Miniatures on Ivory the prices will vary likewise from £3 3s. up to £10 10s.

With every portrait in either branch such prices include a handsome Morocco Case, with gilt metal mat and plate glass.

(Otago Witness, 3/2/1855) (First photographer's advertisement in Dunedin.)

A Public dinner took place at the Royal Hotel on the 25th ult., to celebrate the anniversary of the birth of Robert Burns. About 40 sat down to an excellent dinner, and paid Mr. Smith the compliment of doing ample justice to the fare prepared.

Mr. J. Barr, of Halfway Bush, as chairman, and Mr. Kilgour as vice-chairman, did the honors of the evening.......

A variety of toasts were proposed ; and the entertainment of the evening was varied by many good old Scotch songs, sung in a genuine style by several members of the company. " Auld langsyne" having been sung by the company in chorus, the meeting broke up between 11 and 12.

The meeting appeared to give universal satisfaction, and passed off admirably. We regret that we are unable to give a more full report of it, and that we have mangled the chairman's remarks, which were delivered with so much enthusiasm, and with so much broad Scotch as to be beyond us altogether.

(Otago Witness, 10/2/1855) (First annual Burns dinner.)

Only one Authorised ! !

ROB—LAFFECTEUR.

THE Rob of Dr. Boyveau-Laffecteur, the only one authorised in France, Belgium and Russia, is very superior to the sirups of Cuisinier, and of Sarsaparilla. It replaces the Cod's Liver Oil, the Antiscorbutic Sirup, the essences of Sarsaparilla, as well as all the preparations having iodine, mercury, &c., as their basis. Of easy digestion, agreeable to the taste and smell, the Rob is recommended by the medical men of all countries for the cure of Dartres, Abcesses, Cancers, Scalds Heads, Ulcers, the consequences of the Itch, Scrofula, Scurvy, as well as for Syphilitc diseases, whether old or recent, and which have resisted the effect of mercury and the iodure of potash. The Rob of Boyveau-Laffecteur was approved of by the old Royal Society of Medicine, by the decree of An XIII, and furnished to the French Navy in 1788 and 1793 ; in 1850 it was approved of in Belgium by the Minister of War for the sanitary service of the Belgian army, and latterly it has been officially authorised for all the Russian Empire. The Rob has been admitted into all the hospitals of the French Navy since 1788.

The General Entrepot of the real Rob Boyveau-Laffecteur is exclusively at the house of Dr. Giraudeau de Saint Gervais, 12, Rue Richer, Paris, to whom applications must be addressed to obtain Agencies for the sale of the Rob de Laffecteur.

In order to procure the Rob de Laffecteur, bearing the signature of Dr. Giraudeau de Saint Gervais, application may be made in confidence to

MR. A. S. WILSON, Chemist, Princes Street.

(Otago Witness, 10/2/1855)

Dunedin, Saturday, March 31, 1855

The seventh year of our existence as a community has just passed, and the statistics which have been obtained by the local Government, although not completed in all points, enable us to contrast the state of the Province at this period with its state at the close of the first year of the settlement of Otago.......

At the close of the first year of the settlement of Otago, March 31, 1849, there was a population of 745 souls within the Otago Block, of whom 426 were males, and 319 females : there are now within the whole Province, exclusive of Maories, 2557 souls, 1408 of whom are males, and 1149 females— shewing a slight improvement in the balance of the sexes.

The extent of land in crop in 1849 was only forty-two acres, chiefly in gardens : this has increased to 3168 ; but the most remarkable increase has been in the quantity of stock. In 1849 there were 35 horses, 375 horned cattle, 2430 sheep, and 50 goats (exclusive of the districts north of Port Chalmers) : there are now 435 horses, 6511 horned cattle, 58, 902 sheep and 251 goats....

On the whole, therefore, our progress may be said to be satisfactory, not rapid, certainly, when compared with the colonies of modern times. Australian colonies and California have so far exceeded anything that has gone before them, that rapidity in this matter has quite altered its meaning ; but still, whilst we cannot boast of rapidity of progress, we can of steadiness. It would not be seemly in us to point to individual instances of what has been attained in a few instances, but we may say that there are numerous instances of men who came amongst us as labourers who are now men of considerable property. We cannot point out any who have made splendid fortunes, such as we hear of in Melbourne and Sydney ; but, on the other hand, it would be equally difficult to find a case of extensive failure.

(Otago Witness, 31/3/1855)

FOR SALE

A TWO-YEAR OLD GELDING.
Apply to Mr. M'Gibbon, Caversham.

(Otago Witness 5/5/1855)

FOR SALE

THAT Quarter Acre of Town Land, No. 48 Maclaggan Street.

Apply to MR. M'GIBBON, Caversham

(Otago Witness 19/5/1855)

Otago on the move

While conditions in Dunedin were not good during 1850, the economy still grew a little. Nevertheless, Cargill was probably a tad optimistic in a January 1852 letter, published in the August 1852 edition of the propagandist Otago Journal: "Our progress during the last year has been very decided; the harvest is now on, promising, with a little wheat brought in for barter from the neighbourhood, a full supply for our own consumption, whilst of potatoes we have already had a surplus for export; small fruits in exuberance and peaches, are nearly ripe in the open air. The wool clip has done well."

Business also increased in 1852 and 1853, although there was a period of deep community gloom in the winter of 1852, when no ships called at the port for over four months. Business slowed to a crawl. The Witness complained about lack of both news and advertising revenue and said: "We might all go junketting, but the roads are so muddy it is best to stay at home. There is nothing doing in the police court, no accident or offence, or fires – in fact, 'no nothing'."

Excellent harvests in 1853 and 1854 helped put the community's mood, and economy, back on track.

In 1855, Condamine Carnegie, a Philip Laing alumnus, reported that Otago had "...advanced from a paltry poor place to a bustling place of business." Carnegie had quit Dunedin for Sydney in 1852 because he said the town was "...fast going down the hill," and because of his opposition to the Cargill clique.

Dunedin progressed steadily for the rest of the 1850s. The first formal bank, a branch of the Union Bank of Australia, was established in January 1857. Before this, Macandrew, and then John Jones, had provided a limited banking function. They bought produce such as wool and grain with 1/- and £1 promissory notes which could be redeemed at their stores.

Otago revenues almost doubled between 1857 and 1858, to £46,000. Considerably more money was spent on education, emigration, steam, streets, roads out of town and other public works. Work began on a new courthouse and jail.

The £2,000 spent on streets included a cutting through Bell Hill, which had acted as a barrier between Princes Street and the Octagon. Spoil from the cutting was used to begin land reclamation in the harbour. There was even talk of a municipal water supply, though this did not eventuate for several more years.

Revenues more than doubled the next year, to £100,000, and were stable in 1860, at £98,000. The following year, under the stimulus of the goldrush, they jumped to £220,000.

Otago's population at the end of 1858 was 1,700. By 1860 it had increased to 12,000, and in the next, goldrush year, it trebled to 30,000. ■

Cartoonist James Brown's drawing of the Reverend Thomas Burns braving the Dunedin elements. Burns was the spiritual leader of the young Otago settlement.

Dunedin's original First Church and School House opened in September 1848 near the beach in lower High Street. This Free Church of Scotland structure was the only purpose-built house of worship until an Anglican church was completed in 1855. The early First Church carried on the severe tradition of its Scottish parent church. No hymns were permitted and psalms were sung in the very unmusical 'lining out' fashion. This curious form can still be heard today, in BBC Scotland broadcasts of the Gaelic Church service. The Dunedin church contained no organ, which was regarded as a "kist o' whistles" – an instrument o' the Deevil. The Free Church did not celebrate Christmas Day or Good Friday, considering them to be normal working days.

The severe approach to religion may not have been out of place in Scotland, but in Dunedin it contrasted strongly with the attitudes and activities of the substantial Anglican minority, and contributed to community tension. The first Anglican services were held in the town jail in January 1851, by Reverend Charles Creed, a Methodist missionary based at Waikouaiti. The first Anglican minister appointed to Dunedin was the Reverend J A Fenton, in 1852. He held services in the Courthouse until a church was built. The first schoolmaster was James Blackie, who came to Dunedin with Thomas Burns in the Philip Laing. This was the only school operating when the McGibbon family arrived in Dunedin, and the older children may well have attended.

Dabbling in politics

As already mentioned, the detail of Dunedin's politics of the 1850s is beyond the scope of this book. However it is interesting to look at the relatively minor involvement of John McGibbon. One event at his home is a nice illustration of the curious electoral practices of the day.

McGibbon first nailed his political colours to the mast in 1853, when he was named with Macandrew and others to a committee of 'gentlemen'. The committee's aim was to promote Cargill clique candidates for the first Provincial Council elections.

The next published political connection was in November 1855, when the McGibbon house was advertised as the polling place for the election of an Eastern District representative to the Provincial Council. The same month, McGibbon was included in a list of 47 Dunedin gentlemen who urged Macandrew to put himself forward for re-election to the General Assembly of New Zealand. The following month his name appeared on a similar list of worthies who urged Cargill to stand for the Assembly.

In March 1857, Ambresbeg was

also the venue for an apparently unsuccessful meeting of Eastern District electors seeking to select a representative for the New Zealand House of Representatives.

James Macandrew, from a bust outside the Otago Settlers Museum in Dunedin.

One month later an interesting election for Eastern District representative on the Otago Provincial Council took place at Ambresbeg. As with other elections at this time, there was no secret ballot, and eligible voters simply strolled up at the appointed time and announced their preference in a show of hands.

On this occasion, John McGibbon actually proposed the Scottish candidate, David Howden, while William Cutten proposed William Carr Young, an Englishman. On the show of hands, Young won by 15 to 13. Howden then, as was his right under the electoral system, demanded a separate poll, and individuals then came by the house to vote throughout the day. The progress tally was announced every hour. By 3 pm, Young was well in front, with 34 votes to Howden's 17. As the afternoon wore on, Howden supporters drifted in from the Taieri, and by the close of polling had narrowed the gap: Young, 40; Howden, 31.

One week later, the losing side held a dinner at Ambresbeg, and consoled themselves with stirring toasts and speeches which included allegations of voting irregularities in the Cutten/Young camp. Needless to say, these allegations were not reported in Cutten's newspaper, the Otago Witness. The Macandrew-backed Otago Colonist did cover the occasion, and its report is reproduced as facsimile on page 141. The meeting formed a committee which aimed to purge the electoral roll, but the outcome was never reported by the Dunedin press. ∎

NEW ZEALAND FOR ME

I love bonnie Scotland, and England's blest shore,
But I love the new land of the Maori more,
Where labour's a blessing, and freedom's supreme,
And peace and contentment endears every scene.

    With its flax, and its fern, and rare cabbage tree,
    Its freedom,–its blessings;–New Zealand for me!

Like a child of old Ocean, surrounded by sea,
Is the land of New Zealand, the home of the free
Its wide-spreading valleys, and cloud-capped hills;
Its beautiful rivers, and blythe-sounding rills.

    With its flax, &c.

The land of the goi tree, mapu, and pine,
The stately totara, and blooming wild vine
Where the birds, sporting cheerily all the day long,
Make the woods ring and echo the voice of their song.

    With its flax, &c.

Where the Englishman's cot rises sweet to the view
Surrounded with flowers of each varying hue ;
And his fields, waving yellow with earth's golden spoils,
Make his home circle happy and sweeten his toils.

    With its flax, &c.

Bright land of the south! fairest gem of the sea!
Like branch from the stem of old England the free,
May thy name be enrolled in the annals of fame,
And spread a halo around the old English name.

    With its flax, &c.

—John Blair, Green Island, Dunedin, 1861

Southland beckons

By 1858, John McGibbon had evidently developed quite a taste for the land, and decided to take on large scale cattle farming in the inland open country administered by the Waste Lands Board. At the beginning of the year, with his 19 year old son Thomas and 150 head of cattle, he travelled south to the large 90,000 acre (36,000 hectares) Otapiri Run along the northern slopes of the Hokonui Range in Southland.

According to Thomas McGibbon's reminiscences, there was a partnership arrangement with James Macandrew. The partnership must have been informal, as only Macandrew's name appears in the Waste Lands Board records of the time.

After six months, the pair returned to Dunedin, apparently not liking the roughness and isolation of the squatting life. Thomas says his father did not "...feel warranted in transporting his wife and young children from a comfortable home to a sod hut or whare on the outskirts of civilisation...In these circumstances, my father decided to surrender his share of the run."

His attitude may well have been influenced by the death of his son David during the absence at Otapiri. Perhaps it was also influenced by business dealings carried on behind his back by James Macandrew, in Dunedin. The Otapiri Run was notorious for murky speculation by Dunedin property barons, and Macandrew bought and sold his own interest in the run no less than four times between 1858 and 1859. He first relinquished the run in June 1858, so if John McGibbon had no formal partnership arrangement, he may have been sold down the river.

Thomas McGibbon's account of the Otapiri experience is on page 148, and a discussion of the commercial finangling is on page 157.

Southland again

John and Thomas McGibbon returned to Dunedin in July 1858, perhaps wondering what to do with themselves next. An answer came less than two months later, when the Otago Provincial Council advertised for offers for the lease of the Mataura Ferry and Accommodation House, in Southland. Associated with the ferry was 1,000 acres of potential farmland.

McGibbon won the contract, and on 4 December he posted a bond of £200. Mentioned on the document as jointly standing surety for the bond was none other than James Macandrew, plus Macandrew's brother-in-law, William Hunter Reynolds.

Later that month the McGibbon family left Dunedin in a bullock wagon trek that became celebrated in the annals of Southland history. Thomas McGibbon's description of the journey is on page 159.

We will leave it to Jane McGibbon's contemporary, Mrs Bannerman, to close the chapter of life in Dunedin:

"But further effort was yet in store for [Jane McGibbon]. The land in Mataura was thrown open for occupation, and nothing daunted, this heroic woman prepared to accompany her husband and with her family begin pioneer life anew, undertaking the journey overland.

"In 1858 she and her husband arranged their affairs, gathered together their cattle, put the fowls in crates and packed up all their household goods, and one bright morning bade adieu to the home which had sheltered them for eight happy years.

Not without some heartache did this brave woman lock the door of the now empty house, home no more, with so many fond

Jane Bannerman (nee Burns), who wrote about Jane McGibbon's departure from Dunedin.

memories of hopes and fears, struggles and hardships, times of rejoicing and times of sickness all crowding on her memory.

"The last look was taken of the fireless and deserted house, and stepping into the wagon beside her children they started, the corner was turned, the old life was a thing of the past, and she set a brave heart to the long weary journey which stretched away before her." ∎

David McGibbon died in Caversham while his father and eldest brother were living at Otapiri Station. David had the distinction of being the first person buried in Dunedin's newly opened Southern Cemetery. The headstone no longer exists at the cemetery.

SACRED
TO THE MEMORY OF
DAVID FOURTH SON OF
JOHN M¢ GIBBON
WHO DIED 20TH MARCH 1858.
AGED 6 YEARS & 4 MONTHS.

£250 POUNDS REWARD

(F)

WHEREAS a person by the name of JAMES MACKENZIE and others did, on or about the 1st March last, steal and drive away about 1000 Sheep from the Timaru Station, and as there is reason to believe that the same men have, on previous occasions, stolen both Sheep and Cattle, and driven them away. The owners are of the opinion that there is a regular organized gang of thieves and receivers either in this or the Otago Province.

£100 of the above reward has been paid on the apprehension of M'Kenzie, and the remainer will be paid to any person or persons who shall give such information as will lead to the conviction of all the parties concerned, and the recovery of the Stock.

R & G RHODES
Lyttelton, March 15th.
(Otago Witness 19/5/1855) (First advertised reward in the Witness regarding the celebrated Canterbury sheep thief.)

DUNEDIN TIME.—In consequence of the extreme inconvenience which has been experienced for some time past, there being no means of ascertaining the correct time, His Honor the Superintendent has ordered the old custom of firing a gun at 12 o'clock at noon on Saturdays to be resumed.
(Otago Witness, 26/5/1855)

Thursday the 24th inst., Her Majesty's Birth-day was celebrated with every manifestation of loyalty. The day was kept as a general holiday...The day's rejoicing concluded with a dinner at the Royal Hotel, to which between 50 and 60 of the settlers sat down. Captain Bellairs occupied the Chair, and W. H. Reynolds, Esq., acted as Vice. " The Health of Her Majesty," " The Army and Navy," " The Heroes before Sebastopol," and " Our Allies" were received with enthusiasm, and responded to with deafening cheers.
(Otago Witness, 26/6/1855)

Superintendent's Office,
Dunedin, 21st August, 1855.

HIS HONOR THE SUPERINTENDENT has been pleased to direct it to be notified that the following gentlemen were, on Monday the 20th inst., duly elected Members of the Dunedin Town Board :—

Mr. John Jones
Mr. James Kilgour (F)
Mr. Alex. Rennie
Mr. James Macandrew
Mr. John Hyde Harris
Mr. William Henry Cutten
Mr. John M'Glashan
Mr. Charles Robertson
Mr. Robert Williams
By his Honor's Command,
JOHN LOGAN,
Clerk to the Superintendent.
(Otago Witness, 25/8/1855) (First Dunedin Town Board)

" Nothing extenuate, or set down aught in malice."

J. NICOLSON, (F)
(Late of the Deptford Theatre),

BEGS respectfully to announce to the inhabitants of Dunedin and Suburbs, that by request he will give a

DRAMATIC READING

in the Odd-Fellows' Hall, on the evening of Friday, August 31st, 1855.

The Play selected for the occasion is the *Merchant of Venice.*

Tickets of admission 1s., to be had of Mr. Smith, Royal Hotel.

Open at 6½, to commence at 7.
(Otago Witness, 25/8/1855) (First visiting theatrical.)

BEST CAST STEEL SPADES

THE Undersigned has just received a Shipment of Hawkes' Best Cast Steel Garden and Ditching Spades Nos. 2, 3 and 4, all warranted.

JAMES PATERSON
Princes Street.
(Otago Witness, 1/9/1855)

SHEEP NETS

JUST RECEIVED a few of the above, 45 yards long, with ropes to suit.

JAMES PATERSON
Princes Street.
(Otago Witness, 1/9/1855)

TO FLOCKOWNERS AND OTHERS

FOR SALE, Fifty Sheep Hurdles, Wool Box, full size, one Canoe made of Totara, will carry one ton firewood.

Apply to John Cormack, South Taieri, or at the ferry.
(Otago Witness, 1/9/1855)

The " Gil Blas" from Melbourne, arrived in this port on the 3rd instant. She made the passage to the heads in 8 days, but the wind being unfavourable for her entering the port, she was blown off the coast for 14 days.
(Otago Witness, 8/9/1855)

FOR SALE, EX " CAROLINE AGNES"

ONE Patent 2 Horse-power THRASHING MACHINE, complete, with extras for Barnwork, and Gear.

J. JONES.
(Otago Witness, 27/10/1855)

CONTRACTORS WANTED

TO Mould and Burn 80,000 Bricks. Apply to MR. SPEED, at Carisbrook, or to

J. MACANDREW & Co.
(Otago Witness, 27/10/1855)

THE Subscriber is prepared to receive Cattle on terms.

WM. FERGUSON.
(Otago Witness, 1/12/1855)

EUROPEAN INTELLIGENCE

LATEST TELEGRAPHIC DESPATCHES
(From the *European Times*, May 21st)

A telegraphic despatch from the Prince Gortschakoff has been received in Berlin. The Prince writes, that nothing very important had taken place in any part of the Crimea. The fire of the Allies before Sebastopol, he says, is very moderate.

The Allies have made a new battery and effected certain repairs. The night of the 11th, and early on the morning of the 12th, the Russians made a sortie from the Redan and the position before it, and spiked several guns in the English batteries. On the 12th the Allies exploded several camoulets before the Flagstaff Bastion, but did little harm.

RUMOURED BATTLE

The Press Orient reproduces the rumour of a violent engagement having been fought between the Russians and Turco Egyptians, near Balaklava. The Turks behaved admirably. They stood their ground for eleven hours, until the arrival of the Allies decided the victory.

(Otago Witness, 29/9/1855)

Fire.—A fire occurred at Dunedin on the afternoon of Monday, by which the gaol was entirely consumed. It appeared that the fire originated from Mr. Monson's (the gaoler) having thrown some ashes and lighted embers down the cess-pool, with the object of purifying it. The flames when first discovered were but a few inches high, but spread with such astonishing rapidity, that, before water could be procured the fire had caught the gable end of the gaol, and, passing up between the weatherboards and the lining, defied all efforts to extinguish it. In less than ten minutes about 100 persons were on the spot ; whose assistance for a time was comparatively useless, the building being surrounded by a high paling...At the time of the fire there was but one prisoner confined for a petty offence, who laboured so assiduously to save the building, that he was much burned...This is the first occasion of a fire of any extent having occurred in Otago, and it would be well for the public to take some steps to procure necessary implements to extinguish fire... (F)
(Otago Witness, 27/10/1855) (First serious fire in Dunedin.)

WE have so long been anticipating information of the fall of Sebastopol the the news of the repulse of the allied forces on the 18th June comes upon us with tenfold bitterness. It is impossible for us, in this distant part of the world, to form any idea of the correctness of the censure cast upon the leaders of the British forces, or to say whether the assault of the 18th was a wise or an unwise measure. [More]
(Otago Witness, 27/10/1855)

KIA RONGO

Kia Nga Maori heitonganga mea o te Teira o Koputai Kia utu ngatanamea o tera marama o Nowema.

NA TEIRA.

(Otago Witness, 27/10/1855)

TARANAKI.

We have received from the Taranaki Herald of the 12th of September, announcing the arrival of the Duke of Portland from Wellington,with 200 rank and file of the 65th Regiment, and several field peices. This has had a very salutory effect upon the Natives. [More]

(Otago Witness, 3/11/1855)

NOTICE

The following places have been appointed Polling Places for the Election of Members of the Provincial Council for the Province of Otago, for the undermentioned districts, namely-

For the EASTERN DISTRICT-

At the residence of Mr. John M'Gibbon, Caversham Vale, near Dunedin.

For the WESTERN DISTRICT
[etc]

A. CHETHAM STRODE, R.M.,
Returning Officer

(Otago Witness, 3/11/1855)

To the Electors of the Eastern District

(Comprising the East Side of Harbour, Anderson's Bay, Green Island, and Caversham)

A MEETING of the Electors of the above District will be held at the house of Mr. John M'Gibbon, at Caversham, on Wednesday next, 7th inst., at ½-past 5 o'clock precisely, for the purpose of considering as to the most fit persons to represent the district in the Provincial Council.

It is hoped there will be a full attendance, and Electors are earnestly requested not to pledge themselves to any candidate whatever until they have had an opportunity of conferring upon the subject.

(Otago Witness, 3/11/1855)

DUNEDIN HARMONIC SOCIETY

A GENERAL MEETING of the Members of the above Society will be held in the hall of the Mechanics' Institute, on Friday the 23rd inst., at ½-past 6 p.m. precisely. A full attendance is particularly requested.

L. LANGLANDS
On behalf of Members.

(Otago Witness, 17/11/1855)

TOWN SECTION FOR SALE

THAT SECTION, situated in Maclaggan Street, No. 28, having fifteen months of a lease to run.

Apply to Mr. M'GIBBON, Caversham.

(Otago Witness, 24/11/1855)

DUNEDIN, SATURDAY, NOVEMBER 24, 1855.

OF all places in the world at an election time, we believe Otago is the slowest. The election of the Superintendent passed off in the quietest manner possible. A stranger would scarcely have known that an election was to take place, and the meeting for nomination was as dull an affair as we have ever witnessed ; not a question was asked, nor a remark made. This might have arisen from the method of proceeding, Captain Cargill having made his remarks after he had been declared duly elected, when of course it was useless to ask questions.

(Otago Witness, 24/11/1855)

The description of the southern country near the Mataura (which we publish in today's issue) comprises but a small portion of the available country to the south. [more]

(Otago Witness, 24/11/1855)

1856

THE news of the Fall of Sebastopol was received in Dunedin on the 9th inst. Flags were immediately hoisted, the bell set ringing, the services of our one gun, an eight-pounder, called into requisition, and a salute of (we do not know how many guns) fired — the latter an ebullition of loyalty and enthusiasm which will be fully appreciated when we state that the powder cost 4s. 6d. per lb....

(Otago Witness, 12/1/1856)

THE Undersigned is a Cash Purchaser of every description of Produce, deliverable at his Stores in Dunedin or Port Chalmers, or will advance liberally on shipments made to his correspondents in the neighbouring colonies.

J. JONES

(Otago Witness, 1/3/1856)

MISSIONARY BOXES.—On the evening of Thursday last week, the children attending the Dunedin Sabbath School met in the School-room with the teachers, when the Missionary Box belonging to the School was opened and found to contain the sum of £5 10s. 8d., which the children by vote apportioned to the following schemes, viz., to the Jewish Mission, £3, and to the Foreign Missions, £2 10s. 8d. On a subsequent evening, the Box belonging to the Anderson's Bay School was opened, and the contents, Sixteen Shillings, equally divided betwixt the same two schemes. The whole has been remitted home by the Convenor of the Sabbath School Committee.

(Otago Witness, 1/3/1856)

IRON HOUSES FOR SALE

NOW LANDING EX " CHALLENGER," @ Melbourne—
Four Commodious Iron Houses, with Cooking Stove and Chimneys, complete.

J. MACANDREW & CO.

(Otago Witness, 15/3/1856)

FOR SALE, Two Bull Stags, broken in to dray and plough. Can be seen at Mr. Cargill's station, Tokomairiro. Apply at the Printing Office, or to Walter Miller, Tokomairiro.

(Otago Witness, 15/3/1856)

FOR SALE,

TWO Large Reflecting Brass Telescopes 1 Pair Globes—Terrestrial and Celestial
2 do. Improved Revolvers
2 do. Double-barrelled pistols
1 do. Single do.
10 Shares in Sheep Company
4 Shares in the Property Investment Co.
A Mare and Foal—and 7 bullocks fit for breaking or the butcher. Apply to JAMES REID, Princes Street.

(Otago Witness, 22/3/1856)

WE have to notice the arrival of the " Thomas and Henry" from Sydney. By her we have news of importance, excepting the markets. The prices of farm produce are low, and were quoted on the 1st March as follows :— " Fine flour £28, seconds, £26. Wheat 10s. 6d to 11s. 6d. Oats 4s. 6d to 5s. 6d. Bran 1s. to 1s. 3d. Potatoes 4s. 6d. to 6s."

(Otago Witness, 22/3/1856)

THE " Gil Blas" sailed on Thursday from this port for Melbourne direct with a cargo of wool, valued at £3777.

(Otago Witness, 22/3/1856)

PLOUGHING MATCH

THE Tokomairiro Agricultural Meeting and Ploughing Match will be held on Friday, April 18, 1856—Ploughing to commence at 10 o'clock, when Prizes will be given for the best Ploughing of Half an Acre of Land, furrows 9 by 4.

1st Class—To the best Ploughing with either Bullocks or Horses—one Prize.
2nd Class—with 2 Bullocks in harness.
   .1st Prize   .2nd Prize
3rd Class—With Bullocks in yoke, with Driver.
   .1st Prize   .2nd Prize
4th Class—With Horses, and without a Driver.
   .1st Prize   .2nd Prize
Entrance, 10s. per Plough.

Prizes will also be given for the best sample bushels of Wheat and Oats, and for the best cwt. of Potatoes grown in the District, the produce of the present harvest.

Subscriptions in aid of the prizes will be received by the Committee, or by their Treasurer, Mr. Thomas Balfour Thom.

Dinner will be provided for the Competitors and Visitors by the Owner of the Land.

JOHN HARDY,
Secretary

Tokomairiro, March 26, 1856

(Otago Witness, 5/4/1856) (This may have been the first ploughing match in Otago.)

NOTICE.

WHEREAS the practice of Harbouring Prisoners escaped from the Gaol of this district has of late been very prevalent, whereby in many instances the ends of justice have been defeated,—This is to Give Notice that all persons in future found guilty of committing the above offence will be prosecuted with the utmost rigour of the law.

Otago

Notice is also given that the mark ↑ has been put on all articles of clothing worn by prisoners under sentence in Dunedin Gaol, and any person purchasing, or having in his possession any of such clothing after this notice, will be punished as the law directs.

A. CHETHAM STRODE,
Sheriff.

Sheriff's Office, Dunedin,
16th April, 1856.
(Otago Witness, 26/4/1856)

MARRIED.

IN the Manse, Dunedin, on the 21st instant, the REV. WM. BANNERMAN, Minister of Tokomairiro and Clutha, to JANE, second daughter of the Rev. Thomas Burns, Dunedin.
(Otago Witness, 31/5/1856) (Jane Bannerman, who wrote about Jane McGibbon in Dunedin, is pictured on page 136.)

SEVERAL gentlemen have during the week arrived from Nelson, having travelled overland. It appears that the route from Nelson to the extreme south of the Middle Island has become much frequented, and the journey is now a comparatively easy one.
(Otago Witness, 7/6/1856)

PURE COCHIN CHINA FOWLS
For sale in pairs.

PARTIES wishing to keep the above splendid Fowl can be supplied on application to Messrs. Jones & Williamson.

Early application is necessary, as but few will be parted with.
(Otago Witness, 7/6/1856)

EX THOMAS HENRY

1 CASE BONNET RIBBONS 2 cases Ladies' and Girls' Straw and Leghorn Bonnets, and Children's hats.
J. JONES.

(Otago Witness, 28/6/1856)

TO ARRIVE
PER " SIR EDWARD PAGET,"

A LOT of " All-Wool Clan Tartan Cloakings and Plaids of the Newest Fashions, and selected from the Best Manufacturers.

ROSS & KILGOUR.
(Otago Witness, 28/6/1856) (Ross and Kilgour occupied the site of the original McGibbon store.)

MACAULAY BURNT IN EFFIGY.—The Highlanders of Glenmore, in Inverness-shire, feeling aggrieved and indignant at the slanderous charges brought by Mr. Macaulay against their predecessors, in his last volume of the History of England, assembled together, and, headed by a piper playing the

" Rogue's March," proceeded to the Black Rock, near Glenmore House, and there burnt in effigy the distinguished historian. The assembled crowd gave three shouts of execration as the effigy was consuming. Macaulay, when in the Highlands, resided for a considerable time at Glenmore House.
(Otago Witness, 26/7/1856)

TO BE SOLD,

A First-rate Young PIG DOG of a strong and heavy stamp, the Owner having no further use for him.

Apply to WM. JOHNSTON, Kuri Bush.
(Otago Witness, 2/8/1856)

FOR MELBOURNE DIRECT

THE fast-sailing brig " GIL BLAS," John Nichol, Commander, (under engagement to the Provincial Government) is expected to arrive here about the 10th August next, and will be despatched for Melbourne direct within 14 days after arrival.

For Freight or Passage apply to
J. MACANDREW & CO.
(Otago Witness, 9/8/1856)

NOTICE

WE, the following Requisitionists, beg to call a meeting of the Inhabitants of Caversham, to be held in the house of Mr. Hugh Calder, on Wednesday 15th instant, at 6 o'clock p.m., to consider the necessary steps to be taken to erect a School in the District.
JOHN ANDERSON.
DAVID CALDER.
JOHN M'GIBBON.
W. BLACKIE.
DONALD REID.
HUGH CALDER.
(Otago Witness, 4/10/1856) (The meeting was reported on by the Otago Witness on 18/10/1856. The Education Board was condemned for not including Caversham in the places for building a school. There appeared to be about 30 ratepayers and 60 children living in or near Caversham, and it was impossible for them to attend school in Dunedin. "The meeting therefore prayed the attention of the Board to the subject, at the same time expressing its willingness to render such pecuniary aid as was in its power toward establishing a school in the district.")

BIRTHS

At Ambresbeg, Caversham, on the 7th inst., the wife of Mr. M'Gibbon, of a son.
(Otago Witness, 18/10/1856) (Archibald Alexander)

KINDNESS.—Deal gently wth those who stray. Draw them back by love and persuasion. A kiss is worth a thousand kicks. A kind word is more amiable to the lost than a mine of gold. Think of this and be on your guard, ye who would chase to the grave an erring brother.

A LESSON FOR MOTHERS.—A mother once asked a clergyman when she should begin the education of her child, and she told him it was then four years old. " Madam," was his reply, " you have lost three years already. From the very first smile over an infant's face your opportunity begins."

BREVITY.—If you would be pungent be brief, for it is with words as with sunbeams, the more they are condensed the deeper they burn.
(Otago Witness, 25/10/1856)

IMMIGRATION.

TWENTY THOUSAND POUNDS having been voted by the Provincial Legislature of the Province for promoting Immigration from Great Britain to Otago, parties wishing to get out their Friends are requested to make immediate application in the form annexed.

Printed copies of the form may be had on application to this office.

By his Honor's command,
JOHN LOGAN
Clerk to Superintendent.

Superintendent's Office, Dunedin,
19th December 1856.

To his Honor the Superintendent of the Province of Otago.

I hereby apply for the undermentioned persons to be brought to Otago as assisted Immigrants under the Government Scheme; and I hereby bind and oblige myself, jointly and severally with said Immigrants, to pay the cost of their passage by instalments, to such extent, and within such time, as may be agreed upon by the British agents for the province, or by any person duly authorised to make such agreement.

NAME.	AGE.	TRADE OR CLASS OF LABOUR.	ADDRESS.

*(Name and address of Applicant)*_____

_____ } *(Witnesses to Signature).*
(Otago Colonist, 2/1/1857)

UNION BANK OF AUSTRALIA.

THE DUNEDIN BRANCH of this Establishment will be OPENED for the Transaction of General Banking Business THIS DAY, the 2nd of January, 1857.

Temporary Office at MR SIBBALD'S Private Hotel, Stafford-street.

Office Hours—from 10 A.M. to 3 P.M. Saturdays , from 10 A.M. to 1 P.M.
ALFRED JACKSON,
Manager.

Dunedin, Dec. 24, 1856
(Otago Colonist, 2/1/1857)

To Wool Growers

THE Undersigned have just imported a large assortment of material for Sheep Wash, consisting of—

Tobacco
Sulphur
Spirits and Oil of Tar
Mercurial Ointment
Corrosive Sublimate
Arsenic

J. Macandrew & Co.

(Otago Colonist, 2/1/1857)

Dunedin Academy

This Scholastic Institution will Meet again, after the Christmas Recess, on MONDAY, 5th January, 1857.

The Scale of Charges and time of payment stand thus:–

PER QUARTER,

And Payable Always on Entrance:

I.   English Reading – Writing – the Principles of Arithmetic..............£2 2

II. Above specified Branches, with Grammar–Geography, sacred and profane–the Fundamentals of History–Practical Composition and Elocution–the higher departments of Arithmetic–Biblical Biography.. 5 5

III. Above enunciated Divisions, with Mathematics throughout all its Ramifications–Antiquities–Biography–Mythology–Greek and Latin Composition, both in prose and verse–Philosophic History, Ancient and Modern...................... 6 6

J. G. S. GRANT,

Rector.

(Otago Colonist, 2/1/1857)

SCHOOL BOOKS.

JAMES PATERSON & CO. have just received a supply of the following school books :—

School Bibles and Testaments, with Psalms and Paraphrases
M'Culloch's Course of Reading
Third and Fourth Irish Lessons
Chambers' Rudiments of Knowledge
    "   Introduction to the Sciences
    "   Matter and Motion
    "   Rudiments of Geology
    "   "   Chemistry
    "   "   Hydrostatics
    "   "   Mechanics
    "   "   Zoology
English Grammar
Complete System of Geography
Modern Geography
First Arithmetic
Practical ditto
Mensuration
Appendix to ditto
Elements of Bookkeeping
Key to ditto
Algebra
Plane Geometry
Rudiments of Latin, by the Edinburgh
   Academy
Latin Delectus
Mair's Tyro's Dictionary
Hallard's French Grammar
Well's French Fables
Elements of Greek
Greek Exercises
Greek Testaments
School Atlas
Fulton & Knight's Dictionary
Sheets of Syllables
First Initiatory Catechism
Mother's   ditto
Brown's   ditto
Shorter   ditto
Ditto, with proofs
Thomson's Sacramental Ditto

Catechism on the Principles and Constitution of the Free Church.

(Otago Colonist, 2/1/1857)

Wanted

A PRECENTOR for the Free Church, Dunedin. Salary £120 per annum. Candidates are requested to send in their applications in writing to the Clerk of the Deacons' Court on or before the 1st February.

DAVID TAYLOR

Clerk to the Deacons' Court.

Hope-street, Dunedin.

Jan 7, 1857.

(Otago Colonist, 9/1/1857)

Wanted

A YOUNG MAN, well acquainted with Farming and general Agriculture, and who understands the management of horses. None else need apply.

R. H. JEFFREY,

The Forbury

(Otago Colonist, 9/1/1857)

RESIDENT MAGISTRATE'S COURT.

The following is an abstract of a return of all cases disposed of in the Resident Magistrate's Court, Otago, from the 1st January to the 31st December, 1856 :—

	Conv.	Dism.	Settled	Total.
Assault..................................	7	0	2	9
Drunkenness...........................	50	4	0	54
Felony.....................................	1	1	0	2
Malicious injury to property....	0	1	0	1
Merchant Seamen's Act..........	34	0	0	34
Sureties to Keep the Peace......	2	0	0	2
Offences against Harbour Regulations.........................	0	5	0	5
" Cattle Trespass Ordinance..	23	0	0	23
" Summary Ejectment ditto...	2	0	0	2
" Licensing ditto....................	0	1	0	1
" Destitute Persons Relief do..	0	0	1	1
" Dog Nuisance ditto..............	3	0	0	3
" Passengers Act....................	2	0	1	3
Totals	135	12	4	151

Of the above, one case of assault was between a Maori and a European, and five charges of drunkenness were against Maories.

Under the civil jurisdiction, eight claims against Maories, amounting to £123 3s. 2d., were settled out of court. Of 138 cases between Europeans, for claims amounting to £1295 15s. 11d., 54 were settled in favour of the plaintiffs, 662 were settled out of Court, and 22 were dismissed.

Total number of civil and criminal cases, 297.

(Otago Colonist, 30/1/1857)

HUNDRED OF DUNEDIN.— The meeting for the election of wardens for this Hundred was held in the Land Office on Tuesday last, the Commissioner of the Waste Lands Board presiding. A number of parties were proposed, but declined to accept.

The following individuals were elected:– Messrs David Hood, David Calder, Alex. Chalmers, John Stoddart, Adam Begg, John M'Gibbon, and John Muir.

The Commissioner briefly directed the attention of the wardens to the duties devolving upon them, pointing out the importance of immediate action, and stating that the amount of the licence fees, somewhere about £50, was at their disposal, and ready to be handed over on application. The wardens therefore resolved to enter upon their functions at once, with which view a preliminary meeting was held forthwith, at which Mr. David Hood was elected secretary. Ⓕ

(Otago Witness, 21/2/1857)(First announcement that the Dunedin Hundred had been constituted.)

N O T I C E.

To the Purchasers of Wearing Apparel at the Sale by Messrs. James Macandrew and Co., on the 25th September last, of the Effects of James Bennett Sinclair, deceased, intestate.

HAVING been informed by the relatives in Scotland of the above-named decease, that when he left Scotland he sewed or quilted into one of his coats a sum of 10 or 12 sovereigns ; the undersigned has to request that parties who purchased at the above sale, or have in their possession, any garment of the above description, will make a careful inspection of the same ; and if they find any money secreted therein, that they will hand the same to the Official Administrator, on account of the Estate.

ROBERT CHAPMAN,

Official Administrator.

Official Administrator's Office,   Dunedin, March 5, 1857.

(Otago Colonist, 13/3/1857)

To Contractors and Others.

TENDERS will be received by the Clerk to the Town Board of Dunedin, on or before the 31st. day of March, 1857, from parties willing to cut a new channel across Princes-street, above the Survey Office ; to make a Stone Culvert, with turned arch ; to fix a self-acting floodgate at the lower end thereof ; and to cut a new channel in front of the Commercial Inn.

Also,

From parties willing to Repair and Improve the Road from the Survey Office, Dunedin, to the Bridge at the Water of Leith ; in both cases according to plans and specifications, to be seen by applying to

MALCOLM GRAHAM

Clerk to the Board.

Dunedin, 11th. March, 1857.

(Otago Colonist, 13/3/1857)

A lecture on Mesmerism, especially with reference to its efficacy as a curative agent in cases of disease, was delivered by Mr. Moir, on Tuesday evening, at the Mechanics' Institution, which was crowded. The lecture was a rather desultory affair; and a patient, who, in compliance with invitation, came forward to be operated on for rheumatism, did not appear to be very strongly sensible of the efficacy of mesmeric agency.

(Otago Colonist, 20/3/1857)

FIREARMS

CAUTION

WHEREAS complaints have been made that several boys and other idle persons have late been in the habit of prowling about the outskirts of the town of Dunedin and upon the Town Belt, and trespassing upon suburban land adjoining said Belt, with loaded guns, in pursuit of wild pigeons and other wild fowls, and of recklessly discharging the said firearms at said fowls, to the great annoyance and terror, and in some cases, even to the imminent danger of the lives of the inhabitants residing in the vicinity of said firing.

NOTICE IS HEREBY GIVEN, that all parties in future so offending against the law shall be prosecuted with the utmost vigour the law directs.

Police Office, Dunedin
26th March, 1857

Otago Colonist, 27/3/1857

DINNER TO MR. HOWDEN

Yesterday evening the friends and supporters of Mr. Howden entertained him to dinner at Mr. M'Gibbon's, the polling place, where a tent had been erected for the occasion . There were upwards of 40 individuals present—chiefly electors in the Eastern District. The chair was occupied by Mr. W. Martin, M.P.C., and the vice-chair by Mr. John M'Gibbon.

We regret that the limited time precludes our inserting a full account of the speeches and proceedings at the meeting, which was one of the most harmonious and enthusiastic gatherings of the kind which has been for some time witnessed in this Province. The meeting was one of a thoroughly practical nature, and was wound up by resolving itself into a District Association for purging the electoral roll, which, it appears, even in this small district, is greatly in need of revision. In the course of the evening it was clearly shown that Mr. Howden had lost his election by the votes of those who do not reside in the district, and who have no legal qualification to vote. It appears that of the voters of this class 12 voted for Mr. Young, and only two for Mr. Howden. Some of the speakers expressed themselves very warmly at the injustice which had been inflicted upon the *bona fide* residents in the district, who had been swamped and overborne by what they termed light cavalry, some parties having voted for

Mr. Young who have had no property in the district for years. It was made manifest that, with the roll thoroughly revised, another election will find Mr. Young in a minority, unless he propitiate the goodwill of those who are now opposed to his principles.

After the usual loyal toasts had been duly honoured, the CHAIRMAN briefly proposed the health of the guest of the evening—Mr. Howden. They had heard a good deal lately about "scholar-like" and "gentlemanly" qualifications; but it had been well said that true nobility consisted in virtue and usefulness; and in this point of view Mr. Howden was one of Nature's noblemen, for he was always to be found foremost in every good work.

The next toast was "The Agricultural Interest of Otago," in speaking to which Mr. M'ANDREW took advantage of the fact that so large a number of the grain producers in the district being assembled to point out the loss and inconvenience to which not only the growers of grain, but the producers, are subjected, in consequence of there being but one flour mill in the Province. He shewed the advantages which would result from having a mill on the Kaikorai. The company, to a man, reciprocated Mr. M'Andrew's views; and, to shew that they were in earnest, a Joint-stock Flourmill Company was formed there and then, and capital to the extent of £450 subscribed on the spot.

Mr. JOHNSTONE proposed "The Pastoral Interest," and observed that a great mistake existed amongst the flockowners, viz., that anybody would do for a shepherd. This would lead to the most serious results, as, while ignorant persons were employed as shepherds, no remedy against disease could be effectual. It was indispensably necessary, with a large prospective increase in our flocks, that trained shepherds should be regularly brought from home. By this means, and having fenced lands for the flocks at particular seasons, New Zealand wool would soon rival the best German clips.

Mr. M'GLASHAN proposed the health of Mr. Seaton, coupled with the cause of education—a cause very dear to his heart. Much misapprehension existed on this important subject, and parties had lately endeavoured to cast a stigma upon men of far more sagacity and practical knowledge than themselves, but who were supposed to want a scholastic education. But all were comparatively new to their duties here, and practical knowledge and sagacity were of the greatest importance, and in these he believed Mr. Howden to be by far the superior of Mr. Young. But let them not neglect the education of their children, or they hereafter be put in the background by new settlers. Mr. M'Glashan then referred to some gross mis-statements, made for election purposes by Messrs. Cutten and Young to the inhabitants of Anderson's Bay, to the effect that certain members of the Education Board were opposed to the erection of a school in that district, and which had been

secured only through the influence of the two first-named parties. This was altogether untrue, as it was only proposed that the inhabitants should first decide between remaining under the Dunedin Committee, or being erected into an independent district.

Mr. SEATON returned thanks.

The next toast was "The shipping and mercantile interest," coupled with the health of Mr. Macandrew.

Mr. MACANDREW returned thanks.

Mr. M'GLASHAN proposed "The Press," which was responded to by Mr. LAMBERT.

The health of the District Road Trustees was proposed, which brought up the subject of roads. Considerable dissatisfaction was expressed at the conduct of the Town Board of Dunedin, which, it was alleged, is spending the public money in a way which will be perfectly useless to the country settlers in so far as regards the coming winter, while it was by no means certain that the road through Rattray-street would be the best line, even after it might be made available for the country settlers, which it was not likely to be for some time, and not without a very large sum being expended beyond the town belt.

The proceedings were varied by a few suitable songs—one of which, composed for the occasion, was sung by the author. The party broke up at ten o'clock, all apparently highly pleased with the "feast of reason, and the flow of soul," mingled with so much that is calculated to be practically beneficial to the general progress of the district.

(Otago Colonist, 10/4/1857)

PUBLIC LECTURES

The want of intellectual instruction and entertainment having hitherto been much felt in Dunedin, it has been suggested, with a view to supplying this desideratum, that a series of Popular Lectures should be delivered during the ensuing Winter Evenings:

Civilization and Christianity

The influence of Character, and the Responsibilities devolving upon Young Men in Reference thereto.

Natural Theology.

The Present State of Europe, &c.

The Influence of the Physical Agents on Human Organization.

Popular Sketch of Astronomy.

Popular Physiology.

The Sources, Properties and Results of Heat or Calorie.

Origin and Progress of Printing.

A Popular Résumé of the Foregoing,
[*More*]

(Otago Witness, 18/4/1857) (First announcement of a new series of lectures intended to restore Dunedin's flagging interest in intellectual matters.)

JOHN MOLLISON,

HAS ON SALE, EX "DUNEDIN" — 1 Case of Boots and Shoes, made up to Order, consisting of —

Men's and Boys' Watertight Boots
Wellington, Clarence, and Blucher do.
Women's Girls' and Boys' Lacing-up do.
Ladies' Cloth and Leather do.
Ladies' Cordovan and Carpet Slippers

&c &c &c

LIKEWISE

Oatmeal, Pearl Barley, and Split Peas
Black's spades, Nos. 3,4, and 5
Potatoe and Dung Forks, Plough Traces
Patent Hooks and Scythes, Hay Forks
Harrow Mountings, Wheat Riddles
Barrow Mountings, Padlocks, &c., &c.

ALSO

Ladies' Paisley and Wool Shawls and Plaids
Do. Alpaca Robes and Dresses
Do. Cashmere, DeLaine, Poplin and Lustre Dresses
Ladies' and Misses' Mantles
Misses' Black, Brown and Drab Felt Hats
Ladies' Black and Blue Lace Falls
Crochet Collars, Edging, Bordering
Misses' Victorines, Muffs, Gloves, &c.
Bonnet Ribbons, &c.

(Otago Witness, 24/4/1857)

ON SALE

JUST LANDING, EX " DUNEDIN"

20 BARRELS Best Scotch OATMEAL
10 Barrels best Scotch Pearl Barley
10 Barrels best Split Peas
15 do Archangel Tar

CROCKERYWARE - consisting of Dinner,
Breakfast, Tea, and Toilet Sets, Jugs, Bowls &c.

ALSO

Mustard, Pickles, Sago, Arrowroot, Salad Oil, Raspberry and White Wine Vinegar, Sardines and Confectionery.

JAMES PATTERSON & CO.

(Otago Witness, 24/4/1857)

GARDEN OPERATIONS FOR MAY.

A garden being an ornamental, as well as a useful, appendage to every dwelling, this is now about the best time of year to make new gardens, and alterations and improvements upon old ones. Drain, trench, and manure it well. From this time up till September is the safe month for removing and planting trees, shrubs, and plants of all kinds.

In removing trees let due care be observed in taking up the tree or bush ; it is in preserving the smallest thread-like rootlets, that we rely upon for its future growth. In planting, spread the roots regular, and at full length ; plant the finest soil about the roots, with a good watering, so as to establish them the better in their new position.

The growth of vegetation will now be almost suspended for this and the following months, so the sooner hedges are dressed, and trees and bushes pruned, and the whole garden thoroughly cleaned up the better. That being done now, instead of being delayed until Spring, will enhance the pleasure of the garden during the dreary months of winter.

Look over fruit, roots, and seeds that are stored past, and see whether there is anything wrong, which is sure to be the case if in a close, moist, and warm apartment.

Slight frosts may be expected towards the end of the month. Any tender plants likely to fall victim should be protected by spreading bush boughs over them, or placing them under glass. Where any new flower-garden is contemplated, or shrubs to be planted, now is the time to set about getting it done.

Fine serene weather still continues ; all busy threshing and carting wheat to the mill, and oats for shipment : but in terror of the roads getting bad before we get our flour from the mill and oats into town. We certainly longed to get the management of the roads in our own hands ; we got that, and made but a poor acknowledgement. Has not the Government the power to stop the frantic career of the Town Board?—who are wasting the means at their disposal in the gully, and in every bye-path they can find, and leaving undone what every body needs, viz., the principal street from the head of the swamp, and away along towards the mills.

(Otago Colonist, 8/5/1857)

HUNDRED OF DUNEDIN

NOTICE IS HEREBY GIVEN, that at a Meeting of the Wardens, held on 31st March, 1857, in the Odd Fellows' Hall, Dunedin, the under-mentioned BYE-LAWS were agreed to, and being submitted to the Waste Land Board, received their assent on the 11th day of April, 1857 :

INTIMATION IS HEREBY GIVEN, that from and after the First day of June next, these Bye-Laws will be put in force.

By Order
JOHN M'GIBBON
Secretary to the Wardens
Ambresbeg, Caversham
24th April, 1857.
(Otago Witness 25/4/1857)

FOR SALE

AN EXCELLENT cow in calf, warranted a Good Milker. Also, a young HEIFER. Apply to
JOHN M'GIBBON
Caversham
(Otago Witness 9/5/1857)

CRICKET BATS, BALLS & WICKETS Several sets of the above (by Clapshaw, Son, & Co., City Road, London) may be had at

CHARLES ROBERTSON'S
Princes St.
(Otago Witness, 1957)

COURT NEWS

TUESDAY, MAY 5

Three little boys, whose names we shall not give, were charged with being guilty of throwing annoying and offensive matter (human excrement) upon the door and doorstep of the house occupied by William Statiford on Tuesday, the 28th April last.

The charge was denied by the juvenile defendants, and, the proof not being sufficient, the case was dismissed.

TUESDAY, MAY 12

William Henry Cutten, of Dunedin, was charged on the information of John Shepherd, Chief Constable, with permitting two cows, his property, to wander at large within the limits of the town of Dunedin on 1st May instant.

Defendant fined 5s. for each animal and costs.

(Otago Colonist, 15/5/1857) (Cutten's own newspaper, the Otago Witness, neglected to report this court case...)

ORIGINAL POETRY

As I cam' thro the Wakari Glen
    All in an Autumn gloamin',
My heart was licht and fancy free,
    Nae thocht had I o' roamin',
But there I met a bonny lass,
    She set my heart a dancing,
The blood ran hot thro' my veins
    Like mettled steeds a prancing.

Her cheeks were like the blooming rose,
    Her een as black's a raven ;
Although 'twas but a moment's glance,
    It's in my heart engraven,
Fore love will mak' the bauldest man
    Bind at the shrine of beauty,
There's honour in the homage paid—
    It's a commanding duty.

But fancy free was I nae mair,
    For Cupid had me fairly,
His dart it pierced my heart right thro',
    And noo I'm altered sairly.
But should this nymph prove kind and leal,
    My heart would pound with rapture
When led by Hymen's silken cord,
    Fast bound unto my captor.

Away frae me ye heartless crew,
    That lo'e nae bonny lasses,
Ye gat yere clue frae Minstrel Burns,
    Wha ca'd ye senseless asses.
I trow he lo'ed the bonny dears,
    As seen in mony a sonnet,
He wadna pass a bonny lass
    Till he took aff his bonnet.

J. B., South Craigielee

(Otago Witness, 23/5/1857) (J.B. is John Barr, Dunedin's unofficial poet laureate of the 1850s.)

ADVICE TO YOUNG WIVES.— Let me especially recommend to a young wife a considerate attention to whatever her husband will require *when* he comes home *before* he comes home, in order that, on his return, she may have nothing to do but to share in the comfort and enjoyment for which she has provided, and may not be running about after his usual and reasonable requirements, exposed to his reproaches for her negligence, and to those of her own conscience, if she has any.— *Home Truths for Home Peace.*

GAY DRESS.—Beauty gains little, and homeliness and deformity lose much, by gaudy attire. Lysander knew this was in part true, and refused the rich garments that the tyrant Dionysius proffered to his daughters, saying, "That they were fit only to make unhappy faces more remarkable."— *Zimmerman.*

QUITE UNANSWERABLE.—An old lady combated the idea of the moon being inhabited by remarking with emphasis that the idea was incredible to believe—"For," said she, "What becomes of the people of the new moon when there is nothing left of it but a little streak?"

BOTH OF ONE MIND.—A subscriber writes to an American editor in the west :—"I don't want your paper any longer." To which the editor replies :—"I wouldn't make it any longer if you did ; it's present length suits me very well."

A machine for digging potatoes has been lately in successful operation in several parts of Scotland and Ireland.

THE SUNDAY.—A correspondent of the *Notes and Queries* says the only words in English for the first day of the week, before the existence of Puritanism, were Sunday and Lord's-Day. The former of these expressions was used by our Saxon ancestors, with all Teutonic nations. The latter was adopted from the Christian form of Southern Europe. Saturday in Italian still retains the name of Sabbato. The word for Sunday, in Russian, means resurrection— "Identifying the day, as the Southern nations do, though more significantly, with the great triumph of the Christian faith."

DOWN AS A HAMMER.-A Vermont editor gives this advice to the ladies.—"When you have got a man to the sticking point, that is when he proposes—don't turn away your head or affect a blush, or refer him to Pa, or ask for more time ; all these tricks are understood now, but just look him right in the face, give him a hearty smack, and tell him to go and order the furniture.

FEAR OF EVIL.—In the commission of evil, fear no manas much as thine own self. Another is but one witness against thee ; thou art a thousand. Another thou mayest avoid, but thyself thou canst not. Wickedness is it's own punishment.

(Otago Colonist, 5/6/1857)

THE COST OF THE AFFECTION.—Never, perhaps, are children dearer to their parents than when the price of bread and meat is excessive.

ADVICE TO THE FAIR SEX.—A Lady has no occasion, when she has a new bonnet, to buy any bonnet-trimmings for it, for she has only to take it to church the first Sunday, and her friends are sure to trim it well for her.

A **YOUNG** Lady (of the age of six-and-thirty) declared the other day in strictest confidence to her maid-servant, that she would sooner dye than let a single grey hair show itself.

A **SHORTCUT TO METAPHYSICS,—**What is the Matter?—Never mind. What is Mind?—No matter.

(Otago Colonist, 19/6/1857)

COMMON EXPERIENCE,—John Wesley says :—When I was young I was sure of everything ; in a few years, having been mistaken a thousand times, I was not half so sure of most things as I was before ; at present, I am hardly sure of anything but what God has revealed to Man."

(Otago Colonist, 26/6/1857)

COSTLY ORNAMENTS.—It is stated that the wife of one of the most distinguished physicians of Paris wears a ring made from iron that was extracted from the blood taken from her husband during some disease with which he was afflicted. But this is not more remarkable than the set of jewellery a lady wears, which was produced perfect by the sweat of her husband's brow.

HOW TO FIND FAULT.—Find fault, when you must find fault, in private, if possible ; and sometime after the offence, rather than at the time. The blamed are less likely to resist when they are blamed without witnesses. Both parties are calmer, and the accused party is struck with the forbearance of the accuser, who has seen the fault, and watched it for a private and proper time before mentioning it.

(Otago Colonist, 14/8/1857)

J. WILSON
PHOTOGRAPHIC ARTIST
MEDICAL HALL, DUNEDIN.
PORTRAITS TAKEN DAILY FROM
10 A.M. TILL 3 P.M.

(Otago Witness, 27/6/1857)

PUBLIC LECTURES

THE Ninth lecture of this series will be delivered by DR. PURDIE, on Wednesday vening first, and hald-past Six o'clock.
SUBJECT:—
" Popular Physiology."
Collection at the door on behalf of the Dunedin Library.
For the Committee.
JAMES BARR,
Secretary

(Otago Witness, 27/6/1857)

SQUATTING IN THE SOUTH
BY ONE OF THE FIRST SETTLERS

Hard living in the South at first,
 Tho' hungry one would feel,
There was nothing but potatoes,
 And "give the dogs the peel!"

Perchance at times a little flour,
 But seldom any meat;
Tho' always tea in plenty there,
 Yet sugar was a treat.

Then when we'd flour we had no yeast,
 But scones and Johnny-cake,
Of flour and water (that's the tack!)
 As tough as we could bake.

Then came the beef — ah glorious times!
 Oh how we did pitch in!
"There's tea and sugar, spuds and beef,
 "All ready, now begin!"

Time sped on ; and sometimes we'd plenty,
 And sometimes scarcely knew,
How we should manage to exist,
 Until the 'tatoes grew.

But now these times I find have chang'd,
 And plenty of good things,
The *Star*, in plying back and fore,
 Sure from Otago brings.

We've tea and coffee, raw and good,
 We've herrings from Lochfine,
We've rice and sugar, candles too;
 Sit up till half-past nine.

Besides, we've beef and mutton here,
 The 'tatoes too have grown,
And greens and turnips now we have,
 Hard times I guess have flown.

The more we have, the more we want,
 For tho' we've got good feed,
I'll tell you still what we should like,
 Some jolly books to read!

Murihiku, May 19.   H.S.
(Otago Witness, 27/6/1857)

Hundred of Dunedin.

DOGS WORRYING CATTLE

COMPLAINT having been made to the Wardens, by settlers in Anderson's Bay and Town districts, that a gang of Dogs, numbering from four to seven, and recognized as belonging to Dunedin, have been repeatedly observed worrying the Cattle depasturing on the Waste Lands of the Crown in the said districts :
 NOTICE IS HEREBY GIVEN, that after this date, all Dogs so offending will be shot.
By order,
JOHN M'GIBBON,
Secretary to the Wardens.
June 29, 1857.
(Otago Colonist, 14/8/1857)

Hundred of Dunedin

THE WARDENS are requested to MEET, in the Odd Fellows' Hall, Princes-street, Dunedin, on THURSDAY, the 1st October next, at half-past 4 o'clock afternoon.

Business of importance will be laid before the Meeting.

By Order
JOHN M'GIBBON
Secretary to the Wardens

(Otago Colonist, 11/9/1857)

SALE OF HORSES.—Mr. W. H. Cutten held a Sale by Auction yesterday and disposed of a considerable number of Mares at prices varying from £30 to £65, the average being rather about £41 each. The result of this sale shows that horses of superior quality (especially of a stamp for draught) continue in full demand.

(Otago Witness, 12/9/1857)

SITUATION WANTED

A YOUNG LADY, lately arrived in Otago, is desirous of obtaining a Situation as GOVERNESS in a respectable family.

For particulars apply to MISS BELL, Blythswood Cottage, Dunedin.

(Otago Witness, 12/9/1857)

AXTELLE'S THEATRE
OF AND
FUN MIRTH

By special Desire of General Hope and Colonial Expectation.
A PERFORMANCE
Will take place at the Royal Hotel, Dunedin, ON MONDAY, THURSDAY, AND SATURDAY NEXT.
MR. C. S. AXTELLE begs most respectfully to inform the Public of Otago that a series of Amusing Entertainments will take place on the above Evenings, consisting of Acrobatic Evolutions, Pyramidical Positions, Antipodean Exercises, Somersault Throwings, Juggling and Tumbling, Corde Volante, Trampoline Performances, with a variety of Singing, Dancing, Pantomimes, &c.

Doors open at 7 ; commence at half-past.

Admittance :—Reserved Seats, 4s. : Adults, 3s. ; Children, 2s.

(Otago Witness, 26/9/1857) (First travelling show to come to Dunedin.)

NOTICE

THOSE persons residing in the Caversham and Town District who paid the Depasturing Licence for the Dunedin Hundred, are requested to meet on FRIDAY, 13 November, at 6 o'clock, in the house of Mr. John M'Gibbon, Caversham, to advise as to the best way of laying out the district proportion of cash in the improvement of the Run.

DAVID CALDER,
JOHN M'GIBBON
Wardens

(Otago Witness, 7/11/1857)

FOUND

A YEARLING BULL. If not claimed and removed within eight days by the owner, it will be sold to pay expenses.

JOHN M'GIBBON
Caversham

(Otago Witness, 7/11/1857)

GOLD FIELD.

REWARD OF £500

THE Provincial Council of Otago having voted the sum of £500 for the discovery of a remunerative Gold Field within the Province of Otago—Notice is hereby given, that the above Reward will be paid to any person or persons who may discover a remunerative Gold Field, and give information of such discovery to his Honor the Superintendent. One moiety of the reward will be paid when a quantity of gold exceeding 100 ounces, the *bona fide* produce of such Gold Field, shall have been brought to Dunedin, or exported from the Province, within one year, under certificate of the Collector of Customs at Invercargill or Dunedin ; and the balance will be paid when 500 ounces shall have been brought to Dunedin, or exported from the Province, within one year, under certificate of the Collector of Customs at Invercargill or Dunedin.

In the event of more than one claim being made for such Reward, the Government will beat liberty to make such a distribution of the Reward as may appear to them just and equitable.

By his Honor's command,
JOHN LOGAN,
Clerk to the Superintendent.
Superintendent's Office, Dunedin,
Dec. 10, 1857.

(Otago Colonist, 11/12/1857) (First announcement that a reward would be paid for the discovery of substantial goldfield in Otago.)

1858

LESSONS IN MUSIC.

MISS REDMAYNE will be glad to give Lessons in the Piano-Forte and Singing, according to the principles taught in England. Apply to MISS REDMAYNE, Langlands' Cottage.

Also, MISS REDMAYNE will be happy to make up Ladies' Dresses, Mantles, Jackets, Bonnets, and all kinds of Needlework.

(Otago Witness, 23/1/1858) (First advertised piano lessons. Miss Redmayne had newly arrived in town, and would become a mainstay of the Dunedin musical establishment. She was also a regular contributor of poetry to the Otago Witness.)

PLAIN SEWING.

MRS. FAZAKERLY and Daughters will undertake all kinds of Plain Sewing.

Apply at Mr. David Millar's, Moray Place.

(Otago Witness, 23/1/1858)

CONCERT.

MISS REDMAYNE begs to announce to her Friends and the Public in general of Dunedin, and its Vicinity, that she intends giving a GRAND SACRED and MISCELLANEOUS CONCERT.

Further particulars will be duly announced.

(Otago Colonist, 2/4/1858) (First concert of 'serious' music.)

H. PERRING,
WATCH AND CLOCK MAKER

(FROM FRENCH'S, ROYAL EXCHANGE, LONDON)

Begs to announce to the Public generally that he has commenced Business in the above Line, and hopes, by punctuality and attention to business, to merit a share of the patronage.

(Otago Colonist, 2/4/1858)

NOTICE.

THE PARTY who took a small Meerchaum Pipe from the Long Room, Commercial Hotel, can have the Case belonging to the same, by applying to MR. DUNCAN.

(Otago Colonist, 2/4/1858)

NOTICE.

WILLIAM HEPBURN, Veterinary Surgeon, M.E.V.C., F.E.V.M.S., takes the liberty of intimating that he is now practising as a Veterinary Surgeon in the Province of Otago.

All letters addressed to him in the meantime, to the care of Messrs. Ross and KILGOUR, Merchants, Dunedin, will meet his attention as far as possible.

(Otago Colonist, 16/4/1858)

MATAURA FERRY.

THE PROVINCIAL GOVERNMENT having agreed to establish a FERRY at the Mataura River, opposite Mr. Rich's station, two miles below the falls, and to grant a lease thereof for 5 years.

TENDERS, in duplicate, will be received at this Office, until MONDAY, the 31st day of May, 1858, from parties willing to lease the same.

The Government does not bind itself to accept the highest, or any, of the offers that may be made ; but in the event of a suitable offer being received, £200 will be advanced for buildings, &c.

Further information will be given, and the conditions of the lease shown, on application at this Office.

By Order,
JOHN LOGAN,
Clerk to the Superintendent.
Superintendent's Office, Dunedin,
26th April, 1858.

(Otago Colonist, 7/5/1858) (Evidently there were no takers, because this was advertised again in September.)

Notice to the Public.

I HEREBY Caution all Persons against supplying either Goods or Money to my wife, Mrs. Mary Williams, after this date, as I shall not hold myself responsible for the same, she having voluntarily left my house.

PETER WILLIAMS.

Dunedin, May 19, 1858

(Otago Colonist, 21/5/1858)

The number of births over deaths for the year ending 31st December, 1857, is 158; the increase from immigration during the same period being 369. Since the commencement of the present year, we have had upwards of a thousand additional immigrants, which will make the total European population of the Province at this moment nearly 6000, being 50 per cent increase, since the census of 1856....

....With regard to the capital of the Province, "Dunedin," there are now evident signs of enlargement. For some years the place has been almost stationary ; now, however, one who has been absent for twelve months cannot fail to perceive great changes. Several outlets from the town towards the suburban districts have been opened up. We see numerous houses peeping out among the trees in all directions. This place bids fair to become something like a town ; we know of few more picturesque positions—combining commodious sites for commercial purposes, as well as for villas and private residences. In our next annual summary we hope to be able to point to some public buildings worthy of the place ; at present there is nothing deserving of the name, not even a Town Hall, that most essential requisite in all societies. A handsome church and spire, to be built of freestone, is about to be erected on Church-Hill, an elevated position overlooking the town and harbour.

The population of Dunedin is composed chiefly of the officials of the Government, merchants, storekeepers, and tradesmen. It is the seat of the Provincial Government and Courts of Justice ; and the channel through which the whole exports and imports of the province pass. The amount of business done is much larger than the appearance of the place would, at first sight, indicate. There are four Hotels in the town—two Printing Offices—three places of Public Worship—a High School, with its Rector, one male and one female teacher, supported by the Government—besides a private Academy ; there are two Breweries in the neighbourhood, which promise to make the place celebrated for its ale, the climate being peculiarly adapted for brewing. There is one Flour Mill in operation, and another Flour and Oatmeal Company

have commenced to build on the Kaikorai Stream, some four miles from the town. There is a third Flour Mill in the Tokomairiro Plain : they are all driven by water power. A Candle Manufactory has recently been started, which turns out very superior candles.

(Otago Colonist, 7/5/1858)

RAINTON AND WHITE,
BAKERS, PASTRY COOKS, &C.,
RATTRAY STREET, DUNEDIN,

RESPECTFULLY inform the Inhabitants of Dunedin and vicinity that they have commenced Business as above, and trust, by strict attention to all Orders they may receive, to merit that which they solicit with confidence—the support of the Public in general.

N.B.—Orders for BRIDES' CAKES, FANCY BREADS, SHIP BISCUITS, &c., executed with care and despatch.

(Otago Colonist, 23/7/1858)

£18 REWARD

A REWARD of £3 per Head will be paid by the Undersigned, for the immediate Apprehension and placing in Custody of all or any of the six seamen named as under, who have deserted from the " Jura" ;—

Archibald Ballintine.   Charles McLean.
George Middleton.   Alexander Taylor.
Robert Lamont.   Duram Liston.

J MACANDREW & CO.

Agents for the " Jura"

(Otago Colonist, 23/7/1858)

THE INDIAN MUTINY FUND

A GRAND VOCAL and INSTRUMENTAL CONCERT in aid of the above Fund will take place on MONDAY EVENING, July 19, in the Schoolroom.

PROGRAMME.

PART I.

"Napoleon's Grand March". For Flute, Violins, Saxhorns, Cornopeans, and Accordeons.

Duett—"The Minute Gun at Sea." Miss Redmayne and Mr. Christie.

Trio—"Favourite Air," For Saxhorns and accordeons.

Scotch War Song—"The Pilbroch." Miss Redmayne, with Saxhorn accompaniment by Mr. Begg.

"Will you come to the Bower." For Flute, Violins, Saxhorns, Cornopeans, & Accordeons.

Ballad—"By the Sad Sea Waves." (By particular desire) Miss Redmayne, with Pianoforte, and Concertina accompaniment by Mr. Richardson.   *(Benedict)*

"Favourite Waltzes." Flute and Pianoforte. Mr. Briscoe and Miss Redmayne.

AN INTERVAL OF TEN MINUTES

PART II.

"Louden's Bonny Woods and Braes." For Flute, Violins, Saxhorns, Cornopeans, & Accordeons.

Solo—"Favourite Airs." Flute. Mr. Briscoe.

Duett—"Ye who shun the haunts of care." Scotch song. Mr. Christie.

Song—"The Swiss Girl." Miss Redmayne, with pianoforte, and Concertina accompani-

ment by Mr. Richardson.   *(Linley)*

Solo. For Concertina. Mr. Richardson.

Duett—"Damon and Clora." Miss Redmayne and Mr. Christie.   *(Dr. Harrington)*

Georgian Ballad—"I had a Dream." Miss Redmayne, with Concertina accompaniment by Mr. Begg.

Imitation Bagpipes. Messrs. Begg and Richardson.

"Scots Wha hae." For Flute, Violins, Saxhorns, Cornopeans, and Accordeons.

Finale. "God Save the Queen," Solo and Chorus.

Miss Redmayne will preside at the Pianoforte, and a large number of Amateurs have kindly promised their assistance.

Tickets may be had at the *Colonist* Office ; Mr. Healey's, Paterson's, Curie's, Jones & Williamson's, Wilson's, Dick's, Sinclair's, Ross and Kilgour's, and Bog's ; and at Miss Redmayne's, Maclaggan-street.

Admittance 3s. Reserved seats 4s. Family tickets, to admit 4, 10s. 6d. Reserved seats, ditto, 12s. 6d. Doors open at Half-past Seven; Concert to commence at Eight.

(Otago Colonist, 16/7/1858)

Marriage of the Princess Royal

THE ILLUSTRATED LONDON NEWS contains splendid illustrations of the above, with a coloured Portrait, and an original Bridal Song, with Music.

The Illustrated London News supplied regularly, to the latest dates. Also the Illustrated Times, Punch, British Workman &c.

W. LAMBERT

Bookseller and Stationer

Stafford-street

(Otago Colonist, 18/6/1858)

To the Editor

SIR — I shall feel greatly obliged if you will please inform me, through the "Witness", what has been done with the money, which, I believe, amounted to upwards of £50, that was paid last year for Depasturing Licences for the Dunedin Hundred. I have made enquiries, but cannot find that one shilling of the above sum has in any way, been expended for the benefit of the Licence Holders.

I am, &c.,

AN OLD SUBSCRIBER

[The Wardens of the Dunedin Hundred certainly pursued an extraordinary course. We believe, in some cases, they returned the Licence fee to those who had paid it; but, as their accounts have never been published, we are, like our correspondent, in ignorance of what was done with the whole sum. At the last meeting for the election of Wardens for the Dunedin Hundred, not a single elector attended. We may, therefore, assume that they are indifferent upon the subject, and do not appreciate the advantages and privileges of the system of Hundreds, — an indifference which, we believe, they will some day regret.

— ED.]

(Otago Witness, 12/6/1858)

MATAURA BRIDGE

CONTRACTS in duplicate will be received at the Land Office, Invercargill, until noon of Saturday, the 4th day of September next, and at this office until noon of Saturday thereafter from parties willing to Erect

A WOODEN TRUSSED GIRDER BRIDGE

at the Falls of the Mataura River, according to a Plan and Specification to be seen at the Office of the Civil Engineer, Dunedin, a duplicate of which may be seen at the said Land Office.

By Order,

JOHN LOGAN

Clerk to Superintendent.

Superintendent's Office,

Dunedin, 6th August 1858.

(Otago Witness, 7/8/1858) (The bridge was not proceeded with.)

THE OTAGO WITNESS

DUNEDIN, SATURDAY, AUGUST 28, 1858

THE most important event which has occurred for some time in the annals of the Province of Otago, is the arrival at Dunedin, yesterday evening, of the steamer "Queen," from Melbourne, via Wellington and Canterbury. Being the first steamer which has ever anchored off Dunedin, she was welcomed with a salute of 20 guns. We understand that she brings a considerable number of passengers anxious to view this Province. The "Queen," it is said, has come on a voyage of speculation, and in search of employment, but what may be the proposals of her owner we do not know.

(Otago Witness, 28/8/1858) (The Queen was brought to Dunedin by James Macandrew. A more effusive article appeared in the rival Otago Colonist, which supported Macandrew.)

MATAURA FERRY

TO BE LET FOR A TERM OF YEARS

OFFERS for the LEASE will be received at the Land Office, Invercargill, till 12 o'clock on SATURDAY, the 2nd day of October, 1858, and at this office, till 12 o'clock on the Saturday thereafter.

The Government will not be bound to accept the highest or any of the offers that may be made.

The terms of the lease will be shown at this Office on and after the 10th, and at the Land Office, Invercargill, on and after the 17th inst.

By order,

JOHN LOGAN,

Clerk to the Superintendent

Superintendent's Office,

Dunedin, September 2, 1858

(Otago Witness, 4 September 1858) (This advertises the contract won by John McGibbon.)

TO BE SOLD OR LET

A VERY DESIRABLE PROPERTY, consisting of 30 acres of LAND, all fenced round, with a large DWELLING HOUSE, Barn, Stockyard, and abundance of timber and good water for domestic purposes. A considerable quantity of the ground is under grass, nearly 8 acres ploughed and ready for seed.

Persons connected with Dunedin by business, will find the said property exceedingly useful.

Terms and particulars by applying on the premises to the Proprietor,

JOHN M'GIBBON

Caversham

(Otago Colonist, between 8/10/1858 and 5/11/1858) (This is the family's home property called Ambresbeg.)

LOST

TWO BULLOCKS, branded G Y on the off hip : one three years old, white and brown spotted, with strawberry neck ; the other is two years old, dark red. They were traced to the head of the Waihola District. A reward of £1 per head will be paid for such information as will lead to their recovery.

JOHN M'GIBBON

(Otago Witness, 27/11/1858)

Treat for Christmas and the New Year

SALMON, FROM THE TWEED. Herrings, from Lochfine.

Roast Veal, from Smithfield Market.

FatHens and Eggs, from the North-East Valley.

ON SALE AT

ROBERT MILLER'S STORE,

Great King Street, near the Water of Leith.

N.B.—the inhabitants of Dunedin leaving the cares and close atmosphere of the crowded town, and for a day breathing the sweet pure air, of the North East Valley, and with pleased eye gazing on the romantic beauties of hill and dale, river and stream, would acquire an appetite for the above viands. This, closed with a dish of strawberries and cream at Gebbie's Gardens, and a draught from the pellucid liquor flowing from the Water of Leith, would conduce greatly to the advantage of their health, their pleasure and their morals.

(Otago Colonist, 31/12/1858) (The McGibbon family missed out on this opportunity, having removed themselves to Mataura Falls to begin hard pioneer life anew in a hastily constructed mud hut.)

Hocken Library

*Princes Street looking south, in 1858. The building marked * is where the McGibbon family lived for part of 1850, and had their shop until late 1851. Shortly after this photograph was taken, Ross and Kilgour erected a two story builing on the site, which is on the north-west corner of Rattray and Princes streets. The building with a central chimney, on the left side of the street, is the Mechanics' Institute, where the Cargill Memorial now stands. On the right, men are beginning work on a cutting through the steep Bell Hill, which was a considerable barrier between Princes Street and the Octagon. In these days, before harbour reclamation started, the beach was close to the east side of Princes Street.*

GOING ABROAD
Part four: Southland

■ Contents

John and Thomas MacGibbon established in a wattle and daub hut at Otapiri Station, 1858.

'MacGibbons' accommodation house at Mataura Falls, 1864.

'MacGibbons Corner', Gore, 1905.

The fruits of commercial success: John Jr's home in Gore.

Thomas MacGibbon in the New Zealand Legislative Council, 1914.

Taking up the Otapiri Run

I have read with great interest the articles dealing with the early days of Muruhiku, or Southland as we call it now. As I have been in this part of the Dominion since January 1858, it seems but fair that I should add my quota to the information at present being collated.

By Thomas MacGibbon, written in 1909

I have no diary to refer to, so the incidents I have recorded are simply reminiscences recalled by memory. As the events occurred 51 years ago, it does not do to be over-critical, but I believe they are correct.

The stories of the early days of this fair young land are worthy of preservation, and I trust that these notes may be of a little service in helping on the object in view.

Early in January, 1858, my father entered into an agreement with the late Mr James Macandrew to go shares with him in the Otapiri Run, which extended along the northern slopes of the Hokonui Hills from East Peak to the Oreti River at the point where the

Thomas MacGibbon, ca 1880

Thomas MacGibbon's pioneer experiences in Southland, 1858/59

In the early years of this century, the Mataura Ensign in Gore made a wonderful contribution to New Zealand pioneer history by publishing a column of pioneer recollections collected by local historian and journalist Herries Beattie.

Thomas MacGibbon had many interesting memories to recall, and as one of the more able writers among Southland's early pioneers, he was persuaded on several occasions to write for the Herries Beattie series. He was the major single contributor to the first omnibus edition, in 1909. Later contributors to the Ensign's Pioneer Recollections included Thomas's brother John Jr, and John Jr's son Hugh.

Thomas first travelled to the future Southland province in January 1858, when he was 19 years old. Leaving the rest of the family behind in Caversham, Dunedin, he joined his father John, in driving a herd of 150 cattle to the Otapiri Run, a 90,000 acre run which extended along the northern slopes of the Hokonui Range above the Waimea Plains, from East Peak near Gore, west to the Oreti River.

Here, in his own words, are Thomas's tales of early Southland. They make interesting reading, not only from a family point of view, but also for the broader picture they give of early pioneer conditions and activities in this part of New Zealand.

Permission from the Gore Publishing Company to use material from Herries Beattie's books is gratefully acknowledged.

In this section of the book, the family name is spelled MacGibbon, rather than McGibbon. The family made this change themselves, shortly after moving to Southland.

railway siding called Caroline is now.

We, that is my father and myself, accompanied by William Barr and John Souness, started from Dunedin for the south driving 150 head of cattle and also a team of bullocks and a dray to carry provisions and other necessaries.

There were no roads formed after leaving 'Hope Hill' on the Taieri, and we had to flounder through swampy creeks with small cuttings in them, and which took our team all its time to negotiate. The track occasionally ran along a steep siding, which made it difficult to avoid capsizing the dray. Indeed we did go over just before we reached the native village at Henley, but fortunately very little damage was done.

We were giving Mrs Logie, wife of the sheep inspector, a lift as far as Mr Gerrard's place at Waihola. I happened to be driving at the time, and seeing the nature of the ground, I asked Mrs Logie to alight. Fortunately she acted on my suggestion, as immediately after, the dray capsized and our tilt was flattened out 'as flat as a pancake'. However this mishap occasioned very little damage and we duly arrived at the Taieri Ferry, which was then kept by the late Mr James Harrold, afterwards well-known at Stewart Island.

Here we had to swim all our cattle across the Taieri River, and a trying

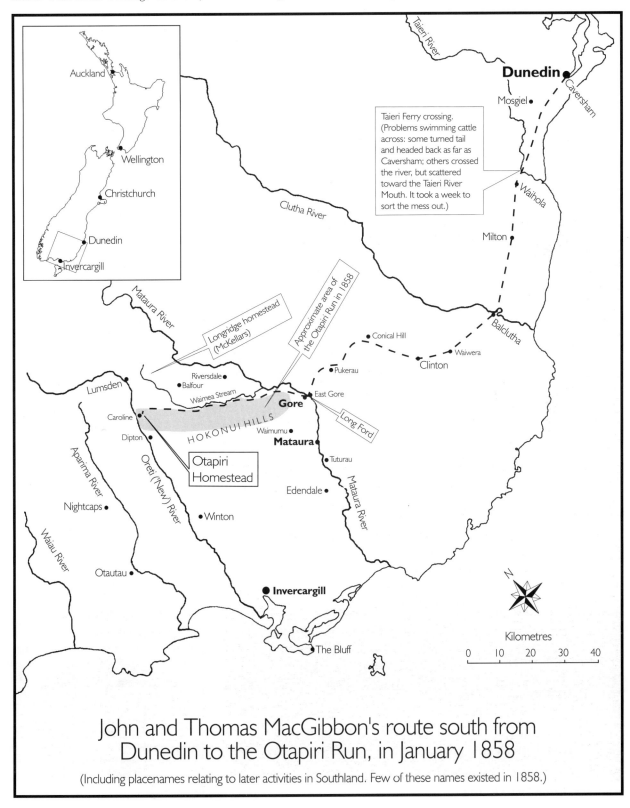

Taieri Ferry crossing. (Problems swimming cattle across: some turned tail and headed back as far as Caversham; others crossed the river, but scattered toward the Taieri River Mouth. It took a week to sort the mess out.)

John and Thomas MacGibbon's route south from Dunedin to the Otapiri Run, in January 1858

(Including placenames relating to later activities in Southland. Few of these names existed in 1858.)

In January 1858, John and Thomas MacGibbon, and two assistants, drove 150 cattle from Dunedin to the Otapiri Station in Southland. The most difficult part of the journey was here at the Taieri Ferry, where problems getting cattle across the river caused a week's delay.

time was had. We endeavoured to drive as many animals as possible into the water after the 'decoy' but our endeavours were often futile, and so we had to adopt other means to force across the ones that would not 'take the water'. We tried roping and towing them at the stern of the boat, and even this method was not always successful.

The crossing was a most tedious job. Night fell with the task uncompleted, and we had left some of the cattle behind. We left them in a stockyard, which proved to be unsafe. Next morning, all hands had to hunt for the missing beasts. We picked them up eventually, scattered all over the country as far as Caversham.

It took us a whole week to gather our stragglers and get them safely over the river, and then we had to search for those which had crossed over on the first day. These we found scattered in small mobs over the rough hills that lie between the Ferry and the Taieri Mouth.

At last we got the whole mob collected and continued our journey towards the distant Hokonui Hills.

Infant Balclutha

Passing Lake Waihola and the Tokomairiro plain, we put up at Meadowbank, then occupied by John Cargill. Thence the road — or rather track, for road there was none — led up the ridges towards Miller's Flat, crossing Lovell's Flat, where Mr Lovell had a small accommodation house — the only house between Tokomairiro and the Molyneux ferry.

Here we were more successful and expeditious in crossing. The ferryman, Mr John Barr, with his assistants, joined us and we drove the cattle up to a spot above the bend of the river and launched the whole mob by dint of shouting, stockwhip-cracking and dogs barking. The current set across the right bank, so as soon as we got the cattle afloat, they were helpless and were carried right across.

In this way we avoided the tantalising experience we had had at the Taieri, where often when the mob were half-way across, they would turn back for the shore they had just left, and the whole work had to be gone over again and again.

We had two days at Johnnie Barr's place, and the cattle luxuriated amidst the rich pasture and splendid flax that grew on the site of Balclutha. The swamp that lay between the flat and the ridges was impassable, and with the river, acted as a boundary to this great natural paddock. The neck at the northern end was fenced off by a couple of chains of post and rail fencing, so we felt that our cattle were safe.

Mr John Barr's accommodation house and Mr McNeil's private house were the only buildings on the flat where the town of Balclutha now stands.

Into the unknown

After our two days' rest we started on another portion of our journey to the 'far South' and now entered an almost trackless country very little known. We needed a guide, and obtained the services of Mr Tom Martin, of Te Houka, who had been as far as what is now known as Tapanui.

The first night out from Molyneux ferry we camped at Waiwera, where a few panels of fencing had been run across a bend of the creek, forming a handy paddock.

The paddock was too small for our mob, but by camping at the ford after the mob had been driven across, we were able to prevent them from returning. As the country was strange and the grass luxuriant, we found the stock pretty handily in the morning.

I remember that night, because it was really the first we had experienced out-of-doors. Our assistants, both strong young men, disdained getting under the dray, but wrapping themselves in a blanket, bivouacked in a large flax bush, declaring they would be 'all right'.

My father and I slept on the dray under the tilt and spent a comfortable night, but we heard our two fellows about very early in the morning, and as a consequence we had an early breakfast and start.

The night, although a January one, was very frosty – so much so that there was ice the thickness of a shilling on the water in the billy. Our young fellows, after their 'beauty sleep' was over, found that Jack Frost was about to such an extent that they could not stop on their flaxen couch, but had to stir around to get their stiffened limbs supple again.

We had a laugh over their disappointment, but the experience led them to camp comfortably under the dray every night afterwards. We used to cut a lot of silver tussock and store it in the dray for the night's repose. The tarpaulin being let down over the wheels and back formed not a bad shelter.

Next day we passed through the Popotunoa Run, which was then owned by a Mr Fuller. That night we camped at the Wairuna Creek.

Our route after this led through Captain Mackenzie's run past Conical Hill, so that we might strike the leading ridge, which we followed down past the Landslip to Pinkerton's ford on the Waikaka.

Gore's first inhabitant

Pinkerton's Ford is now known as Howe's Ford, and here we camped for the night. Our dogs had caught some young pigs during the day, and at supper we enjoyed a repast of roast suckling pig. I might mention here that during the journey we were able to vary our diet by catching the eels which were plentiful in all the creeks.

Our route then led us to the top of the leading ridge, which we followed over the saddle into what is now known as East Gore. We crossed the 'Long Ford' on foot, the Mataura River being so low that the water scarcely covered the gravel. Then we boiled our billy on the west bank, right on the site of what is now the famous town of Gore.

We were joined here by 'Jacky-Jacky' (Mr Glendenning), who owned a run on the eastern side of the river and shepherded his own sheep. He was a fierce-looking, big-bearded 'Hielandman', in most uncouth garb and with long unkempt locks. However his manner belied his looks and he greeted us courteously. We in return extended him the rites of hospitality by

giving him a good stiff tot of rum and a pannikin of tea.

Jacky-Jacky's abode was a 'mai-mai' of the simplest kind, being merely two forked sticks set up seven feet apart and a ridge pole placed resting on the forks. Over this a blanket was thrown and pegged down to the ground, leaving both ends open. Health officers of the present day would have been able to pass the abode as 'sanitary' had it come under their inspection.

Moving on from Gore

From the Long Ford, we drove over the 'Cemetery Hill' and across the flats and low ridges, crossing innumerable little creeks, most of which we were able to get over without cutting fords. One or two creeks happened to be too wide, and we had to bring the spade into requisition. In a few minutes in most cases, we would dig a place where the wheels could drop into the creek, and we slightly sloped the banks on the other side where we came out of the creek.

The only visible buildings were Mr McNab's hut and woolshed at the edge of the bush to our left, but as we had plenty of provisions with us, we did not call.

The Hokonuis

The country through which we were passing until we reached the

Enjoying a "good stiff tot of rum and a pannikin of tea" with local squatter 'Jacky-Jacky', are John and Thomas MacGibbon on their journey to Otapiri Station in early 1858. Jacky-Jacky, wrote Thomas, was an uncouth looking hielandman whose manners and hospitality belied his appearance. The first resident of what became East Gore, Jacky-Jacky was one of only a handful of Europeans then living in inland Southland.

John and Thomas MacGibbon establish themselves at Otapiri Station, on the northern flanks of the Hokonui range. They arrived in early 1858 to establish the station in partnership with Dunedin businessman and politician James Macandrew.

Otamita Stream was Mr McNab's, and was very richly grassed. There were no rabbits in those days and the face of the Hokonuis was covered with verdure – in contrast with the bare, rocky slopes that present themselves nowadays as one journeys up the Waimea Plains.

Our next halting place was on the Otamita Creek, not a great way from where the Wantwood homestead now stands.

The country from this to the East Peak was part of the Reaby Run, owned by Messrs Chubbins and Gunn. These two men afterwards divided the run between them, Mr Gunn taking what is now known as Wantwood, and Mr Chubbins retaining the homestead at Reaby, which he afterwards sold to Mr J R Davies, of wooden railway fame.

Mr Chubbins is still living and resides at Hunterville in the North Island. He must be well over 80 years of age.

Mr Gunn was a jolly bachelor and his hut at Otamita was a regular place of call for travellers, a state of things that finally became too heavy a tax when the Switzers diggings broke out. I have seen over twenty visitors in the hut at one time, and as there were not enough bunks to accommodate near this number, each man rolled himself in his blanket and lay down on the floor, feet to the fire. The apartment was filled from wall to wall.

Mr Gunn was afterwards very successful in his run speculations. Having sold Wantwood to Mr Wentworth at a good figure, he bought into the Tapanui Run with Mr Tom McKellar (or Tom Pepper, as he was familiarly called). He subsequently purchased and almost immediately sold the Switzers Run, making a lot of money over the deal without even occupying the place.

Ultimately Mr Gunn disposed of all his property and went to live in Melbourne, where he married. I met him long after, when he was on a visit to New Zealand, and we had a long chat together. He told me that he no longer owned an acre of land, nor a hoof of stock, but had invested all his capital, which was considerable, in securities. I was sorry to hear of his death some years later, for he was a genuine man. Indeed, it would have been difficult to get two better men, physically or socially, than Messrs Chubbins and Gunn.

In due course we reached the Otapiri Bush, where we pitched our camp. Our stockmen gave us a hand to erect a whare before they returned home.

We had a lonely and a rough life before us. The country was exceedingly rough and the hills were covered with a most luxuriant growth of fern, mixed with sowthistle, tutu, matagourie and speargrass of both kinds – Spaniard and Wild Irishman.

Travelling in this dense, thorny vegetation soon told on our habiliments, which gave evidence of rough usage. We had to patch and patch with sacking or anything convenient to prevent ourselves from being reduced to primitive 'Eden' garb.

Our neighbours were not so near as to trouble us by being too close proximity. The closest were Messrs Peter and David McKellar at Longridge, twelve miles distant. These gentlemen, originally from Argyllshire, Scotland, but more recently from Victoria, were first-rate fellows. Both were bachelors at that time.

Peter McKellar came over to see us and bade us welcome. His dress was certainly not a 'dress' one. ■

Carting wool to Invercargill

Peter McKellar of Longridge Run asked if I would take a load of wool down to Invercargill for him with our team, as he and his brother only had a two-horse team.

By Thomas MacGibbon

That trip took us just three weeks. and was full of the little incidents unavoidable in a journey of over 90 miles with no track and no culverts.

At Mr McNab's station we were joined by the station team, also conveying a load of wool, and driven by Mr Archie McNab. Our first camp was at the Waimumu Ford, which was a very narrow cutting, and pretty deep. It required considerable care to get safely over, but we accomplished the feat and camped on the southern side.

Next day our journey was down the winding track along the top of what is known as the 'high terrace', there being no road along the Mataura River flat where the Invercargill road is now.

Our day's march was made without any special difficulty until we reached what is known as the Steep Pinch. This was indeed a formidable obstacle, more particularly as we were driving top-heavy, wool-laden drays. By skidding the wheels however, and observing the usual precautions, we got down safely and camped on the Invercargill side.

Next day we arrived at Half-way Bush – now known as Dacre – about noon, and found a Mr Hughes just making dinner in the usual camp fashion. He courteously invited us to partake of his meal, which we were nothing loth to do, and we had a pleasant dinner party.

Mr Hughes had been mate of a stock ship called the Northern Star, which was wrecked at the New River entrance. He was busy erecting the first accommodation house at Dacre, and had got the walls of split and hewn slabs erected, but so far had put none of the roof on.

'Remember the Sabbath'

Bidding goodbye to Mr Hughes, we started on the trek again, having resolved to stay for the night at Woodlands, as it is now called. We needed to get across a narrow and very steep cutting through a swampy creek before camping.

Mr McKellar and I also resolved that as the next day was Sunday, we would camp for the whole day. Not so our companions, who scoffed at the idea of losing a fine day on account of its being the first day of the week. They were determined to proceed on the journey towards Invercargill notwithstanding our attitude on the question.

However, 'man proposes but God disposes', and as it happened, our friends did not travel on Sunday.

*M*an proposes but God disposes', and as it happened, our friends did not travel on Sunday.

When we reached the dreaded cutting, Mr McKellar with his horse team went first and my team followed next, and we both got over without mishap.

The next team swerved slightly as they rushed down the cutting, bringing the top-heavy dray somewhat side on. Over the whole load went to the bottom with a crash. "The best laid plans of mice and men gang aft agley".

The next day, Sunday, was not spent in travelling, as it required the whole day to set matters straight again – no light job with 12 bales of wool on.

Camped alongside us was Mr Wilson, known as 'Long Wilson'. He

*W*e had to patch and patch with sacking or anything convenient to prevent ourselves from being reduced to primitive 'Eden' garb.

was on his way northward with a large number of sheep to take up and stock the Victorian Company's runs on Wendon and Wendonside. Mr Wilson, poor fellow, was later drowned in the Mataura River near Keown's Ford.

Bullock-punching

On the Monday morning we followed the track (there was no road), skirting the edge of the bush until we got to Garrie's at the north end of Myross Bush.

Here we turned down to the Waihopai Creek and were rejoiced to find that it had just recently been spanned with one of the primitive bridges of the early days: heavy logs thrown across the creek and saplings nailed to them. Consequently our crossing was much easier than we had anticipated, although even then it was not what you might call easy, as the ground on either side was very swampy.

This necessitated much expert use of the bullock-whips and not a little rather sulphurous language. Bullock-drivers generally believed both accomplishments to be essential to success in the craft.

By bush and swamp

From the Waihopai 'bridge' we soon got into the leading ridge near Mr Copland's farm and followed its windings past Mr John Oughton's farm on what is now called Mill Road. From there we followed the bays of the bush until we got to Robinson's now Adamson's place.

In this locality there were some very bad swampy creeks to negotiate, and the district had an unenviable reputation among teamsters. It was impossible to head the creeks, as they rose somewhere in the bush, so we camped for the night to give the bullocks a proper chance in the morning when fresh, to tackle the apparently fathomless swamps which lay between us and the town.

Invercargill

In the morning, with much labour and anxiety, we got through our 'sloughs of despond' and on to the dry ridge which took us along the side of what is now Forth Street, Invercargill.

Tay Street was all bush at the east end, and as much of it had just been felled, the road was impassable for wheeled traffic. We finally drove into Tay Street just where Nith Street intersects, and it was plain sailing to Mr Calder's store at the west end, where the Bank of Australasia now stands.

Alongside Lind's Waihopai Hotel there was a stable which, although not completed, had a roof, and in this building we deposited our loads of wool. The present Albion Hotel, opposite the Post Office, stands on the site of Lind's building, which was the first, and for a time the only, hostelry in Invercargill.

Lind's hotel stood a little way off the line of Dee Street and was a composite building. The larger part was constructed of slabs with a thatched roof, while the smaller portion, which was new, was built of weatherboards and roofed with shingles. Here we put up for a couple of days, and the host, Mr Lind, and his good lady made us very comfortable.

A one-horse place

Invercargill was a very one-horse place in those days. The houses, or rather huts, were few in number. The two stores were primitive in character.

Dee Street was a mass of dense bush which extended right down to the back of the hotel. The only street which showed any sign of man's improvement was Tay Street. This improvement amounted to the bush having been felled the width of the street.

In those early days the town went generally under the name of Waihopai. The name Invercargill was bestowed some time afterwards when at a meeting of notables it was proposed to name the town Cargill in honour of the first Superintendent of Otago. The then Governor of New Zealand, who was present, suggested he prefix 'Inver', so Inver-Cargill it was and remains. The unfortunate part, however, is that the prefix 'Inver' means 'at the mouth of', and the creek on which the town is built is the Waihopai, as it happens.

However, what's in a name? – and Invercargill has thriven remarkably despite the misnomer. Since those days of 'auld lang syne', it has grown to be a place of importance.

Swapping reminiscences

On our way back to the Waimea Plains, I picked up about 600 feet of sawn timber which had been left for me at the edge of the bush about the end of what is now McMaster Street. I carted this timber up to the Halfway

Bush to form part of the new accommodation house being erected by Mr Hughes.

On our way, we camped alongside Mr John Oughton's house and spent the evening indoors with his family.

After a pleasant evening, David McKellar and myself adjourned to our 6-by-8 tent. I remember that during the night we had a fight with rats, which were present in swarms and had attacked the sheepskin rug on which we lay.

After leaving Halfway Bush we had a regular southerly buster which confined us to our tent for a couple of days. We beguiled the time by swapping yarns and telling anecdotes.

Mr McKellar had a great deal to tell about his first trip with stock, from Mokomoko to the station at Waimea. The snowgrass was so long that he needed to take a small cut of the main flock of sheep, and drive them ahead a half-mile or so to make a track along which the main flock might travel.

This procedure made progress very slow, and it is not surprising that the Messrs McKellar did not reach their run at Longridge for a year or more after starting out from the Bluff.

In a previous article in this series, Mr W H S Roberts described how the McKellars camped for a considerable

Invercargill in July 1859 — it would have been even more primitive when Thomas MacGibbon visited early the previous year.

time at the scrubby manuka bush on the Charlton Flat.

Stamina

Mr McKellar described some of the hardships they encountered on the trip. His experiences are worthy of record, if only to show the stamina of the men who pioneered this country.

One of the chief impediments to travelling was the snowgrass [red tussock], which grew luxuriantly and to a great length. In places where it had escaped burning, I have seen it eight feet long, so that it will be seen that it was a serious obstacle to rapid progress over the plains.

During the winter the weather alternated between frost and sleet, and with the snowgrass being saturated with moisture, it requires no stretch of the imagination to know that the travellers' clothes were anything but dry and comfortable.

McKellar told me that after a thorough soaking all day and a hard frost at night, he sometimes found his nether garments frozen so stiff they would stand on their own! The only course was to get a good fire started and dance around to keep warm until the heat of the flames had thawed out the garments and made it possible to get into them.

Squatters

In recent years, we have heard many unkind remarks about the squatters and their holding of such large tracts of country. However I am convinced that the detractors would not be prepared to undergo the risks and hardships which those hardy pioneers endured. They were a kindly, hospitable race, and if they made any money, they earned it the hard way. Their day is past, and the country is being thickly settled, but we owe a great deal to the men whose hardihood and courage enabled them to plunge into the unexplored wilds of the country.

All honour to them – they sowed, and the present occupiers reap.

A plague of rats

In due time we reached the Croydon Station on our homeward return, and were kindly and hospitably entertained by Miss McNab and her brother, the father of the ex-Minister for Lands.

From Croydon to McKellars at Longridge was a two-day drive, and we felt glad we had got back, particularly as a heavy fall of snow came on and covered the country deeply for several days.

Time hung somewhat heavily on

After a thorough soaking all day and a hard frost at night, he sometimes found his nether garments frozen so stiff they would stand on their own!

our hands, and the only recreation was reading, varied with an occasional rat hunt. This latter pastime afforded a great deal of amusement and excitement to us and our canine assistants.

Doubtless if the unfortunate rodents themselves could have expressed themselves, their words would have been, "It may be fun to you, but it is death to us".

In the vicinity of the station there were immense clumps of speargrass, and as the roots are edible and much appreciated by the rats, they congregated there in considerable numbers.

The order of the day was to get all the station dogs around while we poked poles into the base of the speargrass. This startled the rats out, and the dogs, who were eagerly awaiting this part of the performance, joined in the fray.

The rats gave the dogs many a good chase, but the result was usually a considerable number of victims.

Another method of rat killing was to keep a candle burning in the sleeping tent, which was erected on the top of sod walls so as to give more head space. Crumbs of bread and meat were laid down as bait, and we waited with loaded revolvers to pop off the rats that appeared.

As I have previously stated, the rats were literally swarming, and it was very difficult to keep stores from their voracious maws.

Longridge Station

The McKellars' station was very simple in character – a slab cooking and eating hut, and tents such as I have described, for bedrooms. This was the only accommodation for several years. There was also a woolshed and sheep-yards for the work of the station.

The whole menage consisted of Peter and David McKellar, and a Maori boy named Paul. Paul was a very intelligent lad who performed the duties of cook and general rouseabout.

While I was staying there, Paul nearly settled the lot of us by putting part of the contents of a bottle of strychnine into some damper bread, under the impression that it was soda. Fortunately for us all, Peter McKellar happened to take down the bottle of strychnine to use some for poisoning the wild dogs, which were troublesome. He noticed that the contents were materially reduced, and then it came out what Paul had done. Needless to say, we did not eat that damper.

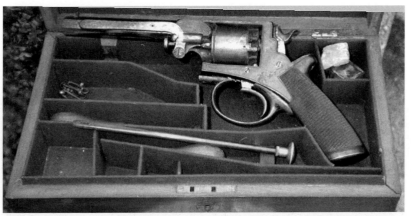

"Another method of rat killing was to keep a candle burning in the sleeping tent, which was erected on the top of sod walls so as to give more head space. Crumbs of bread and meat were laid down as bait, and we waited with loaded revolvers to pop off the rats that appeared." (This revolver is believed to have belonged to Thomas, and may well be the rat blaster.)

John MacGibbon Senior, ca 1865

Poisons were handled very carelessly on stations in those days, and the wonder is that more casualties did not occur. In this case, the poison was on the shelf over the fireplace, along with other tins containing soda, acid and other culinary necessaries.

The district's first wheat crop

While staying at Longridge, I helped David McKellar harvest his crop of wheat, which he had grown in a bend of the Mataura just below the Waikaia Plains station. The crop was not ripe, having been sown late for chaff. As far as I know, this was the first wheat grown in the Mataura district other than a few square yards grown by the Maoris at the Tuturau kaik.

Before we left Longridge, Mr Wilson arrived with his sheep for the Wendon runs, and we had some good exercise swimming the flock across the Mataura River. Of course a good many got drowned in crossing, but this was only one of the incidentals in opening up the 'back blocks'.

Adieu to runholding

My father and I did not take very kindly to the squatting life with such rough surroundings. This was particularly so as my mother and the younger members of the family were still in Caversham. My father did not feel

warranted in transporting his wife and young children from a comfortable home to a sod hut or whare on the outskirts of civilisation.

The nearest doctor lived at Invercargill, 80 miles away — not much in these days of railways and good roads, but an impossible distance where there were no roads, no bridges and railways not thought of in our wildest dreams.

In these circumstances, my father decided to surrender his share of the run, and Mr William Johnston was sent to take delivery. In July 1858 my father and I handed over the station and the stock and returned to Dunedin.

There are many more adventures by 'field and flood' which might be added, but I shall conclude this period of my experiences at this point. Perhaps should the afflatus of old-identity remembrances again descend on me, I may pen another chapter later on. ∎

To the South! To the South! To the
  land of the free,
Where the mighty Mataura rolls
  down to the sea;
Where a man has but to tickle the
  waiting soil,
To receive sure reward for his labor
  and toil.
    —ANONYMOUS "LOCAL BARD",
      QUOTED BY HERRIES BEATTIE

There's work enough to do, boys.
And that same work is rough;
There's ploughing and there's
  ditching.
From Waitaki to the Bluff.
    —JAMES BARR
A land without a past?
Nay Nay, I saw it fifty years this day.
Nor man, nor beast, nor tree:
Wide empty plains where shadows pass,
Blown by the wind o'er whispering grass
Whose sigh crept after me.
    —WILLIAM PEMBER REEVES

VIRGIN COUNTRY

The first white settlers found that much of Southland was already tussock and grass country, with fern and flax common in the lower and wetter areas. But not long before, most of the province appears to have been covered by bush. Large areas of this bush had been burned off. Some of the fires may have been accidentally started by Maori groups, but natural causes such as lightning strikes are a strong posibility, with local Maori lore telling of great fires which devastated large areas of Otago and Southland, destroying flora and fauna, including the moa. The Otakaramu Hills, east of Gore, were treeless when the run was taken up, but were dotted with charred stumps.

W H S Roberts, an early runholder and recorder of local history, described vegetation in the Waimea Plain in 1856: "The ground was well grassed, but the speargrass was too plentiful. The pasturage was very good. There was a good deal of scrub in the bends of the Mataura known as 'wire plant' (Olearia Virgata). There were also manuka and koromiko. Maoriheads, a kind of grass tree about three feet high, abounded in the swamps, and in some we saw toitoi grass and raupo. We did not pass any cabbage trees today…we reached a rich flat covered with luxuriant herbiage, just the country for cattle. Most of the land was soft, but it must be remembered it was the middle of winter and the ground had never been trodden by cattle. We proceeded slowly through tomatakuru scrub, speargrass, Spaniard, snowgrass and other native grasses…we camped in a bend with good feed at the Elbow and a swamp on one side. Maori cabbage* abounded…" Part of the MacGibbons' first Southland run, Otapiri, was on this Waimea Plain.

The hill areas of Otapiri were described by Thomas MacGibbon as being "…covered with a most luxuriant growth of fern, mixed with sowthistle, tutu, matagourie and speargrass of both kinds — Spaniard and Wild Irishman."

Called Pora by the local Maori. It was a kind of wild turnip with long leaves and a thin wiry root. The leaves were eaten.

John MacGibbon, James Macandrew et al and the Otapiri Run

John MacGibbon Snr's connection with the Otapiri Run is linked with Dunedin businessman and politician James Macandrew, and with a murky period in Otago's early commercial history.

John MacGibbon was evidently a business partner of James Macandrew. Family tradition has it that MacGibbon, as an upright Scot and honourable business partner, felt obliged to bail Macandrew out of a serious personal debt in the late 1850s. To raise enough money, MacGibbon had to sell most of his reputedly considerable Dunedin assets. Having thus impoverished himself, he decided to make a fresh start in Southland, leaving in late 1858 to take up the ferry and accommodation house contract at Mataura Falls advertised by the Otago Provincial Council.

One thing is certain: the MacGibbons first went to Southland at the beginning of 1858, and it was for reasons other than the Mataura ferry.

When the lands of the world-old darkness are quick to the rising sun,

And the men who break the trail for us
their life-long work have done,

They'll pierce the realm of Further-Out,
to find themselves among

The tribes they left in the hidden West in the days when the world was young.

So, then, the last camp-fire they'll light
upon the widening trail,

And sling the blackened billy in the
shadow-laden vale;

While thoughts of home and days gone by their fleeting spirits rend,

With never a wail they camp on the trail
and wait for the coming end!

—ELSDON BEST

When all the world is young, lad,
And all the trees are green,
And every goose a swan, lad,
And every lass a queen;
Then hey for boot and horse, lad,
And round the world away;
Young blood must have its course, lad,
And every dog his day.

—KINGSLEY

They went to the Otapiri Run, as partners of James Macandrew.

It is possible that MacGibbon was given a share in the run in return for helping Macandrew out of one of the holes he regularly fell into, as Dunedin's most enthusiastic speculator. If so, the arrangement must have been informal, because MacGibbon's name is not associated with Otapiri in Otago Waste Lands Board records. It also seems likely that John MacGibbon was far from being a pauper when he left Dunedin.

A public saga

In any event, with or without MacGibbon involvement, dealings concerning the Otapiri Run became an ongoing and very public saga in Dunedin financial circles.

The run itself was originally applied for by Edmund Davidson, at the end of 1855 or early 1856. The gazetted area was 90,000 acres, and the Otago Waste Lands Board stipulated that a minimum of 3,288 sheep had to be run on the property. It appears Davidson could not provide the stock, and a licence was never issued. The gazette notice described the property as Run 146 – 'Mataura West'.

Then on 10 June 1857, a new applicant, John Parkin Taylor, was advertised, with the locality now given as 'Hockanui Ranges'. The annual lease was to be £7. At that time, leases were based on one penny for each sheep, and so the £7 would have represented 1,680 sheep – only half the original requirement. Taylor never took up the run, so the first occupiers were probably John and Thomas MacGibbon, who arrived early in 1858.

Taylor transferred his right and interest in the run to James Macandrew. The transfer was sanctioned 23 April 1858, but probably gazetted toward the end of 1857.

Between 1858 and 1859, Macandrew bought and sold his right and interest in the run no less than four times.

Macandrew first relinquished the property – to John Hyde Harris – on 18 June 1858, while John and Thomas

MacGibbon were still living there. We don't know what role, if any, John MacGibbon had in the transfer, but it seems likely that it was done behind his back.

Clue

A brief but tantalising clue is contained in Herries Beattie's notes from his 1909 interview with John MacGibbon Jr: "They left because Macandrew was shaky. They lost their cattle owing to Macandrew's financial straits."

These enigmatic clues may point to the real story behind the family tradition that MacGibbon bailed out Macandrew. The bailout may well have occurred in Southland, rather than in Dunedin. MacGibbon's contribution to the partnership may have been the cattle herd, which was now lost.

A year later, on 31 May 1859, the Otapiri run was transferred back to Macandrew. Then on 4 August of the same year, Macandrew transferred his right and interest yet again, in favour of John Jones, of Waikouaiti and Dunedin. Jones climbed off the merry-go-round on 20 June 1861, when he transferred the run to Duncan McCallum.

In *The Southern Runs*, Herries Beattie notes that "...[Otapiri] was one of the runs about which great yarns used to be spun dealing with artful business manipulations in Dunedin. It will be noticed that the list of owners includes two Superintendents of Otago and one of Southland, and the redoubtable Johnny Jones."

Dealings over the run were publicly aired by people anxious to point accusingly at Princess Street pastoralists.

Was John MacGibbon a pawn in the process, or one of the artful dodgers?

There is an interesting footnote to the relationship between MacGibbon and Macandrew. When MacGibbon signed the lease for the Mataura Ferry, it was Macandrew and Macandrew's brother-in-law, William Hunter Reynolds, who put up a bond of £200.

Conscience money? ■

William Adam and the Johnston family at Otapiri

Herries Beattie collected reminiscences of his uncle William Adam, who came to Otapiri in 1858 as William Johnston's hired hand. Johnston spent two years at Otapiri, managing the run for James Macandrew, who presumably became sole owner after John and Thomas MacGibbon departed.

Adam describes a six-week southward journey which was similar, though more problematical, to that undertaken a few months later by the full MacGibbon family. Mr and Mrs Johnston had three children, and travelled in a bullock dray. With them were Mrs Johnston's sister and a bullock driver.

Like the MacGibbons, they lost their bullocks at Waiwera. Unlike the MacGibbons, they never found their bullocks, and had to borrow replacements from Alex McNab at Knapdale Station. Then their dray collapsed and they had to borrow another to complete the journey.

Mrs Johnston and her sister were probably the first European women to cross the Mataura River at Longford (Gore). Previously, women who travelled to the southernmost parts of Southland had gone by boat around the coast.

No doubt the party was given a warm welcome at Otapiri by John and Thomas MacGibbon, who would have been keen to hand over the reins of the property and get back to their family at Dunedin. However the new arrivals would certainly not have been able to rest in comfort.

Imagine the scene...

Imagine the scene: mid-winter in what was then one of the most isolated and least-known parts of New Zealand. A party of eight people arrives at the homestead, on the edge of the Otapiri bush about four miles from the Oreti River and 70 miles north of Invercargill. But the homestead is only a one-room wattle and daub hut, doubtless lacking any of the amenities travellers would long for at the end of such a tiring journey.

The area around the homestead can only be imagined, but probably included little other than primitive stockyards and a rough hut to store equipment. Close at hand would have been some of the fledgling station's greatest assets: the bullocks. Thomas appears to have had a particular affinity and love for these beasts of burden, which had already taken him on several colourful adventures – with many more to come. Introducing a touch of culture to the wilderness, Thomas had given the bullocks names from Greek mythology, like Jupiter and Hercules.

Natural state

William Adam said the country around Otapiri was in its 'natural state', and he also found traces of Maori habitation. This included a raised food storehouse high in the bush. It needed to be raised to stay clear of the Norwegian rats which swarmed over the area. He also found a Maori skull, a broken axe and a paua shell.

The run had some milking cows, and Mrs Johnston once made a large cheese which William Adam carted 70 miles to Invercargill on a bullock-drawn sledge. He sold the cheese for a "high price" and spent the money on provisions to take back to Otapiri.

Animal life at Otapiri included numerous wild Maori dogs ('kuri'), described by Adam as long haired, short-snouted, ugly white and yellow brutes about the size of a small collie. The dogs did not bark, but gave a "long lugubrious howl", which "on a dark night was quite sufficient to give one an eerie feeling". These dogs killed many sheep on local stations, Mr Adam said. However that was not a problem at Otapiri, where only cattle were run.

Native birds were very numerous, and Maori hen (wekas), pigeon, and particularly quail were part of the station diet – no doubt a welcome change from the standard station fare of mutton and damper bread.

"Mrs Johnson was very fond of them as table birds, and would ask the men when they came in if they had brought any home," Herries Beattie reports Mr Adam as saying. "They were so plentiful that Mr Adam generally had one or two in his pocket. As he laughingly says, 'We were living in the wilderness, and quail were easily provided, but manna was another matter, as we had to go to Invercargill (70 miles), or to the Clutha (80 miles) for flour.'."

The Waimea Plain, being off the beaten track, was a vast bird sanctuary, William Adam remembered. Every stream "...harboured vast colonies of water fowl, and the plains thronged with woodhens and quail. The young [quail] were beautiful wee chicks, and it was quaint to see them play hide-and-seek in the grass if a hawk hovered overhead."

Yet by 1911, Herries Beattie was bemoaning: "The teeming millions of native birds have vanished as if they had never been." ∎

The hills in the distance are the eastern end of the northern flanks of the Hokonuis. Otapiri Run began near near the eastern end of the hills, and extended for 40 kilometres – ending well off-camera to the right. The run also included flat land extending to the southern bank of the Waimea Stream (near the base of the hills, but not visible in this photograph). The township of Gore is near the left hand end of the photograph.

We travelled in a slow but sure manner, for if you owned a team of good bullocks they would take you through almost anything in a new, roadless country.

Down south again, with the family in tow

By Thomas MacGibbon

Shortly after my father and I had left the Otapiri Run and returned to Dunedin, we found that the Otago Provincial Government had advertised tenders for a seven years' lease of the newly established ferry or bridge at the Mataura Falls, together with a run of over 1,000 acres in connection therewith.

As both of us had been much impressed with the luxuriance of the 'feed' in the South, my father tendered for the lease and was successful.

For the ensuing month or two we were very busy getting everything ready for the 'exodus'. In this, we were considerably assisted by the experience we had gained on our first trek down South. We were able to provide for the 'camping out' many little conveniences of which we had been entirely ignorant on our first journey.

Our bullock dray was provided with a comfortable 'tilt', and we also secured a good tent which could amply shelter our whole family while on the tramp.

The party consisted of my father [49], mother [41], two sisters [Jessie, 16; Jeannie, 14] and three brothers [John, 9; Ebenezer, 4; Archie, 2]. [Thomas himself was 19.]

Also with us was a young friend who was a shipmate from the Old Country and an old schoolmate of mine in Glasgow. He was engaged to accompany us and give us a start in our new home.

Leaving Caversham

We left Caversham, where the family had resided for eight years, in the latter end of December 1858, and commenced what was quite an adventurous journey even in the early days.

On this occasion we had a small mob of cattle and with them a quiet cow in milk. We bailed her up night and morning to the dray wheel and we had a plenteous supply of the lacteal fluid to make our tea more palatable.

In addition we had a large coop filled with fowls suspended from the end of the dray. As some of these birds were laying, we were able to be quite epicurean in our dietary scale.

Fish, as I stated in my notes of the previous journey, were plentiful in every creek in the shape of eels, and ducks were to be shot in every lagoon and stream. So we were able to restock our larder almost every day.

There was no legal shooting season then, and as the Acclimatisation Society had not been established, there was no-one to let or hinder our sport with either gun or bob.

Catching eels with the 'bob'

I do not know whether many of our young people will quite understand what I mean by the 'bob'. It was a favourite method of catching eels by means of some frayed strips of green flax attached to a short stick. Large worms were threaded on the flax strands, which were looped up. The fisherman allowed the bait mass to rest in the water where eels seemed likely to be present. Usually it was not long before a smart jerk and tug would be felt, when the fisherman would adroitly flick out the prey before it could disentangle its teeth from the frayed flax composing the bob.

The sport must be followed at night, and it is good fun if the fish are plentiful. By this method I have caught eels weighing up to 10 and 12 pounds.

Eels were almost the only fish to be found in the creeks then, as the only other variety seemed to be what we called 'cockabullas'.

[Cockabullas is no doubt a corruption of one of the Maori names for the grayling or native trout, kokopura. This was a fish somewhat like a trout, but the flesh was soft and not over-palatable.]

However, the eels were rare good eating and they could be kept for a day or two hanging to the body of the dray, so they were nearly always available as one of the courses of our camp feasts.

Slow but sure

As we had young children in our party, our progress was not rapid. In any case, travelling per bullock dray was not so speedy as present day motoring, but from what I notice in the newspapers concerning the death rate from motor accidents in America, I consider it was at all events much safer.

We travelled in a slow but sure manner, for if you owned a team of good bullocks they would take you through almost anything in a new, roadless country. The patient ox was man's best friend in this respect, for horses were too fiery and jerky, breaking the harness in their plunging. This was a consideration where there were no saddlers to mend broken gear.

The bullocks were always driven yoke and bows, and a simpler mode of attaching the animals to the load it would be difficult to imagine. At the worst, if you did get bogged it would generally mean a split yoke or a broken chain. It was usual to carry a spare yoke and an extra chain to provide for such emergencies.

At a pinch, if there was no spare yoke, a round sapling, smoothed where it rested on the bullock's neck, and a couple of auger holes at each end to pass the iron bow through, could be made in half an hour. Sometimes these makeshifts did better service than the elaborately finished ones.

The bullocks as beasts of burden are passing out, like many of their erstwhile masters. The placid, slow-moving team will soon be only pictured in memories.

Our progress was slow and it was over a week before we reached Waiwera, having had a very pleasant journey with nothing worthy of notice in the way of experiences. At Waiwera, however, we lost our bullocks.

As I mentioned earlier in these notes, there was a fence across the ford so that stock put across on the further side from their home would not usually stray. In this case we were deceived, as in the morning no bullocks were to be found, although all the rest of the cattle were there.

> *P*ower did the business, and we began to feel that we could move almost anything with our bullocks.

We hunted the whole country from the Molyneux Ferry to what is now Clydevale, then occupied as a run by the Messrs Archibald Bros. At last a passing traveller informed us that he had heard of a team of working bullocks having been seen on Mr Alex Chalmers' Otakaramu run. My assistant and myself set off at once, and found our lost bullocks in a bight of Taylor's Creek a few miles nearer Gore than Pukerau.

Of course the names Pukerau and Gore were not known then. The former was not named, and the latter was then designated 'Longford', on account of the long shallow ford at the crossing, which was a short distance below where the railway bridge now spans the Mataura River.

As may be imagined, we lost no time in collecting our cattle, and next morning we started back for the camp, 25 miles distant. Immediately on reaching camp, rather late in the afternoon, we yoked up, and covering a few miles of our journey, camped for the night at the Wairuna Creek.

During our absence, my father and mother had ridden up to Mr Alex. McNeil's farm to spend the day. His place was situated under the Kaihiku

Hills, not a great way from our camp at Waiwera. On their return to the Waiwera camp they found it deserted, but judging we had found the missing animals, they followed onward and late in the evening joined us at the camp at Wairuna.

Our new home

From this point we had a pleasant journey, the weather being fine. In due time we reached and crossed the Longford, and although we were then only eight miles from Mataura, we had to make a lengthy detour to reach it.

We travelled up the leading ridge to the Croydon home station then occupied by Mr Nat. Chalmers. Here we camped for the night, and next day followed the leading ridge as far as the ford mentioned in my notes about the trip to Invercargill. From here we travelled down the left bank of the Waimumu Stream and were obliged to cut scrub to make crossings over the numerous swampy creeks flowing into the Waimumu.

On reaching the site of what is now the town of Mataura, we made a camp. We found that the house which we were to occupy had not even been commenced, as the contractors, Messrs Nicol and Kay, were busy constructing the bridge first.

We learned that the Provincial Government's boat, which we were to take possession of, was on the river at Tuturau, just below the Maori kaik.

Next day we proceeded down the bank of the river to the site of the ferry. We cut a ford on the Waimumu, and a good one we got, as we found the bed to be lignite. With banks being low, we had no difficulty in crossing. We had one more difficulty at the next creek (a small one deep down between precipitous banks), but a little spade work and careful driving got us over that also.

At last we reached our destination on the bank of the river opposite Maori Bush. We proceeded to construct a mud hut as a temporary accommodation house, and this we occupied for several months until the 'government house' at the falls was completed.

As showing the kindly nature of the Maoris, we were not there long before they paid a visit to welcome us. There were six Maoris I think – Solomon [Teko Hutu] and his two wives Huko and Pi, with three children – one a grown girl and the other two a small girl and a boy. [The girl was Toki Reko, also known as Queenie. She ended up in a MacGibbon photo album.]

Expressing their sympathy with us in our lack of fuel, they supplied us with some good dry kowhai which they had collected in their bush, carried down to the river and boated over. We greatly appreciated the kindness, which was quite spontaneous, and we were ever after on very friendly terms.

At the time of our arrival, the Tuturau Station had just changed hands. Mr George Lloyd, of Green Island, had sold out to Mr Edwin Rich, a son-in-law of Sir John L C Richardson (later Superintendent of the province). The late Mr J P Joyce, later editor of the 'Southland News', was stockman in charge of the run, and had Mr Tommy Littlewort as an assistant. Both these gentlemen were pleasant, hearty fellows, always ready to bear a helping hand to the newcomers. We became very friendly, both then and in after years.

Log hauling

Messrs Nicol and Kay, contractors for the new bridge and ferry house, were busy getting timber for both, cutting it in the Maori Bush.

The logs for the new bridge were heavy, long trees cut to the required size. The contractors had difficulty in transporting them to the bridge site, which was just over the falls, where the paper mill and freezing works now stand.

They had only two bullocks, and even with the loan of four more from the [Tuturau] station, their team was not strong enough to drag the logs through the dense vegetation and miry swamps between the bush and the falls. I was enlisted in the work, with my team of six powerful bullocks, and with ten animals hauling, we got the logs up to their (what afterwards proved) temporary resting place at the falls.

It was rough work tearing a way through the swamp grass and fern, but 'power' did the business, and we began to feel that we could move almost anything with our bullocks. In fact, we felt that we were almost ready to rival the feat of a Yankee teamster who bragged that his team had dragged a two-story house and then he had gone back and drawn the cellar!

An old-time bridge

The bridge was a very primitive concern consisting of two heavy logs placed on bearers at either end, and braced by diagonals tied across the top. It did not go across straight, but turned after crossing the widest chasm (which was about 70 feet wide) at an angle on the centre rocks. Then there were two more logs to span the smaller chasm. On these logs, 8x4 decking was laid diagonally, and the whole was railed at the sides about 5ft high.

> *We travelled in a slow but sure manner, for if you owned a team of good bullocks they would take you through almost anything in a new, roadless country.*

The bridge was only intended for pedestrians and horse traffic, and its width was about six feet. We found some difficulty in getting mobs of cattle over it until we had trained some of our bullocks to act as decoys. [Thomas's brother John Jr recalled that cattle would sometimes become jammed in the angle in the middle of the bridge.]

Unfortunately the bridge did not last long, as it was swept away by a high flood in April 1861. Some of the timber was seen for several years after being stranded where the town of Wyndham now stands.

It was evident from the first that the structure was in danger during every flood, as frequently we could not approach it from the Otago end. It was only about 18 inches above the level of those rocks which were bare at the normal condition of the river, so it was not surprising that it was eventually carried away.

The bridge vanishes

Shortly after the bridge was completed, the authorities, recognising the inevitable destruction of their property if something were not done to save it, endeavoured to avert the threatened calamity by adopting various protection measures.

Mr James Marchbank, father of Mrs Graham, who now lives in Gore, was sent down with a gang of men and they sank strong iron bolts into the rock alongside the logs on each side, and placed a band over the logs at each end.

As a further protection, the gang blasted the edge of the falls away from a considerable distance above, but all these efforts only delayed the catastrophe, as the flood which I have referred to lifted the bridge bodily and hurled it downstream. In the morning, all we saw was one of the beams on the centre rock anchored by the bolt at one end and hanging forlornly down. Of the rest of the bridge there was not a vestige remaining.

Symbolic event

A peculiar coincidence in connection with the carrying-away of the connecting link between Otago and Southland was that the messenger conveying the proclamation of the severance of Murihiku [Southland] from the province of Otago had only just passed over the bridge the previous day, on his way to Invercargill.

On his return, the messenger had to stay with us several days until the waters had abated sufficiently for us to ferry him across in our boat, his horse swimming at the stern.

This mode of swimming horses over was the only way of crossing for several years when the river was unfordable, as the bridge was not replaced for a long time after.

It was about 1867 or 1868 when the present wire suspension bridge was built, and I think I was the first to cross it in a buggy. This was before the guard rails were put on, and I was on my way to my father's home at Kelvingrove, on the Hokonuis, as I had just returned from my visit to the Old Country. [Bringing his new bride, Bella, for whom crossing the narrow bridge without rails must have been a hair-raising experience.]

During our occupancy of the Ferry, we met most of the early settlers of the district. When my father was appointed postmaster, our house was frequently visited by people from far and wide. The Mataura Post Office was the only one in the Eastern District outside of

Invercargill, and people came from as far as Manapouri to transact postal business.

The duties of the post office were not great, and I may state that there was no 'morning delivery'.

Until the outbreak of the diggings at Gabriel's Gully, we led a rather quiet life. The traffic was not great. Indeed it was so small that the few travellers experienced great difficulty in keeping to the track from Popotunoa and making the Ferry House at Mataura. This was owing to the ridgy nature of the country and the deep fern and vegetation which clothed the ground.

Many a poor weary traveller who had taken the wrong spur found himself a long way out of his bearings when the riverbank was reached.

To remedy this state of things, the Provincial Government engaged my father to draw a plough furrow along the most available route, starting near where Mr A Macaulay's station now is, and continuing until within sight of the Mataura Falls bridge.

On the Southland side, the furrow was continued to Halfway Bush (now Dacre) and served its purpose well. Travellers, seeing the work of the ploughshare, kept close to this mark of civilisation and thus a defined track was soon formed.

Golden days

As I have already mentioned, it was not until gold was discovered at Tuapeka by Gabriel Read [May 1861] that there was any traffic passing through to speak of, but the gold discoveries made a great change in this respect.

Most of the able-bodied men in the province left their homes to try their luck on the new fields, and as a result, our house was filled night after night. We were forced to erect additions, and even then our place was insufficient to accommodate the travelling public.

We had to pass over the river nearly all the male population of Southland on their way to the 'Land of Promise'.

Messrs Roebuck and Blacklock stayed with us a month or two and prospected up and down the Mataura River. They obtained 'colour' everywhere, but nothing sufficient to warrant a 'rush'. The only place where there was a better prospect than elsewhere was just below the Maori Bush on the banks of the river, and there the indications were so good that a party was formed to work the ground.

They got to work with cradles and long toms, and for some time were very sanguine of establishing a goldfield and claiming the reward offered by the Provincial Government for the discovery of a payable field. But after working for a month or two and only winning about a pound weight of fine scaly gold, they also gave it their best and left the district.

That plenty of gold existed in the valley of the Mataura was evident, but it was also apparent that it had been sown so thinly that the ordinary methods of working were unprofitable, and it was left to the enterprise of these modern days to win the precious metal by dredging.

I have seen good gold washed out by my young brothers on the Waimumu Stream when we were digging lignite for fuel. The boys used to dig out the sand between the layers of lignite, then wash it in a long-handled shovel or tin dish. The result was sometimes nuggets as large as pinheads. [Gold dredges operated in the Waimumu Stream and Charlton Creek between the 1890s and the 1930s. Most dredging ended by 1914. The total amount of gold mined from the two streams was 39,000 oz, at an average loss of eight shillings an ounce.]

After getting fairly settled in our new home, we broke up a paddock, which we sowed in oats for the stable. We cropped this several times.

I believe it was my misfortune to be perhaps the first to sow sorrel — that pest to farmers. We had got a quantity of seed oats from Tokomairiro, and when sowing these in the old-fashioned way from a sheet slung in front of me, I noticed a quantity of small yellow seeds at the bottom. Never having seen sorrel seed, I took these to be clover. Alas! it was not so, and we had as prolific a crop of sorrel as one could wish for.

It so happened that gold was discovered that season at Switzers (Waikaia) and the Lake districts, and trade by wagons became brisk between Invercargill and the goldfields. The wagoners, as they passed, purchased the sheaves of oats then in stook, and afterwards, wherever they made their camps, sorrel sprang up and spread to the tussock land, causing many people to say, incorrectly, that sorrel is an indigenous plant. The oat sheaves paid us well – we got one shilling each for them handed over the fence. ∎

"We proceeded to construct a mud hut as a temporary accommodation house, and this we occupied for several months until the 'government house' at the [Mataura] falls was completed."

John Junior remembers the big trip south

While Thomas MacGibbon did a man's job during the big trip south, his brother John Jr, then a boy of 10, evidently took a boyish delight in the whole trip. Interviewed in 1909 by Herries Beattie for his first series of Mataura Ensign pioneer recollections, John Jr said the weather had been warm, and the journey like a "picnic to the young fry".

"They had plenty of food, and their stock of provisions was supplemented by the toothsome flesh of various native birds and by succulent roast pork provided for their delectation by unwary wild pigs," Beattie wrote.

"The narrator [John Jr] distinctly remembers a camp at the Waikaka, for, boylike, he spent his spare moments fishing – for 'cockabullies'. Next morning the party found the right track and, crossing over the ford, passed what is now known as Sheddan's and the Pinnacle, and came through the notch in the hills behind East Gore School.

"From the notch, the party had a splendid view of the Mataura Valley, and the narrator says it was just as he had pictured it in his imagination. There was the river winding about, the long, level plain with not a house in sight, and the luxuriant growth of flax and other vegetation covering the plain."

Croydon Station

"The party crossed the pellucid Mataura at the Long Ford [near present-day Gore] and made for Croydon Station, where Mr Nathaniel Chambers had the homestead. Mrs Chambers was a very nice woman and was very kind to Mrs MacGibbon and the children.

"From here the party crossed the Charlton Creek near the present Croydon Bush School, and the journey was continued down the ridges to the Mataura Falls."

In his private notes, Herries Beattie said the family's trip to Mataura was only the third made by a bullock wagon from Dunedin to Southland. The first wheeled venture into the trackless wilderness had been the journey of John and Thomas MacGibbon to Otapiri Station in January 1858. The next such journey was undertaken six months later by the William Johnston family, which took over at Otapiri. On the second MacGibbon trek south, it was possible to follow some of the previous wagon tracks. Thomas had the job of riding ahead to find them.

Beattie's article in the Mataura Ensign says that when the MacGibbon family arrived at Mataura Falls on 6 January 1859, "...they found the Provincial Government, with that delay which so often characterises governing bodies of all kinds, had not even started the promised accommodation house." The party moved on down the river bank to a site in what was known as Maori Bush, opposite the Maori kaika at Tuturau.

"The family continued to live for a few more days as it did on the trek," wrote Beattie. "At night the tent was requisitioned, while a tarpaulin slung over the dray made an additional 'room'. Then a sod hut was made and this unpretentious mansion was occupied for five to six months until the accommodation house at the Falls was ready for habitation.

"The nearest white neighbours were Messrs Joyce and Littlewort, who were working on the Tuturau Run."

A crowded sod hut

Beattie's notes contain an amusing recollection of John Jr concerning life in a crowded sod hut. One wet night they were visited by two men, one of whom was Reverend William Bannerman, the second Presbyterian minister to arrive in Otago. The weather was bad, and the MacGibbons made 'shakedown' beds on the floor for the travellers. The tiny two-room 'inn' already contained eight family members, and that was not all, as the reverend gentleman discovered. Jane MacGibbon had brought poultry with her from Dunedin, and she took great care of them. She was particularly protective of a "gigantic" Cochin China rooster, and brought it inside the hut each night so it would not be lost or killed. In the morning, the rooster did what roosters do in the morning – it let out a deep bass crow which reportedly nearly scared Rev Bannerman out of his wits. ∎

Demonstrating advantages of a reaping hook over a butcher's knife (p164).

Maori woman from an old MacGibbon photo album. She may be Toki Reko, aka Queenie, from the Tuturau kaika. Toki was a daughter of Reko and Pi.

The kaika at Tuturau

The MacGibbon family evidently had a fair degree of contact with local Maori, who lived a short distance south of Mataura at a kaika called Tuturau. This was a small village whose population varied considerably at different times of the year. There were 20 residents when the MacGibbons arrived in 1858.

The permanent residents were descendants of a Ngai Tahu chief called Reko, who migrated to Tuturau in 1827, after Te Rauparaha destroyed his pa at Kaiapoi. Reko had died a year before the MacGibbons arrived, and his two wives, Huko and Pi, had a new husband, Teko Hutu (aka Solomon).

During the kanakana season, Tuturau's population swelled considerably. The kanakana (lamprey eels), ran up the river every year to gorge themselves on whitebait, and then attach themselves to the rocks at the Mataura Falls. It was said to be the largest concentration of kanakana in New Zealand before the fishery was decimated by mining pollution. Maori dried the captured eels for later use.

In the 1909 interview with Herries Beattie, John MacGibbon Jr told some interesting tales about the kaika. Some of this material was published by the Mataura Ensign, but much is from unpublished notes in the Hocken Library's Beattie Collection.

First contact with local Maori came on the day the MacGibbons arrived at

Mataura. The boys were collecting dry flax stalks (korari) to make a fire, when some Maori women, up from Tuturau to inspect the newcomers, offered a better substitute. Saying the boys needed rakau (sticks), they went into the bush and soon returned carrying bundles of wood.

John Jr recalled the family's appreciation of this kindness, which marked the beginning of a friendly relationship. John MacGibbon Sr was able to help his Maori neighbours shortly afterward, when he showed the advantages of a reaping hook over a butcher's knife for cutting wheat. Beattie noted: "McG. had a reaping-hook and he did the work with it, much to the gratification of the dusky aborigines."

There was one awkward moment when the MacGibbons arrived. This was in connection with the ferry operation, which John MacGibbon had been contracted to establish. The Provincial Government had evidently already supplied a boat for river crossings, and the Tuturau Maori had been ferrying people across for payment. Initially they would not hand the boat over, but, as Beattie noted: "...they must have heard of this [Government] authority, for when he mentioned his name, opposition vanished and they said 'Kapai' (good)".

Sources of mutual wonderment

Living close to people with such a different culture was a fascinating experience for the MacGibbons. No doubt the Maori found the MacGibbons equally curious. John Jr related a number of impressions and incidents to Herries Beattie.

The Maori were very superstitious, said John Jr. They kept a sacred fire burning and considered certain trees to be tapu.

One day as he passed the kaika, John Jr heard great merriment, and called in to investigate. He found a mischievous Maori boy called Kaitai imitating the white man's wearing of spectacles, and "...going into great explosions of laughter." Kaitai had found two pieces of green glass and had woven a frame for them from grass.

The main house, or whare, was long, with no chimney. Smoke from the cooking fire had to percolate out of

the whare through the flax and raupo roof. John Jr said he needed to stay near the floor, for fear of suffocation.

An old hut was used for catching kaka parrots, which were then a plentiful and favoured item of food. According to John Jr, a kaka would be caught, brought inside the hut and made to scream. Other kaka, attracted by the noise, would land on the roof and be pulled inside by their legs.

The same hut was the scene of an incident which greatly disturbed the Europeans. Huko, one of the old chief Reko's surviving wives, "...had rheumatics very bad", and her family shut her up in the hut to die. It was not a willing death, and her screams and moans attracted the attention of John Sr, who sent her food. The food was intercepted by Huko's son, Jim, who would not let her eat it.

John Jr spoke of an old Maori called Abraham, whom they knew as 'Daddy'. Daddy was heavily tattooed and looked "very fierce", but "...he was not as bad as he looked.." Old Daddy went mad every full moon, and at such times he would sometimes visit the MacGibbons, talking excitedly to himself.

Usually when these lunar moods were upon him, Daddy would retire out of harm's way to the old kaka-catching hut. One day, John Jr peeked inside. Beattie's notes record the boy's shock: "He stole up to the hut and there was Daddy, mouth frothing, eyes rolling in a frenzy, meanwhile performing a haka with a butcher's knife in his hand. The narrator did not disturb 'Daddy' but crept away silently."

Maori battle lore

Tuturau is well-known in Maori battle lore, for it was here, in 1836, that possibly the last act of inter-tribal warfare took place in the South Island. Te Rauparaha, from Otaki in the Wellington province, had conquered and terrorised many Maori communities in the South Island. A group of his war party, led by Te Puoho, travelled as far as Tuturau and took over the kaika. However a hastily-assembled group of Muruhiku Ngai Tahu, led by Tuhawaiki, successfully counter-attacked, killing many of the invaders and making slaves of the rest. ∎

'MacGibbons' was no Ritz on the Mataura

It had been a bone-aching day in the saddle, and Edward Jackson was looking forward to a restful night at 'MacGibbons' accommodation house. He came over the brow of the hill overlooking the Mataura River, and as his horse picked its way through the tall red tussocks, he spied a line of tattered flags beside a rough track. He followed the track down to the river bank, where the only sign of human habitation was a crude sign hammered to a pole. "Raise the flag to request a river crossing," it read. On the bank opposite, a rowboat was tethered to a stake.

Jackson raised the flag and waited.

And waited, stamping his feet with impatience.

After an hour, the ferryman arrived by horse and rowed across to collect him. Jackson asked how his horse was to cross the river and was told it would have to swim.

The pair travelled one mile downstream to a small weatherboard and shingle-roofed house, where Jackson found facilities and a welcome that were notably less than he had anticipated. At least that was how the traveller reported his experience in a November 1861 letter of complaint to the Superintendent of Southland Province.

"Sir, I beg to bring to the notice of the Government an evil which is generally acknowledged by travellers between Invercargill and Dunedin," Jackson wrote.

"I refer to the very inferior entertainment provided by Mr McGibbon of the Mataura Accommodation House."

Mr Jackson's catalogue of complaints started with his steed. Had MacGibbon pointed to the local ford, the tired horse could have waded across the river instead of having to swim.

On reaching the accommodation house, a mile further downstream, his mount had to use a stable that was "...over-run with fowls" and "...unfit

'MacGibbons' accommodation house at Mataura, ca 1864. The photograph was taken by a photographer called Ross, who brought his camera gear from Invercargill, pushing a little barrow which was harnessed in front to a dog (which can be seen in the photograph, in front of the standing men). Sitting on the ground at left are young MacGibbon boys, Ebenezer and Archie. Standing are John Jr, John Sr, and Eric McKay, the family's live-in tutor. There are two main buildings in the photograph, joined in the front by a verandah. The two-storied building on the right was erected in 1863, and contained higher class accommodation with private rooms. The MacGibbons had two upstairs bedrooms in the older building, and shared a public room with travellers. Guests in the older building slept in a communal dormitory. Guests ate with the MacGibbon family, and had to wait for John MacGibbon Sr to say grace before beginning their meal.

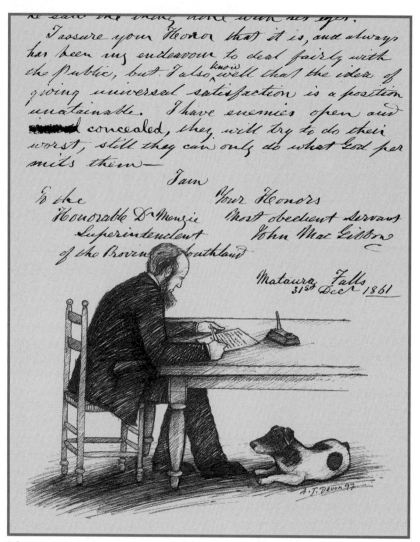

John MacGibbon Senior writes to the Superintendent of Southland Province, answering allegations that he was running a sub-standard operation at the Mataura Ferry and Accommodation House. This business was being run by the MacGibbon family under contract to the Provincial Government. The MacGibbons were reported several times in the early 1860s, with allegations including poor accommodation standards, and a 'want of civility' on the part of John and his eldest son, Thomas. Police inspectors found the accommodation standards were reasonable, but agreed with complaints about attitudes toward guests.

It is known that the family was extremely busy during this period. Not only did they run the ferry and accommodation house, but they were the postal centre for a large area of Southland which not only included the Mataura Valley, but extended west to Manapouri. After the Otago gold rushes began in 1861, a huge increase in numbers of travellers – many of whom were rough characters – would have put pressure on the operation.

for horses to rest in." To make matters worse, no horse feed was available.

Conditions were little better for Jackson himself. His feather bed was damp, smelled "disgustingly" and he was forced to leave in the middle of the night.

Summing up the experience, and claiming to represent the views of nearly every traveller on the road who had the misfortune to put up at the MacGibbon establishment, he advised the Superintendent that "The deportment of the man and his Son in Charge of the House is often offensive and uncivil to travellers..."

This was the second letter of complaint the Superintendent had received from travellers. A month earlier, Justin Aylmer had drawn his Honour's attention to "...the insufficient and bad accommodation at McGibbon's on the Mataura."

Aylmer complained that fowls had taken over the only shed, and no hay was available for his horse. MacGibbon supplied little more than a quart of poor quality oats, for which he charged two shillings – a price Aylmer evidently considered excessive.

The house was not large enough to hold both the MacGibbon family and travellers, Aylmer said. The family should not have been living there, he said. No private rooms were available for travellers, who had to doss together in a communal bunkroom.

It was the dirtiest and dearest house without exception from Dunedin to Riverton, Aylmer opined, winding up his letter with a suggestion that his Honour should "...inquire into the matter."

Please explain...

His Honour certainly did, and fired off a 'please explain' letter to John MacGibbon. The letter is missing from National Archives files on Southland Ferries, which contain the complainants' letters. John MacGibbon's response is in the archive, and it reads:

"Yours of date 18th Dec I have perused. The first point of it 'Absence of comfort and neatness in the house.' The food put on the table is decidedly of good quality. Travellers are under a mistake if they expect to get fresh Beef steak or Mutton chops, daily. Any reflective person may readily perceive that, isolated as the Mataura house is, the absence of fresh meat, except at killing time is not surprising. Cleanliness is a principle always in real operation, both as regards Food etc, and likewise to the Beds. My wife and daughters have enough of respect for themselves, to be guilty of carelessness on this point. Further, when I go to market I always purchase the first quality of goods.

"I invite any person, however much prejudiced against me, to inquire at the stores I deal with in Invercargill and Dunedin, & bring proof that I at any time bought goods of inferior quality merely to save money.

"A word more about the beds. I am perfectly alive to the fact, that I require a few more private bed-rooms; and I will have them as soon as I can procure timber and a builder.

"The Stable is not up to the mark. It will be improved when I get timber. I at no time ever charged for Stabling. I only charge for the Oats that are ordered, and these oats are always the best I can buy.

"The two last charges are very grave, but unfortunately for the credit of the defamer or defamers, cannot be supported by facts.

"Persons at all acquainted with the Mataura Ferry know very well that the boat is placed as near the house as is consistent with safety to man and beast, the distance being a little over one mile, therefore tho' I see people coming down the hill to the river I do not know they want my assistance or not, till they hoist my flag.

"Let it be remembered that the Ferry is not a legalised Ferry, therefore I in no case travel up to the boat till called upon by the hoisting of the Flag. To enable me to go up to the boat on the shortest notice I keep a horse at the house.

"The public sometimes expect more than is reasonable from one in my position; for instance, about three months ago, five men came with 2 horses and a loaded cart. At their request I showed them how to take the Ford, and charged them for my trouble one shilling, which they did not pay, as they could not perceive I had any right to do so, tho' I left the work I was at, went up to the ford and directed them.

"How it comes that incivility toward travellers is set against me, I am at a loss to understand. In taking a retrospective glance at my dealings with the public since I came here, I really cannot charge myself with such unbecoming conduct. The only approach to incivility on my part occurred about three weeks back. A person named Mr. Ervin or Irvan C.E. did damage to a cooking Stove of mine by throwing his horse rope over it. The horse shied, dragged the stove and broke part of it. I pointed it out to him, and said he would require to pay me 20/- on account of repairing at Invercargill. He declined to pay the damage, on which I believe I told him he was no gentleman. However strange it may appear, I still hold the opinion I then expressed, simply because he saw the thing done with his eyes.

"I assure your Honour that it is, and always has been my endeavour to deal fairly with the Public, but I also know well that the idea of giving universal satisfaction is a position unattainable. I have enemies open and concealed, they will try to do their worst, still they can only do what God permits them."

Who these enemies were, and what their beef was, is a mystery. The archives contain no evidence of immediate follow-up by the Superintendent. But the complaints kept coming.

Eighteen months later, a Mr Swanston complained of his treatment at MacGibbons. By this time, the accommodation house had been extended, with a separate wing containing eight bedrooms and a private parlour.

Arriving cold and hungry after a 45 mile ride over bad roads, Swanston and a companion booked into the new wing, and had a fire lit in the parlour. They ordered a meal. An hour later, MacGibbon came in ringing a bell, and announced that dinner was ready in the public dining room.

Swanston asked to have his meal brought to the private parlour. MacGibbon refused, assuring his guest that there were "…no rowdy characters in the other room."

"But we still insisted upon having tea where we were," Swanston continued. "Then McGibbon in a most rude manner turned upon his heel, and said, 'Well you must waste my time.' I followed him out, not being quite sure that I had heard him correctly, and asked him what he said, his reply was 'Yes you must wait until this tea is over' or words to that effect. At the time – nearly seven – Kennedy and I walked over to Mr Turnbulls at "Tuturau", it raining hard and a horrid road – with Mr Turnbull and McDonald of Isla who happened to be present at the time – rather than put up with McGibbon's impertinence."

This was not a solitary instance,

The book kept there for the purpose of entering any complaint against the Ferry or Accommodation House, had been turned to the purpose of caricaturing private individuals, and in fact filled with filthy and obscene representations.

John MacGibbon's return of ferry crossings, to the Southland Provincial Government.

Swanston claimed. Nobody stopped at MacGibbons if they could help it, he said.

His final shot read: "...his house is the most unpleasant and uncomfortable one to stop at on the road – as much on account of McGibbon's incivility as anything else."

Another complainant was Bishop Harper, who wrote to the Superintendent about "… wretched accommodation and meals."

The complaints were substantial, and must have been at least partly justified. John MacGibbon was evidently not a believer in the old adage that 'the customer is always right' – Given his background in retailing, his attitude toward customers was a little surprising.

Excuses

Charles Muir, in his excellent local history, *Mataura, City of the Falls*, offers some excuses: "To do him justice, John MacGibbon was a busy man and had other things to do besides his accommodation house. There was the sometimes dangerous job of ferryman to attend to. This involved boating travellers across the river. A further duty was to keep an eye on the fords, one above the Falls and the other in the vicinity of the Maori Reserve, travellers relying on his recommendation as to whether or not it was safe to cross. He also carried out the duties of Postmaster." [For £5 a year.]

MacGibbon also had 1,000 acres associated with the ferry lease, and presumably he was trying to develop it as a farm. A less onerous task, which came with the position of postmaster, was that of marriage celebrant. Couples would travel from as far away as lakes Te Anau and Manapouri to be married at MacGibbons.

Gold miners

The operation became very busy from 1861, when the Otago gold rushes started. Diggers were travelling to the Nokomai and Switzers fields, and further on, to Central Otago. Traffic on the 'road' soared, allowing the MacGibbons to "rake in the shekels at a great rate," pioneer Alfred Duncan recalled to Herries Beattie.

Around eight to ten people were taken across the river each day, and many would have stayed at the accommodation house.

The goldminers were a tough lot who undoubtedly put great pressure on the limited facilities at the accommodation house, and very likely strained their hosts' patience.

William Chubbin told Herries Beattie that some of the diggers ("rough customers") would eat meals and then refuse to pay. John MacGibbon then made it the rule that meals had to be paid for before they were served. Beattie wrote: "Mr MacGibbon liked good value for his money, but [Chubbin] had many dealings with him and always found him to be a 'square man'."

Duncan said Thomas MacGibbon kept the books, and remembered one day when, after travellers at the crowded table had eaten their three shilling meal, John Sr called out, "Tummas, come and report progress!"

Problems with rough-necks were detailed in a note from John MacGibbon to the Provincial Government: "In reference to the enclosed statement of Mataura Ferry Traffic, I beg to remark that rather more than one fourth must be put down as unpaid. Again I am very often bounced and in danger of being treated to a knock-down for asking the fare, by some of the roughs who pass. I have often thought that a Police Officer here would be a benefit."

The original wing of the Accommodation House, all that existed when the travellers' complaints began in 1861, had two upstairs private bedrooms for the family. Downstairs was a bar/parlour, and kitchen. A communal sleeping area for travellers was in a loft above the parlour. Other than the bedrooms, the kitchen was the only room where the MacGibbons could have had any private family life.

In October 1861, when the first complaint was laid, the MacGibbon family numbered nine, including baby Colin, then less than two months old. Complainant Aylmer was undoubtedly right in suggesting that John MacGibbon should not keep his family in the crowded accommodation house.

Given the pressures and tensions that must have existed, is it any wonder that the MacGibbons lost their cool from time to time?

Police reports

Complaints from the public did result in police investigations. An April 1864 report by Sergeant Butler discounted allegations about the accommodation. The house was not inferior to any other house on the road, he said.

"In the wing of the building set apart for the more respectable travellers, the bedrooms are small but perfectly clean, the bedding being of a superior description. On the ground floor is a sitting room which is invariably kept as clean as circumstances will permit.

"In the other wing of the building is a dining room with furniture of a rather coarse description. Overhead this dining room is a bedroom or garret for the accommodation of working men and

Cobb and Co's two-day coach service between Dunedin and Invercargill began in 1864. Passengers stayed overnight at the Mataura Accommodation House. (Illustration from E M Lovell-Smith's Old Coaching Days, *reproduced by permission of the Lovell-Smith family.)*

so forth. The stables are just now abundantly supplied with every description of forage."

Butler thought the food was only so-so, but presumably typical of such road houses. But he supported complaints against the character of the MacGibbons:

"With regard to the provisions supplied by Mr McGibbon, as far as Sergeant Butler can judge, they are rather of a coarse description. But it is not so much of the provisions supplied, as the manner in which it is put on the table, that persons complain of, and also the way in which Mr McGibbon and his son abuse anyone that ventures to make the slightest remonstrance.

"This principally is what causes Mr McGibbon to be so universally disliked."

Sergeant Butler noted than on an earlier occasion, he "…found that the book kept there for the purpose of entering any complaint against the Ferry or Accommodation House, had been turned to the purpose of caricaturing private individuals, and in fact filled with filthy and obscene representations."

This intriguing book is not in the National Archives and does not seem to have survived – more's the pity!

Moving on

During his tenure at Mataura Falls, John MacGibbon made two bids to buy the Accommodation House and its associated 1,000 acres of land on the Waimumu Flats. His first offer, in a letter dated 12 May 1864, included an opinion that the accommodation house was poorly located, being too far away from the ferry operation.

The files contain no official answer to the purchase proposal. Nor is there an answer to a second offer, in January 1866, this time mentioning a sum of £1,354. This offer included a promise to keep the ferry going for up to five years.

At this stage, John MacGibbon had to do something about his situation, because the original seven year lease had expired and the Provincial Government was seeking tenders for a new licence.

The second purchase offer was obviously not accepted, and as the person who received the application bore the name of Aylmer, this was perhaps not entirely surprising. And

perhaps a belief that he was hopelessly out of favour with officials in the Superintendent's office, was the reason why MacGibbon later put forward a derisory tender for the lease of the ferry and accommodation house. His bid of £80 a year was well below the £200 tendered by his eventual successor, Thomas Pollock, who took over in March 1866.

The MacGibbon family moved on from Mataura Falls to Kelvingrove Run in the Hokonui Hills, but not before considerable debate with the Provincial Government over the valuation of improvements at the Accommodation House. ■

John and Jane MacGibbon and their eldest children, during the period they were running the Mataura Accommodation House and ferry: Top left: Jane; top right: John Sr; bottom left: Jeannie; bottom right: Jessie; centre: Thomas. Other members of the family at this time included John Jr, Archie, Ebenezer and Colin.

Mataura River a serious travel barrier for early settlers

Early travel between Dunedin and the south of the South Island was done mainly by small coasting vessels. The few people who ventured into the interior of the province, then still part of Otago, were squatters and runholders. However after Invercargill was established in 1856, overland travel became increasingly common.

Travel was difficult, and dangerous when rivers were high. The Mataura crossing was particularly feared, and claimed several lives before a permanent bridge was built.

On 8 June 1857, 'Viator', writing to the editor of the Otago Witness, noted that the route between Dunedin and the new town of Invercargill was "formidable" and urged that a ferry over the Mataura be established.

".... great delays are and will be occasioned to travellers at both sides of the Mataura and Waihopai Rivers (mountain torrents!) and at innumerable creeks — that at neither of the above rivers is there as much as a house of accommodation should travellers be detained; they are compelled to rush through and take all risks, or they get half-starved and perished; that at nearly every creek of magnitude it is a case of 'wet through', with blankets, saddle, saddle bags, and self, with great risk to a horse; and that between Popotunoa and the Bluff the bogs are so numerous and bad as to render the journey one of much anxiety."

In September 1857, the Bishop of Christchurch was parted from his horse and nearly drowned while attempting to cross the Mataura.

Mataura favoured crossing point

Mataura, rather than the 'Long Ford', was chosen as the crossing point because in those days, the preferred track from Dunedin bypassed the future Gore location.

After Clinton, the track went further south than the present main road, through higher country past Otaraia to Mataura Falls. Here there was one ford above the falls, and a second two miles below them.

The older road still exists, and is known as the 'old coach road'. The route taken by the MacGibbons to Mataura, via the Clinton, Pukerau and Gore areas, was closer to the present main road.

The earliest ferry

In early 1857, there was a short-lived ferry near Mataura Falls, run by John Kelly, one of Invercargill's first residents. Kelly had responded to an advertisement by the Otago Provincial Council seeking someone to run a ferry at Tuturau and build an accommodation house. Kelly and his daughter Kitty walked up from Invercargill, but took such a dislike to the lonely situation that they quickly gave it up and returned home.

During 1857 and 1858, the Otago Provincial Government advertised several times for items connected with a Mataura crossing: a boat to be built for £22 for use as a ferry at Tuturau; a swing bridge to be erected half a mile below the Falls; an accommodation house to be built; a lease to run a ferry and accommodation house; a wooden

Looking northward to the Mataura Falls, after the original bridge had been washed away. The short-lived structure used the centre rock as a pier and was little more than a footbridge. This photograph, probably taken in the late '70s or early '80s, shows a flour mill with a water wheel in front of it, on the site later occupied by the freezing works. (Mataura Historical Society)

John MacGibbon Sr ca 1863, with Archie (left) and John Jr (right). John Jr began taking the mail to Gore on horseback a year earlier.

trussed girder bridge to be erected at the Falls (replacing the earlier bridge tender).

Two of the earliest travellers to stay with the MacGibbons were A A McDonald and A A Cameron, who left Dunedin, heading south, in January 1859. In a letter to Herries Beattie, Cameron said, "We found Mr MacGibbon's accommodation house opposite the Maori Bush consisted of a V-shaped sod whare, erected two or three weeks before. If memory serves me right, we slept in a tent." It is not recorded whether John MacGibbon charged them for the privilege.

Well-known watering hole

The Herries Beattie recollections are full of comments by early settlers about having stayed or eaten at 'the MacGibbons' while heading south, or, more often, heading north to the gold-fields. One of the latter was John Sinclair, travelling from Invercargill:

"The next night we made Mataura (Mr MacGibbon's)...next morning, when we were ready for the road, Mr MacGibbon would not ferry us across the Mataura River, as there was an Act forbidding all cattle to cross from Southland to Otago Province, owing to the rinderpest being prevalent among them.

"At last Mr MacGibbon gave us the loan of his boat, so we made the bullocks ford the river and crossed with the goods and sledge with the boat at our own responsibility."

Arguments

According to the abstract of rev-

enue and expenditure for the Otago Provincial Council for the quarter ended 30 June 1859, a total of £533 5s was spent to construct the Mataura Accommodation House and bridge. Before very long, funds for an extension to the accommodation house were being requested, amid some controversy.

In September 1859, £200 was requested, but it is not clear if it was spent. However in April 1860, a proposal to spend a further £350 on additions to the building caused some discussion. One newspaper* reported:

"The proposed additions caused a discussion. It was agreed that the additions ought not to be made without a higher rent were paid by the tenant. The ferry buildings had already cost between £500 and £600. It was urged by the Government that the lessee of the land had suffered injury from having been induced to take the ferry with the understanding that a toll should be levied on the bridge subsequently put up, and that he was entitled to compensation. The item was then referred to a select committee to inquire into the whole circumstances of the case."

Next day, the select committee reported back, as described by the newspaper:

"On the item £350 for additional erection to the Mataura Ferry House being proposed for reconsideration, Mr Gillies, as a member of committee appointed to inquire into the matter, stated that they had examined the lease, and found that the ferry was leased to Mr MacGibbon for a term of nine years from January 1859, at £40 a year, with the right to relinquish his lease at three months' notice. After discussion, the item was struck out."

Although the Otago Provincial Council knocked back John MacGibbon's request for additions to the accommodation house, they did authorise £70 to build a stable.

Dispute

It appears that John MacGibbon's lease entitled him to charge anyone crossing the river in the Mataura/Tuturau locality, whether by bridge, ferry or ford. A dispute over his right to do so was reported in the Otago Witness of 25 February 1860: "The Government having granted a lease authorising the tenant of the ferry house to levy such a toll, is in the awkward fix of

having entered into a bargain which it cannot fulfil."

The matter was referred to again in the Otago Provincial Council deliberations referred to above.

It is not clear if the right to charge a bridge toll was ever legalised, or whether John MacGibbon continued to 'try it on' and got away with it.

Within a year, the bridge was washed away, and the right to charge for river crossings was undisputed. The charge was sixpence per man and one shilling per horse. Women and dogs were free. (The cost for children and other creatures is unknown.) ∎

Reported in Herries Beattie's fourth set of Pioneer Recollections. The newspaper's name is not given, but was probably the Otago Witness.

Follow the line of flags

TO TRAVELLERS

THE BRIDGE AND ACCOMMODATION HOUSE on the Mataura River are now open. Travellers, by following the line of Flags will find the Bridge.

JOHN M'GIBBON,
Lessee
(Otago Witness, 26 April 1859)

In a separate contribution to *Pioneer Recollections*, W H S Roberts wrote:

"It was a narrow wooden bridge, just five feet wide, and strong enough for a man on horseback to ride over. The spray always kept it wet. On my trip south in May, 1860, I tried to ride over the little bridge, but my horse, a thoroughbred, was so frightened at the roar of the falling, clashing water (for the river was in flood) that I had to walk and lead him. The spray wet me considerably, and on the centre rock the water approached within a few feet of the bridge."

The early runholders

In 1859, and for several years afterwards, the country around us was all occupied by runholders, or 'squatters' as they are usually called — except for a strip of country extending from the Charlton Creek, the boundary of the south of the Croydon Run, and running along the base of the Hokonui Hills to Forest Hill.

By Thomas MacGibbon

This latter area was cut up by the Provincial Government into 2000 acre blocks and sold in lots of one or more at 10s per acre. Only a few of these blocks were sold, and it was not until some years later that the New Zealand and Australian Land Company purchased a large portion, being what is now called the Waimumu Block.

Prior to this, the country around Edendale, south of the Ota Creek, was a pastoral run owned by Mr Robert Stuart. His run was early proclaimed a hundred (called the Mataura Hundred) and thrown open for selection in small sections. Nearly all of it was purchased by the New Zealand and Australian Land Company and added to what they had already acquired. Their extensive holding previously comprised Waihopai Downs, Morton Mains, Seaward Downs and the Mataura Estate, so the magnitude of their possessions will easily be realised.

[Note: In the early 1870s, the Mac-Gibbon family ran cattle on a large area bounded by the Waimumu and Charlton streams and the Mataura River, leased from the New Zealand and Australian Land Company.]

The Eastern runholders

The principal runholders in the district during our first few years' residence in Mataura were Messrs Edwin Rich (Tuturau), Shanks Bros. (Marairua), Dr Menzies (Dunalister), F L Mieville (Glenham), Dr Richardson (Oaklands), George Peel (Waimahaka), Daniel Sinclair (Toi Tois) and Thomas Reynolds (Otara).

On the Upper Wyndham was Mr John Anderson, and higher up, Mr Oliver, of Cairn Station.

Mr Thomas Trumble was at Otaraia, Mr Dalrymple at Islay and Messrs Pagan Jun. and Wilson at Venlaw.

Otakaramu Station was occupied by Mr Alex Chalmers when we came down, but soon after that, Captain Boyd bought it.

The whole of the Landslip Hill country and the Merino Downs were held by Captain MacKenzie.

Next in order came Knapdale, Mr McNab's well-known property on the east bank of the Mataura River. Above the Pyramids was the run held by the Victoria Company, and this included Wendon and Wendonside.

The eccentric Tibbetts brothers at Switzers Run

The country above Muddy Creek was held by Messrs Tibbetts Bros., and a good story is told of these gentlemen in connection with the rough nature of the run.

The country was thickly clothed with scrub, and such great difficulty was experienced in mustering the cattle, that the owners resolved to obtain from Great Britain a mortar and ammunition, so they might 'shell' their missing cattle from the dense cover!

The elder of the two brothers was a retired army captain, and this may account for their proposal to adopt such a novel method of mustering.

A good deal of eccentricity was indulged in by the owners of the Switzers Run which was originally taken up by Mr Switzers, a bootmaker of Dunedin. Their dwelling place was built astride a small creek, and the bunks were ranged along each side of the stream. This was a convenient arrangement. If the occupants were disturbed by thirst, they only had to dip a pannikin into the running water. This saved them the necessity of getting up, and besides, they could be sure that the water was fresh and in no way tainted by the air of a sleeping compartment!

The two gentlemen under discussion figured prominently in a later shooting case at what is now Mr Gillander's homestead. Here the gallant captain made a raid and the unfortunate cook, a Dane, was shot. A few hours later, the unhappy perpetrator met his fate at the hands of his own brother.

[Herries Beattie commented further on this incident, saying that when Captain Tibbetts saw service in India, he had been afflicted by a touch of the sun and would go crazy now and again. Another contributor to the recollections said that on the occasion described by Thomas, Captain Tibbetts went to the neighbouring station looking for strayed horses, got into an argument with the German cook and killed him with a revolver. Shortly afterward he tried to shoot his brother. The brother returned the fire and killed him in self-defence. In remorse, the surviving brother tried to kill himself, but was prevented from doing so by a policeman who was present. The case caused a local sensation.]

Dislodging cattle from the scrub

I had personal experience of the difficulty of dislodging cattle from the scrub that grew in this district [in the vicinity of the Mataura River upstream of Gore]. Mr Archie McNab had bought the chance of eight bullocks that had been lost for a long time and were supposed to be somewhere among the scrub along the Mataura.

He asked me to give him a hand, and so, mounted on good stock horses, and armed with efficient stock whips, we hunted for about a week. At length we succeeded in capturing our cattle, which, from wandering so long in the scrub, were fairly wild.

But we got them out without shelling, although there was a great deal of yelling and stockwhip reports. We got them headed for Mataura and travelled all night, as we dared not leave them until we had them in a place of security.

The 'spec' turned out to be a good one, as the cattle were in the pink of condition, or, as we used to say, "as fat as mud". As soon as possible, they were consigned to the tender mercies of the butcher, and some of them turned the scale at 1,400 lbs.

The northern runholders

During our hunt for the cattle, we stayed a night with the McKellar brothers at their homestead at Longridge. They held the whole of the country from the fork of the Waimea Stream and the Mataura River to the watershed just over Lumsden. Their run was bounded on the east by the Mataura River, and on the west by the Waimea Stream. It was an immense territory and was well-grassed, particularly on the river flats.

The McKellars afterwards disposed of the lower half to the late Mr G. M. Bell, who later sold out to the Agricultural Company.

Above Longridge, a run was taken up by the McNeil brothers, who named their place Ardlussa, by which name it is still known.

Five Rivers station was taken up late in 1859 or early in 1860 by Mr Arthur Hogue, who later sold it to Mr Fitzwilliam Wentworth, a cousin of the Hill brothers of Croydon station.

Glenquoich Station, at what is now known as Athol, was taken up by Messrs Joseph and Henry Rogers.

Western runholders

Centre Hill run was occupied by a Mr Dalzell, and the Moonlight Ranges was occupied by Mr J H Taylor, of Riverton.

While we were at the Otapiri Run,

I remember receiving a call from Mr Shea-Lawlor, the gentleman who drove the first lot of cattle onto the Castle Rock station. He informed us that he had just driven a dozen or two bullocks onto that run so that it might be declared 'stocked' and enable the owner to obtain the pastoral license.

Farther west, several runs were taken up by the Messrs Hankinson, and others right up to Te Anau, but I did not know much about that part of the country, as it was almost a 'terra incognita'. Occasionally, however, I met the gentlemen who had taken up that far-back country, as they used to stay with us when on their way to Invercargill, and as I stated in my previous notes, our house was their post office for some years. They had a young employee named Ellaby who carried the mails from Mataura to Te Anau once a month or so.

Hokonui country

Messrs Chubbins and Gunn owned the Reaby Run in conjunction for some time, afterwards dividing it between them, with Mr Gunn taking the Otamita or Wantwood portion.

On the north-west, this run was bounded by the one my father took up — the Otapiri Run. This is now known as Glenure, a name which was given to it by Captain McCallum, who acquired it some time after we left. The

captain was a genuine 'Hielandman' who despised the 'sassenach trews' and wore the kilt even when riding, whether on the station or on his occasional visits to Invercargill or Dunedin.

The next run extended to the Oreti River and was occupied by Mr Cuthbert Cowan, who I am pleased to state is still alive and resides at Benmore, near Dipton.

A Mr McFarlane owned the Benmore Run on the Hokonuis, south of Otapiri or Glenure Run, and this ran down as far as Dipton now stands. This run later belonged to Mr Hugh McLean, who held it for a good many years.

Across the Oreti River were Messrs Wright and Lee and Mr McClymont's station, afterwards owned by Messrs Morrison brothers.

At Glendhu, on the east side of the Hokonuis, Mr Angus Cameron lived for some years. For a good while he had been a stockman for Mr McFarlane at Benmore, but later became a cattle owner on his own account. When we afterwards lived at Kelvingrove, he was for some years a neighbour of ours, and he and his good wife – both, alas! now dead – were hospitable entertainers and the best of neighbours. ■

[Here Thomas MacGibbon ended his 1909 reminiscences.]

Farming in their own right

John MacGibbon Sr's ultimate intention in moving to Southland was probably to be a farmer. His first attempt, at Otapiri, ended in failure. Later in 1858, he returned to lease the Mataura Ferry and Accommodation House, and with this lease came 1,000 acres of land on the Waimumu flood plain.

The land associated with the ferry lease was part of the attraction. According to a 1933 article in the Mataura Ensign by his grandson, Hugh, John had earlier been "...most impressed with the luxuriance of the feed for stock in the south."

National Archives records are silent about the farming operation, which would initially have been based on a herd of cattle the family brought

with them from Dunedin. Probably they never developed the farmland to any great extent, given the demands of the ferry and accommodation house business.

The MacGibbon family twice offered to buy the 1,000 acres from the Southland Provincial Council, but were unsuccessful. After the ferry lease expired in 1866, they went into full-time farming, buying a 1,000 acre block of land in rolling country bordering on the east Hokonui Hills, under a prominent peak called Ship Cone. It was potentially excellent farmland, although the farm size was too small to generate real wealth for a large family.

They named the farm Kelvingrove, after a favourite park in Glasgow.

The family may have had another

freehold block of land in the area, and they grazed cattle elsewhere in the Hokonui Hills on land within the Mataura Hundred.

At Kelvingrove they built a substantial homestead, which must have seemed luxurious after the cramped conditions they had endured at the accommodation house. It was a two story building of ten rooms, from timber cut locally and hand sawn in a sawpit. The building, which had two dormer windows in the upper floor, was designed by the family tutor, Eric McKay. The house no longer exists, and probably burned down – the fate of many pioneer homesteads.

The family which moved to Kelvin Grove was already reduced by one member. Jessie had married lo-

A wee dram with the neighbours, during the Kelvingrove years: from left, (unknown), John MacGibbon Jr, John Chubbin, W Chubbin, Angus Cameron. Written next to the photograph were the words, "There like our dads o'auld lang syne/Let social glee write us a'/Aye blythe tae meet our mous tae weet/And aye as sweard tae gang awa." Roughly translated, this means, "In that place, as it was for our forebears/Let the merriment of companionship put us in that good frame of mind/Which makes us always eager to gather for a drink/And always reluctant to go away." A shorter version might read, "Any excuse for a drink." John Jr later became a noted abstainer and president of the Gore Temperance Society.

cal runholder James Shanks Jr, and was living with him at Mairarua Run, at Tuturau. Another daughter, Jeannie, would soon move out to marry James Miller of Islay Run, also near Tuturau.

Kelvingrove was next door to the Reaby Run, where the Chubbin family lived. The families were friendly, and in 1867, Thomas MacGibbon would join John Chubbin on a trip to Scotland and Argentina. The voyage would produce a wife for Thomas and give him a life-time taste for travel.

The MacGibbon family was only at Kelvingrove for a few years, and they seem to have run into serious financial difficulties there, probably mainly because they were living beyond the run's means. Thomas's over-

seas trip would have been costly, as it was probably first class all the way. The year after he came back with Isabella, they built themselves a separate house. At the same time, farming returns were starting to decline.

In late 1869, Thomas agreed to buy the property from his father. Shortly afterward, John Sr became concerned that the run was running into serious financial difficulties, and presumably to guard against possible loss of £1,000 he had advanced to Thomas, he wrote a note asking for the money to be returned. Probably he did this as a pre-emptive strike to make sure he was first in any queue of creditors. Interestingly, Thomas had, only nine days earlier, gifted the run's cattle to his wife – presumably also to guard against their being claimed by creditors.

This is speculation, based on two documents which have survived. What *is* known, is that in 1870, Kelvingrove Run was sold to John Elliot, and the family purchased another property, Woodlaw Station, near Nightcaps. It was an unqualified disaster. While they were actually on the road droving their cattle herd the 80 or so kilometres to Woodlaw, they learned there had been a problem with the title deeds. The deal fell through and they were left with their cattle on the 'long acre'.

For the next two years the MacGibbons were almost wandering herdsmen. They were able to lease grazing for their cattle at Yellow Bluff, near Otautau, and later moved to another lease at Tuturau.

In 1872, shortly after moving to Tuturau, John MacGibbon bought a small stone store in Mataura from James Pollock, the man who had originally taken over from him as ferry operator. The family was now back in the retail business, but they still had their animals.

They continued as cattle farmers on a very large area of land leased from the Australia and New Zealand Land Company. The lease covered the entire area bounded by the Charlton Creek, Mataura River and the Waimumu Stream. The only boundary fence needed was a 1.6 kilometre stretch near Mataura. Everywhere else, impassable swamps formed natural barriers for stock.

Forty years later, this land was divided up into small farms, whose

Taking a break from haymaking, with tea and scones, at 'Koromiko', Eastern Bush, near Otautau, in about 1925. Koromiko was farmed by Dave and Bill MacGibbon, who had been financed onto the property after World War I by their father, John MacGibbon Jr. Left to right: Dave and Bell with infant Hugh; Bill, Davey Cupples, Gus Moreton and Tom Glynn.

owners would comment on the large number of bones they found when ploughing. They were the bones of cattle lost by the MacGibbons. Some died in swamps; others were poisoned by the leaves of the tutu plant.

The price of cattle continued to drop in the early 1870s, and it was eventually decided to sell out the whole mob to the Woodlands Meat Preserving Company. The lease was relinquished, and from that time on, retailing became the family's main business.

For the next 60 years or so they continued to own farmland, although for the most part they did not personally farm it. However in 1918, after the end of World War I, John MacGibbon Jr financed his returned soldier sons, Dave and Bill, onto a 450 hectare sheep farm at Eastern Bush, near Otautau.

The farm, named Koromiko, was later split into two halves. Bill named his half Marshburn. His son Angus continued after him, until 1990. Dave retained the Koromiko name for his half, and passed the farm on to Hugh. Hugh later passed it on to his son David, who sold up in 1997, ending three generations of MacGibbons farming at Eastern Bush.

Another returned soldier to begin farming after World War I was Stanley MacGibbon, son of Ebenezer. He established a 300 hectare sheep farm on MacGibbon Road, in the district of McNab, just north of Gore. Two farms operated by his descendants remain in MacGibbon Road, with each containing part of the original block, plus land bought from neighbours. One property, still called Burnley, is being farmed by Stanley's daughter-in-law Margaret, and her sons, Andrew and Stanley. The other property is run by Bob and Hazel MacGibbon and their son and daughter-in-law, John and Susan. ∎

A woman pioneer's life: Fanny Mieville

The first squatter in the Mataura Valley, Frederic Mieville, settled on Glenham Run in early 1854. A few months later he went back to Dunedin, married Fanny Richardson and brought her south on horseback to a life of extreme hardship and loneliness. The recollections Fanny wrote for Herries Beattie give us an idea of what Jane MacGibbon faced four years later, living in a sod hut as the first white housewife in another part of the valley.

Frederick Mieville had already built a house – of sorts. It was a low cottage built of punga logs, lined with clay. It was divided into two rooms and had a clay floor. One of the men hired to help on the run had cut the leather tops off his old boots to make hinges for the door, which was a rough affair made of split ribbonwood palings.

The clay floor and walls were still damp, and when the fire was lit, the room filled with steam. The beds consisted of a pile of ferns on the floor. A table and chairs were improvised from logs. The walls had to be patched and repatched with mud for many months. However eventually the mud dried without cracks, and they even wallpapered a room which earned the "admiration of all travellers."

The rustic setting provided some compensation: "The house stands on the slope of a hill on three sides surrounded by bush, and open in front to an extensive view over grassy ranges studded here and there with bush, and intersected with brooks and rivers…nothing can exceed the beauty of the spot," wrote Fanny.

Plagued by blowflies

While noting that New Zealand had very few drawbacks as a place to settle, she was less than enthusiastic about the bluebottle blowfly, describing its ravages as "beyond belief".

"All blankets and clothes must be securely packed away after use. The usual plan is to tie them up in sacks. Even during the night the flies are busy, and by dawn the blankets in which you may be sleeping are alive with maggots," she wrote.

"A coat or dress hung up for a few hours will be unwearable until thoroughly cleansed. Gun barrels when greased are attractive and it is not unusual to find them full of maggots.

"Nothing is safe, and I know of no remedy except civilisation, which always brings the common house fly, before which the bluebottle, for some reason, retires."

When she ran out of soap, she made her own. She understood that soap contained fat and alkali, but knew none of the details of soapmaking. As usual, she and Frederic improvised. "The camp oven was filled with wood ashes and then as much water added as it would hold. This was slowly boiled for some time, allowed to cool, and the lye poured off and boiled with mutton fat. The result was 'soft soap', most cleansing, but too powerful for ordinary purposes, as it simply skinned one's hands.

"Washing is perhaps the greatest hardship of all, and only those who have tried it know the misery of bleeding hands, which no amount of practice prevents," wrote Fanny.

"After a time we discovered cleansing properties in the stream running just below our house, and it became our custom to put the coarser things into this creek for the night, weighted with stones, and after being rinsed and dried in the sun, they would put to shame the best efforts of a laundress."

At one stage when the supply schooner Endeavour from Dunedin was six months late, they ran out of all food except for mutton from their sheep flock, home-grown potatoes and a small amount of tea, "…which had been wetted with sea water and dried in a bag up the chimney – indescribably nasty, ugh!"

To give variety, she sometimes boiled sow-thistle (puha), which tasted a little like spinach.

Clothes also ran low when the vessel ran late. Fanny had to improvise a skirt from two of the blue serge shirts "…worn by men of all sorts in the bush." A third shirt worn on top completed the outfit, which "…was not by any means a bad costume."

When toes of boots wore out, she sewed leather tips onto the socks which poked out the holes. ∎

Back to the Old Country to collect a wife (taking a side trip to Argentina)

In 1867, Thomas joined neighbours John and Margaret Chubbin and their three children in a trip to the United Kingdom. Part of the visit was spent in Glasgow. Then, temporarily leaving Margaret and the children with relatives in England, the two men sailed across the Atlantic to Buenos Aires. For several weeks they explored the country, checking out its potential for farming. On horseback, they travelled south for about 500 kilometres across the Argentinian pampas. It was the rainy season, and they met flood conditions in several areas.

Chubbin recalled later: "I thought the country had a grand future before it, but considered the Government was bad, like all the other Spanish governments, and this was mainly the reason I did not settle there."

Deciding there was no place like home, Chubbin picked up his family and returned to New Zealand. Meanwhile Thomas went back to Glasgow and secured a bride. She was Isabella Nairn, second daughter of a well-off family whose money came from a joinery factory.

Thomas probably met Isabella on the first leg of his overseas trip, and was now back to continue the wooing process. The match probably had its genesis in Southland, and it is likely that Thomas arrived in Glasgow with a letter of introduction to the Nairn family.

It seems that James Steuart Shanks Sr, Jessie Mac-Gibbon's father-in-law, may have set things in motion. Shanks, also a native of Glasgow, and a friend of Archibald Nairn, probably suggested the match. No doubt he described young Thomas and his prospects in glowing terms.

Thomas would have needed to mind his Ps and Qs in the genteel society inhabited by both the Nairn family, and his uncle, David McGibbon, with whom he stayed. Attitudes and language appropriate to bullock teams and travelling diggers would simply not have done. While Thomas had been leading a rough pioneer existence, Isabella and her sisters had been attending a pri-

vate school for nice young ladies. While Thomas had roughed it on working hacks in Southland, Isabella had dressed up in a riding habit to ride elegantly in the surrounds of her family's country house north of Glasgow at Campsie Junction.

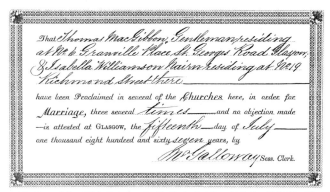

That *Thomas MacGibbon, Gentleman, residing at №. 6 Granville Place St. Georges Road Glasgow, & Isabella Williamson Nairn residing at № 19 Richmond Street there* have been Proclaimed in several of the Churches here, in order for Marriage, three several *times* and no objection made —is attested at GLASGOW, the *fifteenth* day of *July* one thousand eight hundred and sixty *seven* years, by *Wᵐ Galloway* Sess. Clerk.

N.B.—Upon production of this Certificate, the parties will obtain *from the Registrar of the Parish or District within which the Marriage is intended to be solemnised*, a Copy of Schedule C., formerly given out by the Session Clerk.

Thomas's occupation was given in his marriage banns certificate as 'gentleman', but he must have been intensively coached in order to impress the Nairn family.

A family understanding is that the Nairns had considered that their daughter was 'marrying down' to the rude colonial. Nevertheless, they must have been convinced of Thomas's prospects to release their 19 year old daughter to his marriage bed and a new life on the other side of the world.

Thomas had certainly convinced his father-in-law of the merits of New Zealand's farmland. Writing to Isabella shortly after she left Scotland, Archibald Nairn described a visit to a friend's country estate near Birmingham, and added, "You tell Mr MacGibbon that was the only land I have seen that came up to his description of the New Zealand pasture fields."

Archibald's letter was mainly about domestic Glasgow matters, but opened with an appreciation of his new son-in-law: "And promising that ere you see this that you will have arrived in the land of your adoption after a comfortable passage and found your partner in life what I expected him to be, a very good husband." ∎

Thomas and Isabella after their wedding in Glasgow, 1867.

Thomas Smith (bootmaker and saddler)

Saleyards

Post and Telegraph Office (Thomas Palmer, Postmaster)

James Pollock's general store, under construction. (Bought by John MacGibbon and Sons in 1872)

Mrs Hamilton's private school

William Gardiner (blacksmith)

James Pollock's accommodation house and stables

Suspension bridge opened in June 1868

Mataura in 1871. At this date the only other building in Mataura was the original accommodation house which had been operated by the MacGibbon family. It was on the photographer's side of the river. (Mataura Historical Society)

The Rise and Fall of John MacGibbon and Sons

The MacGibbon family developed a substantial merchant operation, becoming big fish in the small pool that was Eastern Southland. They were the biggest show in town for perhaps 40 years, and their fortunes followed a classic pattern: generation one started it all, generation two expanded and consolidated, and generation three lost the lot.

By the time the last shop shut its doors in 1962, the firm had been an Eastern Southland business fixture for 90 years.

Beginnings

It all started on the 22nd of June, 1872, when John MacGibbon and Sons opened for business in a stone store in Mataura, bought from James Pollock. It was the second business exchange between the two men: six years earlier John MacGibbon Sr had passed on the reins of the Mataura Accommodation House to Pollock.

By 1872, Mataura had grown only a little from the days when the locality was known as 'The Falls', and the MacGibbons were the only residents.

There were now a few houses and a stock saleyard, built by people who serviced the rural sector and catered for the needs of travellers on the road between Dunedin and Invercargill.

The earliest surviving photograph of Mataura, apart from the 1864 view of the original accommodation house, is the bleak image above. By now the settlement was known as Mataura Falls.

The photograph, taken in 1871, shows the new swing bridge which had replaced the river ferry in June 1868. Thomas MacGibbon crossed this bridge shortly afterwards, while bringing his new bride Isabella home to Kelvingrove Run.

(Diverting a little, it is interesting to note Thomas MacGibbon's comments on that journey, which was undertaken in stormy conditions. Although by 1868, in Thomas's words, the country had become "somewhat semi-civilised", the journey must have been hair-raising for a refined young lady fresh from Glasgow. Thomas wrote, "Creeks were still unbridged and roads unmade, and in a rainy sea-

son such as we frequently experienced years ago, travelling, especially with ladies in the company, was a serious matter." Mataura had its new bridge, but at that time the narrow structure had no guardrails. Crossing the surging river in a horse and gig would have been something for Isabella to write home about.)

The 1871 photograph shows James Pollock's stone store, still under construction. Left of the store is the settlement's first post office, which opened at the end of 1868. To the right is the biggest business in town, Pollock's accommodation house and stables. This is a different building from the first accommodation house, which was situated on the photographer's side of the river.

Other buildings were occupied by a bootmaker and saddler, blacksmith and the first schoolmistress, Mrs Hamilton. Mrs Hamilton had a private school with five pupils.

The only building on the other side of the river was the old 'MacGibbons' accommodation house, by then owned by Hugh Cameron.

The new store was well placed to receive business. It was opposite an established watering hole for travellers who had come off the hilly Old Coach Road to the Mataura Valley, and needed a break. (In those days, the main road to Invercargill bypassed Gore and cut across rolling country from Clinton to Mataura.)

By the time the MacGibbons took over, John Sr was getting on in years. He was 63, and his wife Jane was 55. Eldest son Thomas was already a mature man of 33, with a wife and three children. His two sisters had both left home to be runholders' wives. His next two brothers, John Jr and Ebenezer were young single men of 23 and 18 years respectively. Rounding out the family were Archie (15) and Colin (10).

The MacGibbons were in the right place, at the right time and with the right experience. The area was opening up to smaller scale farming, after the proclamation of the Mataura and Tuturau Hundreds. The family business developed quickly. It was a classic country general store, where you could buy anything from a bolt of cloth to a pair of shoes, a box of nails and a bag of potatoes. But it was always strong in rural servicing – a forerunner to the stock and station firms of today.

John MacGibbon and Sons traded in rural produce. In the early years this was mostly wool, grain and cattle products. They would have usually sold on farmers' behalf for a commission fee, although sometimes they would have bought produce outright and on-sold it.

After grain markets collapsed in 1890, farming in the district became more diversified, with dairying and fat

lamb farming becoming important.

The company had an agency for the National Fire and Marine Insurance Company of New Zealand, and this would have been a profitable sideline. The MacGibbon stores in Mataura, and later in Gore, all had prominent signs advertising National Insurance, which was based in Dunedin and did excellent business in Southland. MacGibbon and Sons would have received ten per cent of the net value of all insurance policy premiums, including annual renewals.

By the end of the century, the original stone store was replaced by a more substantial building, and the company had expanded to the other side of the river. As well as the main store,

they had a grain store, timber yards and bakery. They even kept horses behind the main store in a paddock named The Saltmarket, after the street where they had lived in Glasgow.

Expansion to Gore

With the Mataura business well established, the MacGibbon family began to look further afield. Thirteen kilometres to the north of them, Gore was on the move. In earlier years, prospects for growth had been limited because almost all the hinterland was in the possession of three large estates: Knapdale to the north, Croydon to the west, and Otakaramu to the east.

The property which had the greatest influence on the prosperity of early Gore was the large Knapdale Run, owned by Alexander McNab. This run, which included the fertile Waikaka Valley region, began to be broken up for closer settlement in 1874. Sales of Waikaka Valley land were held by ballot in 1874, 1875 and 1876, and 75 blocks were taken up by a new breed of small farmer known as 'cockies', who were able to buy on deferred payment terms.

In 1875, the railway from Invercargill to Dunedin reached Gore and the town's future was assured.

Gore's first building, as with its neighbour Mataura, had been an accommodation house. It opened at the end of 1862, to service travellers who

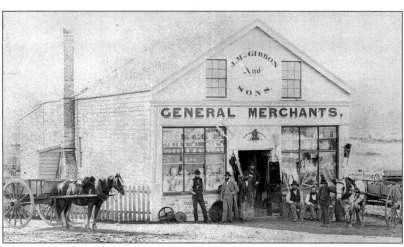

The East Gore shop, probably shortly after it opened in 1878. Standing with a proprietorial air, second from the left is John MacGibbon Jr. Above the door is a sign advertising the company's agency for the National Fire and Marine Insurance Company Ltd.

crossed the nearby 'Long Ford' on the Mataura River. Just as in Mataura, much of the hotel's early business was related to gold. Diggers from the north would ford the river in order to travel west to goldfields at Waikaia, Nokomai and Wakatipu.

It was another land sale in the area which attracted the attention of MacGibbon and Sons. This was in October 1877, when a large number of blocks came available in what became known as the Big Land Sale. It included farm blocks at Otama to the north, but also a number of town subdivisions across the river from Gore where Alexander McNab had his first homestead. This locality was to become known as East Gore, then Gordon, and finally part of Gore Borough.

The second shop on the Mataura site. The family lived upstairs.

The Tammany Ring conspiracy

According to Herries Beattie's notes from an interview with John MacGibbon Jr, some Gore businessmen, including Thomas Green and a Mr McCaughan, felt that development across the river would "mar" the existing township. (This probably meant they wanted to stifle potential competition.) They determined to buy the land up and keep it vacant, in a conspiracy which became known as the 'Tammany Ring'.

John MacGibbon Sr's son in law, James Shanks (who had by then switched from runholding to auctioneering), heard of the plan. Acting on Shanks' intelligence, a group of Mataura residents including John MacGibbon Jr, Dr McAffer, W G Forbes, Hughie McLean and a Mr Brown, determined to break the 'Ring'. They succeeded in this by outbidding the Gore contingent at the beginning of the auction. The first two sections went for £200 and £120, and then the price dropped to £50.

The MacGibbons could see that East Gore was strategically placed for servicing farmlands opening up north and north-east of Gore. John Jr and Ebenezer moved up from Mataura to found a general store. The first building in East Gore, it opened for business on 14 January 1878, initially selling groceries and drapery.

Within a year, John Jr and Ebenezer were joined by other general stores, a saddler, wheelwright, blacksmith, tinsmith, baker, butcher, tailor, land agent, watchmaker, public hall, two hotels and a branch of Bank of Australasia. East Gore was beginning to rival original Gore, across the river. The fears of the Tamany Ring conspirators were being confirmed.

MacGibbon and Sons was the principal business in East Gore, and within six months, with his financial and social position secure, John Jr would marry Mary Ward, from Oteramika Bush near Invercargill. Two years later his brother Ebenezer secured the hand of Mary Latham, whose family had moved into the area, buying 400 acres of land at nearby Waikaka Siding in 1878. The Latham farm, named Burnley, is now split among Ebenezer and Mary's descendants. ∎

The East Gore shop, ca 1900. Left to right: (unknown), (unknown), (unknown), Mrs P Banks, (unknown), Mrs Jamieson, Alec Simpson, Miss Bennetts, Mrs Simpson, Ebenezer MacGibbon, Dave MacGibbon, Walter McKinnon, Percy Banks, Andrew Watt. The exterior looked much the same when the shop closed in 1951.

MacGibbon and Sons established a third branch in 1883, buying this store on the corner of Gore's Main and Mersey streets from Kelly and Mullaly. The Gore Oddfellows are marching past to their 1885 picnic.

MacGibbon's Corner

East Gore almost caught up with Gore across the river, but by the 1880s it became clear the older settlement would prevail. The west side of the Mataura was better placed to take advantage of the railway. Indeed, Gore was poised to become the 'Chicago of the South' opined one of the town's two newspapers, the Southern Standard. (The prediction was just a tad over-optimistic. Today, over a century later, Gore's population is nudging 8,500, compared with greater Chicago's six million. In 1880, Gore's population was 600, compared with Chicago's 503,000.)

John MacGibbon Jr saw the advantage of having a foot in both camps, and in 1883 he was able to buy an existing general store operated by Kelly and Mullaly on a strategic site at the corner of Main and Mersey streets. A natural meeting place in the town, it soon became known as MacGibbon's Corner. Some older residents still call it by that name. John Jr moved to the new store, while Ebenezer stayed at

the Gordon branch. (In 1882, East Gore had been renamed Gordon, a name it retained until 1890 when it became East Gore again.)

By the end of the decade, MacGibbon and Sons was a household name with a reputation for integrity and fair trading. The company might also have been described by contemporaries as solid, unpretentious and more careful than most with its money (see the panel story opposite). An uncharacteristically elaborate advertisement in Stone's Otago and Southland Directory of 1888 described them as "General merchants, grain dealers, commission agents etc.; agents for sawmills, brickfields and the National Fire and Marine Insurance Company, etc. etc. etc.".

Business structure

In attempting to unravel the commercial history of MacGibbon and Sons, the author was not helped by the fact that, only a few years ago, officials of the Companies Office in Inver-

cargill destroyed almost all records. All that remain are index cards which list initial company structures, registered instruments and liquidators' statements. None of the actual documents have survived.

Initially John MacGibbon and Sons was a private company, and the 1888 will of John MacGibbon Sr shows that he, Thomas, and John Jr had equal shares in the land and buildings of all three stores. Ebenezer owned no bricks and mortar, but shared equally with his brothers in other assets (stock, monies, goodwill etc) of the Gore and Gordon stores. After his death, John Sr's share of land and buildings was divided equally between Thomas and John Jr, except at Mataura, where Thomas received the full share.

In 1894 there was an unsuccessful attempt to turn the family company into 'MacGibbon's Co-operative Stores Association Ltd', with a capital of £40,000. The prospectus, reproduced on page 186, notes that the firm is "...well-known throughout all

Southland, having been in existence for a quarter of a century, and no puffing up is required to convince anyone it has been a very successful and lucrative business for many years."

In 1903 the two Gore businesses were incorporated as a public limited liability company called MacGibbon and Company Ltd. It had a nominal capital of £20,000. Two years later the Mataura business was registered as a private company called John MacGibbon and Sons Ltd, with nominal capital of £5,000.

The Gore and Mataura businesses then operated as separate entities, although there were cross shareholdings.

Business miscellany

Three shops were built on MacGibbon's Corner. The original wooden structure burned to the ground in 1900, and newspaper accounts said the building had been insured for £2,500 and the stock for £4,200. The company rebuilt bigger and better, with a three story brick structure which cost £4,000. Four years later, the new building was lost in a second blaze that destroyed 27 shops in the vicinity. An identical replacement still stands today.

Compared with their competitors, the MacGibbon businesses were very restrained in their newspaper advertising. There were no display ads, and in the 1880s, they specialised in small advertorials (page 184). Then, around 1920, they began almost daily display advertising for the Main Street shop. The ads were full page width, and as much as half a page deep. They seemed to have a continual sale: "Great Slaughter Sale" was a typical headline. By the 1930s the advertising was more restrained, but there were frequent large ads for fashions, drapery and furnishings. At this time, their main advertising competitors were Thompson and Beattie, and H&J Smith. The latter's ads, as with their shop, had rather more class than the MacGibbons. From the 1940s, MacGibbon and Co did little advertising unless suppliers such as the Modaire corset company paid most of the cost.

Staff tended to be very loyal, and there were many long-serving employees – notably Bob Fisher, who worked for the firm for 50 years and became manager of the Gore branch. Surviving staff remember a strong family

Tight, or just Scotch?

The MacGibbon businesses were canny, if not tight, but there was a generous side.

In pioneer times, people had to be careful with their money and possessions – it was a matter of survival. In Otago and Southland, this pioneer imperative was amplified by traditional Scotch cannyness.

Even in a Scottish community, the MacGibbon stores were renowned for being particularly tight, if not mean in their approach. And for being canny.

The best stories are about Ebenezer MacGibbon, who managed the East Gore business. The stories are undoubtedly exaggerated, and may be more apocryphal than real, but where there was smoke there was probably fire.

Eb would measure a pound of nails to the very last nail. And if that last nail took the weight over the pound mark, he would substitute a smaller nail. He would cut a potato in half, if the whole potato was likely to take the measure over the specified amount.

The full flowering of Eb's cannyness came on the day he found a rat drowned in a barrel of treacle. He kept bulk treacle to fill billies, which customers would bring to the store. Did Eb throw the barrel out? Not likely! He picked the rat up by the tail and squeezed the last drop of treacle back into the barrel. Then he threw the *rat* away.

While the MacGibbon stores were tight, their proprietors were certainly generous when times were tough in the community. During the Great Depression of the 1930s, they extended a great deal of credit to local farmers, to their own serious detriment.

Earlier than that, the family's quiet generosity was acknowledged. In 1915, a Mataura Ensign obituary for Ebenezer MacGibbon noted: "It could be said of him that his left hand did not know what his right hand did. Many a poor creature in this town never knew where help came from in their hour of distress. The orphans never knew who supplied their physical wants. Neighbours never knew how many times the heart of their brother went out in sympathy and practical form towards them."

When John Jr died in 1925, the Mataura Ensign wrote that he had also "...practised hiding from his left hand the welldoing of his right." The obituary continued: "Many in and around Gore and Mataura can vouch for his goodness and self-sacrifice, once his sympathies had been enlisted. These traits he never advertised, but a large number today will mourn the passing of one who in their direst need proved a friend indeed."

One day, at the store in East Gore, Ebenezer MacGibbon saw a man steal a pound of butter and hide it under his bowler hat. Eb had the last laugh, after he invited the man to a warm corner for a long chat...

Frenzied activity at 'MacGibbon's Corner' at the intersection of Main Street and Mersey streets in Gore, ca 1885. This was once Gore's most popular downtown meeting place.

atmosphere. Social events were held, including an annual ball. In 1935 the last company ball was held at the Theatre Royal in Gore. Allan Garrick, then a parcel boy at the Main Street store, remembers dragging sacks of oats around the floor to polish it up for dancing. The Troubadours Dance Band played, and admission was 4/- for Gentlemen and 2/6 for Ladies.

Staff would not have been given more than the barest statutory annual holidays, judging from a 1901 Ensign report of a Gore Retailers' Association discussion on the subject. John MacGibbon Jr informed the meeting that holidays were a "serious matter". "He said he was not sure whether it would be better to have a week's holiday and be done with it," wrote the Ensign's reporter. "Such a course would be better than having so many holidays between Christmas Eve and Easter time. In the old days they often had bread a week old, and salt junk for three

months. It would do some people good if they had that now." It should be remembered that John Jr came from a family which had worshipped with the Free Church of Scotland, in the days when that church did not observe Christmas or Easter holidays.

Stan Catto, who joined the East Gore shop in 1939 as a parcel boy, drove an old van on country delivery to Knapdale, East Chatton, Waikaka Valley and Wendon. He took 120 loaves of bread on the Waikaka run, and called on 38 farms. Similar large delivery runs were a feature of both other MacGibbon shops.

Stan's first job in the morning was to go to the railway station, and he was only allowed to make one trip, no matter how many parcels were waiting. When opening parcels he wasn't allowed to cut the string, which had to be saved along with the paper.

"We had everything there, from a needle to an ashtray," Stan remembers. "During the war, when people had to get their kerosene lamps out again, we still had the lampshades to fit them!"

The East Gore store was a favourite target for thieves – many of whom were borstal escapees. The most celebrated heist was in July 1901, when dynamite was used to blow open two safes. Cheques worth £600 were scattered about and £67 in cash was taken.

On a Sunday in 1921, the Mataura store was plundered by three 10 and 11 year old boys who forced open a window with an iron bar. They helped themselves to a large quantity of goods valued at £40. The Mataura Ensign reported that almost all departments had been visited, and the assortment of purloined articles would have made fine stock for a hawker's cart. The boys put their plunder in packing cases and

planted them in a right of way beside the building. The job was proceeding nicely until a shop employee came to feed the horses, and found the loot. Said the Ensign, "The goods were secured, and as far as is known, there is nothing missing. The boys will appear before the court in due course." Did anyone catch up with the fathers?

The MacGibbons were principled to the nth degree. One example, celebrated in the local press, came in 1889 when the Borough Council asphalted footpaths in the Gore business district. They sought to recover half the cost from shopkeepers in the street, and presented John MacGibbon Jr with a bill for £2/11/4. While other businessmen paid up, John Jr refused to do

Ebenezer MacGibbon, about the time he co-founded the East Gore branch.

so, on the grounds that the Council had not advertised its intention to levy a separate rate, made up a ratepayers' roll or called for objections.

The Council took him to court, but was unable to prove its case. While John Jr appeared to have won the battle – at least temporarily – he lost the war. The Ensign weighed in strongly against him, commenting sarcastically that, "We have no manner of doubt whatever that [the ratepayers] will be duly thankful; and the next time Mr MacGibbon comes forward as a candidate for municipal honours, they will show their gratitude by placing him at the head of the poll, or even a little higher than that, for has he not been shown a true patriot, by throwing the cost of his asphalting upon the shoulders of his neighbours, and in this, standing the crucial test of patriotism –

John Jr and Mary MacGibbon in 1880, with their first-born child, named Mataura.

a readiness to sell the last drop of his brothers' blood in defence of his own fondly cherished principles."

Within a week John Jr paid up, claiming that the Council had '…received a lesson to avoid such high-jinks in future." The incident did not affect his standing at the polls, for the next year he was elected first mayor of the amalgamated town districts of Gore and Gordon.

Decline and fall

It is not clear when the MacGibbon businesses began to decline, but they probably reached their zenith around 1914. They remained locally substantial until the late 1920s, but were seriously damaged by the Great Depression of the 1930s.

A problem common to all three MacGibbon businesses from the 1930s, was that few of the family shareholders still lived in the Mataura Valley. They were in Dunedin and Invercargill, and two key directors lived in Christchurch. The directors took a very short-term attitude toward the businesses and seemed more interested in extracting capital than reinvesting for much-needed modernisation.

Thomas and John Jr, the second-generation powers behind the MacGibbon businesses, stepped aside as hands-on managers early in the century. When the public company was formed in 1903, John Jr retired from active management in Gore, and concentrated on other business interests, Liberal politics, the Southland Education Board and the temperance movement. His oldest son, Hugh, was press-ganged by the family into becoming managing director, but his heart was never in it.

"My father was no businessman," said his daughter, Marylyn Akroyd. "He enjoyed the figures side of it, but he hated the shop. But he wasn't bitter about it – he just accepted that it was his job in life."

Effective control of the Gore shop fell into the hands of Bob Fisher, whose management was far from progressive, and contributed to the decline.

Thomas moved to Dunedin in 1909, and from then on, his involvement in the business was only part-time. His son Archie became the Mataura manager, but absentee company directors gave him little autonomy and no development capital.

The Mataura store in the 1920s. It had men's and women's departments, a shoe store, drapery and grocery. The shop even employed a full-time milliner who made ladies' hats.

Debts unpaid

Archie's son Bruce recalls that farmers would run up debts at the store and never repay them. "People were more mobile by then, and although they owed us plenty of money, they'd avoid our shop by driving to Gore or even Invercargill to buy their stores."

Customers at the Gore stores also had problems paying their bills, and Marylyn Akroyd said MacGibbon and Co was as much a philanthropic organisation as a business.

To subsidise the philanthropy, the family's once extensive town and country land holdings in Southland were sold off, block by block.

At the end of 1938, the directors resolved to wind up the Mataura business, and appointed a liquidator. The store continued to trade until 1941, when the doors closed. Final wind-up was in 1944. The liquidator would have found it impossible to sell the business as a going concern, because the Second World War was on. Archie MacGibbon left Mataura in 1940 and moved to Dunedin.

The East Gore branch was the next to close, in 1951. Considering it had never changed from being a dingy, old-style store, it did well to last as long as it did. After a substantial road bridge was built across the Mataura River in 1896, East Gore had declined rapidly as a commercial centre and had become a residential suburb.

In 1951, MacGibbon and Co was the last store in once-bustling East Gore. It had survived because of its large country clientele, and it had be-

come a community centre. But it could no longer compete with the more modern shops across the river, or with the motor car.

The last branch of the business, in Main Street, Gore, limped on until 1962 when company directors accepted an offer by Southland Savings Bank to purchase the building, and sold part of the business to the outgoing manager, Theo Smythe. ■

H stands for Hunter of Hunter and Brett,
As bumptious a blockhead as ever was
   met.
He went to the goods shed, some wagons
   to load
And said he would see all those
   MacGibbons be blowed.

They should not get any wagons that
   day,
But he very soon found 'twas the Devil
   to pay
For the MacGibbons came down like a
   wolf on the fold
To load trucks in spite of this Hunter so
   bold.

There was but one truck, so to it they
   freized,
Hunter the other end instantly seized.
So one pulled, they both pulled, they
   cursed, and they swore,
They pulled and they pulled, and they
   swore a few more.

Though the struggle soon ended the fun
   was quite glorious
But numbers prevailed and the Macs
   were victorious.
And the end of it was, at least so it is said,
That Hunter was hunted right out of the
   shed.

—ANONYMOUS (GORE MUSEUM ARCHIVES)

SHEEP SALE, GORE

SATURDAY, 17th MARCH.
At 1 P.M.

GREEN and SOUNESS have received instructions from A. MacArthur, to sell by Public Auction at their yards, on SATURDAY, 17th, MARCH,
At 1 P.M.
1000 MERINO EWES, in lots to suit purchasers.
(Mataura Ensign, 9/3/1883)

That enterprising firm of John MacGibbon and Sons is extending its borders, and the latest addition to its establishments is of no mean order. They are now fairly established in Gore, in the store lately occupied by Wilcocks and Co., where they are disposing of a Bankrupt Stock marvellously cheap. Men's suits, 20s ; tweed trousers, 6s. They now keep a full stock of Ladies' hats and dress trimmings and fancy goods of all descriptions at Gore, Gordon and Mataura.—Advt.
(Mataura Ensign, 11/5/1883)

The truck question is exciting a great deal of attenton in this district, and the railway department now seems quite unable to cope with the grain traffic, albeit they do the best with the material at their command. Grain now arrives at Gore in large quantities in covered and uncovered railway trucks from the Waimea Plains, and long lines of settlers' teams daily reach the towns on both sides of the river. On the eastern bank we understand that Messrs MacGibbon and Sons alone have 2000 bags of grain, some of it in the open air ; and although promised trucks some time ago these have not yet come to hand.
(Mataura Ensign, 18/5/1883)

Terms Cash! The following goods are on hand and must be sold out to make room for new stock:—Galvanised roofing iron ; Nos. 8, 9 and 10 fencing wire ; raw and boiled oils and paint. Tea in half chests and boxes, also 1lb packets ; men's long leggings, 15s, men's coats and trousers, 20s upwards ; boys' and youths' suits, 16s upwards ; ladies' trimmed hats and jackets. Unreasonably cheap, and all of sterling value. These goods at sale price, cash only.—J. MacGibbon & Sons, Gore and Gordon.
(Mataura Ensign, 28/5/1883)

GIFT AUCTION.

THE MATAURA PRESBYTERIAN Church Committee intends to hold a Gift Auction in aid of the Building Fund, in Humphries Hall on Friday, 14th September.
Contributions will be received at the stores of Messrs MacGibbon and Sons and Park and Winning.

ROBT. WINNING,
Sec.
(Mataura Ensign, 31/8/1883)

THE FREAKS OF A MADMAN
◆

During the early part of the week, there was a great deal of excitement in the Chatton district over the freaks of an unfortunate fellow named Hugh McPeak, who lately made his way to the Knapdale Station. He has for some time been employed in the neighborhood of Gore and was generally regarded as weak-minded. His health was far from good, and lately by a shilling subscription, funds were raised to send him to Invercargill for better treatment than he could obtain hereabout. It is said that he was in the hospital there and from there went to the asylum at Dunedin, but upon this point we have no definite information. At any rate in due time he turned up at Knapdale and showed decided symptoms of lunacy, divesting himself of his clothing and otherwise differing in habits from his fellows. On Monday night he was secured by residents in the locality and placed in a hut for safety, but from this he made his escape, only to be re-captured on Tuesday and lodged in one of the queerest dungeons we ever heard of—none other than the wool-press at the sheds on Mr McNab's station! Within four massive walls of considerable height, with scarcely room to occupy other than a standing position, and without a stitch of clothing, he passed the night, his behaviour being at times very noisy. On Wednesday Constable Pratt was called for and on his arrival on the scene that lunatic was released from his impromptu lock-up, dressed, and brought to Gore, thence to be taken to Invercargill for medical examination.
(Mataura Ensign, 31/8/1883)

Not a comet! Now to be seen at MacGibbon & Sons, the largest stock of summer goods ever exhibited at Gore or Gordon. The ladies of the district are specially invited to inspect our goods before purchasing anywhere else. Over 100 pieces of print to choose from. Saddle cloths and Roslyn and Kaiapoi tweed suits in stock in large quantity. Invalids can purchase hop bitters, or any other drugs or medicines of us. Flower and vegetable seeds in an astonishing variety. Turnip seed, Aberdeen yellow and purple top greystone, purple top Swedes, &c., &c. Oamaru barbed wire on hand.
(Mataura Ensign, 28/9/1883)

STOCK SALE, GORDON

SATURDAY, 17TH NOVEMBER,
At 1 o'clock.

Shanks & Barr (in conjunction with J. MacGibbon and Sons) will sell by Public Auction at their Yards, Gordon, on the above date, at 1 p.m.—
1 Shorthorn Yearling Bull
7 Quiet Dairy Cattle
Mixed lot of Ewes and Lambs
Horses, &c.
(Mataura Ensign, 13/11/1883)

WANTED KNOWN.—The Gospel of the Grace of God will be Preached in the Temperance Hall, Gore, on Sunday, 18th September, at 7 p.m. All are earnestly invited. Seats free. No collection.

MANDEVILLE QUADRILLE Wind-up Dance, Friday, 23rd September. Good music. Refreshments galore, Tickets, 1s 6d ; Ladies cordially invited. Dancing at 8 p.m.—H. Horrell, Hon. Sec.

WANTED.—Youth to cook for three men. Apply by letter, " Bachelor," Ensign Office.

CARPETS and Floorcloths. We hold the largest stock in Gore. Well worth your while inspecting this department.— J. MacGibbon and Sons.

OUR Dressmaking Department a great success. So it should be, when we make well-finished dresses for 12s 6d.— J. MacGibbon and Sons.

LIVING to Dye, and Dyeing to live.—J. Davies, American Dye Works, Dee and Leet Streets, Invercargill.
(Mataura Ensign, 17/9/1898)

MacGibbon and Sons have an ingenious contrivance called The Torpedo Washer— one of the few machines which have been invented in order to assist the housewife in the multifarious duties of her calling. There is often a reproach to the inventive genius of mankind that, while the machines are yearly coming to his aid to lessen the weight of his labours, no mechanical genius has yet brought forth a contrivance to assist the housewife in the darning of her socks, the baking of her scones, her combing of her children's hair or such other duties and, perhaps, there never will. But the Torpedo Washer makes play of the laborious duties of the wash-tub. As its name signifies, it is torpedo shaped, of galvanised iron about 15 inches in diameter and 3 feet 6 inches in length. The washer stands on an iron frame of suitable height from the ground to enable the operator to work it with comfort. The feature of the machine is that the clothes are washed with compressed air. The half-revolving motion of the washer causes the hot water inside to compress the air which is forced through the clothes cleansing them without any rubbing whatever. The washer is a Huddersfield patent and is used extensively at Home. Several have been used locally and ladies who have had experience of them testify their great effectiveness, in one instance three blankets receiving three thorough washings in 18 minutes. An attachment is affixed to the stand whereby an ordinary wringer can be used and the machine is seen as one which will gain in popularity with the housewife. A trial of the washer will be held at Messrs J. MacGibbon and Sons East Gore premises tomorrow afternoon.
(Southern Standard, 17/12/1901)

MISCELLANEOUS NOTICES

WE stock Thorley's Food for Cattle and Horses. Thomson's Anti-Mammitis and Cow Cleanse.—MACGIBBON AND CO., LTD., Gore and East Gore.

WE stock Pratt's Animal Medicines, consisting of Colic Cure, Cough Cure, Condition Powder, Worm Powder, Cow Tonic, etc., etc.—MACGIBBON AND CO., LTD., Gore and East Gore.

CHIMNEYS Swept at shortest notice by Tom Green. Orders may be left at 'Ensign,' Morton's Ironmongery ('phone 174), or private address, Wellesley Street.

WE stock Gilruth's Calf and Chicken Foods, also Crushed Linseed and Co-coanut.—MACGIBBON AND CO., LTD., Gore and East Gore.

H BALDWIN is prepared with a competent assistant to commence his Castrating Tour at once. Orders left with him or W. Rainbaum, East Gore, will be promptly attended to.

WE are Agents for the Lister Separators, British made, which stand unrivalled amongst Separators for ease in driving, efficiency in its work and lasting qualities.—MACGIBBON AND CO., LTD., Gore and East Gore.

EVERY HOUSEWIFE should have a look over the Bargains at Christie's New Venture Cash Sale; they're great.

WE can show you a large assortment of Bird Cages, at prices ranging from 5s to 9s 6d, also Cage Fronts, Bird and Parrot Seeds.—MACGIBBON AND CO., LTD., Gore and East Gore.

AN invitation is extended to every woman to visit Christie's China Palace, where many choice articles are being opened up.

OUR Furniture Department is now replete with everything that is required from the cottage to the mansion.—MACGIBBON AND CO., LTD.
(Mataura Ensign, 15/11/1911)

You'll like our new makes in Ladies' Collars and Ties. They comprise goods of the most artistic styles of the season, in a variety of desirable materials for Summer Wear. All are elaborate in design and trimming. We have also received direct from our London buyers an interesting collection of the ruling fashions in Belts. There are many novelty lines in Silk and Leather. Undoubtedly the most elegant and correct assortment we have ever had the pleasure of submitting to you.—MACGIBBON AND CO., LTD., The Main Street's Busy Corner.

A SPECIAL display of Ladies' Neckwear at W. LEWIS AND CO'S., The Leading Drapers, Gore.
(Mataura Ensign, 18/11/1911)

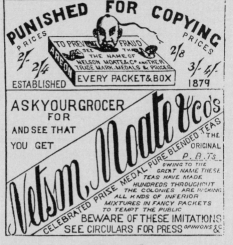
THE spaces on either side of our heading, on page 1, are occupied by recommendations to "Drink Spring Blossom Tea." We understand that Messrs John MacGibbon and Sons have made arrangements for regular supplies of this celebrated tea, which is packed in air-tight nett-weight tins only. Spring Blossom has proved a favorite tea wherever introduced, and no doubt its reputation, which has preceded it, will bespeak that fair trial which it is claimed ensures constant use.
(Mataura Ensign, 5/8/1897)

PROSPECTUS

— OF —

MACGIBBONS' CO-OPERATIVE

STORES ASSOCIATION,

LIMITED.

Registered under "The Company's Act, 1882," and Amendments.

CAPITAL – – – – £40,000,

In 8000 Shares of £5 Each,

Payable as follows:—10s per Share on application, 10s per Share on allotment, balance in sums of not more than 10s per Share and at intervals of not less than three months, but no more than the above 20s per Share will be called up in 1894 nor more than 20s in 1895.

It is not intended to call up more than the above £2 per Share unless agreed at any General Meeting of Shareholders.

PROVISIONAL DIRECTORS:

Thos. MacGibbon, Mataura ; James Paterson, Waikaka ; James Clement, Otaria ; John Kirk, Chatton ; Alex. Dickie, Tuturau ; J. Sloane Miller, Knapdale; Walter McKinna, Otama ; P. F. Monaghan, Croydon ; Thomas Falconer, Chatton ; G. F. Johnston, Waikaka ; Robt. Gardyne, Waikaka ; Ebez. MacGibbon, Gore ; Lawrence Gillespie, Knapdale ; John McGill, Wendon Valley ; Mark Miles, Wendon Valley ; James Harvey, Knapdale ; W. A. McCaw, Gore; Robert Dodds, Otama ; Joseph Townshend, Mataura ; James Donald, Chatton ; Andrew Balneaves, Mataura ; George R. Elder, Chatton ; J. S. Shanks, Jun., Mataura ; Thomas Graham, Otama ; James Marshall, Chatton ; David Wadell, Wendon Valley ; Francis Milne, Chatton; Alex. Smith, Mataura ; Donald McGregor, Wendon ; Donald Robertson, Otama; Finlay Mackay, Tuturau ; Samuel McIntosh, Waikaka ; James Aitken, Waikaka ; David Lawson, Chatton; Andrew Martin, Sen., Gore; Alex. Stewart, Otama; Matthew Dickie, Tuturau;

Alex. Peter, Knapdale ; Adam Johnston, Waikaka ; D. J. Smith, Wendon Valley ; John Jones, Chatton ; Hugh Young, Otaria ; John Dillon, Otama ; Wm. Black, Greenvale ; Thos. McGowan, Mataura ; David Dun, Charlton; John Latham, Gore ; Wm. Paget, Mataura; Alex Barclay, Wendon ; Thos. Logan, Otama; Alex McKinnon, Gore ; Alex Keir, Charlton ; James Cleland, Otama ; John MacGibbon, Gore ; J. H. Perkins, Mataura; Andrew Mason, Pukerau ; W. D. Stewart, Otama; John McCartney, Chatton ; Charles Stroever, Chatton; N. S. Kingdon, Croydon ; Michael Dillon, Gore ; Gavin Whitefield, Merino Downs ; George Wood, Wendon ; David Cumming, Kaiwera ; Geo. Aitken, Wendon Valley ; James Hay, Waikaka ; Wm. B. Reid, Tuturau ; John Gerkin, Knapdale ; E. D. Bust, Gore ; John Irvine, Knapdale ; W. M. Anderson, Wendon Valley ; Andrew Aitken, Gore; Thomas Barclay, Wendon ; John Shanks, Gore; Alex. Simpson, Gore ; John Waddell, Tuturau.

BANKERS :

Bank of New Zealand and Bank of Australasia.

SOLICITOR :

Arch. Fletcher.

The Registered Office of the Association will be in Gore.

This Co-operative Association is being formed to take over the old-established business of John MacGibbon and Sons, General Storekeepers at Gore and Mataura.

This firm is well-known throughout all Southland, having been in existence for a quarter of a century, and no puffing up is required to convince anyone it has been a very successful and lucrative business for many years.

It started business 20 years ago at Mataura, and as the district began to fill with settlers it became necessary in order to keep pace with the requirements of their many clients to open branches at Gore and Gordon. These places have now been opened for years.

The trend of the age is manifestly in favour of Co-operation, and being for some time so strongly impressed with this view by many of their old clients, the Messrs MacGibbon have decided to meet them now as the present time is most favourable for starting a Co-operative Association.

The Association being worked on co-operative principles only, all profits accruing from the business of the producers and consumers will consequently be participated in by the Shareholders.

The Shareholders, having in view that their own interests depend on their hearty support, will be eager to put all their business through the Association.

With this object in view an agreement has been entered into with John MacGibbon and Sons (which may be seen at the office of the Solicitor) for the leasing of their business premises at Gore, Gordon and Mataura, together with the taking over of the Stock in Trade, Plant and Goodwill of the Business.

The value of the Stock in Trade and Plant is to be ascertained and fixed by duly qualified persons nominated by the Directors and the Vendors.

The fact that the firm have decided merely to lease the premises—the rent of which has been fixed at a very moderate figure—and also to take a large interest in the Association, is sufficient guarantee to intending shareholders of the thoroughly *bona fide* character of the undertaking.

The Association has also secured the Vendors' services as Managing Directors, which gives an assurance that they will leave no stone unturned to make the concern as successful in the future as in the past.

There are two or three special features in this agreement very seldom granted, and that is that they are not asking the Association to put all or any money into bricks and mortar by having to buy the stores ; also, they are not asking the Association to take over the firm's book debts and liabilities ; neither do they— still further to show intending shareholders the *bona fides* of the business—propose taking any dividend or bonus on the shares they receive for the goodwill unless the Association show a clean profit of 8 per cent in the balance-sheets for two years.

Another point in the Association is they will on no account deal in wines or spirits.

The Association will take over the business on the 1st January, 1894, or such other date as the Directors may fix.

(Mataura Ensign, 9/1/1894)

Too much of a good deal?

In 1894, an attempt was made to form a farmers' co-operative in the Mataura Valley, based on the existing MacGibbon businesses. It would have bought and sold produce for shareholders, and provided home and farm supplies.

The venture does not appear to have got off the ground. No follow-up advertisements or news items were carried by local newspapers. Many farmers were struggling financially at the time, but perhaps potential subscribers also felt it smacked too much of a good deal for the MacGibbons.

It certainly looks as though the family would have done rather nicely out of the proposal. They would have received a lump sum of £16,000 for their stock-in-trade, plant and goodwill, and they could have used this capital to try their hands in new business and farming enterprises.

At the same time, the MacGibbon family would have retained ownership of the land and buildings, and received rent from them. The family would also have had considerable control over the Association's business, as the prospectus terms guaranteed them positions as managing directors.

An interesting feature of the proposal was that the Association would "...on no account deal in wines or spirits." The stricture was probably the work of temperance campaigner John MacGibbon Jr, and probably turned off some potential subscribers.

By the 1890s, there was a growing movement toward rural cooperative associations. While the MacGibbon venture did not get off the ground, a business along similar lines was formed in Gore by farmers from the Riversdale district, in 1901. This was the Southland Farmers Cooperative Association, which is still in business today. ∎

Establishment, institution, but not a business

"It was an establishment and an institution, but it definitely wasn't a business," says Margaret Carter of the Main Street branch of MacGibbon and Company.

By 1953, when Margaret – then Margaret McColl – joined the office staff at MacGibbons, the business was already well in decline. East Gore branch had closed two years earlier, while the original store at Mataura had folded in 1944.

"It was such an old shop! Bare floors, oiled once a month," recalls Margaret. "You'd walk in the front doors, and it was so dark. They had 40 watt bulbs, and those ceilings went up forever.

"The first thing you'd pass as you came in the door were a couple of forms holding boxes full of socks and other things, and you have to get past those boxes, which were all lined up.

"There was a high glass counter in the front made of heavy glass, with wooden beading along the edges and sliding doors at the back. We would display things like embroidery, gloves and handbags, and there were drawers full of things like cards with ribbon around them.

"That counter was really old – you could still see the mark on it where floodwaters reached in 1913. Nothing was ever replaced unless it was absolutely necessary."

Margaret laughs – "Yes, they were careful. It was the Scottish ancestry – *careful!* I mean, we never had such a thing as a coal bucket. It was always a kerosene tin they'd put handles on. And we just about had to go on our hands and knees to plead for a new pen."

At stocktaking time, every roll of ribbon had to be unrolled and measured.

The shop was always cold during Southland's bitter winters. There was only one open fire on each floor, and to make matters worse, the basement flooded in winter. The permeating damp was tough on staff and customers, but the dark waters did keep the rat population down. Former staff still see bodies bobbing in the bilge.

Long after other shops had switched to mannequins for showing off fashions, MacGibbons stuck with their old wooden hanger-stands – even for window displays.

There had been times when the MacGibbon shops were reasonably up with the play. In 1884 they were even technology leaders, installing Gore's first telephone service to communicate between the two shops. The glass

(Mataura Ensign, 29/6/1940)

counter at the shop entrance probably garnered a mention in the Mataura Ensign when it was new. And at some date in the misty past, the office had been equipped with adding and book-keeping machines.

By the time Margaret worked in the office, the machines were museum pieces. "How the MacGibbons ever bought a book-keeping machine, I don't know, but anyway it was hopeless. And the adding machine must have been at least 40 years old. It was a great big thing – you'd stand there and pull the handle on it."

Even in the later years there was only one cash register in the building, in the grocery department. Whenever customers bought items, change would have to come from the office on the second floor.

Railway

Ask any former staff and customers about the shop, and one of the first things they'll recall is the old 'railway' change system. No doubt the wonder of its day, it had become an intriguing anachronism which adults gaped at and their children adored. It had two rails, between which was an endless, constantly moving cord. Small 'carriages' with hinged lids, about the size of a packet of cigarettes, but deeper, would clip onto the rails. The carriages had terminals on their lids which could be set to identify which branch rail they should divert to.

Margaret Carter was on the receiving end, sitting at a high desk in the office: "The little carriages would come shooting into us. You'd take them off, stamp the docket, put it back in the carriage with the change, clip the carriage on the rail, and away she'd go."

The railway was always breaking down. "Bob Fisher [the store manager] would come racing into the office, and of course he always said it *was* my fault. Mind you, half the time it was – I can't even put staples into a staple gun."

It wasn't the only system of its kind in Southland, but it was kept going long after other stores had moved to pneumatic tubes for intra-store communications, or direct to cash registers.

The railway system had other uses. Margaret had a good friend downstairs in groceries who would send her small blocks of cheese for morning tea. Once the cheese was followed by a carriage containing a dead mouse.

Another memorable occasion was the great carriage pile-up when the first electric blanket came to Gore. Margaret tells the story:

"The office had a big glass front on it, and people would come through from the mantles department or up from groceries to pay their accounts – we were agents for National Insurance, and people could renew their Southland County Council drivers licence with us.

"Theo Smythe had taken over from Bob Fisher as manager, and he had a very good friend, Mr Van Ralta from Dunedin. Mr Van Ralta said, 'Theo, why not be the first in Gore to have an electric blanket.' Theo wasn't too sure. Mr Van Ralta replied, 'Theo, why not just try one – they're marvelous.'

"We set up a double bed outside the office, and put the electric blanket

Margaret Carter, who worked at Mac-Gibbon & Co between 1953 and 1962.

and a couple of Fairydown quilts on it. One Friday evening when Hughie MacGibbon was away for tea, my girlfriend in the mantles department and I decided to hop in the bed and try it out. Some time later, Peter Burke from the fish shop came up to renew his licence and found us both asleep in the bed and a racket going on. All the money carriages from different departments had come in and they were all stacked up on the railway in the office. Everyone downstairs was banging, wondering why they weren't getting any change. Oh dear...to this day I blush about it!"

Departments

The shop had two floors of merchandise, while the third floor was largely unused but had housed a thriving dressmaking business in the early 1900s.

Haberdashery was the first department you met on the ground floor. It had the celebrated glass counter, with high chairs in front of it. There were big polished brass bars with embroidered cotton, ribbons and lace draped over them. Moving on from haberdashery, you passed through materials (MacGibbons had once been *the* place to buy materials), footwear and hardware. Through a fire door was men's clothing, and then another fire door led to groceries.

The grocery department was in grand old country store style: barrels, lots of little mahogany drawers for small items, goods such as milk billies dangling from the ceiling. A great round of cheese on a wooden block with a cutting wire. Lines of biscuit tins: "The last job at night for the junior was to go around and knock down the lids on the tins, to keep the biscuits fresh," recalls Margaret.

"I also remember girls sitting out the back of the grocery breaking open boxes of dates. Kerosene was kept out the back, and you'd have to put on a coat to go out and get it – frightful frosts."

MacGibbon's Corner in Gore, 1905. This building stands today. (Gore Museum)

On the second floor was the office, home furnishings, and women's fashions, which included departments with old fashioned names like mantles, corsetry and millinery. Hugh MacGibbon's office contained heirlooms from his father's home – about eight glass cases of stuffed birds, a big family bible on a stand, a beautiful old music box and a spinning wheel.

Fear and fascination

The third floor held both fear and fascination for young women on the staff.

"The ladies' toilet was up there, and there was only a dim light on the bottom of the stairs," says Margaret Carter. I hated going up because the building used to creak. It was the spookiest place, and we preferred to use the men's toilet behind the grocery department."

But then Margaret found fascination in a disused storeroom on the third floor – an Edwardian time capsule of dressmakers' materials and knick-knacks. Nothing had ever been thrown out from the days when there were resident dressmakers.

"We found 40 cartons of the little bones they'd used to make high-necked blouses and frocks. There were rolls and rolls of fringing – deep purple and variegated colours. Buttons stuffed with cotton wool and covered over with very fine black crochet. Dressmakers' dummies. And the feathers! Ostrich plumes in different colours. But most of the stuff up there was rotten."

Another person who knew the third floor well was Jeremy Salmond, now an architect in Auckland. Jeremy worked

The last MacGibbon family to operate the Mataura branch of John MacGibbon and Sons, off on a holiday weekend to Fiordland, ca 1934. Left to right, standing: Archie ('Cocky'), Mary, Alan, (Ray Williams), (Joe Russell), Bunty (the author's father). In front: Hugh, with Digger, the family fox terrier. Family members not in the picture are Catherine, Struan and Bruce.

after school, writing sale tickets for the shop below. It was lonely up in the Gods amongst the junk, and, "…my best friend, as a callow youth, was an old dressmaker's bust wearing a corset".

Compensations

The shop had become a working retail museum, and people would say to staff, "You mean to say you work at *MacGibbons?*"

But there were compensations. In spite of everything, former staff agree there was a great staff atmosphere. They were particularly loyal to general manager Hugh MacGibbon, who was universally adored. They may also have developed unity in opposition to the store's resident ogre, manager Bob Fisher.

During the thirties, jobs were hard to come by, and staff were loath to leave. But even in the 1950s, when jobs were two a penny, the staff stayed on.

"It was just like a big family," says Margaret Carter. "People got on well together and it never entered your head to leave. You were happy in your work, and that was it."

For young persons, the shop's location was a bonus. Being on a busy corner, it was a great place for keeping an eye on what was going on around town.

Bob Fisher

"Frosty Bob" Fisher is generally blamed for the firm's downfall by family and former staff. He ruled the roost, and Hugh MacGibbon was general manager in name only. Fisher was a shareholder and director, as well as

being store manager. There is a suggestion that he may have bought a controlling interest in the company when shares came available during the First World War, while Hugh was overseas.

If the MacGibbons were 'careful' with their money, Fisher was an out-and-out tightfist who wouldn't even let his wife keep a budgie. Leafy Horrell, who worked in the office for a decade until 1952, remembers heads of department, all well past retirement age, frightened to death of the man. Margaret Carter said the staff would shake with fear whenever Bob was around. "He didn't miss a trick!"

In later years Hugh MacGibbon was quite unable to counter Fisher's influence. By then an elderly man, Hugh was frequently absent from the business. He went to two funerals a week and attended meetings for Gore Hospital Board, Gore High School Board and the Southland Education Board.

Fisher refused to modernise the shop. The building and fittings sorely needed attention, but equally problematical was his attitude to the stock he sold and the customers he sold it to. He was quite blind to the colours which were becoming fashionable in the 1950s,

Hugh MacGibbon, last family member in the MacGibbon merchant enterprises. He retired at the age of 81 when the Gore shop closed in 1962.

Another batch of bread about to be delivered from John MacGibbon and Sons' Mataura bakery. Ewen Balneaves is the delivery boy, and D Wilson is the resident baker.

and staff would sometimes sneak in colours for customers behind his back.

Margaret Carter: "Commercial travellers would come in and they'd open up their boxes and show all the new colours – there was even purple and lime green. Bob would say, 'I'll have six of black, two of navy and one of white' – that was it. One day the traveller swapped the order round and sent him all these bright colours. Bob just about had a fit on the spot."

Customers had no greater love for Bob Fisher than did his staff, and would try to avoid being served by him. He was inclined to go off to the Gentleman's Club for a drop of whisky, at 10am. Coming back into the store, he would reach into a jar for cloves to disguise his breath. One day someone swapped the cloves for cayenne, with spectacular results.

Even in earlier years, Bob Fisher was less than generous to his staff. In the 1930s, Allan Garrick was given a traffic ticket for not having a light on his bicycle while delivering for the firm. Allan took the ticket to Hugh MacGibbon, who gave it to Mr Fisher. Fisher gave it back to Allan, saying "This is yours". Allan had to go to court, where he was fined five shilling by none other than Bob Fisher, Justice of the Peace!

Bob Fisher retired from the business at the end of the 1950s, and was succeeded by Theo Smythe, who had the temerity to suggest modernising.

"What a fight he had on his hands!" says Margaret Carter. "There were far too many shareholders who didn't want him to spend. They were too used to getting a handout themselves, and no-one wanted to re-invest in the business.

"We all knew it had to close one day. Then one Friday, Hugh whispered in my ear that they would close the following Friday. The rest of the staff were told on Monday."

An offer by Theo Smythe to buy part of the business was accepted, and the MacGibbon family interest was over.

"It was a funny week of discovery, opening boxes – what a sale Theo had," recalls Margaret. "Odd boots, whalebone, old men's longjohns, all kinds of things. Two for the price of one – I couldn't close my arms for days!" ∎

Dealing in land

The MacGibbon pioneers bought and sold a great deal of land in Southland, according to records in enormous bound volumes at the Justice Department's Lands and Deeds Division in Invercargill.

In the period before 1872, we know they bought the 1,000 acre Kelvingrove Run in the Hokonui foothills, as well at least one other block of freehold farmland.

Between 1872 and 1926, the family registered a whopping 511 separate Southland land transactions. What we *don't* know is the split-up of these transactions into purchases and sales. But even if everything they bought was sold again during the period, this small family would have made at least 255 separate land purchases. Clearly they were actively speculating in land.

Land speculation was a popular activity among some early Southland families who had money, or access to it. You didn't need vast capital to get started. Land was fairly cheap, and if you could actually live on on your block, it was a snip: a deferred payment system introduced by the Land Act of 1877 (abolished in 1892) let people buy suburban land at ten per cent down and repayment over five years, and rural land at five per cent down and repayment over ten years.

Plenty of money could be made if you timed the purchases and sales right, but some family land empires collapsed like a stack of cards when they were caught with too much land on hand in a falling land price cycle.

Some MacGibbon properties in Mataura and Gore would have been used for their own homes and retail businesses, and a certain amount of other land was retained until the 1930s and later. So the number of original land purchases must have been a good deal higher than 255. Unfortunately it has not been possible to return to Invercargill to analyse the figures in detail, in order to separate out the land sales or to calculate the total area of land involved.

Most transactions took place before 1900, and almost three quarters involved the first two generations: John Sr and his sons Thomas, John Jr, Ebenezer and Archie. A further 12 per cent were registered to John Sr's daughters-in-law.

Thomas was the biggest land dealer, with 172 transactions, and his wife Isabella had 35 in her own name. Next most active was John Sr with 97 transactions, followed by John Jr (59), Ebenezer (36) and Archibald (25). The youngest son, Colin, had only four transactions, while the two daughters had no land transactions recorded under their maiden names.

Two-thirds of the land blocks were in towns, including Mataura (174), Gore (74), East Gore (72) and Invercargill (14). There was also a good deal of land in country districts, especially Tuturau (47), Waikaka (40), Chatton (32) and Hokonui District (14). Smaller numbers of land blocks were held in most Southland country districts. Some of the country land blocks would have been smaller town sections, but it is known that the family owned a number of farms, which they would have leased. ∎

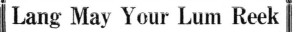

Serving the community

Three members of the second MacGibbon generation – Thomas, John Jr and Archie – had outstanding records of community service, not only within the Mataura Valley, but also within the wider Southland and Otago regions. They were on school committees, town boards, borough councils, the Southland County Council, education bodies, hospital boards and charities. They dispensed justice and ministerial services as Justices of the Peace, were office-bearers in the Presbyterian Church, and promoted local economic development. Thomas and John Jr both had a tilt at national politics, and Thomas eventually made it to Wellington.

Hon Thomas MacGibbon, MLC, JP

Thomas, the eldest son, had the broadest record of community service. It started in the 1870s, when he joined the Mataura School Committee. Shortly afterwards he began a long tenure with the Lyndhurst Roads Board.

Building on his Roads Board experience, he was elected in 1878 as Mataura Riding representative on the Southland County Council. He remained on the Council until 1889 and was its chairman in 1883 and 1884.

He was a member of the Southland Hospital and Charitable Aid Board.

Education was a particular interest, and he progressed from the school committee to membership of the Southland Education Board, which he eventually chaired. It is not known what his achievements were on the Board, but one area of signal failure was his inability to persuade fellow members that all schools should display the Bible's Ten Commandments on classroom walls.

After moving to Dunedin in 1909, Thomas became a member of the Otago School Commissioners' Board, and the boards of John McGlashan and Columba Colleges. Then in 1913 he was nominated by the Southland Education Board as its representative on the University of Otago Council. He retired from that position in 1920.

The extent of Thomas Mac-Gibbon's own education is unknown. He would have attended school in Glasgow until he emigrated as a ten year old in 1849. He probably attended

From pioneer to businessman: by the 1880s, Thomas MacGibbon had moved on from bush-whacking to become one of Southland's business and political leaders. He had been instrumental in building the family company into one of Eastern Southland's major mercantile enterprises. He was also a tireless promoter for other business development in the region. He was a founding director of the Mataura Dairy Factory Company, in 1887. The following year he travelled to the United Kingdom to seek markets for the new company's cheese. While in Glasgow he took time out to have his portrait taken in the Macnab studio in West Nile Street – the same street his father had visited 39 years earlier to arrange the family's emigration to Otago through the Lay Association of the Free Church of Scotland. Other significant Mataura industries Thomas had a hand in establishing included the Southland Frozen Meat works and a paper mill.

the School House in Dunedin during the year or so the family lived in Rattray Street. After they moved to the outer wilderness of Caversham suburb, his formal education probably ceased. Some years later when the family established the Mataura Falls Accommodation House, they engaged a live-in tutor, Eric McKay. Although Thomas was in his twenties by then, he undoubtedly took advantage of the education opportunity.

Thomas was certainly a strong proponent for education, and he sent three of his five sons to Scotland for further study – two in engineering and one in medicine. The other two sons received high school education and went into business. Thomas was a product of his age, and his enthusiasm for higher education didn't extend to the female sex: his six daughters got Brinsmead pianos in lieu!

Local body politics

In pioneering times, public spirited men of energy and initiative were always in keen demand by local settlers, to help develop communities. It was not surprising that, when Mataura established its first town board in 1882, Thomas was elected to it. He remained a member – including chairman – until the Board was reconstituted as a borough council in 1895. Thomas then served on the Mataura Borough Council until 1903. He was mayor between 1898 and 1902.

He was Mataura's first Justice of the Peace, but apparently he was too busy to do the job adequately. According to 'Justice', who wrote to the Mataura Ensign in 1883, Thomas was the only JP in town, and although in every way qualified, he was "…quite unable to overtake (sic) the arduous duties connected with the office. He is often away from home, and parties wanting to sign declarations, &c., have repeatedly to go elsewhere to make an affidavit."

While Thomas MacGibbon was developing the family firm, he was tirelessly promoting other business opportunities for the district. He was particularly concerned with the dairy and meat processing industries.

He was a founding director of the Mataura Dairy Factory in 1887, and one of its early chairmen. He remained a director until 1910. In 1888 he travelled to the United Kingdom to "open up a market for company produce",

Love of luxury, pleasure and indulgence ruining the modern generation!

By 1911, Thomas MacGibbon had settled into the role of elder pioneer and was harrumphing about the new generation. In a letter to Herries Beattie at the Mataura Ensign he wrote:

"I sometimes wonder whether the easier conditions of these modern days are tending to produce a race equal to the one which is 'passing out' and which has laid the foundations of the settlement so deep and broad. I fear not!

"The love of luxury and pleasure is dominant and there is not the same go-aheadism and endurance which characterised the early pioneers.

"The 'moderns' are, in many instances, quite contented to profit by the labours and self-denial of their forbears and to enjoy a 'good time'. This lack of thrift and the love of pleasure and indulgence is at the bottom of much of the industrial unrest and discontent of today."

Continued on page 194

The Mataura Election

◆

MR T. A. MACGIBBON'S ADDRESS.

At Woodlands on Friday evening, Mr T. A. MacGibbon, the Opposition candidate for Mataura, addressed a meeting of electors. Mr M. Leith presided, and there was an attendance of 70 or 80 electors, including several ladies.

Mr MacGibbon, who was warmly received, said that he had very little idea of coming forward at the election until he was requested to do so by the Opposition party of Mataura, and he had only yielded to the representations made on the score of duty. So far he had found it a very pleasant duty. He had been connected with public bodies for over 30 years, and his name was familiar as a member of the Education Board and some years ago the County Council. His first essay in public life was as a member of a school committee, and then he went through the other bodies—road boards, county council, etc. He held that it was an advantage to those who intended going into Parliament to go through the humbler phases of public life.

He had no axe to grind, and he was there in the interests of no party except the opposition, whose principles he was in sympathy with. (Applause). There was no office or portfolio held out to him, and he was not ambitious ; but he simply desired to do as much good as he could if he got into Parliament for his country. If he were sent there he would use his experience of 30 years in assisting to make and amend, if need be, the laws of the land. He was

AN OPPOSITIONIST.

He was opposed to the Government, not from any factious feeling, but he had the conviction that they had been too long in office. It might be said that that was not a crime, but it might be a very serious and grave mistake for the colony to allow one set of men to occupy the Government benches for too long a period. Absolute authority was exercised by the Premier [Hon Richard Seddon]—it had been called a "benevolent despotism"— and the Ministry was apt to cultivate a feeling of self-sufficiency, forgetting the prudential policy which was followed when they first went into office. The people had no opportunity of proving whether the statements made by the Ministry were correct or not.

No one could say that the opposition were unnecessary. They were the colony's guarantee of good management and faithful administration on the part of the Government. Their function was not to give a policy, as was suggested by the Government's followers. It was time for them to divulge a policy when they occupied the Government benches. Their function was to vigorously criticise, censure, or defeat any efforts or proposals made by the Ministry which they were not, as they were conceived, in the interests of the people at large. (Applause).

The Opposition should have 35 out of the 80 members of the House, leaving the Government with the remaining 45, which would give them a working majority of 10. Under these circumstances, if the Government brought in wild-cat or foolish legislation, they would run a risk of sustaining a defeat which would be fatal to their administration. He (the candidate) offered the electors an opportunity to make the Opposition stronger.

If elected, he would not be a blind follower of Mr Massey. He was prepared to accept him as leader, on the lines on which he announced himself, and judging from his past. However he played second fiddle to no man, and he would never follow any man blindly, be he Seddon or Massey. (Applause).

His objection to the Government was, that as a result of their lengthy term of office, they had become

WASTEFUL AND RECKLESS

in their system of expenditure. Small things indicated the general trend, and if they found a man wasting the shillings, they had their doubts about whether he took care of the pounds. That held good with the Government as well as with the individual. The visit of the Premier to England some years ago as the colony's delegate cost £1700, and there was an additional £130 for his secretaries. The premiers of other colonies received only £1000, and expressed themselves as more than paid. The Premiers' Conference in Hobart, extending over three or four weeks, cost £300 or £400. The people in Hobart told the speaker that "that Premier of yours is a jolly good fellow ; he makes money fly round like water." (Laughter and applause). It should be remembered that it was the colony's money which was being so lavishly spent. Coming to later times, they found that the same system prevailed. They could look for an instance at the celebrated

MAPOURIKA TRIP.

The Mapourika was granted by the Union Co. to members for a trip to the Cook Islands. The Government fitted up the steamer most luxuriously, and some 30 or 40 members took the trip. He (the speaker) had also taken the trip, and it cost him something like £35. He enjoyed himself, and he supposed the members enjoyed themselves more, as it did not affect their pockets. (Laughter). There was one item of £150 for albums which the colony paid for, and every luxury that could gratify the eye and the senses was provided. In case members went wild, a Minister went with the party. He was paid a salary of £1200 a year, and even while away drawing his salary, he charged 30s a day travelling expenses. So fine did he cut it that when he landed in Wellington on the 50th day of his trip, he charged his 30s. (Laughter).

These were small things, but when the Ministers had control of millions of money and were not careful in such respects, what guarantee had they that the millions would be spent properly? The same system of reckless expenditure was being followed in regard to the

PUBLIC BUILDINGS,

which were too magnificent. They were paid for by borrowed money, not by the colony's earnings. While the colony had to borrow, the buildings should be plainer in style, and built consistently with requirements. Some of the buildings were ornamented sufficiently to adorn a Swiss chalet or a bride's cake. (Laughter). The example of the municipality of Glasgow, which had paid for its town hall costing one million, and other municipal conveniences, out of revenue should be imitated by this colony, and the electors should put in another set of men who would check this wasteful expenditure. (Applause).

It was remarkable also that Mr Seddon, with all his loyalty and talk of preferential trade (which he gave by increasing the duty on foreign goods instead of by a remission on British goods) had the roofs of the new railway stations covered with tiles made in France, instead of employing Welsh slate or some other British product.

Another charge he had to make referred to the

UNFAIR DISTRIBUTION

of the public funds. The Government had fallen into a method of unfair distribution of votes, and one could not help but be struck with that unfairness. Westland, the favoured district, had £10 5s per head of the population spent on it in roads and bridges, whereas Auckland only had £2 19s, Wellington £2 15s, Otago 15s and Canterbury 5s. He would appeal to them if that was a fair distribution of money. The only reason for Westland's undue share was that it had returned Mr Seddon.

THE SURPLUSES

were talked about, but there was always a suspicion about them...No treasurer had the right to boast about surpluses, as they were on a totally different footing to the ordinary commercial surpluses. The Treasurer's revenue consisted of the taxation of the people, and if there was a surplus, it was evident there was too much taxation.

The colony had been

BORROWING

far too strongly. The public debt now amounted to [£]60 millions, which practically mortgaged every acre of arable land in the colony for 30s to the foreign bondholder, and every acre of pastoral land for 10s. The public debt per head was £68 11s 3d, and the interest per head per annum was £2 12s 6d. New Zealand was the premier colony for debt at the present time...If it had not been for the prosperity of their colony, the people would not have been able to bear it. The Government was not responsible for this prosperity, which was due to events and conditions utterly beyond their control, such as the Australian drought, Boer War and Russia-Japanese War.

(Southland Times, 27/11/1905)

(Sections of this newspaper report have been edited out for reasons of space. Other topics which Thomas MacGibbon covered included cooperative labour, the Public Revenues Act, defence of the administration which had preceded Mr Seddon's Liberal administration, land tenure, the question of a railway line to Tokonui which would benefit only two or three farmers (Thomas could not "give a very definite opinion" on that matter) and the licensing laws (he would oppose any alteration to the present system — a view which would have put him at odds with his prohibitionist brother, John Jr).)

There is rest and comfort for the worn out mothers at last. A Paris physician is "incubating" infants just now. By a process similar to that upon which chickens are artificially hatched, the new born babe is placed in the incubator and there allowed to remain for about six months. It is carefully nourished and at the end of the period named is turned out as strong and well-grown as a child a year old. It is stated that 300 infants have been experimentally treated at a foundling hospital with great success.
(Mataura Ensign, 2/3/1883)

MUNICIPAL MEETING

A meeting convened by Mr T. Green for the purpose of considering the advisableness of forming the town districts of Gore and Gordon into a municipality, was held last night at the Courthouse, Gore. There was a very large attendance, both sides of the river being well represented.

Mr T. Green took the chair and briefly explained the object of the meeting. He thought the two towns now contained enough inhabitants to form one municipality....

...Mr J. MacGibbon moved that a committee be appointed and steps be taken to form the towns of Gore and Gordon into a municipality....

...The chairman suggested that the present was a suitable time for choosing a name for the municipality.

Mr MacGibbon moved that the name be Longford. He thought that dropping both the names of Gore and Gordon would tend to sink old differences.

Mr Fraser seconded.

Mr Canning moved as an amendment that the name be " Gore."

Mr Piller seconded *prop (sic) forma.*

The motion was lost by 19 to 17 votes.

The chairman suggested that a committee be elected to carry out the necessary details.

Mr Henderson moved, and Mr Canning seconded that the following gentlemen be the committee :—Messrs Green, Smaill, Brown, Canning, Roy, Henderson, Dolamore, Milnes, Beattie and J. MacGibbon, five to form a forum.

Mr Beattie muved (sic) and Mr Hanson seconded that the two Town Boards be the committee. The motion was carried almost unanimously.
(Mataura Ensign, 2/11/1883) (The two communities remained separate until 1890, when John MacGibbon Jr was elected first mayor of the combined borough.)

ROAD SKATES.—The cycle is said to be threatened with a rival in the shape of a pneumatic skate, which is being placed on the market by a Scotch firm. The new skate has only two wheels, which are placed in line, one behind the other. With this aid to locomotion it is said that ordinary roads can be travelled with ease. The skates have, it is said, already been seen in some of the Midland towns, where a speed of from six to seven miles an hour has been attained with them in ordinary thoroughfares. We are informed that something of the kind is being made in Invercargill for an inventor. The tires in this case will be solid rubber. The idea is an old one, minus the rubber. A Frenchman designed a thing of the kind 25 years ago, indeed he had only one wheel for each leg. The foot stood on a letter L stirrup which was strapped to the leg, and on a stud pin, on the long limb, a wheel of considerable size revolved. It looked well—on paper.
(Southland Times, 8/2/1894)

The town [Gore] is having a plethora of musical entertainments from all sorts of conditions — from blind musicians to the most artistic and sacred melodies, and always on Sunday evening. The Council have come alive to the fact that they are being "had" in the matter of a charge being made for the Sunday evening gatherings which are proving more attractive to outsiders than the churches. Better the music hall than nowhere.—Own [Gore] correspondent.
(Southland Times, 19/7/1894)

LECTURE ON BIMETALLISM

Mr W. B. Anderson's lecture on Bimetallism could not with justice be summarised. He explained that what was desired was both a gold and a silver currency with fixed relative values, and both or either of which should be legal tender among all trading nations, or at least among the leading nations, and then would come the millennium of trade prosperity. But his audiences have not yet digested the subject. The nations may listen to the voice from the Gore Town Hall. Why not? The lecturer deserves much credit in any case for the compliment he paid his audience in assuming their intelligence and reading was equal to so abstruse a question.—Own [Gore] correspondent.
(Southland Times, 4/8/1894)

The Gore Brass Band, under the baton of Mr Richardson, is being revived and will be an alternative to the Salvation Army Band, "...which has made us a garrison town. Our own band will not, I think, turn out on Sundays. There is nothing particularly sanctimonious about a Gorean youth, rather otherwise, but he declines harness on Sunday."
(Southland Times, 4/8/1894)

and was particularly successful in establishing trading links with Glasgow.

He was a director and one of the first investors in the Southland Frozen Meat Company, which established a large freezing works on the site once occupied by MacGibbons Accommodation House near Mataura Falls.

Thomas also had a hand in the establishment of another large industry in Mataura, the paper mill.

The Church

Another important community institution, the Presbyterian Church, had the benefit of Thomas MacGibbon's involvement. He was superintendent of the Sunday School for 30 years, an elder, and an occasional lay preacher. After moving to Dunedin he became an elder of Knox Church.

In 1905, Thomas stood as Opposition candidate against sitting member Robert McNab for the Mataura seat in the New Zealand House of Representatives. He lost, polling 2,356 votes to McNab's 2,791. A newspaper report of Thomas's campaign meeting at Woodlands is reproduced on page 193. Thomas's allegations of rorts and extravagance in the Liberal administration have a familiar ring to them – the more things change in politics, the more they stay the same.

In 1914, Thomas MacGibbon finally arrived in New Zealand's capital city, through a Reform Party appointment to the Legislative Council. His period on the Council is described on page 209.

John MacGibbon Jr, JP

John MacGibbon Jr's community service was similar in many ways to that of his older brother. He was heavily involved in local body politics and the church. Like Thomas, he was a JP, and both a member and chairman of the Southland Education Board. They were both on the Southland Hospital and Charitable Aid Board, for which John Jr was at one time chairman.

John Jr was second mayor of the Gore Town Board, in 1886. When the Gordon and Gore town boards amalgamated in 1890, he was first mayor of the combined municipality. Elections were held every year in those days, and he won the 1891 mayoralty as well, on the casting vote of the returning officer.

Evidently he was a no-nonsense mayor, with no love of pomp and ceremony. It is not clear whether he was defeated in the 1887 mayoralty election, or didn't stand, but his successor, Ian Simson, was evidently more to the taste of Mataura Ensign columnist 'Cyclops', who wrote: "We [now] have at Gore a Mayor who thoroughly appreciates the dignity of his position. It is quite time we had. The last Mayor did not seem to be so profoundly impressed with his honours as he ought to have been."

In business outside MacGibbon and Company, John Jr was connected with the Gore Dairy Factory, and was its chairman in 1898.

Religion and morality

He was a long-term Sunday School teacher, and an elder of the East Gore Presbyterian Church for 22 years. As with all the early MacGibbons, with the possible exception of younger brother Archie, there was a strong religious moral undertone to most things he did in life.

He campaigned long and hard against liquor and was in several different temperance organisations, beginning with the Gore Gospel Temperance Society which was formed in 1883. He was president of the Society, at least in 1896.

In 1899 he chaired a temperance convention in Gore, and urged the delegates to be persistent in their work. The Prohibitionist journal reported him saying that "During twenty years experience in the district, he had seen professional men and others in flourishing conditions of life brought to the lowest status through drink."

In 1905 he presided over the Mataura Valley Temperance Reform Council.

Religion and wowserism were stronger sentiments in the community than they are today, and they received a good deal of coverage in both Gore newspapers. But in reality, John Jr and his cohorts were swimming against the tide. Most residents were considerably

more secular in their outlook, and liquor prohibition was a non starter.

In 1894 the temperance forces mounted a campaign aimed at securing a 'no-license' for the Mataura electoral and licensing district in a forthcoming poll. Had they succeeded, Gore's seven pubs would have had to stop selling liquor. Reporting on the campaign, the Southland Times' Gore

---

TENDERS.

Cheesemaker.

TENDERS for the position of CHEESEMAKER for the Gore Dairy Factory, at per 100lb of cheese made, will be received by (and all particulars obtained from) the Undersigned up to THURSDAY, 22nd September, 1898.

JOHN MacGIBBON,
Chairman.

(Mataura Ensign, 17/9/1898)

---

correspondent reckoned local prohibition would make little impact, as private supplies of liquor would easily be obtained from Dunedin or Invercargill.

Attendances at public temperance meetings were patchy, and on at least one occasion a lecture was abandoned because hardly anyone turned up. During the 1890s the Salvation Army and its Band of Hope were standard bearers for the movement. Although few in number, they were a noticeable and controversial presence in the town.

The same Southland Times correspondent, evidently no temperance supporter, reported with undisguised pleasure in March 1894 that at long last the Gore Brass Band was being revived and would be an alternative to the Salvation Army Band, "...which

has made us a garrison town. Our own band will not, I think, turn out on Sundays. There is nothing particularly sanctimonious about a Gorean youth, rather otherwise, but he declines harness on Sunday."

Later in the year, the reporter noted that church attendance was not the only sabbath activity in Gore. There were now "...Sunday evening gatherings which are proving more attractive to outsiders than the churches. Better the music hall than nowhere."

Liberal politics

Again like his older brother, John Jr was keenly interested in national politics, though from the other side of the political fence. Whereas Thomas was a Reform Party supporter (which meant that on most issues he was conservative), John Jr supported Richard Seddon's Liberal Party.

In the early 1890s, John Jr campaigned on behalf of women's electoral emancipation. Several MacGibbon women, including John Jr's wife Mary, had signed the 1893 national women's franchise petition which preceded the Electoral Bill of 1893. That bill made New Zealand women the first women in the world to vote in a national election.

It was one thing to have the vote, and another to exercise the right. Voters had to register, and in Gore, a meeting of franchise campaigners in the Temperance Hall set up three teams of two men and two women to canvas the town. John MacGibbon Jr was in the group which canvassed in the East Ward. His companions included a Mr Smith, Margaret Buchanan (founding vice-president of the Gore Women's Franchise League) and Mary Ann Morgan. Miss Morgan was a teacher and singer who would later be involved with John Jr's daughters and nieces in the Gore Girls' Literary Society.

In July 1899, John Jr chaired a meeting which formed the Gore Liberal League. The League's objective was to "...discuss social and political questions, Liberal ideas, assist in passing Liberal legislation". Vice-president was John Penny, Thomas MacGibbon's son-in-law.

John Jr stood as an Independent Liberal for the Mataura electorate in the

John MacGibbon Jr presides over a Temperance Society meeting.

1911 election, but his 2,239 votes were not enough to dislodge the sitting Reform Party candidate, G J Anderson, who was returned with 3,096 votes. It would have been difficult to defeat a sitting candidate in any event, but in this year there was a strong national electoral swing against the Joseph Ward Liberal Government.

While John Jr promoted women's electoral rights, his attitude toward the female sex could also be very patronising. At one of his 1911 election meetings in Gore, he was presented with flowers by young women in the audience, and the Ensign reported: "Mr MacGibbon said he would almost think he was going to be married when he looked at the beautiful bouquets…He had to thank the ladies who had presented him with the flowers, and he hoped that in the course of time they would receive beautiful bouquets on a great occasion – the occasion to which every young lady looked forward."

In 1918, at a Southland Education Board discussion on the need for instruction on home management in schools, John Jr said there was a surprising amount of ignorance on the subject, even from some mothers. The Mataura Ensign reported, "He had once seen a woman, who in her girlhood days had not received any instruction in home management, washing the dishes with her gloves on. She had learned since, however, and now knew how to manage her home properly. He would like to see girls educated as much as possible, but the one great essential for a girl was to be a good housewife."

At a 1922 high school prize giving ceremony he put his views more succinctly: "I give these prizes because I believe that unless a girl has a thorough grounding in domestic science, she is jolly little use as a wife."

John Jr's public life did not revolve entirely around business, politics and morality. He was one of the Hokonui Lawn Bowls Club's leading skips, and took his turn as club president. He was interested in local history, and in 1924 was president of the Gore and Surrounding Districts Early Settlers' Association.

John MacGibbon Jr was in a team which canvassed Gore women, encouraging them to register for the first election after female emancipation was attained in 1893.

Archie MacGibbon, JP

Seven years younger than John Jr, Archie was cut from different cloth, temperamentally and politically. They were both in business, but whereas there was a religious undertone to almost everything John Jr did, Archie was a businessman pure and simple. If religion informed his life, he made no public show of it. He and his wife Georgina ('Aunty Tot') took a great interest in secular activities, and were known as entertainers. Religion gets no mention in his newspaper obituaries, whereas his siblings' obituaries are full of it.

Archie was elected to the Gore Borough Council in 1897, and served till 1899. He was elected mayor in 1901, and then, between 1902–1904, he was a plain councillor again. He was later mayor in 1906, 1908 and 1909.

Archie first stood for mayor in 1899, but was defeated, 291 votes to 265, by Mr Ballintine, a local bootmaker.

The contest stirred up class conflict in the town, judging from comments made by the victor to the Mataura Ensign. Ballintine was reported as saying, "…all the 'toffs' and 'would be toffs' had opposed him by fair or foul means and he felt glad that

he had beaten them. It made him feel quite six inches higher and 20 years younger. The fight was a straight issue between a working man and a 'toff', and a working man had won. Such a thing had never been done in Gore before. Mr. MacGibbon had said that he would not sit in the council except as Mayor. Mr. MacGibbon would have to sit under him now for his impertinence, and that served him right."

Archie was an active Reform Party member, while his brother John Jr belonged to the nominally more progressive Liberals. But on the Borough Council, the brothers' positions were reversed. Archie was one of the more progressive early mayors, while John Jr tended to opt for the status quo.

Archie was frequently in the news in the early 1900s, as he battled ratepayers and councillors, including his brother, who regularly blocked attempts to raise loans to develop lighting, water supply and drainage.

Life was never dull when Archie was mayor – even when dullness threatened. On one occasion he was opening the Gore Fancier's Club show and was well into a speech about all the good things to be gained by entering such shows, when suddenly his voice was drowned out by a chorus of sounds from the feathered visitors. As if acting upon some pre-arranged signal, ducks quacked, roosters crowed, dogs barked and the audience laughed. The Mayor took the hint and cut his speech short.

Business community

Well-known in the town's business community through being local manager for National Mortgage and Agency Co Ltd, Archie was a prominent member of the Gore Chamber of Commerce. He was a local representative on the Southland Electric Power Board.

He was a JP for 35 years, and a leading member of Gore's Lodge Harvey.

During the First World War he and his wife were active in the local committee which helped prepare local recruits for overseas service.

Earlier, when living in Mataura, he was clerk of the Waimumu Roads Board, helped establish the Mataura Dairy Factory and was one of the (unsuccessful) promoters of a woollen mill for the town. ∎

'Aunty Tot' MacGibbon was one of Gore's characters

By Jean Smith, President, Gore Historical Society

For more than 50 years, Georgina MacGibbon was one of Gore's best-known characters. "Aunty Tot", as she was called by family and friends, Georgina was never the little wife in the background. Married to Archie MacGibbon, businessman and mayor of Gore, she definitely made her own mark.

She was born Georgina Begg, one of 12 children in a family of tea-importers who made door-to-door sales. She lived briefly in New Caledonia when she was 16, and was educated at Clyde.

Georgina was a social leader, and in her early days she was recognised as a superb hostess and her parties were legendary. A grandniece says she was a fabulous cook. Her home and garden were very popular for garden parties and relatives recalled the days when carriages would sweep up the drive to her front door.

She was a keen bridge player who also enjoyed a game of bezique. An older resident said that at one time Georgina had two well-trained fox terriers. She was heavily rouged and mascarad and wore a kiss curl on her forehead – she wore it from childhood, and in the latter days it was singed by cigarette smoking. Her fingers, laden with rings, were nicotine stained.

Red was her favourite colour, and one day when going to bridge which she so enjoyed, she dressed in red from head to foot, a scarf around her head gypsy-fashion. At this stage, she had let rooms and sent her tenant out looking for a red handkerchief to complete the ensemble. If she wore white, she dyed her hair red and was known as

'Wedding Cake'. One time when my husband went to her house on business, he said he was distracted by a red blind in the room which gave it a Dante-like atmosphere. She also had a great fondness for hats.

There is a story of a surprise party for her husband's 60th birthday, but she got wind of it and when the guests arrived, they were met at the door by husband and wife in nightgowns and caps and carrying candles. When she was entertaining, she would post her husband to watch for the guests and when shown in, to give the impression that she, the organised hostess had been ready and waiting for ages.

Although she had alcohol in the house, I believe she never drank herself.

Aunty Tot was an avid reader who claimed she could read two lines at a time. She was also a competent carver and had a handsome chair and whatnot she had carved. She had worked intricate designs into furnishings which

were still in her house when she died.

She was an active participant in sports of tennis and croquet and worked for the Red Cross in World War One. She became a voluntary cook in charge of the feeding of large crowds of patients at the makeshift hospital at Gore during the influenza epidemic in 1918.

She became more eccentric as she grew older and when, as a young bride, I first met her, she was an old wizened lady – badly made up, with nicotine stained fingers. A far cry from the hostess of former days.

In 1950, she had been invited to the family wedding of Marylyn MacGibbon and Bill Akroyd, at the Gore Anglican Church. In the rush and bustle, no-one had remembered to collect Aunty Tot, and the intrepid old woman made her own way there – quite a walk. I saw her in flowing black, looking like the old woman from Hansel and Gretel, tapping her stick angrily between the trees to the church door.

In latter years, when she was almost blind, she would sit quietly and when asked what she had been doing, would reply, "I've been thinking about all the characters I have met in the books I have read", oblivious to the fact that she was a character in her own right. She told of going into hospital and being asked her age by a young nurse. "Don't be cheeky – I don't want to know how old you are, and I'm not letting you know how old I am," she replied.

Georgina died on 16 April 1960, and was referred to in her obituary as one of Gore's oldest and best known residents. Her old home in 26 Main Street South was demolished, and the expansive grounds, scene of many former social gatherings, are now part of the Resthaven complex. ∎

The MacGibbon Golden Wedding, Mataura, November 1888

An interesting event, not only to the family, relatives and friends, but as a fact in our colonial experiences useful to the future historian, was celebrated in Mataura on Friday evening — the golden wedding of a pair who came to Southland "in the early days" when no commercial traveller with belltopper and silk stockings came about as now in steam and sofa carriages for "orders" : that of Mr and Mrs John MacGibbon.

Mr MacGibbon learned and prospered in business on the banks of the Clyde, which, however, he left with his wife and a young family as one of the pilgrim band which, under the auspices of the Free Church of Scotland, had formed the Otago settlement. He landed in Dunedin 38 years ago when it was not much of a city...

...The company that met by invitation on Friday evening in Humphries' Hall had assembled under difficulties. Like weather, for midsummer, not even an old identity could recall. Ebenezer MacGibbon and his family had been water-stayed at his new home in Gordon by the rise in the Waikaka, and many old friends who would like to have been present did not venture. Those who did assemble — altogether nearly 200 — thoroughly enjoyed themselves.

The Mataura Ensign
December 1888

Jane MacGibbon (nee McConachy) 1817-1901

John MacGibbon 1809-1891

Married in Glasgow, 31 October 1838

A1 Archibald (Archie) MacGibbon, 1856-1935
A2 Georgina ('Aunty Tot') MacGibbon (nee Begg), 1866-1960
E1 Ebenezer (Eb) MacGibbon, 1854-1915
E2 Mary (Polly) MacGibbon (nee Latham), ? - 1931
E3 Maud MacGibbon, 1881-1931
E4 May MacGibbon, 1883-1951
E5 Ida MacGibbon, 1885-1971
E6 Florence MacGibbon, ca1887-1975
JS1 Jessie Shanks (nee MacGibbon), 1842-1920
JS2 James Steuart Shanks Snr, 1835-1911
JS3 James Steuart Shanks Jr, 1864-1906
JS4 John MacGibbon Shanks, 1865-1938
JS5 Jane (Jean) Shanks, 1867-1916
JS6 Eleanor (Nell) Shanks, 1868-1953
JS7 Isabella (Bell) Shanks, 1870-1942
JS8 Charles Shanks, 1872-1944

JS9 Elizabeth Shanks, 1874-1944
JS10 Colina (Maud) Shanks, 1876-1955
T1 Thomas MacGibbon, 1839-1925
T2 Isabella (Bella) MacGibbon (nee Nairn), 1848-1923
T3 Catherine (Kate) MacGibbon,1869-1945
T4 John MacGibbon, 1870-1945
T5 Colina MacGibbon, 1872-1956
T6 Mary MacGibbon, 1873-1943
T7 Eve MacGibbon, 1875-1963
T8 Archibald (Archie) MacGibbon, 1877-1947
T9 Thomas Arthur (Tommy Arthur) MacGibbon, 1878-1958
T10 Ernest (Ernie) MacGibbon, 1881-1933
T11 Eleanor (Nell) MacGibbon, 1882-1958
T12 Jessie MacGibbon, 1884-1932
T13 Roy MacGibbon, 1885-1947

C1 Colin MacGibbon, 1861-1928
(Married Emily Hawson in 1889; six children)
J1 John MacGibbon Jr, 1849-1925
J2 Mary MacGibbon (nee Ward), 1861-1912
J3 Mataura (Tau) MacGibbon, 1879-1947
J4 Hugh (Hughie) MacGibbon, 1881-1969
J5 Mabel MacGibbon, 1883-1955
J6 John (Gordon) MacGibbon, 1885-1953
J7 Francis (Frank) MacGibbon, 1887-1952
Not yet born in this family:
Angus (Bill) MacGibbon, 1890-1958
David (Dave) MacGibbon, 1892-1973
Missing from John and Jane MacGibbon's family:
Hugh MacGibbon, 1841-1841
David MacGibbon, 1851-1858
Jeannie Miller (nee MacGibbon), 1844-1886

Mataura touched by Bohemia

By the 1890s, Mataura was beginning to reach beyond the practicalities of pioneer life, to consider a little culture beyond Scottish song and dance, church music and brass bands. But even the tentative intellectuals in the town were probably taken aback by the arrival of Isabella MacGibbon's brother, artist James Nairn, in 1890. Nairn burned like a bright candle in their midst for several months, painting and taking part in local musical entertainments.

James Nairn had been a member of the 'Glasgow Boys', a group of artistic rebels who pioneered the Scottish impressionist style. His attitudes probably caused a good deal of comment, if not shock, in the southern town. His politics were relatively radical for the day, and one imagines some interesting conversations took place with his brother-in-law Thomas, whose politics were strongly conservative.

Nairn stayed for a short while with the MacGibbons before moving permanently to Wellington and establishing himself as one of New Zealand's foremost painters.

Below are two press mentions Nairn received while living at Mataura:

AN ARTIST AT MATAURA

◆

(From our own Correspondent)

We have had living among us at Mataura for some months a young Scotch artist, Mr. James M. Nairn, a member of the Glasgow Art Club. He had been in somewhat indifferent health for some time before leaving the Old Country, and came out partly on that account, but principally to visit a near relative with whom he is now staying here. His studio is situated near the bridge in one of Mr. MacGibbon's buildings. He commenced life first in an architect's office in the City of Glasgow, where he remained five years, and at his profession he might have done remarkably well, but his great love for,

Painter James Nairn begins a portrait in oils of Jane MacGibbon. Nairn, who had belonged to a celebrated group of Scottish impressionists known as the Glasgow Boys, emigrated to New Zealand in 1890 and initially lived in Mataura with his sister, Isabella MacGibbon.

and devotion to painting caused him to abandon architecture, and give rein to the bent of his inclination—painting. That he has been successful in it one only has to view his studio and inspect his work. The portrait of Mr. J. MacGibbon, sen., is natural and life like, and to those who have seen him in his home, the posture and expression are indeed true to a degree. Master Roy Gregor MacGibbon, whose name would be apt to betray his nationality wherever he went, is a grandson of the old gentleman above named, and the faithful likeness shown of the youth is at once admitted by all who have seen it. Those two portraits are a striking contrast—young Roy Gregor is only four years old, quite in the morning of his life; his venerable grandfather in the evening of his life, is over 80, but remarkably hearty at his age....

...He intends shortly to visit Dunedin and Wellington, in both of which cities the merit of his work will doubtless be appreciated by lovers of art. It will be a pity if he cannot be induced to pitch his camp somewhere in this colony, where subjects for the painter are so numerous and varied.
(Mataura Ensign, 4/7/1890)

CONCERT AT MATAURA.—A concert was held on Thursday evening, 15th inst., in the Oddfellows Hall in aid of the fund for improving the recreation grounds. There was a full house and the chair was occupied by Mr. Thos. Culling. Misses Bond and Williamson opened the programme with a duet on the piano. Songs were rendered

by Mesdames McKay and Reid, Misses Bond, Palmer, Louden, M. Cameron and R. Palmer, Messrs. Clark, Findlay, Houston, Knight, Maw, Hescott, Wassell, Nairn and Preston. A trio was executed by Misses Colina and Mary MacGibbon and Mr. Nairn. Mesdames MacGibbon, McKay and Misses Cameron, Bond and Palmer played the accompaniments. At the conclusion the chairman announced that after paying all expenses they would be able to wipe off the debt of the recreation grounds and have a small balance in hand. Votes of thanks were passed to the performers, to the chairman and to the committee.—Own correspondent.
(Southland Times, 20/5/1890.)

Dance programme for a Mataura ball, executed on brown wrapping paper by James Nairn. The woman seated in the foreground is Nairn's niece, Kate MacGibbon, while standing to the right is Kate's future husband, John Penny.

James Nairn portraits of John Sr (detail) and Roy MacGibbon, mentioned in the Mataura Ensign article.

MATAURA TO THE FRONT

Some few months ago, we wrote, snowing the great advances made in our sister town— commonly known as the coming "Manufacturing city of the South" in the way of new industries, new business houses, and private dwellings. Since then, a marked change has taken place in the town. For instance, old friends who always enjoyed a trip to see the falls in their rustic beauty, will be sorry to learn that all this has departed, having had to make way for business requirements. Now appears, on one bank of the falls, a very large and handsome structure for the Southland Frozen Meat Co.; while, nearing completion, is Mr. Culling's new paper mill. These two works alone will use up capital to the extent of £50,000. This will give some idea of what these buildings should be like in size.

During the last week, the business places have been connected by telephone, and the town is now in communication with Gore, Riversdale, Invercargill, Bluff, Riverton, and Winton. This is a great stride for the township, as it brings it into touch with all the centres of business.

The chief streets in the town are assuming quite a business look, being all asphalted, and nicely lighted with new lamps.

We notice in Bridge-street, during the last month, Messrs. MacGibbon and Sons have put up two new shops ; and, just by the side of these, Mrs. Bauchop has put up a good, substantial shop, and we are glad to see they are all let to tenants. On the opposite side, is being built an office for Mr. Fletcher, solicitor, of Gore, who, with his usual business tact, sees it is policy to give his Mataura circle of clients the facility of doing business with him in their own town.

The next new arrival will be a doctor, to settle amongst us, who, in answer to an advertisement appearing in the Scotch papers, will soon be at Mataura.

Even in these go-ahead days, Mataura seems anxious to excel others in the rapid way she is putting up new buildings, tenders being already accepted, and the others preparing, for some twelve new residences, Mr. Tweedie's tender for a house being procured by Mr. Dempster, who has also put up a fine large shop in Bridge-street. He has also secured the building of Mr. Connor's house, Mr. Barclay's house, and Mr. Hay's house. Mr. Main secured the building of Mr. Scott's house, and Mrs. Bauchop's shop. Tenders for the other places will not be in till next week. It is quite a treat to see the way the townsfolk have wakened up to the capabilities existing, made by nature for them, and only requiring brains and money to bring, in time, great wealth.

We are glad to see Mataura's worthy stationmaster about again, after a very severe illness. He is again having quite a busy time with the trucks of timber arriving. We do not think he will have cause to grumble at dull trade the next time his balance sheet is made up.

(Southern Standard, 28/7/1893)

Obituary:
John MacGibbon Senior

It was reported in this journal a few days ago, that Mr MacGibbon Senr, had been attacked by illness while travelling by rail from Balclutha to Mataura on the 23rd inst., and that when the train by which he was a passenger reached Gore he was taken to the residence of one of his sons, Mr J. MacGibbon. Medical aid was promptly obtained, and the sufferer recovered somewhat, but the improvement was only temporary, and on Saturday morning the seizure, an effusion of blood on the brain, terminated fatally. By Mr MacGibbon's death, Southland loses one of its oldest residents, and the district of Mataura one of its pioneer settlers — one who through himself and his family, has left his mark on the place which was for so many years his home.

Mr MacGibbon, with a wife and young family, left Glasgow for New Zealand in 1849 forming one of the several ship's companies who under the auspices of the Free Church of Scotland, took part in the establishment of the Otago settlement. For some time after his arrival in Dunedin he carried on business as a store keeper, afterwards relinquishing this in favour of farming. In 1857 he came south and was among the first settlers in the Mataura district. His only neighbours being Mr McKellar at Longridge and Mr McNab at Croydon. Mr MacGibbon took up a piece of country now known as Glenure [then Otapiri] and engaged in stock farming for a time. He subsequently removed to Mataura Falls, where he spent the rest of his life.

In partnership with his sons, he established and carried on for many years an extensive mercantile business, with branches at Gore and Gordon. For some years after his settlement at "the Bridge" he also had an accommodation house, which proved a welcome place for travellers in the days where roads were practically unknown, and dwellings few and far between. In 1887, Mr MacGibbon, who had then passed the allotted span of three score and ten by some years, exchanged business activities for well earned repose, and had since led a quiet retired life. He enjoyed fairly good health till struck down by the illness which ended a long and useful career.

Mr MacGibbon, who was in his eighty third year when he died, was an elder of the Presbyterian church, which possessed in him a warm and liberal supporter. He was much respected in the district, and was esteemed by a very wide circle of friends.

Shrewd, painstaking and persevering, he combined in himself the qualities which make the successful colonist, and throughout all the changes of colonial life his business concerns prospered and when he ceased to take an active part in their management he did so with the knowledge that in his sons he had capable successors.

Mr MacGibbon is survived by his wife and five sons and one daughter, wife of Mr J. S. Shanks, and was pre-deceased by another married daughter, Mrs Miller. Three of the sons — John, Thomas and Ebenezer, carry on the business with which, as already indicated, they have been for many years; Archibald is in business as an auctioneer and stock agent in Mataura; and Colin occupies a responsible position in one of the banks in Invercargill.

Mr and Mrs MacGibbon were married on the 1st of November, 1838 [incorrect — it was 31 October], and they celebrated their golden wedding on the 14th of November, 1888, their date being altered from the 1st to admit of the presence of Mr T. MacGibbon who was returning from a visit to the Old Country. There was a notable gathering at Mataura on that occasion, people from all parts of the district assembling to assist at the interesting event. Over 200 guests were present in Humphries' Hall and a very pleasant evening was spent. Surrounded by his children and grandchildren, the subject of this notice, responding to the toast of his own and life-partner's health, delivered in a short and pithy address, in which reminiscences of his early life and some good advice to the younger of his hearers were happily mingled. His closing sentences have now a pathetic interest. His theme, appropriately enough, was marriage, and in the course of his remarks he advised young people to regard health as of the first importance. With it they could do life's work and the rule of life and of health was found in the Bible, which should have an honoured place in every home, and the reading a portion of which should be a family business. It was the life chart of the family — it fixed the principles of right and wrong; and no young people should marry unless they were at one on these; it gave promise of the life that now is, and held forth a glorious hope.

(Mataura Ensign, March 1892)

Home interests

Archibald Nairn MacGibbon's mother-in-law, Elizabeth Mair, built up a fat scrapbook full of newspaper clippings which had caught her interest. She regularly pasted in items from a column called 'Home Interests'. She did not name the newspapers she clipped from, nor the dates, but some are clearly from the mid 1890s. The Home Interests column was not from her local Invercargill daily, the Southland Times.

A RICH CHRISTMAS CAKE.—Take one pound of butter, twelve eggs, one quart flour, one pound sugar, three pounds currants, one pound raisins, half a pound almonds, half a pound candied peel. Beat the butter to a cream, stir into it the yolks of the eggs, which have been beaten with the sugar, then add almonds chopped fine, with half a pound of spice, now the flour ; add currants, raisins, chopped fine, and peel cut into strips. As each ingredient is added the mixture must be well beaten by hand. Put a buttered paper round the tin and bake for over two hours.

OATMEAL PANCAKES.—Oatmeal pancakes are good for breakfast, and may occasionally take the place of oatmeal in milk so universally served at that meal. Make them with sour milk, with soda to sweeten it. The batter should be stiff. The oatmeal, unless it is ground very fine, should be soaked in water all night.

BAKED APPLES.—A delicious way to prepare baking apples for tea is to cut out the core before baking. When ready to send to the table fill the space left in the apple with sweet cream with a little powdered sugar in it. Quinces are also excellent prepared in the same way. In these, butter may take the place of cream if more convenient.

DELICIOUS BREAKFAST DISH.—For any family of six take three cups of mashed potatoes, one-half a cup of flour, and half a tea-cup of sweet milk, two well-beaten eggs, a little salt ; mix well together, shape them small and drop into hot lard or roll them into little balls, and fry them in a wire basket of boiling lard.

CHESTER PUDDING.—One pint of flour, half a cup of sugar, three tablespoonfuls of cream of tartar, stir well together, place in a pudding boiler and steam an hour and a half over boiling water. Serve with rich wine sauce.

RASPBERRY SAUCE.—One cup and a-half of powdered sugar, quarter of a cup of butter, one cup of raspberry juice, made by pressing fresh fruit, or one cup of raspberry

jam. Stir butter to a cream, add the sugar and juice of one lemon, and last the raspberry juice or jam, beating all well together. Set on ice till wanted.

POTATO CAKES properly speaking should always be fried, never baked, and they are best made with hot potatoes, freshly boiled. Squeeze the potatoes lightly until no lumps remain, put one ounce of beef dripping to every pound, and mix with just enough flour and milk to bind it ; cut into cakes and fry in boiling dripping: drain on kitchen paper, and serve hot.

CHEESE PUDDING.—Take six ounces of grated cheese, a couple of eggs, one ounce of butter, a small tea-cupful of milk, and beat up all together in a basin ; then put them into a small baking dish and bake a light brown.

THE BROOM—If brooms are wetted in hot suds once a week they will last much longer, and always sweep like a new broom.

LEMONADE.—Three pounds of loaf sugar, two ounces tartaric acid, twenty drops essence of lemon, eight pints boiling water, a dessert-spoon of yeast ; bottle the day after making.

OATMEAL BISCUIT.—Take half a pound medium oatmeal, quarter of a pound flour, one dessertspoonful of baking powder ; mix with two ounces butter and half a gill of milk, made hot in a saucepan. Roll out quickly and bake it once in very thin cakes.

TO USE COLD MEAT.—A good way to save and use small slices of cold meat is to chop them fine, add some breadcrumbs, salt, and pepper ; moisten with milk, or with gravy of stock. Make this into flat cakes, dip them in egg, and fry them until brown ; or put the meat in a pudding dish or basin, press it for two or three hours, and slice it for tea.

PLAIN PUDDING.—One cup of molasses, one cup of sugar, one cup of milk, two-thirds of a cup of raisins, three cups of flour, a good tablespoon of cold butter, one teaspoonful of soda and a little salt. Steam three hours. This is very nice. I wish every family would try it and report results.

TO TAKE FAT OFF SOUPS, GRAVIES, JELLIES, &C.—Thoroughly wet a cloth, such as a glass cloth, with cold water, and pour the stock through it ; every particle of fat remains in the cloth, and your stock is as free from fat as if it had been allowed to get cold and the fat removed from the cake. This hint will be found very useful, especially where beef tea, soup, or jelly has to be prepared for invalids, which is often needed

in a hurry. The fat can be melted and clarified, and is quite as good when removed from the cloth as if taken off in a cake. For this information we are indebted to a lady friend in Scotland ; having tried and proved its perfect success, we gladly impart the information to your readers.

———

FACTS WORTH KNOWING

That salt fish are quickest and best freshened by soaking in sour milk.

That cold water and soap will remove machine grease from washable fabrics.

That fish may be scaled much easier by first dipping them into boiling water for a minute.

That fresh meat, beginning to sour, will sweeten if placed outdoors in the cool air overnight.

That milk which has been changed may be sweetened or rendered fit for use again by stirring in a little soda.

That boiling starch is much improved by the addition of sperm, or salt, or both, or a little gum arabic, dissolved.

That a tablespoon of turpentine boiled with your white clothes will greatly aid the whitening process.

That kerosene will soften boots and shoes that have been hardened by water, and will render them pliable as new.

That clear boiling water will remove tea stains ; pour the water through the stain, and thus prevent it spreading through the fabric.

That salt will curdle new milk, hence, in preparing milk porridge, gravies, &c., the salt should not be added until the dish is prepared.

That kerosene will make your tea-kettle as bright as new. Saturate a woollen rag and rub with it. It will remove stains from the clean varnished furniture.

That blue ointment and kerosene, mixed in equal proportions and applied to bedsteads, is an unfailing bug remedy, and that a coat of whitewash is ditto for a log house.

That beeswax and salt will make your rusty flatiron as clean and as smooth as glass. Tie a lump of wax in a rag and keep it for that purpose. When the irons are hot, rub them first with the wax rag, then scour them with a paper or cloth, sprinkled with salt.

———

MINT SAUCE.—Chop the mint fine, then pound it well in a mortar with white sugar or brown according to taste, and add the vinegar gradually, so as to make it into a sort of pultaceous mass, and not as it is often served, a mere dose of vinegar with a deposit of sugar at the bottom. The crushing and pounding of the mint with sugar brings out its flavour.

SARDINE TOAST.—Divide some sardines lengthwise, removing skins, bones, and tail; add a little of the oil from the tin, and put into the oven between two plates, letting them get quite hot. Take some thin strips of bread, the exact length of the sardines, fry them in butter, put half a sardine on each slice, sprinkle on cayenne and salt and a squeeze of lemon juice and serve very hot.

CREAM OF RICE SOUP.—Peel and slice three or four small potatoes. Slice one onion, add salt, a blade of mace, and a teaspoonful of chopped parsley, and one quart of hot veal or mutton stock, boil one hour, strain through a colander, pressing the potatoes into the stock ; add two cups full of hot cream, bring it to boiling point, add half a cupful of freshly boiled rice and serve quite hot.

MUTTON COLLOPS.—Cut some very thin slices from the leg or the chump end of a loin of mutton, sprinkle them with pepper, salt, pounded mace, a small bunch of minced savoury herbs, and minced shallot. Fry them in butter, stirring in a dessertspoon of flour, add half a pint of lour, and a tablespoonful of lemon juice ; simmer very gently about five or seven minutes and serve immediately.

POTATOES A LA PARISIENNE.— Peel the potatoes, and with a vegetable cutter cut as many little balls as possible from each potato ; put them in a wire basket and dip in boiling lard or drippings. Five minutes will fry them. Sprinkle salt over them when cooked, and serve them in a hot dish.

SAGO PUDDING.—Take fruit of almost any kind, apples, rhubarb, raspberries, blackberries, &c. ; stew until soft with water or not as required, and then add sufficient small sago to make it thick, and stew till all is a jelly. It is particularly nice made with rhubarb, and can be eaten hot or cold turned out of a shape.

RAISED MUFFINS.—Melt three tablespoonfuls of butter in three pints of new milk. Add three beaten eggs and a teaspoon of salt, when cold. Stir in flour to make a batter, as thick as you can well stir, add two tablespoonfuls of fresh yeast. When quite light, bake in muffin rings.

An experienced cook says that half a cup of vinegar in the water will make an old fowl cook nearly as quickly as a young one, and does not injure the flavour. The vessel in which it is cooked should be of a material that wine will not affect.

———

REMOVAL OF WARTS.—Warts may be removed by cauterisation. An ordinary pin is thrust through the base of the wart, care being taken not to wound the healthy tissue underneath. Then, the skin being protected, the head of the pin is heated in the flame of a candle. It is said that the wart becomes white and fissured in a few minutes, and comes away on the point of the pin. Dr. Cellier also says that it is only necessary to remove one wart on the hand—that though there may be a dozen, all the others will disappear without treatment.

———

HURRY SCURRY PUDDING.—Cut a stale French roll in slices rather more than ½ inch thick, and soak them in milk flavoured in vanilla or any other essence that may be liked. Place the slices on a strainer and then fry a bright golden-brown colour. Arrange neatly in a dish, and pour over all some jam sauce, or the slices can be served with powdered sugar instead of sauce. Any pieces of light bread can be employed in this way, only they should be all cut the same shape to ensure a neat appearance.

COVERING JAM JARS.—The easiest plan for covering jars is to pass the paper (any paper but newspaper or brown, though clean notepaper is the best) through white of egg—then smooth down on top of the jar by hand. No brandy or fat is needed, and the jam will keep as long as required, by a family at any rate. For travelling, use parchment or even linen in the same way.

TAPIOCA OMELET (VEGETARIAN RECIPE).— Ingredients: Four tablespoonfuls of tapioca, one pound of breadcrumbs, one tablespoonsful of dried sage, three ounces of onions. How made: Soak the tapioca in one and a quarter pints of cold water an hour, then boil half an hour. Mix together the breadcrumbs, sage, onions boiled and chopped fine. Stir in the tapioca, season with pepper and salt. Put in a brisk oven. Serve with brown or onion sauce.—Food Reformer's Cookery Book. ■

Making your own music at home: a popular family activity in the days before recorded music and television. Isabella MacGibbon was an accomplished pianist who loved to get together with her husband Thomas and 11 children, to play Scottish reels and sing songs of 'home' such as My Love is like a Red Red Rose, Kelvin Grove, Ye Banks and Braes, Lochnagarr, Afton Water, Caller Herrin' and Wae's for me Prince Charlie.

A COLONIAL ABROAD:

Descriptions of London in 1900 by Isabella MacGibbon, in letters to her children.

In 1900, Isabella MacGibbon and her husband Thomas travelled to Great Britain on the steamer Kumara. This was Isabella's first trip back 'Home' since she moved to New Zealand in 1867 as an 18 year old bride, fresh from a rather genteel Glasgow household. The 1900 visit may well have been her first ever to London. Thomas had been in the city at least twice before, the last having been on a business trip in 1888. These extracts largely omit family matters such as visits to relatives, and domestic comments and instructions to the eleven children left behind in Mataura. Isabella also visited Glasgow on this trip, but sadly her letters from there contain little other than Nairn family trivia. There is nothing like her breathless descriptions of London below; nor any comment about how it felt to be back in her home city for the first time since 1867.

**London
June 14th, 1900**

We were safe in dock early this morning and everybody was busy packing up until ten, when the Custom House Officer came on board to examine our luggage. He only opened Father's portmanteau, as I remonstrated with him about taking all the things out after I had packed them so carefully – and on deck, where everyone could see the different things. So he contented himself with marking off the other things.

Before we left the ship, we had a lot of goodbyes to say. I felt very sorry to part with our friends, for, notwithstanding my sickness, the voyage was very enjoyable. We had a good Captain and officers, a fine steady quick sailing boat, a good crew and stewards, and lastly a very agreeable company of passengers.

Mrs Dewar has been a friend to myself and everyone on board. Her father, General Hutcheson, and her brother and brother-in-law, came to the Docks to meet her – swells all three. Father and I were passing through the saloon, and she came up to us and said, Father, let me introduce my good Scotch friends, Mr MacGibbon and his wife. And she kissed me with tears in her eyes when we left. It would do you girls good to have seen how your father was appreciated on board the Kumara.

Mr Robson, a shipmate, came with us to this hotel, where we have a large bedroom looking on to the street, and I amused myself looking at the folks passing. In the afternoon, I had a rest on the sofa and Father showed Mr Robson 'round parts of the town. They came back for tea, and then we all went out. We travelled on the top of different cars and had a grand sight of the city and shops. They don't close here until late in the evening.

As far as I can see, there is not such a great difference between the fashions here and in New Zealand. The hats and shirts are more profusely trimmed – cornflower blue the

Portrait of Isabella MacGibbon taken about 1914.

prevailing colour, and blouses like you have are worn on the street. Of course I have not seen the fashionable promenades, but will let you know later on.

Father telegraphed to Aunt Jessie [Isabella's sister] and Robbie came in to see us in the evening. It was late, so he did not stay long. We are going out to see them today, the 16th, when father sees the business folk about money etc, but will not stay with Jessie, as we want to see everything we can before we go north – won't return to London until we are ready to sail for home.

Father and Mr Robson have gone out to find a more moderate hotel than this to stay at. The charges here are too high. Even a bath is charged 6d in the bill.

We went to Tooting in the electric underground tramway, but I did not like it. I felt exactly like what one does when inhaling the gas for tooth extraction. So next time I will go by train. Jessie was very pleased to see us, without making a fuss, and of course we talked of old times till further orders. Mr Aitken and Father got on all right, and had a walk on the Common while we talked. The photo of the family we got out is an excellent one of Jessie and Bob, but Robbie and Gertie have shot up and are quite different. So are Cathie and Cyril.

Gertie, although only 16, has her hair up and wears long dresses. She needs to, as she is employed in a large jewellery warehouse. She gets 9/- a week, and it costs her 6/- for train and tram to the city. She is a stylish looking girl and wears her hair like the others here, combed right up and twisted on top, the hair at the back being pulled quite loose down on the neck, and the short ends are confined with tortoiseshell buckles. Gertie's new dress is black for economical purposes and the whole of the neck down to the shoulders is cream satin covered with guipure lace. There is not much difference in fashions here for plain people. Kate's [Isabella's daughter] hat would be quite the thing, and those turban things like the one in the last Woman [probably Woman's Own magazine] at home are much worn, especially by old ladies with white hair.

Father and Mr Robson went to Mr Parker's church this morning. He is the minister who made the polite remark about the Sultan. They thought him too sensational a preacher and would not like to hear him more than once.

I stayed in resting till they returned, when we had dinner, then took the bus to Hyde Park, riding outside. I could fill sheets with what we saw there. The entrance is orna-mental stonework, and all about the grass are groups of rhododendrons in all colours. The Row was empty, the morning being the time for riders. We walked to the Serpentine, passing ponds with water lilies and other aquatic plants. We took a seat and watched the pleasure boats being rowed about, then we strolled across the grass to the opposite side, passing thousands of people.

About 3.30 the carriages began to arrive – and we had a seat again and watched them passing. Father admired the horses and looked at the people. I can't describe the dresses here, but they were like so many fashion plates, the hats being loaded with trimmings and such a mixture of colours, yet they looked well. Nellie's [daughter] pattern that she fancied is just the style for young girls. Every dress has a coloured or cream yoke. Elderly ladies have light veils in thin black material carried right down the front to the shirt. Girls wear one or two strings of small pearls round the neck over their blouses.

Tell Archie [son] to mangle his best trousers before wearing, as it is de rigeur to have a fold down the front, like new ones. Young Roberts of Dunedin dresses just like the swell Londoners.

One great feature of the Park is the babies and their nurses. The prams

The Handel Festival at London's Crystal Palace. (Illustrated London News, 20/6/1868)

are like small carriages with white covers trimmed with lace, and a canopy overhead. The nurses are all dressed in white piqué dresses and small bonnets with white ties — like the hospital nurses' bonnets, without the veils. Several infants had lovely carrying cloaks, one of thick corded silks with white drawn ribbon scalloped all round.

I have not been to any shops yet, as I am not able to find my way about, and Father has taken us on different buses to see the city.

I think I will finish my diary now, send it away, and defer further description till next week. Father got a list from Mr William here of places to see, and he is to get three tickets for the Handel Festival, where the prominent singers will perform. So that will be a treat for me.

Yesterday we took a river steamer and sailed up the Thames to Kew. After a short walk, we got into the gardens, which are so extensive that in two hours we only saw a corner of them. We saw rhododendrons and all sorts of shrubs in flower. One corner was devoted to irises of every shade and colour, and another to roses, but it is rather early for those last. There are also annuals. Everything is named, but of course one has not the time to make a note of the names. We were too late to see the orchid houses and ferneries, as they close them early, but we mean to go out again and see them.

We started off at two o'clock and

did not get back until 9.30. We returned on the top of the tram and bus, and came a new way here, passing the houses of the aristocracy and the home of Baden-Powell's mother. Baden-Powell is much made of just now. [He was a British general in the Boer War, which was then being fought.]

We passed the great Swan and Edgars drapers, whose windows were a dream of beauty. I have not been near enough to examine the things.

On our way, we got alongside the private carriages going to the theatre, and we could see the ladies inside. The dresses were lovely. One was of thin black stuff all glittering with blue spangles. Another was pink velvet and a lovely pink satin cloak with feather trimming. At one theatre we saw several ladies come out of the carriage on the street with cream brocaded satin dresses and opera cloaks, and their trains sweeping the pavements.

Today we are to hear Madame Albani at the Handel Festival. I will have to go in the dress and bonnet I already have, as I have no time to get new ones.

53 Guildford St
W C London
June 25th, 1900

My Dear Kate,

As promised in my last letter, I now write to you, and you can hand this round to the others.

On Saturday we had a great day at the Crystal Palace, leaving here at 10.30 by train. We got there in time to see part of the grounds and Palace before the Handel Festival commenced. We had reserved seats, which cost 15/- each. We enjoyed the music very much. Even Father was pleased. There was a 40 minute interval, and we walked about outside during that time.

The soloists were Misses Clara Butts (photo in the Woman at home), Samuel, and one other.

I liked Clara Butts best. She was married to Mr Mumford, had titled people at her wedding, and got some grand presents.

After the music was over, we went out into the grounds again, heard a band play, and saw crowds of lovely dresses. At six we had tea in the Palace at a small table, and then walked about, seeing the different courts, and the figures of natives of different countries.

At 9.15 the fireworks commenced, and they were magnificent. We paid 6d and got a nice seat on the terrace outside the Palace. I won't forget the sights of the grounds. Miles of lamps, green, yellow and red in fancy figures. There was a frame larger than the railway goodshed at Mataura, where they showed Gen. Bobs, the battleship Powerful, and a star – all in coloured fireworks. There were two ships, and you could see them firing guns. Two fountains played all the time, and the water turned different colours. The rockets were something wonderful. They shot up to different heights and showers of blue, amber, mauve and green lights fell from them. There was a bicycle race, with the figures all coloured lights. Once the whole top of the frame poured out lights in imitation of the falls of Niagara. Each night's fireworks cost £500.

I forgot to say that the Festival Choir numbered 4,000 and the orchestra 500, which gives you an idea of the volume of sound. The audience was 23,000.

Today Mr Robson, our shipmate, Father and I went out early to Hyde Park to see the riders in the Row. As we were entering the Park, we saw the "Blues" going to receive the

Khedive. Their uniform is blue, with a steel cuirass, and brass helmet with long scarlet plumes. They carry a sword and rifle and one had a battle-axe like those in old history pictures. They were the Second Lifeguards and were mounted on black horses.

After we were in the park, we saw all sorts and conditions of riders and Mr Robson and I thought they would never do to ride our NZ horses. A few ladies had good seats, but whether it was the horses or the girls I don't know, but they rose right up when the horses went past. Tell Eve that she is not to have a riding jacket made. Her blue cloth one is just the shape that all the ladies were wearing – if anything a little longer in the skirt. That cloth like Mary's costume will make the riding skirt, which is worn so short that the foot shows. The bun is the hats, and a few girls were sensible and wore white sailors. I think I only saw

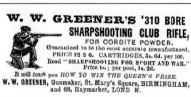
three tall hats among the hundreds of riders. The girls who had no gentlemen with them had a groom riding behind.

After sitting for a bit, we walked round, and saw the carriages and their occupants. We also saw the people on foot, and such a lot of lovely dresses I never saw before. Very delicate Pearl grey is a favourite colour. Picture hats trimmed with yards of silk chiffon or tulle and feathers ad lib. They set off the faces. That black hat Mary got for me is the very newest here, and every lady either wears a feather boa or ruffles like those Mrs Cameron wore when she called to say goodbye to me. I am wearing my blouse with the pink and my black dress, and feel quite dressed enough, as lots of ladies wear plain shirts. And of course others have frills or trimmings on the shirts. Today there were such lovely muslin skirts trimmed with lace. Frills worn by young and old ladies. For the summer you must have a white piqué dress with reefer jacket of the same.

June 24th

Miss Penny called this morning, and we went out together to see some of the shops. There is not as much difference in the prices as I had expected. Tailor-made suits are as dear as in Dunedin. We had strawberries and cream together in a shop in Regent Street. They were delicious.

After lunch, father, Mr Robson and I went off in the underground to see Madame Tussauds. We saw all the Transvaal heroes in wax. The group I liked most was a drawing room held by the Queen. A debutante was being presented in white brocade and satin, and most of the members of the Royal Family were standing around. The likenesses are so good that it is next best to seeing them in the flesh. The dresses were lovely, with pearl embroidery all over the front. There were long trains of brocaded satin, white veils and court plumes. The Duchess of Teck must have been an immense woman, if she is correctly represented. She has a blue velvet train with white petticoats. Her daughter, the Duchess of York,

bids fair to be like her. The young Prince Edward is there – a child of two years, in a lovely cot with blue silk hangings. I could fill pages with description, but I must refrain.

Leaving the Waxworks, we took a bus to Earl's Court to see the Women's Exhibition. Women do everything. They are in uniform, and they act as policemen and play in bands. One group of Welshwomen played very well, and another in Hussar uniform played brass instruments excellently. There are groups of women of all nations, and representations of their dwellings, where they sit at work, talking, reading or embroidering. Every few minutes, one lot will come forward and sing their native songs. They range from English, Scottish and Irish, to Japs, Russians and Soudanese.

The grounds are so immense that we could not go over it all, as I was tired after having been at the waxworks.

I am getting more used to the walking and the weather being cool, and get along not so badly. I will stay in this forenoon and rest, and we are going to St Pauls in the afternoon. We leave for Manchester tomorrow week, and even then we won't have seen all we want to.

The Khedive's visit has prevented us going to Buckingham, as no strangers are allowed there when Royal functions are on.

Miss Penny is to come for me again and go out round town. I expected Lizzie Graham to go with me to the R. Academy, but she has not turned up. We go out to Aunt Jessie's tomorrow and will leave a lot of things with her that we don't require till we go on board again. She had our washing done for us and it cost 7/-. We will want more done before we leave here. Everything gets so black with the smoke.

Give our love to all the girls, your own family and Jack's, kiss my two pets for me XXX and tell Grandma to keep her pecker up. Love to all the Uncles and Aunts, heaps to yourself and regards to all friends as if named.

your loving Mother
Isabella W. MacGibbon

FUNERAL NOTICE.

The Friends of the late JOHN MacGIBBON, Sen., of Mataura, are respectfully invited to attend his Funeral, which will leave the Residence of Mr. John MacGibbon, East Gore, THIS AFTERNOON (TUESDAY), at 1 o'clock sharp, for the place of interment in Mataura Cemetery. The Funeral will pass through Mataura about 3 o'clock p.m.

(Mataura Ensign 1/3/1892)

DEATH.

MacGibbon.—At East Gore, on Saturday morning, 27th February, John MacGibbon, sen., of Mataura, in his 83rd year.

(Mataura Ensign 1/3/1892)

FUNERAL NOTICE.

The Friends of the late MRS JOHN MacGIBBON, Sen., are respectfully invited to attend her Funeral, which will leave her Residence, Bridge Square, Mataura, at 2.30 p.m. on MONDAY, 15 July, for the Mataura Cemetery. Friends will please accept this, the only, intimation.

JAMES SMITH,
Undertaker.

(Mataura Ensign 13/7/1901)

DEATH.

MacGibbon.—On the 12th July, at Mataura, Jeannie, relict of the late John MacGibbon in her eighty-fifth year.

(Mataura Ensign 13/7/1901)

MUTUAL IMPS.

On Tuesday evening, the weekly meeting of the Mataura Debating Class was held, the Rev. J. M. Davidson in the chair. Mr. John MacGibbon, of Gore, delivered his paper on " Land nationalisation," which was spoken to very freely by the following gentlemen: Messrs. J. Lowden, Rogers, Brugh, Hall, Hamilton, J. S. Shanks, and Macandrew. A reading was given by Mr. Shanks. Vocal solos were rendered by Messrs. Hamilton and Stewart. A hearty vote of thanks was accorded to Mr. MacGibbon for his paper.

The usual meeting of the Gore Congregational Society, held on Wednesday evening last, was very well attended. The subject for the evening was a lecture by the President, entitled " Mrs. Grundy." The chair was occupied by Mr. A. Dolamore. Mr. Lewis was very happy in his lecture, as he criticised the customs and shams of society. Mrs. Grundyism, he said, in many respects was an obstruction to progress, and was very often ludicrous in its results. The lecture was interspersed with illustrations and anecdotes, which kept the audience in a good humour throughout. On the motion of Messrs. Drake and Smith, a hearty vote of thanks was accorded to Mr. Lewis

At Gore Presbyterian, on Tuesday evening, a debate took place on the subject, " Is the practice of reading novels beneficial or pernicious?"

(Southern Standard, 21/7/1893) (Mutual improvement societies, referred to as 'IMPs' by newspapers, were voluntary education associations, usually associated with churches.)

AN extended session of the Ivy Dancing Club took place last Wednesday evening at Mataura, when some 45 couples were present. Piano music was supplied by Mrs. Penny [nee MacGibbon], Misses MacGibbon (2), Cameron (2), Shanks, Fowler, and Messrs Blacklock and Dempster (violins). Mrs. Humphries supplied the refreshments to the entire satisfaction of the company. Mr. Arnett made an efficient M.C. The Club will hold a Fancy Dress Ball on the 29th September.

(Southern Standard, 29/8/1893)

WHAT FOLKS ARE SAYING :

That Dr. Hosking, Masterton, seeks patent rights for an " Anti-profanity Carriage Lamp."

That Hosking has apparently hit on something both morally and physically valuable.

That the Mataura Freezing Works has its second refrigerator almost ready for work.

That the Company will then be able to freeze about 750 sheep daily.

That the Mataura Dairy Factory Co. is in soundest financial condition of any similar factory in N.Z.

That average attendance at Gore School during fortnight ending Friday last was 126½

(Southern Standard, 29/8/1893)

THE monthly meeting of the Gore Gospel Temperance Society was held in the Temperance Hall on Tuesday evening. There was a fair attendance and Mr. J. MacGibbon occupied the chair. An address was given by Captain Locke, of the Salvation Army, who at the outset announced himself as being entirely in sympathy with the work, and was a staunch upholder of prohibition, as he believed that was the only sure remedy for doing away with what he considered was the greatest sin a man could commit (that of imbibing strong drink). The Captain dealt at length with the effect it had on the lives of people, and cited several cases that had come under his own observation, where young men had fallen victim to the vile habit of intemperance. He also spoke strongly of the billiard saloons of Gore, and said that drink was disposed of there, as well as in the public houses (" devil houses" was his term for them). He urged all to do their utmost to help out the work in Gore.

(Mataura Ensign, 1896)

Summoned to the Legislative Council

In July 1914, the Legislative Council heard its new member Hon Thomas MacGibbon's master plan for boosting New Zealand's population. A 'populate or perish' proponent, Thomas considered the main reason why New Zealand wives were not breeding fast enough was a serious lack of domestic assistance. Britain's spare women would fill the bill nicely.

At the same time, Thomas agreed with proposals to bring thousands of young men from the "Old Country" to work on farms. Eventually these British lads would team up with the female imports, and boost the Dominion's population even further. The MacGibbon speech came during a debate on the Masters and Apprentices Bill, which among other things, allowed for the immigration of teenage boys to be trained as farm labourers.

"If we had them [the women] coming here in streams, according to requirements, we would as they grew to maturity not only provide the lads with wives, but we would in the meantime provide the mothers of families, now so hard-pressed and enslaved, with the help that is so necessary for them," said the Hon Member.

Several other members referred to the domestic servant shortage, but Thomas MacGibbon was the only speaker who linked the problem to a procreation imperative. No-one followed his lead, and the issue of bringing in young women for training as domestic servants died, after Hon John Fisher, and Hon Francis Bell (leader of the Council and Minister of Immigration), pointed out that experience had shown it was impossible to keep girls down on the farm when they could take jobs in town and have their evenings free.

It had been pointed out that urban families would not take untrained servants, which left only farms as possibilities for taking the young women. England herself had a shortage of trained servants, and any who did want to emigrate, would prefer to go to Canada. The problem of who would take responsibility for single females aged between 15 and 18 was also raised.

Thomas MacGibbon practised what he preached: he had a maid and 11 children.

Called to Wellington

Earlier that month, Thomas MacGibbon had been summoned to Wellington to be a

"There are over a million unfortunate spinsters in Britain, who, through no fault of their own are forced to forgo all the happiness of conjugal rights. I want that million out here."

member of the Legislative Council, New Zealand's former upper house, by the Governor-General, Arthur William de Brito Savile, Earl of Liverpool.

The appointment was an honour, and a deserved reward for over 40 years of extensive public service in the Deep South. It was also convenient for the current Reform administration, which needed to tilt the political balance in the upper house in its own favour. Thomas came into the Council with eight other new Reform party appointees and two Reform Party reappointments. They would serve a standard term of seven years.

During Thomas MacGibbon's Council career, he spoke about 40 times, including a few occasions when he gave valedictory speeches about deceased parliamentary comrades. Given that his time on the Council was during the Great War of 1914-1918, it is not surprising that war issues dominated Thomas MacGibbon's speeches in the house.

He is revealed in the Hansard record as an arch-conservative who gave speeches which could be eloquent and flowery, but which often injected a tone of practical pioneer commonsense.

Patriotism

Most parliamentarians of the period were strong on patriotism, war effort and the British Empire, but Thomas was more rabid than most. He was also virulently anti-German.

He was a strong supporter of military conscription. Speaking to the Defence Amendment Bill in October 1915, he said, "If we want to get the men that we ought to have in a crisis like this – where speed is essential to success – we must have conscription. I am sorry the Government did not embrace the opportunity...to add the power to enforce conscription, so as to bring in shirkers and others who have no desire to exert themselves in this patriotic way..."

Portrait of Thomas MacGibbon taken when he joined the Legislative Council in 1914.

He did not support exemptions on concientious grounds: "It may be a matter of principle in some cases, but there is a spice of cowardice in it, and one feels sorry for a man possessed of such a constitutional or mental aberration."

Up the Empire

Preserving the British Empire was paramount. "We must maintain the Empire at all hazards, even if it means we old men must be called on to handle a rifle. I do not know that I could handle the fatigue very well, but I could still shoot and account for a German or a Turk."

Thomas strongly supported one of the more shameful legislative actions of the 1915 Parliament – a special bill which forced Professor von Zedlitz to resign from Victoria University College on the grounds that his father was German.

Said Thomas, "...he has not us to blame for his position. He has to blame the duplicity and treachery of his own race."

Thomas amplified his feelings about the German race in a 1917 debate on the war. The problem with the Germans was that they were a people "...besotted, a people trained from their infancy to bow their wills to those who rule over them...they are willing to follow [their leaders] absolutely, as they have proved over and over again."

The American entry into the war in 1917 got the Thomas MacGibbon seal of approval. Although critical of their tardiness, he was prepared to forgive and forget: "I have great faith in them. They are given a bit to bragging, but the Yankee is at bottom an Anglo-Saxon, and I believe that blood will tell...I believe that beneath that brag there is a great deal of ability and courage, and that when you scratch an American you find a Britisher."

Fair play

On one occasion, a strong feeling for fair play nearly overcame his moral convictions. The question was whether to give the Wellington Racing Club extra racing days to compensate for days lost while its racecourse was used as a military camp. Though he was a Presbyterian, Thomas had a deep feeling that a racing club was entitled to justice and fair play.

Another member, Hon Mr Barr, chivvied him. Reported Hansard: "He [Barr] was astounded that the honorable gentleman, coming from the country he did, from the part of the Dominion he did, and from the Church that he did, should stand up in the Council and boost up a racing club."

Thomas changed his tune and voted with Barr (and the minority) against the proposal.

Other subjects

Drawing on his long experience in local body administration, Thomas MacGibbon spoke several times on regional issues including local body reform, rabbit and river control and power boards.

Speaking to the Treaties of Peace Amendment Bill in 1919, he gave a long discourse on how to develop Samoa, which had become a New Zealand responsibility after the defeat of Germany. Thomas had visited Samoa and the Cook Islands with a parliamentary group earlier in the year, and he had been there with another parliamentary group in 1895. ∎

Something of an old man's home

The Legislative Council was abolished in 1950, and since that time New Zealand has operated a unicameral parliamentary system – in other words, it has only a single parliamentary chamber, which is called the House of Representatives. The Legislative Council was established in 1852, although it did not meet until 1854. Initially members were nominated for life, but this was changed to seven years in 1891.

The idea of having nominated people in an upper house was never very popular in New Zealand – it tended to go against the egalitarian pioneer grain. At the very start, Wellington's *Southern Cross* newspaper had warned the Council would be "...an assembly of Noodles and Nominees." The *Wellington Independent* had described the concept as "...absurd – so childishly, savagely, brutally absurd."

Being appointed to the Council was a little like being appointed to the United States Supreme Court – you were there for a long stretch, so the government of the day nominated members who would be sympathetic to Administration policies. If lower house bills seemed likely to be rejected by the Legislative Council, the government of the day tended to appoint new members to even up the balance. Long-serving Liberal premier Richard Seddon's appointments reeked particularly of patronage and expediency.

After the 1911 election, the new Reform Party government, under Prime Minister Bill Massey, had its chance to redress the balance and did. It initiated a bill designed to reform the Legislative Council by making its members directly elected, under a proportional representation system. There would also be three appointed Maori members.

In order to make sure the bill was passed, in 1914 the Reform Government appointed nine new sympathisers, and reappointed two retiring Reform supporters for further terms. Thomas MacGibbon was one of the nine new appointees, but he claimed vehemently that he was no mouthpiece for the Government. In his first speech to the Council he said he had advocated Council reform, including direct elections, for the previous ten years. "I rise to repudiate a suggestion…that the new members appointed to this Council are prepared to go on their hands and knees and do as they are told…I have never been led by anyone."

While the Legislative Council Act was passed, it was never brought into operation, being delayed by a series of amendment acts.

After the new appointments of 1914, the Council had around 30 members. Numbers fell by the wayside as members retired and died, and by 1918 there were only 20 left. One of them, first appointed in 1861, was 90 years old. Three were in their 80s, and there were rarely more than 15 members in attendance.

The average age of the 1914 appointees was 70 years. Thomas MacGibbon was 75, and two others were 77. The Council had a deserved reputation as an old man's home. Between 1911 and 1935, 69 per cent of members were more than 60 years old, compared with 19 per cent in the House of Representatives.

And it was a home for old *men*. Although women had been given the vote in 1983, they were still not permitted to stand for parliament. No women members entered the House of Representatives until 1933, while the first two women were nominated to the Legislative Council in 1947. Their presence had been agreed to in principle by the Council in 1914, but not authorised by statute until 1941.

Crusty old Thomas MacGibbon opposed the notion of women in either chamber.

After 1920 the system of patronage – particularly for rewarding retired members of the lower house and other political cronies – became more endemic. During the Labour period of 1935 to 1949, the position of MLC was largely a sinecure for old party functionaries, and the Council became less and less active.

Role of the Legislative Council

Its most important role was to revise legislation from the House of Representatives – drafting corrections, improvements and correcting anomalies which had escaped lower house attention. It didn't even do much of this. For example, in 1916, only 19 per cent of Government bills were amended.

Since the mid 1890s, the principle had been firmly established that the Council was not to interfere in policy matters unless asked. The only time it asserted itself was between 1912 and 1914, in the matter of its own reform.

The Council had the power to reject bills from the Lower House, but rarely did so. Richard Seddon made the mistake of relying on the Council to reject the womens' franchise in the Electoral Bill of 1893. Seddon had publicly supported the bill in the lower house, but he hoped the Council would later reject it, thus keeping his own hands clean. He lost the gamble and was reported to have threatened physical violence to the Council leader after the votes were counted. ∎

Scene outside Parliament Buildings in Wellington on 4 August 1914, when the Prime Minister, Bill Massey, announced the declaration of war with Germany. Thomas MacGibbon had joined the Legislative Council only two weeks earlier. Massey is the stocky balding man in the centre with a silver moustache. (Alexander Turnbull Library)

PEOPLE

Thomas MacGibbon family: back row, L-R: Archie (1877-1947), Colina (1872-1956), John (1870-1945), Kate (1869-1943), Mary (1873-1943). Middle row, L-R: Thomas Arthur (1878-1958), Eve (1875-1963), Thomas (1839-1925), Isabella (1848-1923), Nell (1882-1958), Ernie (1881-1933). Front row, L-R: Roy (1885-1947), Jessie (1884-1932).

Three generations, ca 1870: Jane MacGibbon (1817-1901) with her granddaughter Nell Shanks (1868-1953) at left, and sons Colin (1861-1928), seated and Archie (1856-1935), standing.

John MacGibbon Jr family. L-R: Frank (1887-1952), Gordon (1885-1953), John Jr (1849-1925), Dave (in front, 1892-1973), Mataura (1879-1947), Mary (1861-1912), Mabel (1883-1955), Hugh (1881-1969), Bill (1890-1958).

Four generations in 1894. Left to right: Kate Penny (nee MacGibbon, 1869-1943), Alicia Penny (1894-1970), Isabella MacGibbon (1848-1923), Jane MacGibbon (1817-1901).

Ebenezer MacGibbon family. Back row, L-R: Florence (1883-1975), May (1883-1951), Maud (1881-1951), Stanley (1892-1956). Front row, L-R: Ida (1885-1971), Ebenezer (1854-1915), Mary (? -1931), Hilda (1889-1982).

Jessie Shanks (nee MacGibbon) with her youngest children. L-R: Charles (1872-1944), Jessie (1842-1920), Colina (1876-1955), Bessie (1874-1944). Jessie's children not in the photograph were James, John, Jean, Nell and Bell.

John MacGibbon Sr (1809-1892) with his son Thomas (1839-1925), grandson John (1870-1945) and daughter Kate (1869-1943), ca 1871.

James Steuart Shanks II (second from right), yarning with friends in Mataura.

An old family friend: Rev J M Davidson, Presbyterian Minister in Mataura, 1877-1903. He also preached at Gore until 1884.

John Jr (left) with friends and family in 1912, being farewelled on a grand but tragic trip to the USA, Canada and Europe. His wife, Mary, died of pneumonia in Winnipeg during the trip. Eldest son Hugh (right centre rear) and a daughter were also on the voyage. This was John Jr's only major trip overseas, although he went to Australia several times. His brother Thomas was a keen traveller, in days when trips were long and arduous. Thomas visited the UK four times. First to seek a wife in 1867, then in 1888 on a business trip. In 1900 he combined business with a holiday, and took his wife Isabella. Then in 1910, Thomas, Isabella and their daughter Colina sailed to the UK once more, for the coronation of George V. Thomas also visited Argentina and Australia, and travelled twice to the Cook Islands and Samoa.

Mary Milne, Isabella MacGibbon's maid at Bowmore House.

The Gore Presbyterian Young Women's Hockey Club team in 1907. Back row sixth from left, Maud MacGibbon; second from right, May MacGibbon; front row, fourth from left, Ida MacGibbon; far right, Mabel MacGibbon. (Hocken Library)

The first house built in East Gore by John MacGibbon Jr (Rock Street). Left to right: (a cousin), Mabel, John Jr, Dave (being held by John Jr), Bill, Mary, Gordon (sitting on the post), Hugh (standing in front of the post), Frank. The picture was taken in 1893.

From a family album, this is believed to be Jane MacGibbon's house – it appears to be her sitting on the verandah. The photograph was probably taken in the 1890s after Jane was widowed.

Houses for worship – very familiar territory for the early MacGibbon families. Left: Mataura Presbyterian church (replaced in 1934). Below: East Gore Presbyterian Church.

John MacGibbon Jr's last home in Gore, known as Te Whakahua. Built about 1907, it had 13 living rooms, including three bedrooms on the ground floor and six bedrooms upstairs – crammed full of heavy Victorian furniture. There was an extensive library, a comprehensive collection of stuffed birds in glass cases, and the walls were adorned with numerous paintings, including at least one Goldie. In 1948 the house was sold by the family to the Presbyterian Social Services Association, which converted it into an orphanage called Inglenook. The structure was demolished in 1967. The turret in the right foreground survived the wrecker's hammer and now stands alone as a holiday cottage on a property at Piano Flat in Northern Southland. The house was situated in Huron Street, close to the family's beloved Presbyterian Church, which can be seen to the left rear.

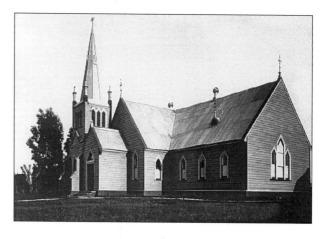

Bowmore House, Thomas MacGibbon's home in Mataura between the late 1870s and 1909. The photograph on the left shows the original shape of the house, which was extensively modified and enlarged to contain the expanding family of eleven children. The 1888 photograph of the extended MacGibbon clan on the occasion of John and Jane's golden wedding (page 198) was taken on the front verandah of the original structure. While Bowmore had grown like Topsy and lacked the style of John Jr's house in Gore, it was commodious. There were five bedrooms, a big dining room, lounge, kitchen with large scullery and a long hallway. A wash house and toolshed were among several outbuildings. Thomas MacGibbon was known to abhor ostentation, and the furnishings and interior decoration would have been less grand than those in his brother John's home.

Family members who died as children were: *Hugh (4/7/1841–19/11/1841) & David (14/11/1851–20/3/1858)*

John MacGibbon Sr
(4/9/1809–27/2/1892)
Jane McConachy
(6/7/1817–12/7/1901)

John was a tobacconist, grocer and tea/coffee dealer in Glasgow; merchant and farmer in Dunedin; farmer, ferryman, hotelier, merchant in Southland (mainly in Mataura).

Thomas MacGibbon
(9/10/1839–27/9/1925)
Isabella Nairn
(16/5/1848–30/6/1923)
Hon Thomas MacGibbon, MLC, JP, lived in Mataura and later Dunedin. Head of MacGibbon & Sons, Mataura branch of MacGibbon & Sons. Member of Legislative Council 1914–1921 (Reform Party). Mayor of Mataura. Chairman of Southland County Council, Southland Education Board, Mataura Dairy Company. Member of Otago University Council, Southland Hospital and Charitable Aid Board, Elder, Mataura Presbyterian Church and Sunday School Superintendent for 31 years.

Jessie MacGibbon
(19/10/1842–19/2/1920)
James Steuart Shanks II
(1835–13/10/1911)
Lived in Mataura. James Shanks, and Sons, with his brother Ebenezer, earlier farming on the Maraiina Run near Tuturau, was a land agent, auctioneer, chairman of the Southland County Council and Member of Parliament for Mataura, 1878–1881.

Jeannie MacGibbon
(31/12/1844–26/6/1886)
James Miller
Jeannie and James farmed at Islay Station, a short distance south-east of Mataura.

Ebenezer MacGibbon
(9/4/1854–3/6/1915)
Mary Priscilla Latham
(?–1931)
Ebenezer MacGibbon co-founded, and managed the East Gore branch of MacGibbon and Sons. Active in the Presbyterian Church.

John MacGibbon Jr
(28/3/1849–7/3/1925)
Mary Ward
(19/12/1861–22/12/12)
John MacGibbon Jr, JP, founded the Gore branches of MacGibbon and Sons, with his brother Ebenezer. He was mayor of Gore, chairman of the Southland County Council, Gore Dairy Company and Southland Hospital and Charitable Aid Board, president of the Gore Gospel Temperance Society and a member of the Southland Hospital Board, Gore Liberal League and Masonic Lodge. He was an elder of the East Gore Presbyterian Church.

Archibald Alexander MacGibbon (Archie)
(7/10/1856–25/10/1935)
Georgina (Tot) Begg
(1866–16/4/1960)
Archie MacGibbon was manager of the Gore branch of National Mortgage & Agency Co Ltd; mayor of Gore; member Southland Electric Power Board and Masonic Lodge; long-time president of the Gore Tennis Club.

Colin MacGibbon
(24/8/1861–2/6/1928)
Emily Frances Hawson
(25/1/1867–12/11/1917)
Colin MacGibbon was a banker, with the National Bank in Invercargill and Dunedin, and with the Bank of New South Wales in Invercargill, Dunedin, Gore, Oamaru and lastly Dannevirke. Active in the Presbyterian Church.

Education: the ultimate legacy

There is an old Chinese proverb about family economic development: "For yourself, plant rice. For your children, educate. For your grandchildren, plant trees."

Old John MacGibbon Sr almost followed the proverb. He laid a strong foundation for business prosperity. And if the trees he planted were beginning to rot by the end of the second generation, he certainly saw the benefits of education for his children and *their* heirs.

The family had been relatively wealthy within its small patch in the deep south of New Zealand. But even if that wealth had been retained and expanded, its value today would have been well diluted among the many hundreds of descendants. A far more powerful legacy has passed down the generations – a family culture which values education.

John MacGibbon Sr had some education – he could calculate, read and write, and he expressed himself well. He brought up his children in an isolated part of New Zealand during a pioneering time when only limited formal schooling was possible, but he showed his belief in education by engaging a live-in tutor.

His children had a continuing thirst for knowledge and ideas, and two involved themselves heavily in local and regional education through membership of school boards, the Southland Education Board, and the Otago University Council. They in turn sent several of their own children on to higher education back in Scotland.

Today in 1997, the adult descendants of John and Jane MacGibbon are extraordinarily well educated when compared with the national average. One third of all descendants aged 20 years or more have university degrees – a proportion that is almost nine times higher than the national average of 3.7 per cent. (The national average is from the latest available census figures, for 1991. The 1996 census figures, when available, are likely to show a rate significantly higher than 3.7 per cent, because the proportion of school leavers going on to university has increased over recent years. However the national rate will still be much lower than the MacGibbon family rate.)

In most countries there is a strong correlation between levels of education and general prosperity. The MacGibbon family came to New Zealand as middle class immigrants, bringing with them both a personal education and a typically Scottish reverence for education.

The family has remained overwhelmingly middle class. They are generally prosperous, though few if any are filthy rich. The family genealogical database shows that probably 80 per cent of working adults are in middle class occupations requiring at least some tertiary education – teaching, medicine, business, nursing, science, engineering, banking,

Thomas MacGibbon in 1920, when he was the Southland Education Board's nominee on the University of Otago Council. Though having limited formal education himself, Thomas was involved in education administration for nearly 50 years.

journalism, home science, music, law, accountancy and so on.

One strong cultural characteristic of the early MacGibbons – their Presbyterian piety – has not lasted as well as education. The first two generations were heavily, narrowly religious, even by the standards of their day. These attitudes began to weaken by the third generation, and most of today's fifth and sixth generations seem little different than the general population, in being largely secular in their outlook. ∎

Distribution of adult MacGibbon relatives, 1997

Auckland City 23%

Provincial North Island 10%

Wellington City/ Kapiti Coast 22%

Nelson/ Marlborough 6%

Christchurch

Canterbury 31%

Otago 5%

Dunedin

Southland 4%

Invercargill

Auckland

Wellington

Overseas
Australia 6%
UK 5%
Other countries 3%

Where are they now?

The MacGibbon family put its first roots down in the southern extremity of New Zealand, but is now spread throughout the country. Most family members – 55 per cent – now live in the North Island. This is still lower than the overall North Island population share, which is 75 per cent.

There has been a strong move north from the original provinces of Otago and Southland, and four out of every five relatives remaining in the South Island live between Christchurch and Nelson.

The move north began early, and the only MacGibbons buried in the Mataura Cemetery are the 'originals': John and Jane.

By the third generation, almost the only family still in Southland were those directly managing the merchant businesses, or engaged in farming. Today the only relatives left in the province are farmers and retired farmers, who have prospered on the best pastoral farmland in New Zealand.

Christchurch has more relatives than any other city, largely due to the high fecundity of a branch of the family descended from Thomas MacGibbon's eldest son, John. ∎

Appendices

- Timeline of major events in the family history of the first two MacGibbon generations in New Zealand.

- Report of Dr William Purdie, Surgeon Superintendent on board the ship Mooltan.

- MacGibbon family ancestors in Scotland – tracing the generations back to 1620.

- Where did they come from – information about the Scottish origins of the family, the name and the clan.

- Mac/McGibbon births and/or baptisms throughout Scotland, 1600-1855, recorded in the Old Parochial Registers.

- Bibliography.

TIMELINE

1809	John MacGibbon Sr born.
1817	Jane MacGibbon born.
1838	John and Jane MacGibbon married.
1839	Thomas born.
1841	Hugh born (dies 4 months later).
1842	Jessie born.
1844	Jeannie born.
1849	John Jr born.
1849	The MacGibbon family emigrates to New Zealand. (Embarks at Greenock on 11 September (ship anchors overnight and sails next day); arrives at Port Chalmers on 26 December.)
1850	MacGibbon store established on the corner of Stafford and Princes streets, Dunedin.
1851	David born.
1854	Ebenezer born.
1856	Archie born.
1858	(January) John Snr and Thomas travel to Otapiri Station, Southland. Return to Dunedin in July.
1858	(December) MacGibbon family travels by bullock wagon to Mataura, Southland, where they are contracted by the Otago Provincial Government to establish a river ferry and accommodation house.
1861	Colin born.
1866	MacGibbons purchase Kelvingrove Run in the Hokonui Hills.
1867	Thomas travels to Glasgow, Argentina, then back to Glasgow, where he marries Isabella Nairn.
1872	MacGibbons establish general store in Mataura.
1878	John Jr and Ebenezer MacGibbon establish branch store at East Gore.
1878 – 1889	Thomas on the Southland County Council; chairman 1883-84.
1882 – 1895	Period of the Mataura Town Board's existence. Thomas a member and chairman.
1883	Additional store established in Main Street, Gore.
1883	John Jr on the Gore Town Board
1886	John Jr mayor of Gore.
1887 – 1910	Thomas director Mataura Dairy Factory; founding chairman in 1887.
1888	Thomas travels to the UK on a marketing trip for Mataura Dairy Factory Company.

1888	Stones Directory advertisement for John MacGibbon and Sons, Mataura, Gore and Gordon; describes the business as "general merchants, grain dealers, commission agents etc, agents for sawmills, brickfields, national Fire and Marine Insurance Company, &c., &c., &c.".
1890 – 1891	John Jr mayor of Gore.
1890	Isabella's brother, artist James Nairn, emigrates to New Zealand from Glasgow, lives initially with MacGibbons in Mataura; paints several family members.
1892	John Sr dies.
1893	John Jr canvasses in support of women's electoral emancipation.
1894	Prospectus issued for MacGibbon's Cooperative Stores Association, capital sought £40,000. Not successful.
1895 – 1903	Thomas on Mataura Borough Council as councillor or mayor. (Mayor 1898-1902)
1897 – 1902	Archie on Gore Borough Council as councillor or mayor. (Mayor 1901-1902)
1898	John Jr chairman of Gore Dairy Factory Co.
1899	Thomas chairman of Southland Education Board.
1899	John Jr co-founder of Gore Liberal League.
1901	Jane dies.
1903	MacGibbon and Company Ltd, Gore, registered as public company.
1905	John MacGibbon and Sons, Mataura, registered as private company.
1905	Thomas stands unsuccessfully for Parliament as Opposition candidate, losing to sitting Liberal member, Robert McNab.
1906/08/09	Archie mayor of Gore.
1911	John Jr stands unsuccessfully for Parliament as an Independent Liberal.
1913 – 1920	Thomas on Otago University Council.
1914 – 1921	Thomas a Reform Party appointee to the New Zealand Legislative Council.
1925	John Jr, then Thomas, die.
1938	John MacGibbon & Sons Ltd, Mataura, in liquidation.
1944	John MacGibbon & Sons Ltd, Mataura, wound up.
1951	East Gore branch of MacGibbon and Company Ltd closed.
1962	Main Street (Gore) branch of MacGibbon and Company Ltd closed.

Report to Captain Cargill by Dr William Purdie, Surgeon Superintendent on the ship Mooltan

Ship Mooltan, Port Otago
26th December 1849

Sir,

Agreeably with the instructions of the Court of Directors of the New Zealand Company, I beg to hand you a list of the Passengers of all classes who sailed from Greenock under my care, and also a list according to the form prescribed by the Directors, of the deaths which took place during the voyage. It is my painful duty to inform you, that Cholera, which was prevailing to an alarming extent in Greenock, as well as over various parts of England and Scotland when we sailed, broke out on board the "Mooltan" on the 21st September when we were in Latitude 31.27 North, and prevailed in many of its most alarming symptoms till we crossed the Line on the 18th October. You will observe from the accompanying table of deaths that from the 25th September till the 15th October there were nine deaths from Cholera.

The deaths in Greenock from Cholera at the time we left were so numerous that every effort was made to conceal the number. The person who engaged to go as Second Mate in the "Mooltan", fell a victim to it a short time before we sailed, as did also one of the Carpenters who was working on board. Captain Chivas was very anxious to get the vessel out of the Harbour lest any of the emigrants should come in contact with the disease on their arrival. Capt. Reaves [?] was himself taken ill with some of the symptoms the night before we sailed and could not come off, as he intended, to bid us good bye.

No symptom however appeared on board until the morning of the 21st September. We had a good deal of seasickness from the time we left till the 20th. I had occasion during that time to reduce dislocation of the under jaw twice, occurring during vomiting in seasickness.

There were also, it is true, a great many cases of Diarrhoea, but there was nothing in any one case different from what is common on shipboard arising, I believe, in a great measure from change of diet and mode of living.

It is also true that McNeil's child's case looked very suspicious, seeing that she died from disease, the prominent symptoms of which were vomiting and purging, lasting all the time till her death. She died from exhaustion, no treatment having the slightest effect on the disease. The mother of the child took ill next morning, with well marked symptoms of Cholera.

It would have afforded me much pleasure to have furnished you with a daily statement of cases occurring during the time that Cholera prevailed on board, had it been possible for me to note the daily or hourly treatment, but that was utterly out of my power. From the time the disease made its appearance among us until it left, I had not a moment's relaxation. There was also another reason why my time was so much occupied, there was no person on board whom I could appoint as my assistant – so that I had both the preparing, as well as the administering of the medicines, and my own health suffered much in consequence.

The following is a brief abstract of the cases which proved mortal and also of the general state of the ship during the period above referred to.

Mrs. McNeil, already mentioned, died about two P.M. same day. The weather had become warm, and there were a good many cases of Diarrhoea. I made a careful examination of all the emigrants and urged upon all the necessity of informing me of the very first appearance of bowel complaint or other derangement of the system.

On the 24th we were off the Island of Teneriffe, in an almost dead calm, the weather becoming very hot and sultry, and the sickly state of the passengers increasing so that my time was spent almost entirely below.

On the 26th at 8.P.M. Mrs. Barr, aged 48, was seized with Cholera. All the most prominent symptoms ceased about 2.A.M. and there was much reason to anticipate a favourable termination, until 11.A.M. when she suddenly started up in bed and laid her hand over her heart exclaiming "I am gone" and died.

I had reason, from the previous state of the pulse, to suspect disease of the heart in her case. I may remark that this person was dancing on deck the night previous.

Many of the passengers now began to exhibit latent symptoms of Cholera. These were a strange painful numbness over all the body, with a tendency to take cramp in their legs and arms when bent. The nearest that I can describe the sensation of numbness, is to that painful feeling experienced when a limb is coming out of that state commonly called 'sleeping'. Some felt as if a discharge of electricity had been received.

The other symptoms were, a most oppressive sensation in the brain, suppression of Urine, a feeling of a heavy load at the Stomach and Heart, Bowel Complaint, overwhelming lassitude and disinclination for exertion.

On the 29th we were in Latitude 20 North, Longitude 19.20 W, the thermometer standing at 85. Two baths were fitted up one for the Adults and one for the children. All the children became affected by 'Prickly heat'. Some adults also became affected by it to such an extent, so as to produce rawness over the surface.

A child of Mr. Geo. Perkins, a full paying Steerage passenger, was at that time dangerously ill with inflammation of the brain – became quite blind with all the usual symptoms of Hydrocephalous. He recovered.

On the 1st October the heat had become so intense that the passengers in the Fore Cabin and Steerage Berths could not endure being below. It therefore was found necessary to provide sleeping accommodation for them on the Poop.

On the 3rd Mr. Geo Perkins, the father of the child above mentioned, was seized with Cholera at 3.A.M. and died after 6.P.M.

Mr. Peter Harrison was seized shortly after Mr. Perkins and died about 10.P.M.

Mrs. Harrison, wife of the last

named Patient, was seized about an hour after her husband and died an hour before him.

After the death of these three individuals, I visited the rest who were then ill, and returned to my cabin to see my own dying infant whom I had scarcely seen since morning. (She died next day – had been ill for some time with disease of the Stomach and Bowels.) I may be permitted to remark that the 3rd was a dreadful day – three deaths in so short a space, and the mysterious disease busy amongst our entire population – scarcely one being free from some symptom or other of it.

On the 6th, Mrs. Proudfoot was seized about 10.A.M. and died at 6.P.M.. Her sufferings were dreadful.

On the 7th, Jeannie Gebbie, aged one year, was seized about 8.P.M. She died on the 8th at 8.A.M. On the same evening Mrs. Kirkland was seized, became quite black, and died at 5.P.M. on the 8th.

On the morning of the 8th while engaged with the last patients, James Gebbie, aged 5 years, was seized the same as his sister. His eyes sunk at the outset. He recovered. I may state that he took convulsion fits after the vomiting and purging ceased, but the kidneys did not resume secretion for a considerable time. He is now quite well.

While I was engaged with the three last cases, the thermometer stood at 89 below. I remained with them from the commencement to the termination.

My wife was now seized with very alarming symptoms – the kidneys had ceased to secrete. Constant and urgent action of the bowels with great oppression of the Brain and numbness over all the body. She ultimately recovered.

One of my daughters – 3 years – was seized with Brain fever, from the effects of the Sun. She recovered, but very slowly.

On the 11th we were in dead calm, with close cloudy weather. The First Mate was seized with Cholera for the second time – and cramped all over. He recovered.

On the 14th, the infant child of Mrs. Kirkland died. She had gradually declined since her mother's death.

On the 15th, Agness Peterson – aged 5 – was seized early in the morning with Cholera – and died at 4.P.M. This was the last case of Cholera which terminated in death, altho many still laboured under the symptoms described above.

On the 17th there were strong breezes and the weather more pleasant, and from the time we crossed the equator, a slow but steady improvement took place in the general health of all on board, with the exception of specific cases of other diseases.

I may remark that it was the opinion of every person of experience and observation on board – as well as my own – that had we remained a few days longer under the same atmospheric influence, the consequences must have been dreadful, it is impossible to calculate the amount of mortality which must have taken place from the weak state to which many were reduced. I for one, was so weak that it was painful for me to walk.

On the 17th Dec. Clarinda Harrison aged 9 months died of Hooping Cough (sic) – which disease prevailed on board from the beginning of October. Almost every child who had not had the disease previously, took it. Four of my children are now ill with it.

During the whole of the voyage there was a tendency to suppuration in cases of injury. Even the slightest scratch of a pin produced it. Besides the Prickly Heat formerly mentioned, the children of all classes suffered afterwards from small blisters breaking out over all the body. Dry scald also broke out upon some of the children and boils upon many of the Adults. But all disease excepting Hooping Cough disappeared a considerable time before we reached the Port, and it is the opinion of all who have seen the passengers that a cleaner and more healthy ship never entered Port Otago.

I cannot conclude this imperfect abstract without expressing the high opinion I have formed of Capt. Chivas. Nothing could express his care and kind attention to all on board and more specially during the trying circumstances we were in during the Voyage. He was always at hand to support and aid me and never shrank from accompanying me in visiting the Cholera Patients.

In presenting the document in support of my claim to remuneration granted by the Court of Directors of the New Zealand Company to the Surgeon Superintendent, I beg to call your attention to the following paragraph in the printed table of Emoluments. "Subject to a deduction of Twenty Shillings for every death."

This rule, wisely intended no doubt to act as a stimulus to the faithful discharge of duty in ordinary circumstances would, if adhered to in the present case, be a grievance of no ordinary kind, when it was considered that my life was exposed and that in the very unfavourable situation of 'tween decks' for such a length of time, to one of the most formidable and mysterious diseases which medical men have at any time been called to contend with. It ought also to be borne in mind that, as stated in the Abstract, I had to perform the duties which properly belonged to Surgeon's Assistant, during the voyage.

I have the honor to be, Sir
Your Most Obedient Servant
William Purdie M.D.
Surgeon Superintendent.

Dr Purdie's list of deaths on board the Mooltan

Name	Age	Date of death	Nature of disease
Ann McNeil	5 years	20 September	Stomach & Bowels
Mrs McNeil	26 years	21 September	Cholera
Mrs Barr	48 years	27 September	Cholera
Mr Geo. Perkins	42 years	3 October	Cholera
Mr Peter Harrison	45 years	3 October	Cholera
Mrs Harrison	25 years	3 October	Cholera
Elizabeth Purdie	3 months	4 October	Stomach & bowels
Mrs Proudfoot	25 years	6 October	Cholera
Jeannie Gebbie	1 year	8 October	Cholera
Mrs Kirkland	26 years	8 October	Cholera
Agnes Kirkland	6 months	14 October	Decline
Agness Peterson	5 years	15 October	Cholera
Clarinda Harrison	9 months	17 December	Hooping Cough (sic)

The MacGibbon ancestors in Scotland

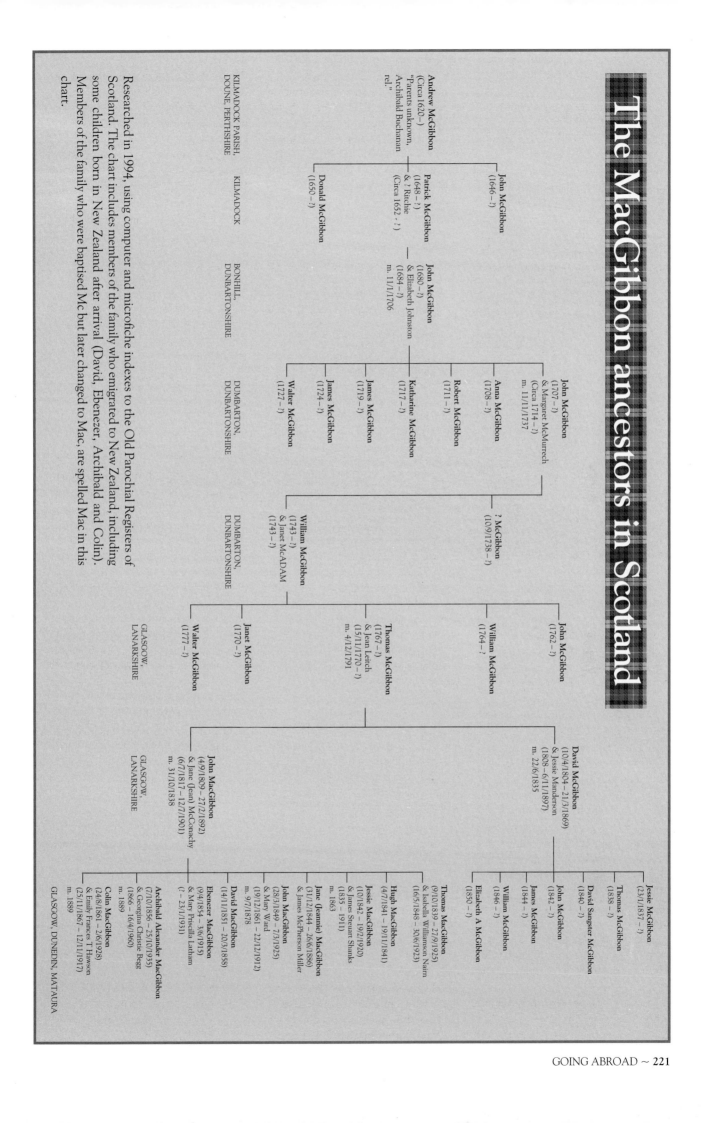

Researched in 1994, using computer and microfiche indexes to the Old Parochial Registers of Scotland. The chart includes members of the family who emigrated to New Zealand, including some children born in New Zealand after arrival (David, Ebenezer, Archibald and Colin). Members of the family who were baptised Mc but later changed to Mac, are spelled Mac in this chart.

Andrew McGibbon (Circa 1620–) "Parents unknown, Archibald Buchanan rel."

John McGibbon (1646–?)

Patrick McGibbon (1648–?) & ? Ruchie (Circa 1652–?) m. 11/1/1706

Donald McGibbon (1650–?)

John McGibbon (1680–?) & Elizabeth Johnston (1684–?) m. 11/1/1706

John McGibbon (1707–?) & Margaret McMurrech (Circa 1714–?) m. 11/11/1737

Anna McGibbon (1708–?)
Robert McGibbon (1711–?)
Katharine McGibbon (1717–?)
James McGibbon (1719–?)
James McGibbon (1724–?)
Walter McGibbon (1727–?)

? McGibbon (10/9/1738–?)

William McGibbon (1743–?) & Janet McADAM (1743–?)

John McGibbon (1762–?)
William McGibbon (1764–?)
Thomas McGibbon (1767–?) & Jean Leitch (15/11/1770–?) m. 4/12/1791
Janet McGibbon (1770–?)
Walter McGibbon (1777–?)

David McGibbon (10/4/1804–21/3/1869) & Jessie Manderson (1808–6/11/1897) m. 22/6/1835

John McGibbon (4/9/1809–27/2/1892) & Jane (Jean) McConachy (6/7/1817–12/7/1901) m. 31/10/1838

KILMADOCK PARISH, DOUNE, PERTHSHIRE

KILMADOCK

BONHILL, DUNBARTONSHIRE

DUMBARTON, DUNBARTONSHIRE

DUMBARTON, DUNBARTONSHIRE

GLASGOW, LANARKSHIRE

GLASGOW, LANARKSHIRE

GLASGOW, DUNEDIN, MATAURA

Jessie McGibbon (23/1/1837–?)
Thomas McGibbon (1838–?)
David Sangster McGibbon (1840–?)
John McGibbon (1842–?)
James McGibbon (1844–?)
William McGibbon (1846–?)
Elizabeth A McGibbon (1850–?)

Thomas MacGibbon (9/10/1839–27/9/1925) & Isabella Williamson Nairn (16/5/1848–30/6/1923)
Hugh MacGibbon (4/7/1841–19/11/1841)
Jessie MacGibbon (10/1842–19/2/1920) & James Steuart Shanks (1835–1911) m. 1863
Jane (Jeannie) MacGibbon (31/1/1844–26/6/1886) & James McPherson Miller m. 9/7/1878
John MacGibbon (28/3/1849–7/3/1925) & Mary Ward (19/12/1861–22/12/1912)
David MacGibbon (14/11/1851–20/3/1858)
Ebenezer MacGibbon (9/4/1854–3/6/1915) & Mary Priscilla Latham (?–23/1/1931)
Archibald Alexander MacGibbon (7/10/1856–25/10/1935) & Georgina Christie Begg (1866–16/4/1960) m. 1889
Colin MacGibbon (24/8/1861–2/6/1928) & Emily Frances T Hawson (25/11/1867–12/11/1917) m. 1889

Where did they come from?

Tracing back through time in the Old Parochial Registers, the earliest family member found who is directly related to John MacGibbon Sr, is Andrew McGibbon. Andrew was born around 1620 in Kilmadock Parish on the outskirts of the small town of Doune, 11 kilometres north-west of Dunblane in South Perthshire. Andrew's parents are not given, but the Register notes that one Archibald Buchanan was a relative.

From this evidence it is reasonable to deduce that the MacGibbon family was allied to the Buchanan clan, whose home territory is east of Loch Lomond, and extends to Perthshire, Stirlingshire and Dunbartonshire.

The MacGibbon family is a recognised sept (branch) of the Buchanan Clan, and is thus entitled to wear that clan's tartan. Some MacGibbons also have sept relationships with the Graham Clan (east and north-east of Buchanan territory), and the Campbell Clan, which is based in Argyllshire to the west of Glasgow.

John MacGibbon Sr's ancestors moved south after two generations to Bonhill, a small village in Dunbartonshire at the southern end of Loch Lomond. The next generation was born seven kilometres closer to Glasgow at Dumbarton, on the River Clyde. Two generations later, the family moved another 21 kilometres into Glasgow city.

William McGibbon, 'our' John Sr's father, was born in Glasgow.

Occupations

We don't know what occupations the early MacGibbons followed. John Sr's father Thomas is the first relative whose occupation is known. He is listed in the 1824 Glasgow Post Office Directory as having a tobacconist business called McGibbon and Son, at 106 Saltmarket Street. The son would have been John Sr's older brother David.

Thomas, David and John Sr were members of the Burgesses and Guild Brethren of Glasgow.

The MacGibbon name

The 'Gibbon' part of the name is a corruption of 'Gilbert', which developed from the Old English personal name of *Gislbe(o)rht*, or 'bright hostage'. There are many other variants of Gilbert, including Gibb and Gibson.

The 'Mac' portion is a Gaelic prefix which translates to 'son'. MacGibbon means Son of Gibbon.

Mac is the full Gaelic prefix, but it is more usually contracted to Mc, or sometimes, as in the early Dunedin newspapers, M'.

Exploding a myth

One hears many bogus theories about the difference between Mc and Mac, and in particular why some families, including the MacGibbons in New Zealand, changed the spelling from Mc to Mac. A popular theory is that Mac = Scots/Presbyterian, and Mc = Irish/Catholic. Therefore people of Scots origin might change their name to Mac so that (horror of horror) they would not be thought of as Catholic. This theory is nonsense, as the preponderance of the Mc prefix in any Scottish telephone directory proves. (Also note that 97% of the MacGibbon births between 1620 and 1855 were recorded as Mc.)

Basically the early scribes were lazy and wanted to save writing an extra letter. In Scotland and abroad, illiterate Macs were often automatically cut down to Mc by official scribes.

John MacGibbon Sr was not illiterate when he came to New Zealand, and he spelled the name Mc until he moved to Southland in 1858.

There is an interesting, and even plausible reason why the change might have been made. Once in Southland, they would have heard about another John McGibbon living in the province. This was John 'Tiger' McGibbon, who lived at a decaying whaling settlement at The Bluff. John Sr may have preferred to distinguish himself from this old whaler, who among other things had a Maori mistress, and an illegitimate daughter by her. Doubtless this would have been an affront to John Sr's puritan sensibilities – more than sufficient reason for him to change his name! ∎

Mac/McGibbon births and/or baptisms recorded in the Scottish Old Parochial Registers, 1600-1855

Total Mc/MacGibbons: 1,392 (of which McGibbon 1,350 (97%), and MacGibbon 42 (3%). Plus 126 people with spelling variants: McGibon, McGibboun, McGibbany, McGibbony, McGibion, McGibban. McGibben, McKibbon etc. (Spelled variously with one or two Bs.)

Major counties where McGibbons were born were: Perth 37%, Lanark (includes Glasgow) 14%, Argyll 11%, Stirling 10%, Renfrew 8%, Midlothian (includes Edinburgh) 7%, Dunbarton 6%, Bute 2%.

Analysis of birth dates shows a clear trend to move south over the period, particularly toward Glasgow in the 19th century.

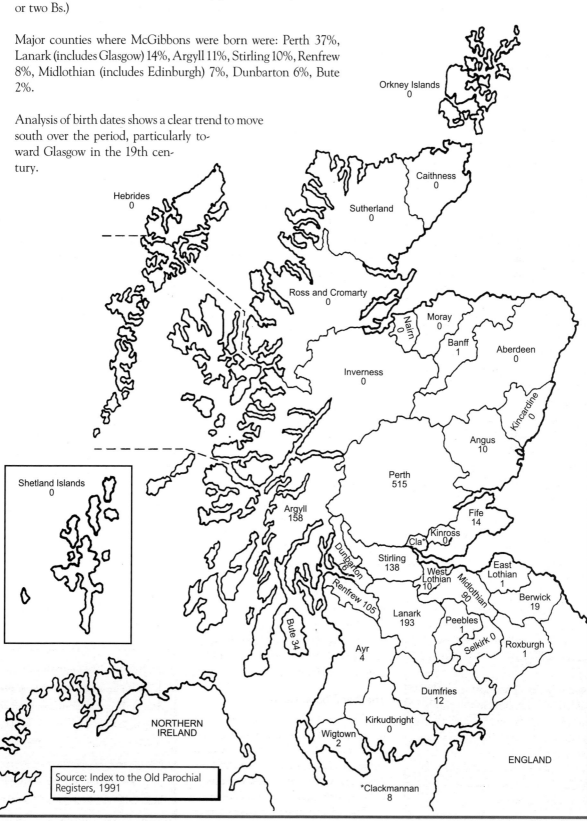

Orkney Islands
0

Hebrides
0

Caithness
0

Sutherland
0

Ross and Cromarty
0

Nairn
0

Moray
0

Banff
1

Aberdeen
0

Inverness
0

Kincardine
0

Angus
10

Shetland Islands
0

Perth
515

Fife
14

Argyll
158

Kinross
0

Cla*

Dunbarton

Stirling
138

West Lothian
10

East Lothian
1

Midlothian
90

Berwick
19

Renfrew 105

Lanark
193

Peebles
1

Selkirk 0

Roxburgh
1

Bute
34

Ayr
4

Dumfries
12

NORTHERN IRELAND

Wigtown
2

Kirkudbright
0

ENGLAND

Source: Index to the Old Parochial Registers, 1991

*Clackmannan
8

Bibliography

■ SCOTLAND

Annan, Thomas, *Photographs of the old closes and streets of Glasgow, 1868/1877,* introduction by Mozley, Anita Ventura, Dover Publications, New York, 1977.

Branca, Patricia, *Silent sisterhood – middle class women in the Victorian home,* Croom Helm, London, 1975.

Brown, Callum, *The social history of religion in Scotland,* Methuen, London, 1987.

Brown, John, *Two short catechisms, mutually connected, to which is added the gospel catechism and an address to children,* Francis Orr & Sons, Glasgow, 1841.

Brown, Stewart J, *Thomas Chalmers and the Godly Commonwealth,* Oxford University Press, Oxford, 1982.

Butters, Lawrence, (reviser) *Fairburn's crests of the families of Great Britain and Ireland,* New Orchard, London, 1986.

Cheyne, A C, *The transforming of the kirk,* Saint Andrew Press, Edinburgh, 1983.

Corrance, Douglas, & Boyd, Edward, *Glasgow,* Collins, Glasgow and London, 1981.

Clyde-built ships – the Dennys of Dumbarton. (Publisher and date unknown.)

Daiches, David, *Glasgow,* Andre Deutsch, 1977.

Denny Dumbarton, 1844-1932, Published by William Denny & Brothers Ltd, date unknown. (Short history of the various Denny family shipyards at Dumbarton. It includes the Denny and Rankine yard, where the sailing ship Mooltan was built in 1849.)

Drummond, Andrew L, & Bulloch, James, *The Church in Victorian Scotland, 1843-1874,* Saint Andrew Press, Edinburgh, 1975.

Dunlop, Eileen & Kamm, Anthony, *The story of Glasgow,* Richard Drew, Glasgow, 1984.

Gibb, Andrew, *Glasgow, the making of a city,* Croom Helm, London, 1983.

Glasgow dramatic review, July 16, 30, 1845, Glasgow. (Article in two parts on the Glasgow Fair.)

Glasgow Green and roundabout – a tourist guide, year unknown, evidently mid-Victorian.

Glasgow observed, Simon Berry & Hamish Whyte ed, John Donald, Edinburgh, 1987.

Glasgow Post Office directories, 1824-1869.

Gorbals Burying Ground records, 1809, 1849.

Guide to Glasgow Fair, Glasgow, 1850.

House, Jack, *The heart of Glasgow,* sixth edition 1987, reprinted by W & R Chambers, Edinburgh, 1993.

Hedderwick, James, *Backward glances,* William Blackwood and Sons, Edinburgh, 1891.

International genealogical index, Church of Jesus Christ of Latter Day Saints, Salt Lake City, 1991, 1993.

Lewis, Samuel, *A topographical dictionary of Scotland,* 1851, (facsimile by Genealogical Publishing Co Ltd, Baltimore, 1989.)

Lockhart, John Gibson, *Peter's letters to his kinsfolk,* ed. Ruddick, William, Scottish Academic Press, Edinburgh, 1977.

MacLaren, A Allan, *Religion and social class,* Routledge & Kegan Paul, London, 1974.

MacLaren, A Allan, *Bourgeoise ideology and Victorian philanthrophy: the contradictions of cholera,* from *Social class in Scotland, past and present,* ed MacLaren, A Allan, John Donald, Edinburgh, no date given.

Mitchison, Rosalind, *Life in Scotland,* Batsford, London, 1978.

Nestor (pseudonym), *Rambling recollections of life in old Glasgow,* 1880.

Old parochial registers, Scotland – births, baptisms and marriages, 1600-1855.

Prebble, John, *The lion in the north,* Secker & Warburg, London, 1971.

Prebble, John, *John Prebble's Scotland,* Secker & Warburg, London, 1984.

Reid, J M, *Glasgow,* B T Batsford Ltd, London, 1956.

Sandy MacIndoe at Glasgow Fair: a character sketch, privately published manuscript, evidently mid-19th century.

Scotland, a genealogical research guide, Church of Jesus Christ of Latter Day Saints, Salt Lake City, no date given.

Simpson, MA, *Middle class housing and the growth of suburban communities in the west end of Glasgow,* 1830-1914, thesis, University of Glasgow, 1970.

Small, David and Millar, A H, *Sketches of quaint bits in Glasgow,* (with descriptons), David Bryce and Son, Glasgow, 1887.

Smith, Donald C, *Passive obedience and prophetic protest,* Peter Lang, New York, 1987.

Smout, T C, *A century of the Scottish people, 1830-1950,* Collins, London, 1986.

Smout, T C (with Wood, Sydney), *Scottish voices, 1745-1960,* Collins, London, 1990.

Statistical account of Scotland, 1792. Number III, Parish of Kilmadock or Doune, by Alexander MacGibbon; Number LXV, Parish of Bonhill, Dumbarton, by Rev Gordon Stewart; Number X, Parish of Barony of Glasgow, by Rev John Burns.

Studies in the history of worship in Scotland, edited by Forrester, Duncan B, and Murray, Douglas M, T & T Clark, Edinburgh, 1984.

The larger catechism, agreed upon by the Assembly of Divines at Westminster, Aberdeen, 1840.

Watts, Isaac, The Young Child's first and second catechism of the principles of religion, to which is added, a preservative from the sins and follies of childhood and youth, R. Farie, Glasgow, 1792.

Weir, J M, A family called Weir. (Contains information about a separate branch of the McGibbon family which emigrated to New Zealand from Argyllshire in 1892.)

Worsdall, Frank, A Glasgow keek show, Richard Drew, Glasgow, 1981.

Worsdall, Frank, The city that disappeared: Glasgow's demolished architecture, Molendar Press, Glasgow, 1981.

Worsdall, Frank, The Glasgow tenement, Richard Drew, Glasgow, 1989.

■ EMIGRATION PROMOTION, THE EMIGRATION VOYAGE AND EARLY DUNEDIN

Adam, James, Twentyfive years of emigrant life in the south of New Zealand, Bell and Bradfute, Otago and Edinburgh, 1876.

Adam, James, Description of the province of Otago, New Zealand, Bell and Bradfute, Edinburgh,1858.

Arnold, Craig, Euterpe: diaries, letters and logs of the "Star of India" as a British emigrant ship, Maritime Museum Association of San Diego, San Diego, 1988.

Association of Lay Members of the Free Church, Account book, 1848-1850, National Archives, Wellington.

Association of Lay Members of the Free Church/New Zealand Company, Applications for land in Otago, National Archives, Wellington.

Bannerman, Jane, Reminiscences. (papers held at the Otago Settlers Museum).

Barr, James, The Old Identities: being sketches and reminiscences during the first decade of the Province of Otago, N.Z., Mills, Dick and Co, Dunedin, 1879.

Brett, Sir Henry, White Wings – fifty years of sail in the New Zealand Trade, 1850 to 1900, 2 vols, Capper Press, Christchurch, 1976. (Reprint of the original 1924 edition by Brett Printing Company, Auckland.)

Brett, Sir Henry, White Wings – Immigration Ships to New Zealand, 1840-1902. Reed, Wellington, 1984. (Based on the original edition above.)

Brooking, Tom, And captain of their souls, Otago Heritage Books, Dunedin, 1984. (An interpretative essay on the life and times of Captain Cargill.)

Brooking, Tom, Out of Midlothian: Scots migration to New Zealand, 1840–1914, conference papers, New Zealand Society of Genealogists Conference, Dunedin, 1989.

Brooking, Tom, Tam McCanny and Kitty Clydeside – the Scots contribution to economic development in New Zealand to 1914, in Cage, Bob (ed.), The Scots abroad: labour, capital, enterprise, 1709-1914, Croom Helm, London, 1985, pp 159-190. Access was also made available by Mr Brooking to working papers for the published paper.

Brooking, Tom, Piping in a rough equality: the Scots contribution to the making of New Zealand culture, contribution to forthcoming publication, Scotland and Empire, John Mackenzie ed., Manchester University Press, publication scheduled for 1997.

Burns, Rev Thomas, Visitation book (Otago Settlers Museum collection, Dunedin).

Cargill, John, Information for the guidance of intending emigrants, Bell and Bradfute, Edinburgh, 1860. Cargill is described as late member of the House of Representatives, New Zealand, and of the Provincial Council of Otago.

Carlewood, Don, The long farewell, Allen Lane, Melbourne 1981.

Chuk, Florence, Somerset Years, privately published, Melbourne, 1987. (Detailed description of emigration to Victoria during the 1840s and 1850s.)

Correspondence and papers relating to a reunion of early emigrants to Dunedin organised by the Otago Witness for 1898. (Otago Settlers Museum collection.)

Davidson, WH, The History of the S.S. Lady Egidia, an emigrant ship of 1860, Lady Egidia Centenary Committee, Dunedin, 1961.

Drummond, John D, Mendelssohn, maidens and monkeys: music and other entertainments in Dunedin, 1848-1862, conference papers, New Zealand Society of Genealogists Conference, Dunedin, 1989.

Dunedin Town Board, Ratebook 1857-62.

Earp, G B, Handbook for intending emigrants to the southern settlements of New Zealand, Geo. Routledge & Co., London, 1852. Butler is described as a former member of the Legislative Council of NZ and one of the senior magistrates of the Territory.

Earp, G B, New Zealand: its emigration and goldfields, Geo Routledge & Co., London, 1853.

Fulton, Catherine (nee Valpy), Autobiography of Mrs James Fulton, 1915. (Privately published; copy in the Alexander Turnbull Library, Wellington.)

Goodall, Maarire and Griffiths, George, Maori Dunedin, Otago Heritage Books, Dunedin, 1980.

Hocken, Thomas Morland, Contributions to the early history of New Zealand (Otago), 1898.

Hocken, Thomas Morland, Flotsam and jetsam Vol IV; historical records connected with the first settlement of Otago (chiefly ships and passengers), Hocken Library, Dunedin.

Lay Association for the Promotion of the Otago Settlement, Collection of account and receipts, 1848-1850. National Archives, Wellington.

Lloyds Register, 1851.

McClean, Rosalind R, Class, family and church – a case study in interpenetration, Otago, 1848-1852, study for BA Honours in History, University of Otago, Dunedin, 1980.

McDonald, K C, City of Dunedin, Dunedin City Corporation, Dunedin, 1965.

McLintock, A H, The history of Otago, Otago Centennial Historical Publications, Dunedin, 1948.

McLintock, A H, *The port of Otago*, Whitcombe and Tombs, Dunedin, 1951.

McLay, John, *Reminiscences* (papers held at the Otago Settlers Museum, Dunedin).

McNeil, Robert & Daly, Diane, *The voyage of the Mooltan*, Alexandra, 1989. (Transcript of F S Pillan's diary of the voyage of the Mooltan.)

Merrington, E N, *A great coloniser*, Otago Daily Times & Witness Newspapers Co., Dunedin, 1929. (Biography of Reverend Dr Thomas Burns.)

New Zealand Company, *The Otago Journal*, Jan 1848, June 1948, November 1948, August 1849, November 1849, November 1850.

New Zealand Company, various papers held at National Archives Wellington, including correspondence, reports and accounts relating to the voyage of the Mooltan and the Pekin.

New Zealand Company, *Annual Report of the Court of Directors*, 4 July 1850. (National Archives, Wellington.)

New Zealand Company, *collection of papers, letters and accounts relating to the sailing of the Mooltan*, National Archives, Wellington.

O'Neill, Judith, *So far from Skye*, Puffin, London, 1993. (Young persons' novel which reconstructs the experiences of a family ousted from Skye during the highland clearances and travelling by emigrant ship to Melbourne in 1852.)

Orbell, Catherine, *Journal of our voyage from England to New Zealand on board the "Mariner" – February 5th, 1849*, Alexander Turnbull Library, Wellington.

Otago News, the, *Handbook to the suburban and rural districts of the Otago Settlement*, Otago News, 1849. (Facsimile reprint by the Hocken Library, Dunedin,1967.)

Otago Witness, *Otago Settlement jubilee number, 1898*, Otago Witness, Dunedin, 1898.

Page, Dorothy, *Finding our lost foremothers: women's lives in nineteenth century Otago*, conference papers, New Zealand Society of Genealogists Conference, Dunedin, 1989.

Parker, J W, *The handbook for New Zealand, consisting of the most recent information compiled for the use of intending colonists*, London, 1848. (Reproduced in *Life in a young colony*, Hankin, Cherry A, ed., Whitcoulls, 1981.)

Soper, Eileen L, *The Otago of our mothers*, Otago Centennial Historical Publications, Dunedin, 1948.

Reed, A H, *The story of early Dunedin*, A H & A W Reed, Wellington, 1956.

Robertson, Joy Matheson, *The Otago Emigrant Ships: social conditions in Dunedin up till 1860*, thesis for Honours in History, University of New Zealand, 1937.

Rutherford, Alma, *The edge of the town*, Otago Regional Committee, NZ Historic Places Trust, 1978. (History of the Caversham suburb in Dunedin.)

Tyler, John, *Passenger diary on the Mariner, arrived Port Chalmers June 1849*. (Diary transcript held at the Alexander Turnbull Library, Wellington.)

Wells, Dr Henry, *Surgeon Superintendent's diary on the Blundell, arrived Port Chalmers 1848*, National Archives, Wellington.

Wilson, John (editor and compiler), *Reminiscences of the early settlement of Dunedin and South Otago*, J Wilkie & Co., Dunedin, 1912.

■ EMIGRATION SHIP PASSENGER DIARIES AND REMINISCENCES

Davis, Fanny, *Conway*, Liverpool to Melbourne, 1858 (reproduced in Carlewood, Don, op cit).

Duncan, George, Elspeth and John. *Reminiscences*. The Duncans were passengers on the ship Mooltan.

Fenwick, John, *Lightning* – Liverpool to Melbourne, 1854 (reproduced in Carlewood, Don, *The Long Farewell*, Allen Lane, Melbourne 1981.

Fulton [nee Valpy], Catherine, *Ajax* – London to Otago, 1848.

Lightoller, Dr H M, *Scottish Bard*, London to Rockhampton, 1876 (reproduced in Carlewood, Don, op cit).

Medical journal of the ship Sir Robert Sale, England to New Zealand, 1847. National Archives ADM 101, 79/1.

Pillans, Francis, *Mooltan* – Greenock to Otago, 1849.

Orbell, Catherine, *Mariner* – London to Otago, 1849.

Tyler, John, *Mariner* – London to Otago, 1849.

Various, *Egidia*, Greenock to Otago, 1860-61 (composite of several passengers' diaries).

Whitby, George, *Pekin* (captain's log), London to various ports including Dunedin, 1849.

Wells, Henry, *Blundell* (surgeon's log), London to Otago, 1848.

(Additional references to passenger diaries and reminiscences have come from previously cited books: Don Charlwood's *The Long Farewell*, Craig Arnold's *Euterpe*, and Joy Robertson's *The Otago Emigrant Ships*. Diaries quoted by Robertson include William Fox (*George Fife*, 1842), Rev Thomas Burns (*Philip Laing*, 1847-48), James Sommerville (*Blundell*, 1849), George Hepburn (*Poictiers*, 1850), Rev Nicolson (*Titan*, 1850-51), Miss McGlashan (*Rajah*, 1853), Adam Wright (*Strathmore*, 1856), Mr Smaill (*Strathallan*, 1858).)

■ WIDER OTAGO, AND SOUTHLAND

Barry, L S & Bown, L C, *In the lee of the Hokonuis*, Lyal Barry Book Committee, Invercargill, 1966.

Beattie, James Herries, *Pioneer recollections, chiefly of the Mataura Valley*, Mataura Ensign, Gore, 1909. (Collected edition of recollections published in the Mataura Ensign between April and November, 1909.)

Beattie, James Herries, *Pioneer recollections, second series*, Gore Publishing Co, Gore, 1911. (Collected edition of recollections published in the Mataura Ensign between July 1910 and May 1911.)

Beattie, James Herries, *Pioneer recollections, third series*, Gore Publishing Co, Gore, 1911. (Collected edition of recollections published in the Mataura Ensign between June 1917 and July 1918.)

Beattie, James Herries, *Pioneer recollections, fourth series*, Gore

Publishing Co, Gore, 1948. (Collected edition of recollections published in the Mataura Ensign between 1947 and 1948.)

Beattie, James Herries, personal interview notes, Beattie Papers (MS582), Hocken Library, Dunedin.

Beattie, James Herries, *A history of Gore and surrounding districts 1861-1962*, Gore Centennial Committee.

Hall-Jones, F G, *Historical Southland*, published by H & J Smith Ltd for the Southland Historical Committee, Invercargill, 1945.

Hall-Jones, John, *Bluff Harbour*, Southland Harbour Board, 1976.

Hood, Lynley, *Minnie Dean*, Penguin, Auckland, 1994.

Lovell-Smith, E M, *Old coaching days, Otago and Southland, New Zealand*, Lovell-Smith & Venner, Christchurch, 1931.

McArthur, J F, *From the kirk on the hill*, Centennial history of the Presbyterian Church in Gore, Gore, 1981.

Miller, F W G, *King of counties*, Southland County Council, Invercargill, 1977.

Muir, D C W, et al, *Mataura, city of the falls*, published for the Mataura Historical Society, Gore Publishing Co, Gore, 1991.

National Archives, Dunedin, land transaction records, New Zealand Company, Otago Waste Lands Board.

Smith, Hallam, *History of the town of Gore, parts 1&2*, Wayland Trust, Gore, 1997.

Smith, Rosemarie, *The ladies are at it again*, Victoria University, Wellington, 1993.

Tod, Frank, *Whaling in southern waters*, Dunedin, 1982.

■ POLITICAL

Grant, Ian F, *The unauthorized version, a cartoon history of New Zealand*, Cassell, Auckland, 1980.

Jackson, W K, *The New Zealand Legislative Council*, University of Otago Press, Dunedin, 1972.

McLintock, A H, *An encyclopaedia of New Zealand*, Government Printer, Wellington, 1966.

Hansard, 1914–1921.

■ RUNHOLDING

Beattie, James Herries, *Early runholding in Otago*, ODT and Witness Newspapers Co, Dunedin, 1947.

Beattie, James Herries, *The southern runs*, Published by the Southland Times, Invercargill, for the Gore Historical Society, 1979.

Eldred-Grigg, Stevan, *A southern gentry*, Heinemann Reid, Auckland, 1980.

■ GENERAL

Beattie, James Herries, *Traditional lifeways of the southern Maori*,

Athol Anderson ed., University of Otago Press, Dunedin, 1994.

Binney, Judith; Bassett, Judith; Olssen, Erik, *The people and the land (An illustrated hstory of New Zealand, 1820-1830)*, Allen & Unwin, Wellington, 1990.

Challice, Dr, *How to avoid the cholera: plain directions for poor people*, pamphlet, Henry Renshaw, London, 19th Century, date unknown.

Jourdain, W R, *Land legislation and settlement in New Zealand*, Department of Lands and Survey, Wellington, 1925.

Macdonald, Charlotte, *A woman of good character*, Allen and Unwin/Historical Branch, NZ Department of Internal Affairs, Wellington, 1990.

Miller, John, *Early Victorian New Zealand*, Oxford University Pressm London, 1958.

Otago Almanac, Mills, Dick & Co, 1893.

Pearce, G L, *The Scots of New Zealand*, Collins, Auckland, 1976.

Scholefield, Guy H, *Newspapers in New Zealand*, A H & A W Reed, Wellington, 1958.

Sinclair, Keith & Harrex, Wendy, *Looking back – a photographic history of New Zealand*, Oxford University Press, Wellington, 1978.

Stones Otago and Southland Directory, 1887.

Watten, Raymond H, *Memoirs – personal experiences with cholera, 1958-1972*, 1997, Kenwood, California, USA, unpublished, personal correspondence with the author. (Watten is a retired US Navy doctor who is one of the pioneers of modern cholera treatment.)

Wise's Directory, 1875/76 and 1892/93.

■ NEWSPAPERS AND PERIODICALS

Evening Star (Dunedin)
Glasgow Courier (Glasgow)
Glasgow Herald (Glasgow)
Greenock Advertiser (Greenock, Scotland)
Illustrated London News (London)
Mataura Ensign (Gore)
Otago Colonist (Dunedin)
Otago News (Dunedin)
Otago Witness (Dunedin)
Otago Daily Times (Dunedin)
Southern Standard (Gore)
Southland Times (Invercargill)
The Prohibitionist (Southern edition)

Index